IMPERIALISM
As Rampant Today
as in the Past

IMPERIALISM
As Rampant Today
as in the Past

Samir Saul

Baraka
Books

Montréal

Impérialisme, passé et présent, un essai by Samir Saul
© All rights reserved.
This English edition was published by Baraka Books in 2025 by arrangement with Éditions Les Indes savantes.

ISBN 978-1-77186-382-7 pbk; 978-1-77186-402-2 epub; 978-1-77186-403-9 pdf

Cover by Leila Marshy
Book Design by Folio infographie
Editing: Robin Philpot
Proofreading: Anne Marie Marko, Rachel Hewitt

Legal Deposit, 3rd quarter 2025
Bibliothèque et Archives nationales du Québec
Library and Archives Canada

Published by Baraka Books of Montreal

TRADE DISTRIBUTION & RETURNS

Canada
UTPdistribution.com

United States
Independent Publishers Group: IPGbook.com

We acknowledge the support from the Société de développement des entreprises culturelles (SODEC) and the Government of Quebec tax credit for book publishing administered by SODEC.

Société
de développement
des entreprises
culturelles
Québec

Financé par le gouvernement du Canada
Funded by the Government of Canada | Canada

PUBLISHED &
PRINTED IN
CANADA

In memory of my father
and of historian Jacques Thobie,
who left us two years apart

CONTENTS

PREFACE

This book revisits the notion of imperialism, establishes a typ- ology of imperialisms and highlights the present-day relevance of the concept. Originally published in French in March 2023, it was written in the first part of 2021, a few months before the world conflict it delineated broke out and slightly augmented in 2022 to take in the conflict in Ukraine. Since then, the processes it analyzed have matured and the systemic conflict anticipated has entered into its active phase. The book turned out to be a preview of what was about to happen.

The translation in 2024 has further updated it as the pace of hist- ory quickened. In October 2023, the century-long conflict in Palestine came to a boil. Both hotbeds remain active, threatening to intensify and spill over into a large-scale wars. The European and Middle Eastern fronts are not separated: a war against Iran poses a threat to Russia's southern flank, even more so than the war against Syria that started in 2011. In the meantime, the confrontation between the United States and China represents a ticking time bomb of world- wide magnitude. Indirect proxy fighting in Ukraine having failed to bring about the desired result, i.e. the "strategic defeat" of Russia and its downfall, it could escalate to a direct clash between Western sponsors of the Kiev regime and Russia. Nuclear sabre-rattling and nuclear war are no longer out of bounds, as the threshold for use is lowered in war planning.

The proxy war in Ukraine turned out to be counterproductive for the West; it backfired. Instead of collapsing, Russia's economy has grown, industrialized further, gained more self-sufficiency, and found new partners to replace Europe. Instead of falling apart, the Russian state is consolidated. Its military production is at full capacity and its armed forces are larger and battle-hardened. Not for the first time in its history, Russia stood up to the West. Until 2022, most Western attention was on China; it was taken for granted that Russia would be a pushover. Such was the hubris inherited from the heady days of United States absolute primacy and Russian impotence of the 1990s. The economic and military consequences of the proxy war in Ukraine made Russia a focal point of the geopolitical and geo-economic reorganization of the world. Isolation of Russia has turned into isolation of the West in a fast-changing international environment.

Western countries are de facto dependencies and satellites of the United States whose ruling classes are stakeholders in American planetary imperialism and US-administered neoliberal globalization with its corollaries such as constant expansionism through war and "regime change," free movement of capital, wholesale privatization of public property, and termination of the postwar redistributive state. This explains why European governments, elites, and media zealously lined up behind the United States despite the economic, social, and political cost their countries incur as a result of such an alignment.

Failure in Ukraine has compelled the United States to seek negotiations with Russia, a tactical fallback that is always reversible if circumstances permit, probably in light of the confrontation with China. The American about turn over Ukraine rattled its Western junior partners and large swaths of its establishment intent on doubling down and clinging to the faltering policy of aggressive unilateralism and forever wars all over the world. Although contrary to the evidence, the Ukraine proxy war looked to them like the long sought-after opportunity at defeating Russia, toppling its state structures, placing it at the semi-periphery of Western capitalism, reducing it to neocolonial status, seizing its immense natural resources and dismembering the country. But reality is stubborn and difficult to dodge; the world hegemon is not capable of fighting two major powers simultaneously and has to limit itself to targeting one at a time.

What was anticipated as a brief proxy campaign using Ukraine to bring down Russia and sideline it in the lead-up to the expected confrontation with China turned out to be an expensive, grinding war of attrition where Europe is the main loser, after Ukraine. One success the United States has registered is the tearing of Europe away from Russia, its cheap gas and its market. The Europe-Russia nexus is broken. Over and above enduring higher energy prices, and militarily sustaining the Ukrainian surrogate by funding, arming and training, European governments wrought havoc on Europe's finances, fueled inflation, and slowed down its economy. While Europe has been undermined, the German economy, dependent on low-cost inputs, was directly sabotaged in September 2022 by the blowing up of Nord Stream, its gas lifeline. It is now in disarray, with its mainstay, industry, gradually shutting down or pressured by high energy prices to migrate to the United States.

Europe is bound to the United States, losing whatever industry it had left and unlikely to be part of Eurasian projects, such as the Belt and Road Initiative. This can be tallied as a success for the United States in the struggle to prolong its hegemony. Should the foreseeable conflict with China induce the United States to force Europe to split with China, it would be plunged in deep turmoil and find itself entirely at the mercy of its American overlord. Its weakened economy and futile chest-thumping against Russia illustrate the descent into irrelevance of the continent that dominated the world for half a millennium.

The lines are more clearly drawn than ever before: the West on one side; the rest of the world, on the other. Beyond the West, historic changes are underway. American injunctions no longer carry the weight they had in the post-1990 era of the "sole superpower." The "sanctions" weapon can be neutralized, the more so as key countries of the world ignore it. The confrontation in Ukraine and the Palestine conflict reveal the new split plainly. The reorganization of the world economy outside the reach of the United States and the range of the dollar is accelerating under the umbrella of BRICS, already representing a larger total GDP than the Western G7 and growing.

At issue is the latest version of imperialism, that of planetary imperialism based on United States-centered globalization of capitalism. Due to its inherent defects and because of opposition, it is showing signs of coming apart. Natural historical evolution has displaced economic, political, and military power away from the hegemon. But empires do not yield willingly, peaceably or gracefully. Our era is that of the dominant power seeking to prevent historical change by all available means, first and foremost by force.

2025 is not 1914. A century ago, several neomercantilist imperial powers vied to establish their primacy over the others. Much water has flowed under the bridge since. Our era is one of planetary imperialism and globalized capitalism where one power, the United States, already exercises hegemony overall. No other power is in a position to replace it, at least for some time. Russia lacks the economic size to be a world hegemon, while China can thrive and is doing so without resorting to imperialism. The issue is not a clash between relatively equal adversaries, as during the First World War, but a confrontation between a hegemonic power and those who refuse its hegemony, between unipolarity-unilateralism and multipolarity-multilateralism.

A last word concerns globalization. Like free trade in the past, it is a systemic pump siphoning wealth from abroad to the economy that props up the entire edifice. It also provides the dominant power based on this economy with the means to bring to heel or harm those who are in a structural relationship with it and who might want to defend their interests. This is why decolonizing countries try to break away from such ties. In the present juncture, rupture was imposed on Russia, leading to a forced delinking with the West. Russia's success in circumventing the West or doing without it, and the example it sets for others, reinforce doubts surrounding neoliberal globalization. The latter has hollowed out economies, deepened social divisions, enriched minorities, immiserated large numbers, destabilized societies, promoted cognitive disorder by massive disinformation and given rise to anger-driven chauvinist politics. Discovery by the West that deindustrialization has left it with a reduced capacity to produce weapons and munitions has raised concerns about delocalized production and prompted calls to reindustrialize. The fact that, against all expectations, China turned neoliberal America-centered globalization to its advantage has revived anti-globalization protectionist urges in the United States itself. Moreover, Western reliance on "sanctions" and punitive rupture of ties are the antithesis of globalization and inimical to its maintenance, so much so that some have brainstormed over the return to economic blocs, endearingly labeled "friendshoring" or, more prosaically, "reshoring."

Can capitalism be deglobalized? The scale of modern production, the need for large markets and the faraway location of indispensable raw materials rule out permanent self-contained, autarkic economies. The bellicose protectionist turn in the United States is really an attempt to extract more from a system that already favors it and to skew even more the rules. It is neither aimed at ending globalization not is it likely to do so. The present phase is one of a contentious and chaotic hegemonic reordering of globalization, much as the interwar years were a hiatus between the pre-1914 and the post-1945 models of globalization. Nationalist rhetoric from the United States does not mean abandonment of its universal imperial ambitions but a way of making "allies" pay more for the difficulty of achieving them. Hectoring, bullying, browbeating and bloodcurdling threats serve that end. Refurbishing neoliberal globalization, unipolarity and planetary imperialism are the predictable outcome of the shake-up ... unless opposition in the rest of the world reduces the exercise to naught.

Bringing the concept of imperialism back

This book deals with a subject that filled the speeches and fueled the debates of the twentieth century. By the beginning of the twenty-first, it had faded from public consciousness to the point where even left-wing or formerly left-wing editors and publishers, who are among those most familiar with the concept (their bread and butter!), no longer understood its meaning. Yet the world continued to evolve and questions about imperialism are returning. This book contributes to the comeback by recalling the relevance and analytical value of the concept of imperialism.

There are subjects in the world of ideas that one would be fool-hardy to raise without offering compelling reasons. Imperialism is one of them. Exasperated by its fluidity, its political undertones and other difficulties, some people prefer to banish it from their vocabulary. This is ill-advised because it responds to a genuine need to identify realities that call for explanation. Such a task is not without risks, given that the pitfalls are not just of a scientific nature. The concept has been an ideological battleground on which successive contingents of combatants have taken up the cudgels, and where confrontations have continued on a minefield of presuppositions, misunderstandings, and imputations of motives. A host of authors have taken pride in unmasking deception, demystifying ideological stances, and dismantling myths. A polemical streak pervaded the treatment of imperialism, even as the complex and malleable concept reflects evolving and unfolding situations.

If the reality of imperialism is not in question, its roots, its driving forces, and its purpose remain matters of controversy. The dilemmas and dichotomies inherent in the question of imperialism invariably recur. They permeate any discussion of the subject. Does it designate only formally constituted empires and colonies, or does it also extend to the de facto trusteeship of politically independent countries through informal control? Does it have a relationship with capitalism or is it foreign to it? Is it integrally linked to capitalism or an incidental epiphenomenon in its history? More generally, does it represent a political or economic fact? A clear-cut divide between politics and economics would lead to an almost Manichean vision of two entities considered watertight and irreducible. Usually, the dichotomy is not so radical and neither politics nor economics are self-sufficient.

Marxist authors, who are very active on the theme of imperialism, consider it to be closely linked to a specific social structure and economic system—a "mode of production"—namely, capitalism. While not exempt of divergences and contradictions, wide-ranging research is carried out in the field of this multidimensional conception. However, if imperialism derives from capitalism in the Marxist perspective, the nature of the link, its degree of necessity or contingency, and the consequences it entails in the regions of the world where capitalism and imperialism are extant, give rise to a variety of interpretations.

Does capitalism have a pressing need for an outlet for its overflow of men, goods or capital, the result of malfunctions intrinsic to its fundamental mechanisms? Going beyond its colonial or imperial origins, is imperialism a historically definable stage of capitalism, the last, as Lenin argued? Who benefits: the entire capitalist economy—the owners of capital in the first place, but the workers too—or specific sectors of the economy which have the ear of state leaders? Is external expansion simply a complement or does it provide capitalism with an essential key to its functioning, even its survival? Are imperialism and colonial domination obstacles to the development of the regions of the world where they impose themselves or, on the contrary, the initiators of their modernization? These questions elicit contrasting answers.

In any case, no redefinition of imperialism can be undertaken without critically assessing the contributions of existing interpretations. None is completely untenable or entirely adequate, given that the concept cannot be understood immediately due to its fluctuating nature. Many of the contributions of the various theorists and the criticisms they leveled at each other are well founded. Both must be sifted through and subjected to criticism with a view to culling material useful to develop a renewed approach.

This book represents an attempt to foster a new interpretation of imperialism, based on a historical approach. Despite the fact that theorization is legitimate and indispensable, here it serves as a companion to history in a project to be understood as theorized history or inductive theorization. If theory can give meaning to empiricism, the latter has the merit of saving theory from turning on itself in a vacuum. History and historical contingency provide salutary antidotes to categorical judgments and overly abstract constructions. It is enough to recall that capitalism, more than once on the verge of passing away, has continued somehow or other to recover and reinvent itself, surprising its supporters as much as its opponents and postponing the day of reckoning.

If this book is not a theoretical treatise on a concept, it is not a history of empires either. Both already exist. The aim is to revisit the phenomenon of imperialism to comprehend it through the lens of history. The goal is to historicize the concept by tracking its occurrence over time, from its origins to the present. The challenge is to observe it from a height that allows us to take into account the characteristics of imperialism in all eras and not, as is most often the case, in just one; in short, to identify a common thread with explanatory utility. Our intention is also to extend the analysis to the present, an era poorly connected to previous ones in the "literature." The book is an effort to reassess imperialism and thereby revitalize it as a framework for reading the past and understanding the present. Finally, it is about pinpointing the economic motive forces of imperialism and their historical manifestations, in other words, the core of imperialism, not about culture, orientalism, perceptions, postmodernism, postcolonialism, New Imperial History, remembrance, societal issues or identities. The contribution lies in reconsideration and reevaluation rather than in theoretical demonstration or empirical research. It is intended to be a fresco and a synthesis written as an essay, halfway between popularization and erudition, unburdened by footnotes, in order to reach beyond specialists.

It is the result of observations, reflections, meditations, ruminations, courses, conferences, and publications which span more than four decades of a life, that of the student, then that of the university professor, who is also a citizen. Imperialism, an ever-present challenge, was taken up regularly and turned over and over in all directions. It is impossible to measure the time and the effort, as well as the multiple trials, needed to find the satisfactory configuration. Finding it for this polysemous concept is no simple undertaking, as the parameters to be integrated are numerous and shifting.

Theories followed other theories, each responding to a particular situation but none to all relevant situations. Liberalism is incapable of perceiving and taking into account, let alone explaining, economic exploitation. Hobsonism (ideas of John Hobson) is ineffectual since, despite the redistribution of purchasing power, imperialism persists. Lenin's thesis accords too much importance to the finance capital identified by Hilferding but not observable anywhere other than in Germany at the beginning of the twentieth century. Hence the interest in seeking a solution in a new arrangement of the entire problem. When theory is at a standstill, it is time to turn to history to overcome deadlocks and impasses by going back to basics.

Our intention here is to reconstitute a theme of great heuristic value and to arrive at an intelligibility of imperialism that is more useful and operational than what is available. A definition of imperialism which highlights the essence of the phenomenon, going beyond the conditions of a particular historical situation, is lacking. There is a need for an interpretive grid that would determine if and when the use of the term imperialism is appropriate, whatever the particular circumstances. To this end, it is proposed to move from focusing on a single period to taking into account the oneness of imperialism across eras. Broadening the focus by looking at the long term to identify the common traits of imperialism means identifying a key feature, which will have variable manifestations depending on the era.

This in no way implies detaching imperialism from the economic, social and political foundations or class relations of each historical era, and even less creating an atemporal entity or an extra-historical abstraction. The object is to demonstrate how these common traits are embodied in the specific practices of each era and how they derive from its material foundations and deep mechanisms. Internal dynamics, specific to each society, are always at the origin of external expansion.

From the study of history, certain general observations emerge. On the international level, there are always inequalities and imbalances between communities and states. These asymmetries of power are objective facts that allow the strongest to exercise coercion on those weaker than them and to gain advantages at their expense, particularly economic ones. Neither a higher law nor an intangible principle, they are nevertheless an invariant observable firsthand from which no period of the past or present is exempt. Whether decision makers flaunt them or strive to conceal them, power relations and their consequences permeate international interactions. Ranging from crude predation to sophisticated siphoning, from tribute to electronic transfer, economic pumping at the expense of the weakest is a part of unequal relationships. There is no imperialism that is purely political without the quest for economic benefits, or purely economic without political coercion. The two dimensions go hand in hand. The economy pervades the state with its logic and relies on it, while the state is rooted in the economy and cultivates it. Politics and economics are in symbiosis; possible disjunctions end up being resolved in due course, one way or another.

An interpretation of imperialism is valid only if it is rooted in history. Imperialist situations involve a relationship of domination or forced linkage that enable the strongest to appropriate wealth (land, raw materials, manufactured goods, capital, or labor generated by a workforce) extorted from the weakest. Politics and economics are always present, intertwined and interdependent. This process is not confined to a single period; it can be found throughout the ages and right up to the present. The mechanisms of political domination and economic plunder change depending on the conditions of each era, the types of societies, socioeconomic structures, geopolitical variables, etc., but the general pattern is the same. This transhistorical vision of imperialism does not hover above history; it gives a central place to historically determined and specific material conditions.

Two corollaries follow. First, imperialism is not a specific stage of history, as Lenin's conception would have it; it exists in all eras since the birth of states. It is modulated according to the societies from which it originates. Capitalist imperialism is only one of its manifestations, admittedly the most elaborate but not the only one. The situation is rather one of stages of imperialism reflecting the evolving template of the societies that produce it. The analysis of imperialism must gain altitude to encompass recurrences in history.

Second, imperialism must be recognized as a primary, rudimentary phenomenon, dating back to the distant past and perpetuating itself in the present. Far from being a product of modernity, still less of the twentieth century alone, imperialism is a legacy of remote times, a remnant of ancestral practices, adapted and updated. Capitalism borrows from precapitalist systems and introduces innovations. It is continuity that takes precedence, even if systemic extraction has overtaken outright plunder. The liberal economist Joseph Schumpeter clearly perceived the atavistic character of imperialism, but he was wrong to believe that it was overcome with the advent of capitalism. This is obvious to the naked eye, and no rationalization can alter reality. Under capitalism, even the use of precapitalist practices, such as chattel slavery and forced labor, is not ruled out.

This book takes as its starting point the observation that any power differential contains the potential of imperialism, both political and economic, and can be its generator. It seeks to shed light both on the backward-looking antecedents of imperialism and on its contemporary extensions. It detaches itself as much from visions which reserve imperialism for the capitalist mode of production, indeed for its most advanced stage, as from those which consider it antithetical to capitalism and consign it to a bygone past whose time is over. Backward, archaic, primitive, much like the state of nature, imperialism refers to the earliest forms of state organization and continues to the present. This book puts forward an analysis which conceives imperialism as a continuum extending from the past to the present.

At the risk of incurring the displeasure of both liberals and Marxists, the definition that derives from all of the above is that *imperialism constitutes a system of international economic transfers based on extra-economic means*. Economic exchanges themselves are not necessarily extortion. They take on an imperialist character when there is appropriation under non-economic pressure, mainly political and/or military coercion. In short, imperialism is the use of extra-economic means for economic ends. Economic depredation is its life blood. Added to facilitate it are political interference, cultural penetration, ideological pressure and, in the contemporary era, the use of mass media. The imperialist relationship is established either out of necessity for the metropolitan economy or out of opportunity to take advantage of the gap in development or power.

The chapters in this book review the fabric of imperialist control since the beginning of states. It goes without saying that the old forms were rudimentary and that they became more complex with the emergence of capitalism. The latter was consolidated as its center of gravity shifted from trade to industry and finance. A major transition took place in the twentieth century when imperialism, until then always embodied in a colonial form, assumed a predominantly non-colonial or postcolonial morphology. At the same time, the spatial scale of imperialism broadened: multiple and territorially defined empires gave way in the twentieth century to an imperialism with a universal scope.

In the background, the international economy, made up of isolated regions and unconnected colonial empires, sparsely crisscrossed by communication networks, densified to become a global economy extending over the whole planet and integrating its various parts. Dynamic and expansionist by its nature, capitalism as a system of production, exchange, and distribution brings the entire world into its fold. No region is supposed to lie beyond it. Every economy is called upon to be inserted, willingly or not, into some phase or other of the movement of the chain of production of goods or exchange of one or more commodities.

The multiplication and geographical extension of international economic relations are processes carried out over a long period of time, requiring prolonged maturation and qualitative changes. Both in volume and in value, cross-border transactions are increasing at a rate that is accelerating over time. From being episodic or limited, commercial exchanges became a constant whose ever-increasing importance makes it an indicator of the state of an economy. In addition to trade, movements of capital and the provision of services give external relations considerable weight in the economies of a growing number of countries. A more advanced stage ushers in the transition from the primacy of international trade to the internationalization of production. The international division of labor is propelled as never before. The circulation of goods through the market gives way to the multinationalization of production.

PART I

Coercive extraction: prehistory of imperialism (Antiquity and extensions)

While imperialism, in the true sense of the word, is a relatively recent phenomenon in the history of humanity, some of its constituent elements have origins that go back into the distant past. Rapine, dispossession, and extortion are types of crude extraction that are part and parcel of relations between human communities. Mirroring the growing complexity of societies, forms change. The primitive and undisguised methods of Antiquity and the premodern era are the crucible. They have the heuristic advantage of revealing with complete clarity the mechanisms in their primary forms, before they are perfected and shrouded by the evolution of socioeconomic organization.

CHAPTER 1

Early agricultural states:
islands in the natural economy

Following the stage of hunting-gathering and the pastoral economy, the emergence of agriculture in the Neolithic Era more than seven millennia ago was the precondition for the formation of states. Previously nomads, human groups became sedentary within a state framework, given that the development of irrigation works, river flood management, waterworks, canals, and drainage required centralization. The first states, born five millennia ago, straddled the fertile valleys of the Nile, the Tigris, the Euphrates, the Indus, the Ganges, and the Yellow rivers. Few in number and enclaves of relative prosperity, they were surrounded by peoples whose mode of organization was that of herders and breeders: tribal, mobile, fluid, subject to the imperative of the search for pastures and, periodically, set in motion by climatic accidents, droughts or demographic pressures on the ecumene. The Asian steppe was the largest source. As in a game of billiards, their migrations directly impacted their neighbors and had a ripple effect on a continental, even intercontinental, scale.

"Civilization" and "barbarism" lived side by side in a tense coexistence. If one depended on the river that supplied it with food, the other was at the mercy of the vagaries of nature, causing frequent and often chain displacements. When tribes were close to sedentary populations, raids on the territories of farmers or attempts to settle on them followed, provoking punitive expeditions in return. States' counter-offensives and their own internal dynamics translated into expansionist and annexationist thrusts. Then began the enterprise of coercive extraction of the resources of the conquered lands, normally by military means. The initiative belonged at times to so-called "civilized" states, at other times to so-called "barbarian" tribes, in an alternation that set the tempo of ancient history and early modern times. Equilibrium was definitively broken after the fifteenth century with the use of firearms capable of mowing down the cavalry of the nomads.

Given the low technological level, the states of antiquity and those of the Middle Ages did not hold a marked or lasting advantage in the balance of power with the tribes. A new means of fighting (bronze weapons, cavalry, war chariot-horse teams) or the weight of numbers were enough to give tribal confederations the upper hand over established states. The phenomenon is verifiable from the assault of the Hyksos on ancient Egypt (seventeenth century BC) to the arrival of the Mongols on the borders of Europe (fourteenth century AD). The age-old struggle between the world of farmers and that of shepherds, between tilled land and desert, steppe and mountain, was a constant of premodern history, explained and theorized by Ibn Khaldun in the fourteenth century AD.

Egyptian pharaohs waged war in Libya and Nubia to seize gold deposits. Those of the twelfth dynasty (1991-1786 BC) took over Nubia by force with the same purpose. From Asia the Hyksos arrived in Egypt, equipped with a new weapon unknown to the Egyptians, light and fast war chariots pulled by horses. From the seventeenth century to 1567 BC, they became the masters of Egypt, demonstrating the fact that ancient states did not outclass nomadic communities. No sooner had Egypt ousted the Hyksos and adopted their fighting methods than it set out to conquer territories beyond its borders. Initially, these strikes were preventive in nature, but the loot they yielded led to their transformation into military occupation.

Egypt pushed northeast to take Palestine and Syria, sources of supplies of trophies, tribute, metals and prisoners of war convertible into slaves. The Egyptian Empire evolved from a rapacious enterprise to a stable and sustainable system of resource extraction. The co-optation of local elements in the Egyptian administration was not uncommon. Having reached its peak in the fifteenth century BC, the Empire was, a century later, able to repel the advance of the Hittites, another Asian people. In the twelfth century BC, it lost its Middle Eastern possessions but successfully resisted the invasions of Libyan tribes and "sea peoples" coming from the Mediterranean. However, Egyptian power was undermined and its decline left the country vulnerable to a succession of conquerors: the Assyrian Empire (eighth to seventh centuries BC), the Persian Empire (sixth to fifth centuries BC), the Macedonian Empire (fourth century BC), the Roman Empire (first century BC).

The kingdom of Sumer, which federated the city-states of Mesopotamia, was formed around 3500 BC. It was constantly subjected to incursions by nomadic populations threatening it on its western and eastern flanks, while a short-lived empire was established in Akkad. A millennium and a half later, around 2000 BC, the destruction of the city of Ur by the Elamites coming from the Persian plateaus put an end to the kingdom of Sumer. Originating from the Syrian desert, the Amorites captured the Sumerian city of Babylon in 1850 BC and founded a dynasty as well as the Babylonian state which would establish its hegemony over Mesopotamia.

Following the destruction of Babylon around 1600 BC by the Hittites of Asia Minor, the Kassites of the Zagros mountains invaded Babylonian territory and ruled it for over four centuries. In the north of Mesopotamia, Assyria was under the tutelage of the Hurrians, an Anatolian people adept at using horse-drawn war chariots, since the seventeenth century BC. It emancipated itself from them in the fifteenth century BC and, in the twelfth century BC, extended its domination towards Asia Minor, before being caught in a vise-like grip by the Aramean tribes to the west and the people of the Zagros mountains to the east.

Recovering in the tenth century BC, the Assyrian Empire went on the path of conquest, equipped with a professional army wielding iron weapons. During the eight and ninth centuries BC, the Assyrian Empire encompassed the Middle East, from the Persian Gulf to Egypt, from Egypt to the borders of the Caucasus, including the island of Cyprus. It was destroyed by the Chaldeans of Babylon and the Medes of the Persian plateau in the eighth century BC, allowing the rebirth of the Babylonian Empire, which took over Assyria's possessions in Mesopotamia, Syria, Phoenicia, and Palestine. In turn, it was conquered by the Persian Empire of Cyrus in 539 BC. The primary function of these military-based enterprises was to extract a constant flow of tribute levied on subject peoples.

In the Indus Valley the cities of Mohenjo-Daro, Harappâ, and Kâlîbangan appeared in the third millennium BC. Equipped with war chariots and horses, Indo-European pastoralists invaded India from the northwest during the second millennium BC. The Indus civilization does not seem to have withstood the assaults of the "barbarians." Around the Ganges, the State of Magadha was formed in the third century BC, followed by the Maurya Empire (fourth-second centuries BC). The Macedonian army crossed the Ganges in 326 BC. In the fourth and fifth centuries AD, the Gupta dynasty unified northern India.

China followed the model of the bureaucratic-military empires of Egypt and Mesopotamia, expanding the territories under its control and fighting off invaders. The Xia dynasty ruled a state from the twenty-first to the sixteenth century BC. That of the Shang (sixteenth to eleventh centuries BC) was at the head of a slave society, which suggests prisoner-producing wars. Agriculture flourished under the Western Zhou dynasty (eleventh to eighth centuries BC), the descendants of invaders. In 771 BC, other invaders having sacked the capital and killed the emperor, the Eastern Zhou dynasty took over (eighth to third centuries BC).

The country was divided into a dozen small states under the sway of feudal princes and was at war with each other until the advent of the Qin dynasty (221 to 207 BC), itself overthrown by a peasant insurrection. The Western Han Empire (206 BC to 24 AD) successfully fought off Hun incursions into China's northern borderlands for more than nine years. It subjugated Korea, Manchuria, and Vietnam to China. In the year 22 AD, major peasant insurrections led to its downfall. A new peasant insurrection broke out in 184 AD under the Eastern Han Empire (25-220 AD). Divided between several kingdoms for two centuries, China was subjected to the penetration of nomadic tribes in the central, northern, and northwestern regions.

The practice of agriculture beyond river societies and civilizations was limited by a harsher or more fickle climate, less fertile soil or a less abundant, regular or controllable water supply than on the alluvial plains. Such was the lot of sub-Saharan Africa, dependent on unpredictable rainfall and arid soil, more often suited to livestock breeding and limited vegetable growing than to large-scale subsistence agriculture. By contrast, the Asian nomads who crossed the Bering Strait found in various places in the Americas—for example, in Peru—the conditions to settle down, farm, and found cities as far back as two millennia BC.

CHAPTER 2

Hellenic variant

Outside of the cradles of the agricultural revolution, farming could not be practiced to the exclusion of other economic activities. Crafts and commerce, also found in the societies of the great rivers, acquired greater importance elsewhere and sometimes supplanted agriculture. Such societies, economies and states were more diverse than agricultural communities. As the sea made long-distance trade possible, maritime societies and states, oriented towards the open sea, competed with land-based societies and states, even challenging their primacy. Navies became a new factor in the deployment of power for economic and military purposes. Born in this context and well placed to take advantage of it, maritime states made their entry into history, a phenomenon destined to be reinforced and to play a growing role in the centuries to come. The extraction of resources from subject regions was no longer confined to coercion by a land army occupying a territory; it now also came from the pressures exerted by those possessing war fleets. Maritime and commercial empires emerged alongside land empires.

Founded on the island of Crete by migrants from Anatolia around 2700 BC, Minoan civilization spread throughout the Aegean Sea. It was the first to depend on export-import trading. Advantageously located in the Eastern Mediterranean at the crossroads of Europe, Asia, and Africa, it specialized in the maritime trade of timber, metals and olive oil. Around 1700 BC, the first Greek (Mycenaean) incursions into Crete began and, after 1400 BC, the island became a component of the world of mainland Greece.

Having mastered the use of bronze, peoples from the northern Balkans ("Achaeans") invaded the Greek peninsula in 2000-1900 BC.

A second invasion took place in 1600-1580 BC. They gave birth to the Mycenaean civilization, which dominated the Aegean world from circa 1650 to 1100 BC. Agriculture on poor soil was no longer sufficient to feed the population; grain had to be imported from Italy, Sicily, and the Black Sea. The counterpart was the export of products in which Greece had a comparative advantage: olives, olive oil, wine, and manufactured goods. The growth of commerce favored specialization. As for Phoenicia, it offered a portrait close to that of Greece; its trajectory was synchronous with that of Greece. In fact, the Greeks first had to emancipate themselves from Phoenician intermediaries before trading on their own account. Known since the second millennium BC, Phoenician civilization acquired its commercial character around 1200 BC and took over from Crete.

These two merchant societies were the initiators of a process of colonization that resulted in dozens of new cities across the Mediterranean and the Black Sea during the eighth and seventh centuries BC. All overlooked the sea or were close to it; many were at the mouths of rivers that facilitated trade with the hinterland. Carthage was founded by Phoenicians in 814 BC. On the Greek side, Syracuse was born in 734 BC (origin: Corinth), Taranto at the end of the eighth century BC (origin: Sparta), Byzantium around 660 BC (origin: Megara), Massilia (Marseille, origin: Phocaea) in 600 BC. Southern Italy and Sicily became Hellenized. The process was competitive and the power of Carthage in the western Mediterranean eventually slowed Greek colonization. In addition to colonization, Greeks and Carthaginians had trading posts, essentially footholds for local trade consisting of a few houses, often simple neighborhoods in existing cities scattered along the Mediterranean coast.

One of the reasons for colonization was the shortage of arable land for a growing population. Tillable areas accounted for just one fifth of Greece's surface area. This was a critical factor as Athens had to source foodstuffs from abroad, including wheat from the northern Black Sea, to feed a population exceeding 300,000 inhabitants. Added to this was social tension: specialization led to the regulation of agriculture by the market, to the decline of food crops and to the expansion of areas devoted to vineyards and olive groves, providing sources of marketable products dependent on an increasing slave labor force. Prisoners of war, the traditional source of slaves, were joined by unfortunate debtors.

Debt-ridden small farmers were driven from their plots to be reduced to servitude or crowded into congested cities. Part of the impoverished or idle urban mass could find an outlet overseas. Political reasons also contributed to colonization since countless civil wars produced losers who went into exile or were exiled.

Whatever the cause, this was not colonization in the modern sense, i.e., the decision of a state to found colonies, or the establishment of overseas dependencies of a metropolis, or of settler colonies linked to a metropolis economically, politically, and militarily. There was no displacement of local populations to install settlers. These ancient colonies were reproductions of their *polis*, samples of their original civilization and means of showcasing it, while being independent in every respect. Although they exported foodstuffs to Greece, they produced what they wanted or could and traded with whomever they pleased, according to their own interests; their economies were not linked to their original *polis* in forced complementarity. Politically they did not come under the latter's authority. They engaged in alliances and military activities without referring to a metropolis. They founded new colonies themselves. The phenomenon was more akin to diffusion than to colonization as it was understood later in history. The expression "Greater Greece" reflected a cultural fact, not a political entity.

Although largely maritime, Athens was also engaged in partly land-based conflicts with other Greek cities. Buoyed by its victories against the Persians at Marathon in 490 BC and at Salamis in 480 BC, Athens seized the opportunity to try to transform itself into an empire imposing its authority on the Greek world, under the pretext of compensation for its sacrifices in the common struggle against the eastern enemy. The navy ensured the city's supplies. Alleging that it provided common defense, Athens sought to finance it by demanding a tribute from its allies, whom it treated as if they were vanquished.

The Athenian economy came to depend on this pumping of resources, characteristic of imperialism. The trend was the same as in Mesopotamia: wars between cities led to the supremacy of one of them. In Greece, it was thwarted by an anti-Athenian coalition which prevailed during the Peloponnesian War (431-404 BC). Philip and Alexander of Macedonia, at the head of a land power mobilizing an army of mercenaries and an elite cavalry, achieved the unification of Greece under their authority. The territories that Alexander conquered from Greece to India (336-323 BC) amounted to a purely military and short-lived construct in the tradition of land empires.

CHAPTER 3

Roman model

Off-center from the eastern Mediterranean, a small region in the middle of the Italian peninsula became the birthplace of the greatest empire of Antiquity. Populated by farmers cultivating land irrigated by the Tiber, Latium was home to the city of Rome, founded in 753 BC, according to legend. Ruled by kings until 509 BC, it became the main city of Latium and took over the leadership of the Latin Confederation, grouping together all the cities in the area. This marked the beginning of a long process of more or less consensual aggregation and especially of annexations via military conquests of increasingly distant regions and countries. Like a wave spreading over five centuries, it made the Roman Republic first the overlord of Italy (265 BC), then of the Western Mediterranean, finally of the Eastern Mediterranean. Unfolding empirically, it responded less to a preconceived plan than to an expansionist dynamic driven by the opportunities that presented themselves and subject to the balance of power. The tool was an army that mobilized citizens and was made up of legions of disciplined infantrymen.

With the Italian peninsula under their control, the Romans set their sights on Sicily and its rich wheat and mineral resources. There they encountered Carthage, the great Phoenician city which dominated the western Mediterranean with its navy and trade. Carthage was tied up with fighting against the Greek city-colonies, but it had to turn its attention to the new pretender. In the First Punic War (264-241 BC), the Romans wrested Sicily, even winning the naval war against the sea power of Carthage. Sicily was the first Roman province. Roman expansionism now extended beyond the Italian peninsula.

In the Second Punic War (218-202 BC), after the scare caused by Hannibal's breakthrough, the Romans took Spain from the Carthaginians and landed in North Africa. The landlubbers of Latium now had a navy which was in command of the western Mediterranean. Corsica and Sardinia were protectorates. Carthage had to pay a huge indemnity and place itself under the de facto tutelage of Rome. But it remained a competitor as a producer of oil and wine. Half a century later, using a pretext provided by its ally, the North African kingdom of Numidia, Rome issued an ultimatum to Carthage, pushing it to revolt.

There followed the Third Punic War (149-146 BC) at the end of which Carthage was razed to the ground, its population enslaved, and North Africa incorporated as a Roman province. Strangely, Carthage, a naval power, won its main victories on land in Italy. Conversely, it was unable to capitalize on its initial superiority at sea or to match Rome's ability to form alliances with potential adversaries of its enemies. Even before the conquest of Gaul (58-50 BC), the western Mediterranean was Roman and would remain so for four centuries, until the disintegration of the Roman Empire.

The very year of the annihilation of Carthage, Corinth was destroyed by the Romans. The Eastern Mediterranean was already attracting their attention. Macedonia was made a protectorate in 197 BC and annexed in 148 BC. Syria was conquered in 189 BC. Taking advantage of the rivalries between the Greek cities, Rome subjugated them all in 146 BC. The states of Asia Minor and Egypt entered into the fold of Rome. Roman power rested on the local aristocracies and elites: everywhere it supported them and, in return, received their support. A vast empire could not be administered without local relays. This model will be that of other empires until the present day. From circa 130 BC, the entire Mediterranean basin became a Roman lake. Master of all its shores, the Roman Empire had no rival in the west or the east. Taking a liking to conquests and territorial acquisitions, the inhabitants of a remote land demonstrated a spirit of continuity generation after generation and imposed their *imperium* on the ancient world.

With the Roman Empire can be discerned the outlines of imperialism in its stripped-down form as a system—both forced and structural—of continuous pumping of distant resources towards the home territory of the empire. Rome followed in the footsteps of its predecessor, the Athenian Empire, but the scale and duration are of a very different order. If the transfer of wealth is a corollary of conquests, the sheer quantity which made its way to Rome was such that it led to long-lasting consequences and changes affecting the foundations of the Roman economy and society. Imperialism transforms those who implement it.

The influx of slaves, ex-prisoners of war, by the hundreds of thousands, of booty, of indemnities, of tribute, of taxes, of requisitions in grain and metals, radically altered the Roman world. A new layer of dealers, middlemen, and hoarders made up of slave traffickers, large grain traders, usurers, and tax farmers (publicans) carved out a special place for itself in the upper echelons of the state. They were complemented by the military commanders and governors who, for their personal account, systematically bled the provinces; Roman control was heavy-handed and without niceties. A large and powerful category of *nouveaux riches* now had a vested interest in the empire; it was wedded to imperialism, providing it with its social base. War was good business and conquest even better. Imperialism became a necessity and an end unto itself.

With unpaid slave labor at their disposal, large landowners expanded their estates. *Latifundia* and plantations covered the best land of Italy and undermined smallholdings. The free peasantry was ruined. Independent soldier-plowers were in short supply. Returning from distant military campaigns, they had to go into debt in order to restore their plots fallen fallow and ended up losing their land to the big owners, thus swelling the contingents of slaves, landless, unemployed, destitute, and idle people. They drifted as refugees to Rome to swell the population of inactive poor wretches, plebeians who had to be fed by distribution of cereals brought in enormous quantities from the farthest reaches of the empire. Rome consumed a lot and produced little. Rome's food supply depended on the possession of foreign territories, notably Egypt and North Africa, the empire's granaries, because the latifundia owners specialized, abandoning grain for vineyards and orchards.

The classic parasitic pattern appeared: with Italy producing less than the provinces, its trade deficit was balanced by tribute extorted from the provinces and subject countries. Also under strain, urban handicrafts could not resist competition from slave labor and imports of manufactured products from the provinces. The outcome was the multiplication of the number of *déclassé* urban dwellers and the spread of pauperism. The old type of proletariat grew as a social category, reflecting the fact that primitive imperialism had reconfigured society from a universe of small-scale producers or tenants (*coloni*) to a slave economy and society.

The economic development of the Roman Empire was extensive in nature. It reached its maximum territorial limit at the beginning of the Christian era. Expansion no longer brought fertile land suitable for large-scale cultivation by slave labor. For the Empire, the issue became one of defending what had been acquired, a task complicated by the incessant civil wars between pretenders to the office of emperor. Border security was less and less assured in the face of incursions by "Barbarians." From then on, the primary obligation was to prevent infiltration and dismemberment of the empire. This proved to be an arduous mission. Civil wars, insecurity, and plague epidemics reduced the population, dried up commerce, depopulated cities, and under-mined production. The tax base shrank, increasing the fiscal burden and exacerbating general impoverishment, while the depreciation of the currency caused inflation. It became difficult to bear the costs of a state apparatus commensurate with a vast empire and an army sufficient to defend it. The crisis was multifaceted: fiscal, monetary, administrative, and military.

A slave economy, based on mass enslavement, requires a perma-nent supply of candidates for servitude. The end of the conquests dried up the supply of war captives and raised their price. As labor became scarce, landowners left their estates unattended. Others reorganized their operating mode, allowing tenants to lease part of their estates (*villae*) and demanding in return payment in unpaid labor (*corvée*), in cash and in kind. In 332, against a backdrop of labor shortages, these *coloni* were forbidden to leave the estates, a measure aimed at attaching them to the land which heralded serfdom. As the state crumbled, these properties evolved into autonomous economic and administrative entities, living in a closed economy. Here lies the genesis of the fief and fiefdom of the medieval period.

Society was unraveling and the state was in dire straits since the third century AD. The capital had to be moved to a safer location,

ROMAN MODEL • 39

sheltered from the marauding tribes that easily entered the *limes* of the empire. Its transfer in 330 to Constantinople (the new name of Byzantium) on the banks of the Bosphorus was not enough. In 395, the empire was split into two parts, each with its own emperor. However, in 405-406, the Germans and Celts were set in motion by the arrival in Europe of the Huns, who pushed them to penetrate deeply into various parts of the Western Roman Empire. The ranks and the leadership of the Roman armies already included "Barbarians." The Western emperor was at their mercy. They sacked Rome in 410 and, when one of their chiefs deposed the emperor and declared himself king in 476, the Western Roman Empire ceased to exist.

The "barbarian invasions" occurred as the Roman Empire decomposed. Its disintegration was punctuated by revolts of ruined peasants and artisans, joined by slaves, even if it did not result from a social implosion, let alone from a military defeat. It fell due to its internal weakening and its proximity to tribal entities, themselves in difficulty. Two factors coincided: on the one hand, the exhaustion of a slave regime and, on the other hand, the dialectic pitting nomadic against sedentary communities, a phenomenon known since the emergence of agricultural societies bordering rivers in Egypt, Mesopotamia, India, and China. On a level specific to the Roman Empire, its collapse was inscribed in its very nature.

In *Considérations sur les causes de la grandeur et de la décadence des Romains* (1734), Montesquieu attributed the failure in the administration of the empire to several factors, mainly to the inadequacy of its institutions. As for Edward Gibbon, he set out in *The History of the Decline and Fall of the Roman Empire* (1776-1788) to identify the causes of the demise, not the least of which was the spread of Christianity. While acknowledging their originality, discernment and elevation, it is important to look beyond these two classic landmark works.

The sustainability of the Roman Empire depended on a permanent process of conquests, essential to supplying the slave labor and material resources needed to maintain it. Once it reached the limits of its territorial growth and adopted a defensive position, the external inputs were no longer available, the system jammed, and the empire lost the wherewithal to reproduce and defend itself. With a size unmatched by its predecessors, the Roman Empire carried the logic of slave empires to its conclusion and revealed their limits. They had to expand, or risk dysfunction and deadlock a prelude to fragmentation. The dismantling of the Roman Empire signaled the twilight of slavery in Europe.

The Eastern Empire spanned the Balkans, Crete, Cyprus, Rhodes, Asia Minor, Syria, Palestine, Egypt, and Cyrenaica. The largest cities were located there: Constantinople, Antioch, Damascus, Alexandria. In the Balkans, it came under pressure from the Slavs, Avars, and Magyars. After the vain attempts of the Emperor Justinian (sixth century) to recover the territories of the late Western Empire, the Byzantine Empire focused on stabilization and self-protection. To the east, it kept up conflictual relations with Sassanid Persia. In the seventh century, in addition to a victory against Persia (637-644), the Arabs took away Syria (634-636), Egypt (640-642) and North Africa (698). They besieged Constantinople in 670, were halted there again in 717 and took Crete and part of Sicily in the ninth century. The Empire was diminished in the eleventh century by the weakness of the emperors and the struggle between the rich elites and the state bureaucracy. The Seljuk Turkic tribes, soon to be Persianized, ousted it from most of Asia Minor after the Battle of Manzikert (1071). Their Ottoman successors seized Gallipoli in 1354, Adrianople in 1362, and the Balkan peninsula (Serbia, Bulgaria, Greece) in 1389. The Empire was reduced to paying tribute to them in 1399 and Constantinople fell to them in 1453. The eastern empire outlived the western one by a millennium.

CHAPTER 4

Post-Roman extraction

A rab expansion is a *sui generis* case. The fact that Bedouin and
Semitic semi-nomads emerge from the Arabian Peninsula to integrate into the established societies of Mesopotamia or Syria and settle
down is hardly original, were it not for the fact that they were, in this
case, bearers of a new religion and driven by the desire to spread it.
Although still present, economic motivations (loot, tribute, etc.) cannot suffice as an explanation for such an outburst. Religious ardor was
a substratum which ensured the geographical extent and duration of
the phenomenon. This extension had a missionary component which
gave it its uniqueness. More prosaically, however, it also involved taking over existing commercial circuits and communications networks.

Stretching from Asia to North Africa, these had as their link and
obligatory crossing point the Arabian Peninsula and the Levant. As
traditional intermediaries, the Arabs became the coordinators of an
intercontinental exchange system linking distant markets. From Syria
and Persia, the Arabs went to North Africa, Spain, and as far as the
south of France. They reached the limits of their advance at Poitiers
(732). After them, other ethnic groups (Turkish, Afghan, Indian, etc.)
adopted Islam and made it the vector of their establishment in the
Balkans, Central Asia, China, Insulindia (the Malay Archipelago)
and Africa south of the Sahara.

Whether it be desert, steppe or sea, wide open spaces are the world
of mobility, where warriors are set in motion by inhospitable nature
or a demographic overflow in relation to the resources available in an
ecosystem. During the ninth and tenth centuries, Western Europe was
subject to raids and demands for tribute (*Danegeld*) from the Vikings
or "Normans" (Danes, Norwegians, Swedes), a Nordic and maritime

version of the tribal land-based incursions that had hitherto originated in the east. It took the offensive against the Muslim world by means of eight Crusades (1095-1270), undertaken by Christianity at the behest of the Papacy and independently of states. Like the expansion of the Arabs, the Crusades were driven by religious fervor; the Seljuk Turks had just taken Jerusalem in 1071 and refused access to Christian pilgrims in 1078.

As for the fabulous riches of the East, more developed than Western Christendom, they aroused vocations that were not solely spiritual. Soon enough faith waned. The religious justification for the Crusades gave way to a taste for conquest, looting and marauding. In a movement foreshadowing the struggles between colonial empires of the future, competing Italian city-states transported, supplied, and financed the warriors, before seizing the conquered cities like Antioch, Jerusalem, Acre, and Tyre. Establishing themselves there, Italian merchants turned their warehouses and trading posts (*fondaco*) into commercial outposts of their mother cities.

The Fourth Crusade (1202-1204) was a thinly disguised economic war. Venice directed it against Constantinople, the largest city in the region with a million inhabitants, where the Genoese competitors and the emperor stood in the way. Free rein was given to hostility towards Greco-Eastern Christianity (the break with Western "Latin" Christianity was complete as of 1054), but the objective lay elsewhere. Stormed by the Crusaders, Constantinople was pillaged, the emperor deposed, and the Genoese dislodged. Having monopolized the trade of the Byzantine Empire and gained a foothold in Egypt and on the Syrian coast, Venice stood out. As master of trade in the Levant, the Eastern Mediterranean, and the Black Sea, it was the leading commercial power in Europe. In 1261, Genoa counterattacked, installed a puppet emperor and deprived Venice of its commercial primacy in the Bosphorus and the Black Sea. But Venice defeated Genoa in the War of Chioggia (1378-1381), then Verona in 1402 and Padua in 1405.

The Crusades confirmed the Italian port cities' stranglehold over the import and export trade of the Byzantine Empire. They provided them with an opportunity to enrich themselves and realize their ambitions to corner trade from the Western Mediterranean to the Eastern Mediterranean and the Black Sea. Merchant vessels were protected by state galleys. Buyers of spices, silks, cotton, fabrics, wines, cereals, etc., Italian merchants had little to offer that would be of interest to more advanced economies; they had to make disbursements in gold and other precious metals. Their deficit was more than made up and losses were recovered by re-exports at high prices to end-buyers in Europe.

Saint Jean d'Acre, the last stronghold erected by the Crusaders, fell in 1291. It was the birthplace of the Order of the Teutonic Knights. When the Crusades ended, these fighters returned to Europe to pursue, in concert with other orders, a new adventure: expansion towards the east, north-east and south-east of Europe. Demographic growth in the twelfth century prompted expansion of the inhabited and useful space in Europe; hence the draining and reclamation of marshlands in Flanders and the Netherlands, as well as the recovery of polders and the construction of dikes in the Low Countries. The eastward expansion, a process punctuated by aggressions and massacres, colonization, Germanic repopulation, and the acquisition of estates and serfs, took place at the expense of the Slavs and the populations of the Baltic.

It portended the colonial expansionism which began with the "discoveries" of the fifteenth century and lasted into the twentieth century. Evangelization served as the justification for this *Drang nach Osten* (drive to the East), with the popes launching Crusades this time targeting the pagans. Christianization and Germanization were added to the annual tribute, the services required from the peasantry, and the installation of Germanic settlers. The invasion was halted in 1242 following defeat in the battle on the ice of Lake Peipus near Novgorod.

In Ireland, the English colonial enterprise unfolded in three stages: the eastern side of the island was conquered at the end of the twelfth century; the entire island came under the domination of the English crown at the end of the fifteenth century, a prelude to land seizure and colonization by English owners; the landing of Cromwell's troops in 1649 led to the massacre of almost half the population, the intensification of land confiscation for the benefit of settlers arriving from England and oppression now worsened by "anti-Papist" religious fervor.

The Russian experience is that of the unification and coagulation of tribal successors of the Scythian and Sarmatian "barbarians" into a state that faced the incursions of other tribal entities to the west and the east, even enduring occupation for more than two centuries following one of the invasions. Although the Slavs were a threat to the Byzantine Empire, they were perpetually on the defensive in the immense Eurasian space. The state they formed absorbed some of its invaders and expelled others in a brutal historical sequence where the stakes were of existential significance. The determining factor was the strength or weakness of the state. There was a striking similarity with the ancient pattern—Egyptian, Mesopotamian, Indian, Chinese or Roman—of centuries-old struggle between sedentary and nomadic peoples. Another similarity was the fact that each conquest resulted in the imposition of a system of tribute payments.

In the fourth century, the Goths threatened from the west, the Huns from the east; in the sixth century, the Finns penetrated from the west, the Avars, then the Khazars, from the southwest. In the seventh and eighth centuries, Swedish Vikings (Varangians) reached southern Russia, settling there to be assimilated with the Slavs. At the end of the nineth century, a state was formed in Kiev. Pechenegs and Cumans put pressure on its southeastern flanks. At the same time as the Teutonic Knights and the Swedes went on the offensive in the west and were driven back, the last great outflow of Asian nomads towards sedentary societies began.

The Mongols (or Tatars) took Beijing in 1215, then Central Asia in 1219, before heading towards Europe. They did not neglect Korea, which they subdued between 1231 and 1257. They burst into south-eastern Europe in 1223 and returned in 1237 to undertake an invasion, a preliminary stage in an occupation of eastern and western Russia which would last until the fifteenth century. Next came Persia and the Abbasid empire, whose fate was the worst. Baghdad was devastated, its population massacred, and the last Abbasid caliph killed in 1258.

The empire of Genghis Khan and his lineage was a military state based on the superiority and mobility of its cavalry mounted on sturdy ponies. Its aim was to extract wealth from conquered lands. While Kiev, Moscow and other cities were destroyed, the hallmarks of conquest were pillage, slavery, conscription into the armies of the "Golden Horde," heavy taxes (capitation) and payment of tribute. The Mongols let the Russian princes administer and collect taxes as they did before the conquest, provided they paid the required tribute.

From 1362, dissensions and conflicts between Mongol khans (princes) allowed a Russian revival initiated by the Grand Duke of the

Principality of Moscow. Russian artillery countered Mongol cavalry. Tatars placed themselves in the service of the Russians in 1452 and complete independence was declared in 1480. The Muscovite state emerged from an effort to repel foreign domination, a phenomenon synchronous with and comparable to the reconquest of the kingdom of France at the end of the Hundred Years' War (1453) and the Spanish *reconquista* (1492). Ivan III married the niece of the last Byzantine emperor in 1472. The fall of Constantinople in 1453 gave him the symbolic status of continuator of the Byzantine Empire and the Muscovite state, which the Kievan principality joined at the end of the tenth century, the role of Orthodox Christianity. This ushered in an era of territorial expansion spanning two and a half centuries, and including colonization in the south, in the southeast and in Siberia.

In northern India, the power of the Gupta dynasty (320-570), whose cradle was the lower Ganges plain near Bengal, gave way to a period of fragmentation and disorder. Divided, the Indian kingdoms were unable to resist the raids of Muslim Afghan horsemen that began in 998. From 1191 to 1200, they occupied northern India. Although it conquered Bengal in 1202, the Delhi Sultanate (1206-1526) controlled only the northern part of the Indian subcontinent, as the resistance of the southern states proved insurmountable. Lacking a bureaucracy and not having effective control over the provinces, the sultanate was unstable. Weakened and breaking up into several small states, it was swept away by a Mongol invasion commanded by Taimur (Tamarlane) in 1398; Delhi was ransacked.

Its renaissance in 1450 was short-lived; a new invasion from the north put an end to it following the battle of Panipat in 1526. Founded by Babur, a descendant of Taimur and of Genghis Khan, the Moghul dynasty dominated India until 1707. Their state was a confederation of warriors, better organized than the one it replaced and equipped with a bureaucratic apparatus worthy of the name. From 1681 to 1690, the kingdoms of the center and south of the peninsula were conquered. For the first time in its history, the subcontinent was unified, albeit briefly because rebellions immediately broke out. The Moghul Empire disintegrated from 1707, existing only formally for a century and a half. In 1858, it was abolished by Great Britain.

In China, dynasties succeeded each other in the wake of peasant revolts and civil wars, while the ongoing struggle between settled society and nomads from the north continued. The Sui dynasty (581-618) exhausted itself and China in military expeditions against the tribes of the northwest and against Korea; a major peasant insurrection led to its overthrow. The Tang (618-907) fought against the Turkish tribes by calling on the intervention of other Turkic tribes (Uighurs). They eventually gave up defending the borders militarily and instead paid tribute to the nomads. Incursions to the north resumed between 936 and 960, although on a lesser scale.

While China was unified under the Song dynasty (960-1127), it had to pay tribute to the northern nomads to ensure its tranquility, which did not prevent the capital from falling into their hands in 1126. The Mongols launched an attack on China in 1234, took the capital in 1276 and were masters of the country in 1279. The Yuan dynasty (1271-1368) was Mongol; its fall was indirectly caused by the Black Death (1348-1349). In 1449, the Ming dynasty (1368-1644) suffered defeat at the hands of the Mongols and the emperor was taken prisoner. At the end of the seventeenth century, the Qing dynasty (1636-1912) was again battling a Mongol tribe. In the case of China, a country in a largely defensive posture, it was the state that experienced drainage for the benefit of nomadic populations.

Retrospect and perspective

As a prehistory of imperialism, the ancient and premodern period came to its conclusion. It faded out without ending or being relegated to the past. The primitive form of imperialism took on the character of undisguised extraction of wealth through coercion. Force carried and conferred its own legitimacy. Depending on the case and the need, it was accompanied by a complementary justification: the proclaimed superiority of one's protective deities or of one's religion. Such was the matrix of imperialism and its original modus operandi. Partaking of confiscation and dispossession, imperialism did not spring from an irrepressible desire to carry out armed proselytism for one's faith or civilization, but it could indulge in it.

Alongside this pre-imperialism, based on the simple diversion of wealth by extra-economic means, emerged a new type of imperialism. It was soon to become the dominant form. While remaining fully operational, the force component left more and more room for structural factors in the functioning of the economy. From being essentially politico-military, imperialism became economic-politico-military. From primarily state-based, it mutated into a field of concerted action between the state and private economic interests.

Its genesis dated back to the prehistoric period of imperialism. Port cities facing the open sea emerged to compete with land-based empires. Carthage, then Venice, were the archetypes of domination through commerce, supported by a merchant fleet and defended, even imposed, by a navy. The maritime model was destined for a promising future as new, fast-growing states embraced it. In the hands of a merchant oligarchy, Venice constituted the forerunner of the capitalist state.

Another configuration appeared as early as the Middle Ages. Flemish manufacture tended to make England a supplier of wool and an importer of textile products from Flanders. The model of specialization between primary economies based on raw materials and processing economies took shape. In 1331, the King of England reacted by inviting Flemish weavers to settle in his kingdom. Protectionist measures in favor of national manufacturing followed: a monopoly of maritime transport for English ships in 1381; a ban on the importation of textiles from the continental Europe in 1464.

Not without irony, given its future role as champion of commercial freedom, England illustrated the importance of protective state action in the emergence of national manufacturing. It escaped the relationship of structural economic dependence that will be the lot of many countries. In any case, although the more economic and modern form of imperialism took precedence over the purely coercive and ancient form, the two variants coexisted, as if history was averse to discard what could always be of use.

PART II

Appropriation by force: colonial imperialism in the modern era

War, the matrix of killings, compensations, reparations, annexations, and looting, has occurred in all eras. At the same time, the crude extraction at the basis of primitive imperialism did not disappear; it perpetuated itself. Territorial acquisitions, brutal occupations, predations, and exterminations of populations punctuate the centuries of the modern period. Colonization and slavery even extended significantly. The Church forbade the enslavement of Christians, but not of pagans and heretics. If the invasive movements of tribal confederations of the past ended, the displacement of populations continued in the reverse, but no less violent, form of settler colonialism as part of the colonial expansion of European countries.

As for tribute, alongside the indirect forms applied by the new European empires, the Ottoman Empire levied it directly until the eve of the First World War at the beginning of the twentieth century. In many respects, German domination of the European continent during the Second World War was a vector of raw extraction and primary imperialism, supplemented by later forms of dispossession, such as depopulation of spaces to be colonized in Eastern Europe (*lebensraum*) and forced integration of the economies of satellite countries. With German eastward expansionism, capitalism and neomercantilist imperialism spawned settler colonialism in Eastern Europe, the bloodiest and most backward form of colonization, an outgrowth of the colonial practices of Western imperialism in the non-Western world. Supremacism, racism, and genocide were constituent features throughout.

However, each historical phase highlights and favors certain methods of appropriation, without necessarily rendering previous ones obsolete. The modern era is characterized by the advent of capitalism and the spread of a more advanced form of imperialism. In a relationship of reciprocity, the two develop concurrently with the emergence of a global market. Capitalism is to be understood as an economic system where private ownership of the means of production, production for the market, and wage labor (labor power as a commodity) dominate.

It does not exclude the presence of other relations, such as serfdom, forced labor or slavery, but they are either residual or subordinate and integrated into its circuits. The establishment of capitalism was a long and cumulative process. In Europe, it extended from the early modern era in the fifteenth century to the nineteenth century. For a long time, it was only embryonic, with simple forms of private property accompanying restricted commodity production. The latter then became predominant, the last stage being the generalization of wage labor.

Always based on force, the imperialism of the modern era included more and more economic ties. From outright seizure by a state of a territory beyond its sovereignty, it transitioned to a siphoning of wealth and a draining of resources by means of an economic system underpinned by force. Furthermore, the militarization of international trade was synchronous with the birth of new European dynastic states for whom it was a source of power, and with the increased importance of the colonial and overseas aspect of trade. The quest for monopoly was paramount. A matter of interest to both the State and individuals, it was more than ever a function of the use of military means and subject to the fortunes of war.

Always legitimized by some rationale, imperialism added to the religious cloak, which it never completely shed, a secular justification that was more unabashedly assertive. The synthesis generated during the Crusades, which blended missionary and economic interests, was to have a deep and lasting impact, as well as many incarnations. Yet, making noble or humanist ideals, first religious then secular, go hand in hand with crass greed and murderous violence constituted an ideological and intellectual challenge which would henceforth be inseparable from the history of imperialism. Limitless ingenuity would have to be called upon to stress the former and obscure or downplay the latter, setting the stage for the later obligation to admit wrongdoing and display repentance, without however paying reparations.

The modern era from the fifteenth to the eighteenth centuries, and its aftermath in the nineteenth and twentieth centuries, is that of a new type of colonialism. Similar to the colonization of Ireland, and that attempted in Eastern Europe in the twelfth and thirteenth centuries, it differed from ancient colonization—Phoenician or Hellenic—in several respects. The new colonialism was the work of states or individuals supported by states implementing a project of national construction or expansion. It was part of their overall economic policy which thoroughly linked the economies of the colonies to those of the European metropolises.

It was explicitly aimed at the economic specialization of both within the framework of nascent capitalism. Finally, where conditions were suitable and always under the aegis of the metropolises, it involved the settlement of European colonists on lands conquered and taken by force from Indigenous populations. Whether colonies or settler colonies, these overseas dependencies were exclusive possessions of their respective metropolises and part of formally constituted empires.

From the end of the fifteenth century, emerging capitalism generated a new type of imperialism based on the acquisition of overseas colonies. Colonial imperialism extended from the sixteenth to the twentieth centuries. Its manifestation depended on the physiognomy and stage of development of capitalism. Commercial capitalism projected itself into mercantilist imperialism from the sixteenth to the eighteenth centuries, the first phase of capitalist imperialism. Industrial capitalism formed the basis of free-trade imperialism in the nineteenth century, the second phase of capitalist imperialism.

From the end of the nineteenth century to the first half of the twentieth century, commercial, industrial, and financial capitalism engendered a neomercantilist imperialism eager for new colonies, but also spilling over into formally independent countries, particularly in the financial sphere. The world wars, the transformations of capitalism, and the liberation of the colonies in the twentieth century ushered in a new era. Colonial imperialism gave way to an imperialism without colonies, postcolonial, and globalist, extending to all independent countries, whether developed or underdeveloped.

The modern era saw a shift in the world's center of gravity, the importance of which cannot be overstated. The main pole in the history of most of mankind, Eurasia, including its Egyptian and Mediterranean annexes, was supplanted by the Atlantic zone. On the periphery of Eurasia, a peninsula of the Asian land mass, Europe—and more so Western and Northern Europe—was originally no more than an appendage of secondary value, a promontory overlooking little-known seas of no tangible interest.

At the end of the fifteenth century, the originality and the first results of internal changes —economic, social, political, military, intellectual—made themselves felt, giving Europe a formidable increase in power compared to the ancient world. Continued and augmented over the following centuries, these transformations would make Western Europe the overlord and pivot of the world for half a millennium. Outflanking Asia, taking possession of the Americas and, then, of most of the other continents, the maritime powers of the North Atlantic, previously countries of secondary status, replaced the former Eurasian land powers and imposed a hegemony on the entire world that is still relevant today.

From that point on, the offensive was unidirectional: from the Western Hemisphere towards the rest of the world. Half a dozen European powers bordering the Atlantic would bring to bear their superior military means, organization, and strategies to achieve their ends. Of an unprecedented kind, modern and contemporary imperialism was the handiwork of these Western countries and their American offspring, with only Japan joining them in the twentieth century. All ancient civilizations were vulnerable and imperiled in the face of a threat for which nothing had prepared them. The consequences of contact, more precisely of clashes, often proved catastrophic for them.

The modern era also witnessed a quantum leap in the formation of an international economy that stretched beyond the immediate area or territory close to it. Trade relations of a regional nature were to be found in Northern Europe, the Mediterranean, the Indian Ocean, and

East Asia. Exchange between these regions was rare and ephemeral. At most, more regular commercial links were established for specific high-value products, such as Asian spices and Yemeni coffee, whose land and sea routes led to Europe. From the fifteenth century onward, the outlines of an international economy began to appear, linking all continents through the movement of goods and precious metals, then of people, and finally of capital. Initially small in scale, internationalization continued to grow in volume and complexity.

CHAPTER 5

Mercantilist imperialism
and economic zones

A tangible model guided cross-border expansion of national economies in formation. Practice and theory existed for a long time
without the terminology to describe the new realities. It was later on,
when the questioning began, that the detractors of the model called it
"mercantilism" in order to label, or even reify, all of the propositions
they intended to refute. Adam Smith, advocate of free trade, was the
first and foremost spokesman for this movement. The expression hit
the mark because it adequately conveyed a way of thinking and the
policies that flowed from it.

a. Mercantilism

As much a toolbox as a doctrine for building and strengthening the
economy of the territorial dynastic state, mercantilism can only be
understood in an international context. Clearly or vaguely, contemporaries perceived that increase in wealth was a component of state
power. Mercantilism was a practical economic doctrine, aimed at
building the state, its *potestas* and its *imperium*. It was a doctrine for
combat against other states and for weakening them.

The reports of Barthélemy de Laffemas and the *Traité de l'œcon-
omie politique* (1615) of Antoine de Montchrestien were early expres-
sions of mercantilism. It was in foreign trade that wealth lay, argued
Thomas Mun, a London merchant and director of the East India
Company, in *England's Treasure by Foreign Trade* (1662). England
had to sell more to foreigners than it bought from them. In the same
vein, another director of the EIC, Josiah Child, published *A New*

Discourse on Trade (1665 or 1668). The goal was a self-sufficient economy capable of providing the resources to wage war and international competition was the yardstick of success.

Exports were desirable and had to exceed imports so that the difference could be settled in favor of the exporting country by means of precious metals. A positive trade balance attracted gold and silver from abroad. Emphasis was placed on the production of manufactured goods, those whose added value in the form of labor allowed more species to be brought home in exchange for exports. Thus mercantilism was both bullionist, even predatory, and incidentally productivist/industrialist.

Matthew Decker, a director of the EIC, made the point in *An Essay on the Causes of the Decline of Foreign Trade, Consequently of the Value of the Lands of Britain, and on the Means to Restore Both. Begun in the Year 1739* (1739):

> Therefore if the Export of Britain exceed its Import, Foreigners must pay the Balance in Treasure and the Nation grow Rich; But if the Import of Britain exceed its Export, we must pay the Foreigners the Balance in Treasure and the Nation grow poor.

At the same time, national power was always sought after. In his *Essai politique sur le commerce* (1734), Jean-François Melon defended mercantilism, protectionism, and slavery.

Tropism towards the Iberian experience in an America overflowing with silver and gold, a bullionist fixation, and a precious metals fetish gave mercantilism its distinctive features. The state needed these metals to finance incessant and increasingly costly wars. Ultimately, the balance of trade and the balance of silver and gold metals were considered to be indicators of the state of health of the economy.

The mercantilist system was, by definition, protectionist. Conflictual relations were at the root of mercantilist thinking because wealth was viewed as originating from outside, while the economy was static, as it had been for millennia marked by scarcity. In a zero-sum game, the enrichment of one economy involved the impoverishment of its rivals. Both the physical product and the precious metals were conceived as fixed at a given point in time. Rival economies shared them in proportion to their ability to snatch markets, aided by the armed support of their respective states. It was the duty of the state and its proper political and military action to capture the largest share of constant global wealth. The wealth of its nationals grew thanks to the interventionism of the state and its protective role.

Mercantilism was closely associated with the quest for colonies. The state's will to power and colonial expansion went hand in hand. The first entailed wars, the second had to provide precious metals to cover expenses, particularly those of war. The desire for self-sufficiency, even the exaltation of autarky, a quest for precious metals, and the promotion of manufacturing were the motivations underlying colonial policy. As appendages of the metropolis, the colonies supplied raw materials and re-exportable products, while serving as captive markets for its manufactured goods. Slavery provided the labor force for colonial plantations. "The negro-trade, therefore, and the national consequences resulting from it, may be justly esteemed an inexhaustible fund of wealth and naval power to this nation," wrote Malachy Postlethwayt, English mercantilist author and director of the Royal Africa Company, in 1746, in *The National and Private Advantages of the African Trade Considered*.

The implementation of mercantilist thinking gave rise to various applications. All chartered companies enjoyed privileges and monopolies in line with the general principles of mercantilism. On the other hand, the degree of state intervention in production processes varied: high in France during Colbert's era, significant in England, low in the Netherlands. The weapon of tariffs was wielded vigorously by England and France, less by the Netherlands which, moreover, did not prohibit the outflow of cash.

A touchstone of the mercantilist system, the protection of the merchant marine led to granting it a monopoly for transport in national ports. In 1651, Dutch shipping accounted for half of English maritime transport. England rigorously enforced the Navigation Acts of 1651 and 1660 against the Dutch commercial fleet, whose tonnage was such that it hardly needed similar measures. France could not afford to promulgate maritime laws at this time, given the inadequacy of its fleet in relation to its needs. In terms of colonial exclusivism and complementarity between metropolises and colonies, all European powers were inspired by the same ideas.

Mercantilist imperialism bore witness to the advent of capitalism in history. It was an outgrowth of capitalism in its prime and the first form of capitalist imperialism, but not the last. It was associated, on the one hand, with colonialism and colonization, on the other hand, with the internationalization of economies. It implied the formation of economic groupings subordinate to a few metropolises and spread overseas on other continents. Although, as a latecomer, Japan did not go beyond Asia, its mode of operation was consistent with the European model. The object was the creation of a compulsory inter-relationship or complementarity between a metropolis and remote dependencies forced to specialize according to its needs.

The colonizing movement got underway with the explorations and geographical discoveries that had followed one another since the end of the fifteenth century. Economic internationalization proceeded simultaneously with colonization. The process of linking previously distinct or loosely connected economies had been developing continuously and irreversibly since the beginning of the colonization of the Americas and of Insulindia in the sixteenth century. Vast and faraway lands were reorganized and shaped *manu militari* as specialized extensions of European economies. Whether carried out within the framework of a policy of settler colonialism (the Americas) or economic colonization (the Indonesian archipelago, India), it was the beginning of a practice which continued into the twentieth century. Establishing settlers had forerunners in Irish and Eastern European history in medieval times. It radically altered the structure of the economies and countries subjected to colonization.

There was another domain whose customs and practices contributed to the birth of the international economy: long-distance trading. Hard-won experience and positions in intercontinental exchanges formed the foundation on which the colonial empires were built. This fusion of trade and colonization marked the decisive phase of the establishment of the international economy and mercantilist imperialism.

For a long time, international trading took place in relatively autonomous geographical areas. Each was made up of circuits that structured and directed the movement of goods. Over the medium and long term, these areas experienced non-simultaneous periods of progress and decline in their activity. Its pace set by the nature of the leading products, this fluctuation was also contingent on the identity of the city or state which imposed itself as the main, often unavoidable, intermediary of one or more regions. In the age of mercantilist imperialism, some areas were to decline, others to expand, so that the relationships between the latter, previously episodic and marginal, became regular and multiplied. Connections paved the way for rapprochements, not excluding the incorporation of one area by another.

In medieval times, before the advent of mercantilist imperialism, the main trading circuits were located in three large areas: the Mediterranean, Northern Europe, and Asia. A fourth would be added in the sixteenth century: the Atlantic world. While Russia bordered on Northern Europe, Persia acted as a land link between its Indian and Ottoman neighbors, and Egypt acted as a maritime link between Arabia and the Mediterranean. As for North Africa, it overlooked the Mediterranean and communicated with West Africa via the camel caravans of Muslim merchants. On the eve of the rise of Atlantic maritime economies, colonization, and mercantilist imperialism, the profile of the areas deserves to be reviewed.

b. The Mediterranean region

In the Mediterranean area, both ordinary and precious goods were traded internationally. Among the former, foodstuffs were of particular importance. Sicily may have been the breadbasket of the Western Mediterranean, but it could not meet all the needs. So cereals were brought from the Ottoman Middle East. Lands of grapes and olives, Spain, Italy, Crete, and Cyprus were at the origin of sustained trade in wine and oil.

Demand was buttressed by the growth of Italian cities, as well as the great eastern cities of Constantinople and Cairo. Spanish wool supplied the factories of Florence and Milan, before being directed to those of Flanders. North African leather was complemented by that of Eastern Europe, then by imports from the Americas. The development of artillery called for the importation of metals. Germany exported copper, while England supplied lead and tin. From Italy came manufactured goods: Milanese weapons, Florentine woolens, Venetian glassware.

From their contacts with the "Orient," the Crusaders brought back to Europe a taste for spices, sugar, coffee, silks, cotton fabrics, and other fine articles. No products aroused as much envy as spices, precious goods par excellence because of their usefulness for preserving food. Light in weight, they were nevertheless of great value and sold at high prices. European demand was high. Pepper, cinnamon, cloves, nutmeg, and ginger were grown in the Malay Archipelago (in the Moluccas) and on the Indian peninsula. Transiting from the cultivation sites to the port of Malacca by way of Chinese or Arab intermediaries, the cargoes were taken by Arab merchants to the Malabar coast in western India.

From there, they were transshipped to take the Red Sea route to Cairo and Alexandria or the Gulf route to Aleppo and Beirut, the last stages before embarking for Europe. Along with the spices traveled highly valued Indian cotton fabrics, Chinese and Persian silks, precious stones, indigo (a dye), and saltpeter (an explosive). Despite breaks in continuity and portages, the sea route via the Indian Ocean proved its worth. It made the search, dating back to the thirteenth century, for a land route across the Asian continent superfluous.

Control of the profitable spice networks fueled intense rivalries in Europe. Mediterranean trade in both ordinary and precious goods was dominated by Venice. Geographically at an advantage over Genoa, it was the Ottoman Empire's objective partner in the international spice economy. Halfway between East and West, mistress of the Adriatic and of the sea in the Eastern Mediterranean, it imposed itself on all as an intermediary, reseller, transporter, and financier, to the great benefit of the oligarchy of the patricians-merchants-bankers that governed it. Their sailing ships crisscrossed the Mediterranean, carrying all manner of goods and pocketing the revenue from freight. They conveyed cereals as well as Asian spices which they loaded in Egypt or in Syria.

International commerce led to a rapid accumulation of profits. What distinguished Europe's distant trade from that of other parts of the world was its interaction with local trade. The Champagne fairs connected Italy and Northern Europe. The Serenissima Repubblica di Venezia was the pivot of European trade, the center of redistribution and re-export of goods coming from the four cardinal points. The Venice-Levant, Venice-Southern Germany and, to a lesser extent, Venice-Flanders axes structured international trade in the Euro-Mediterranean area. Breaking the Venetians' de facto monopoly in the Mediterranean, dislodging them from their privileged situation, and ousting them meant the search for new exclusively maritime routes, more direct and without intermediaries, to the eastern sources of spices.

Unsurprisingly, Genoese competition turned up. Genoa, located on the western coast of Italy, had to cede the eastern Mediterranean to Venice and look towards the Atlantic for a direct route to the Orient. In 1162, the Genoese were trading on the Atlantic coast of Morocco, while the Genoese navigator Lancelotto Malocello discovered the Canary Islands. In 1291, the Vandino brothers and Ugolino Vivaldi, who were merchants and navigators by occupation, attempted to reach the Orient by sailing south around Africa. After passing through the Strait of Gibraltar, their two galleys disappeared without leaving a trace. Two centuries later, the Portuguese, peripheral competitors making an unexpected but logical appearance, given their geographical position and their experience as deep-sea fishermen, set about diverting commercial activity from the Mediterranean world to the still largely unknown—to them—Atlantic zone.

c. Northern Europe

Northern Europe constituted a second group. Despite their specific characteristics, the Mediterranean area and Northern Europe were not watertight worlds, existing in a vacuum. From the Mediterranean region and via the Bay of Biscay, products such as wine, olive oil, salt, and spices were shipped to the North, which in turn sent wood, grains, and salted or dried fish in the opposite direction. Northern exports were its specialties. The Baltic area was a leading supplier of goods such as wheat, herring, iron, lumber, and softwood products. Unlike the Mediterranean area, northern Europe did not have a significant luxury trade, apart from that of furs. North of the Alps, the major traffic concerned ordinary and heavy products, plus woolens.

Flanders, the dynamo of the Nordic economy, played the role of manufacturing core, importing raw materials, and exporting finished products. Alongside the Italian city-states, it constituted Europe's other economic hub. A major consumer of Eastern European wheat and Spanish and English wool, Flanders supplied Europe with fabrics and woolens. Its wool industry began its decline at the end of the fifteenth century.

The primacy of the Hanseatic towns in the northern trade was maintained until the sixteenth century. They were closely linked to the center of the Flemish textile industry, first Bruges, then Antwerp. Well situated on the waterways leading to the North Sea, the Netherlands, and Germany, Antwerp was, at the end of the fifteenth century, the economic metropolis of northern Europe. During the second half of the sixteenth century, Flanders bore the brunt of the war between the Habsburgs of Spain and the Netherlands (United Provinces), which joined the Reformed camp. The Flemish provinces were devastated; Antwerp's artisans and financiers moved to Amsterdam. The center of gravity of northern trade and finance shifted to the Netherlands.

More competitive and aggressive, the Dutch wrested commercial hegemony from the Hanseatic League. Their shipowners, sailors, and merchants learned their skills in the fifteenth century fishing and trading herring, the main staple of the Dutch diet. While they continued to export products from the Netherlands, they above all established themselves as Europe's universal charterers and carriers. Their thousands of ships sailed everywhere. Baltic grain, Scandinavian wood and iron, wines, spices and sugar were just some of the goods they were familiar with. Technically innovative, appearing around 1590, their *fluitschips* (flutes) were designed as cargo ships for common products. With rounded hulls and wide bottoms, they were spacious boats offering high capacity and permitting low freight. They were inexpensive because of standardization and mass production in modern shipyards. Shipbuilders had Baltic raw materials within reach and a cheap credit system to support their activity. It was more sensible for foreigners to buy flutes in the Netherlands than to try to build them.

The Dutch merchant navy took on exports from all, without exception, and provided services between the continent's ports, including the smallest ones. Its availability, reliability, and reasonable rates made it irreplaceable. In the seventeenth century, the Dutch commercial fleet accounted for two thirds of the total number of European ships, despite English and French efforts to compete with it or to weaken it through war. The activity it generated occupied more people than anywhere else in the same field. Having become the European warehouse for products of all kinds and the commercial, financial, and stock market capital of the continent, Amsterdam was not overtaken until the eighteenth century. The struggle that England had been waging since the seventeenth century against the Netherlands for naval, commercial, and financial supremacy was finally crowned with success.

d. Asia

The third economic space, Asia, was the world's largest. Five major regional groupings made up the Asian area: China, Japan, Insulindia, India, and the Ottoman Empire. They carried on lively commercial relations with each other. A wide variety of exports circulated within Asia, and some were transported to Europe.

China and Japan, the former a vast self-sufficient country, the latter an island universe, could be content with episodic foreign trade, proceeding in fits and starts. Foreign trade was a less incidental and more constant activity for their neighbors to the south and east. Insulindia was a point of contact for Indian and Chinese merchant networks. Traders from Gujarat and Coromandel settled in Java and Sumatra, introduced the pepper plant and handled pepper exports to Europe. They made the city of Malacca the crossroads of the South-East, the nodal point of the complex of routes at the junction of the two sides of maritime Asia.

India, a geographical rather than a political entity, was practically a continent divided into several states. Its merchants spread across Southeast Asia. Their networks in the eastern half of the Indian Ocean met those of Arab merchants in the western half, connecting the Far East and the Mediterranean. The port of Surat linked Insulindia with the Gulf, the Red Sea, and East Africa, where Arab merchants were in their element.

Asian goods arriving in the Ottoman Empire, the last link in the chain, were picked up by European buyers for redistribution in Europe. Trade in the Europe-Asia direction replicated the route, reversing the order of intermediaries. Ottoman provinces such as Egypt and Syria exported cotton, silk, wool, and linen items to Europe. Within this vast Empire, active trading took place between the regions: leather and leather goods from North Africa to the Levant and Asia Minor, in exchange for textiles, carpets, and foodstuffs.

The Venetian stranglehold on the spice trade in the Mediterranean inevitably led potential competitors to redouble their efforts to loosen it. Going around the middleman to the source of spices in the East became the primary objective of rivals.

CHAPTER 6

Rise to power of the Atlantic world: Portugal and Spain

After the *Reconquista*, completed in 1415 in Portugal and in 1492 in Spain, the Iberian states set their sights on Africa to the south and the Atlantic to the west. In both cases, the aim was to gain direct access to Asia's spices by taking the Atlantic route. The Portuguese considered the east-west route crossing the Atlantic to be longer than the north-south axis running along the coast of Africa to the Indian Ocean. They preferred the second, even if it was longer than the route across the Mediterranean.

However, this far-flung adventure meant continuing the holy war against Islam in neighboring North Africa. The priority was to conquer Morocco as much for the cause of Christ as for the control of West Africa's gold trade networks. The caravans that took gold from the Niger basin to Tunis and Algiers, from where it passed to Genoa and Venice, would be redirected towards Morocco; Lisbon would then ship it to Antwerp, the economic capital of the North and the place where the product was sold. The Genoese also searched for gold on the West African coast, sometimes in tandem with the Portuguese, sometimes against them.

In the background lay the desire to circumvent Africa to reach Asia and, at the same time, take Islam from the rear through a strategy of encirclement. The idea seemed all the more appropriate as the fall of Constantinople in 1453 and the expansion in Africa gave the Ottoman Empire total command of the traditional routes to the Orient, rendering frontal attacks obsolete. The blockage in the Eastern Mediterranean turned the focus to the Atlantic. The plan was as ingenious as it was ambitious, but it required reinforcements. Hence the hope of finding the legendary Christian kingdom of Prester John, said to be located on the enemy's flank, and of enlisting the help of this co-religionist whose power was exaggerated.

a. Portugal on the imperial path

Portuguese expansion had the appearance of a Crusade updated by its extension from the Mediterranean to Africa and Asia, and by the addition of new, frankly assumed economic objectives. The religious motivation tended to dissipate for the Dutch, English, and French successors, except for the Calvinist, Huguenot, or Puritan dissidents. The opportunity came with a civil war in the Maghreb in 1411-1412. Portugal took advantage of the situation to seize Ceuta in 1415. But the occupation aroused local opposition, which surrounded and isolated the town. In 1437, the landing against Tangier was neutralized and the expeditionary force captured; a new attempt in 1463 met with the same fate. The other positions acquired in Morocco were difficult to maintain.

Pursuing anti-Muslim conquests and achieving commercial goals in Africa seemed out of reach. Already the attention of the Portuguese was turning towards nearby islands in the Atlantic and the West African coast. They visited Madeira as early as 1420, began colonization in 1425 and took possession in 1445; sugar cane plantations were established. Originally from India, cane spread westwards: grown on plantations in Palestine at the time of the Crusades, it reached Cyprus. Sugar from Madeira was sent to Antwerp for refining and export. The Portuguese arrived in the Azores in 1427 and colonized them in 1445; they occupied the Cape Verde Islands in 1456. The Canary Islands were the only ones inhabited; Castile had to overcome fierce and long resistance from the natives to seize them in 1448. With their plantations worked by slaves, the Atlantic islands were the laboratory for the sugar-producing islands of the New World. Neither an end in themselves nor a substitute for Asia, for the Iberians they were springboards to the open sea.

The push out of Portugal and Spain followed on the *Reconquista*. The Iberian Peninsula having been recaptured, many fighters, particularly from the lower nobility, were available and facing idleness.

In addition to the religious motive, the movement was driven by a European impulse for economic revival and enrichment, bringing to an end the era of famine, the Black Death (bubonic plague), and demographic collapse of the fourteenth century. It revealed the socio-economic transformations underpinning the emergence of capitalism and the dynamism of a commercial bourgeoisie ready to broaden the scope of its business.

It also contributed to the birth of national economies and the consolidation of new dynastic states. As they asserted themselves on the continent, they set themselves apart from the mass of principalities, duchies, counties and city-states, too small to defend themselves, to have diversified economies or to represent large markets. The emerging powers benefited from scientific progress and knowledge of all kinds acquired by Europe.

Portuguese Prince Henry the Navigator promoted maritime exploration and experimentation in shipbuilding. The Portuguese had access to the geographical and cartographic knowledge of the Muslim world via Genoa, their ally and the rival of Venice. Like Spain, France, and England, Portugal received help from Italians who understood that the Atlantic states were better situated than Genoa to find an ocean route to the east and to break Venice's hold.

The European states that embarked on expansion on the oceans enjoyed a marked superiority in terms of naval technology and navigation instruments (compass, astrolabe). Methodically, following the Portuguese example, they learned to accumulate lessons, to unite the science of experts and the practical knowledge of seafarers, and to rapidly apply lessons and discoveries for military and commercial purposes. The navy enabled them to undertake long-distance journeys, go on the offensive, make their way into foreign seas and take control of them. From that point, the navy became a lever for European supremacy.

The versatile *caravela* gave the Portuguese a distinct advantage. Light, long and of high tonnage, it could sail far and fast. Entirely sail-powered, it did not require a large crew. This three-masted ship with lateen and square sails was both maneuverable and armed with cannons. A cargo carrier, she was also a shallow-draught exploration boat and a warship equipped with a floating battery of guns. This ocean-going sailing ship, equipped with ordnance that kept the adversary at bay, made galleys and close-quarters combat obsolete. From now on, maritime battles became artillery duels in which technology played an ever-greater role, conferring unprecedented destructive power.

While trying to gain a foothold in North Africa, the Portuguese began exploring the West African coast in 1418 in search of gold and ivory. Year after year from 1441 onwards, voyages followed one another, moving gradually southwards; Senegambia in 1444, Guinea in 1460. Gold and slaves were brought back in 1442. Factories (trading stations or agencies) that were set up along the coast, exchanged cereals, fabrics, trinkets, and horses for gold, slaves, and low-grade pepper. In order to establish a monopoly on African trade, orders were given to sink any foreign ship and throw its crew to the sharks. The Equator was reached in 1471 and Sao Tome colonized; African slaves cultivated sugar cane on that island and sugar was transported to Europe. The slave trade was as lucrative as the gold trade.

A new model of exploitation and colonization emerged, soon to be transposed and amplified in the Americas, with the Guinean coast becoming a reservoir of slave labor. Portuguese merchants swapped their traditional role as fish, wine and salt sellers for that of traders in gold, slaves, sugar and, soon, spices. The mouth of the Congo was reached in 1482 and Angola in 1484. In 1487, the Portuguese rounded the Cape, called "of Good Hope" (that of finding "the Indies"), and entered the Indian Ocean. They reached Calicut (India) in 1498. The Christians they found were Nestorian heretics, not the subjects of Prester John, but there was no shortage of spices. The Portuguese were only the latest arrivals in an Indian Ocean crisscrossed by Japanese, Chinese, Indian and Arab traders ("India to India" or "country trade").

The aftermath was violent, underlining the fact that commerce was inextricably linked to the use of force, that the military and the economic dimensions are part of the same continuum, and that the commercial relationship was fundamentally coercive. The Portuguese prevailed through war. Their navy had mercantile and military functions, and they took advantage of the superiority of European naval technology. The aim was not to carve out a market share or to compete with local merchants according to economic criteria, such as price, quality or efficiency; European goods of the time found no takers on their merit in the East. Nor was it a question of selling at a more competitive price on the European market. The goal was to make the market inoperative by eliminating competition through extra-economic means, in order to take its place upstream and downstream of the spice economy. Commercial success was based on monopoly, wrested by force.

And so it will be for all other aspirants to mercantilist imperialism. Portugal had to maintain its imperialism and defend its monopoly at gunpoint. With its million inhabitants, it confronted ancient Asian empires in their own waters thousands of kilometers from Europe. It had the specialized armament required for its projects, while facing off against states less concerned by the sea. Finally, Portugal benefited from the enmities which separated these states and which were never overcome, preventing them from coalescing against it. This led them to call on Portugal for help against their local enemies. The Portuguese were not averse to taking sides in local disputes in order to subdue first the common adversary, then the ally. All in all, Portugal pioneered methods that other European powers would apply even better than it did and, first and foremost, against it.

Hormuz and Socotra were captured. On the Malabar coast, Calicut was bombarded in 1502 and Goa conquered in 1510. In 1511, the Portuguese failed to seize Calicut but they captured Malacca, the hub of the spice economy, and took Ceylon in 1515. Arriving at Canton in 1513, they set up a trading post in Macao in 1557 for commerce with Canton. The Portuguese became masters of the Indian Ocean and the adjacent seas. Only the Red Sea escaped their control due to the arrival of Ottoman troops in Aden in 1538. Dom Francisco de Almeida was appointed Viceroy of the Indies in 1505. Rather than territorial conquest, the Portuguese Empire focused on controlling shipping lanes, strategically located stations and sites essential to its operations. It made the Goa base its stronghold in Asia and secured a chain of support points, ports of call, trading posts and warehouses (Zanzibar, Mombasa, Mogadishu, Socotra, Hormuz, Ceylon, Malacca, Timor, Macao).

While it did not succeed in completely drying up rival trade routes, it did pose a serious threat to them. The flow of spices transported to Europe started in 1501. Since the beginning of explorations, the state supported economic enterprise with armed force. Almost annually, the armed fleet left Lisbon to return with tons of spices. Having no goods likely to interest the Asians, the Portuguese exchanged the gold and ivory obtained in Africa for Indian cotton goods, and took spices to sell on the European market. The profits were enormous for the Portuguese intermediary who replaced all the others, buying cheap in Asia and selling dear in Europe. With product prices imposed at both ends of the supply chain through a monopoly acquired by force, a new type of imperialist appropriation emerged. It was to set an example, just like the new colonization characterized by plantations and slavery.

As a lasting consequence, Europe's center of gravity shifted from the Mediterranean to the Atlantic. Venice's wealth was threatened, and the city-state saw Lisbon (and, secondarily, Antwerp) take over its status as Europe's spice hub, while the spice trade was diverted to the Cape route. The Portuguese even sold spices in the Mediterranean basin, which had been a Venetian preserve. For all practical purposes, Venice was deprived of supplies of spices. Weakened by the wars against the Ottomans and Habsburgs, its vitality was spent. The spice trade which it had monopolized by force and by virtue of its geographical location, was taken away from it. It became the prerogative of the Cape route held militarily by a newcomer. The Venetian patriciate, like the Genoese, recycled its accumulated wealth and established itself in the role of banker of Europe. As much as Venice, the Ottoman Empire suffered from this diversion, while the ancient silk road linking Asia and Europe was abandoned.

Portuguese domination lasted a century. The causes of decline were twofold. In Portugal, the profits from the oriental trade were mainly used to import food and manufactured products, discouraging or driving national products from the market. The depressive economic effect was compounded by the introduction of bonded labor which advantageously competed with national production. Sudden enrichment emanating from abroad was detrimental to the economy, which tended towards rentierism. Overseas, Portugal seemed less capable of ensuring the proper functioning of its imperial system. As early as 1540 and despite obstacles, shipments of spices made their way back to the Mediterranean. The administration of Asian possessions was plagued by inefficiency and corruption.

Finally, the Asian jackpot aroused the envy of other European countries in the Atlantic area. The entry of the Dutch on the scene in 1595 and the English in 1600 sounded the death knell for the Portuguese Empire. Countered in Asia, Portugal reoriented itself towards its Brazilian domain in America, where a colonial enterprise of a different nature, based on sugar cane, plantations and slaves, took over from the spice trading posts.

b. Spain pounces on gold and silver

In the meantime, an even more sizable empire came into being in the fifteenth century. Spain became less of a rival to Portugal because it was concentrated in the Americas. Its expansion followed in the wake of that of its neighbor with a delay of a few decades. If the Portuguese Empire laid the foundations of mercantilist imperialism, other empires completed the model, in particular the dimension relating to settler colonization.

The Genoese navigator Christopher Columbus took part in African journeys in search of gold and a passage to the Orient. Believing the route to the west across the Atlantic Ocean to be shorter, he proposed it to Portugal in 1481-1482. But Portugal was satisfied with its progress on the southern route and his project was rejected. Columbus submitted it to Spain which agreed to sponsor him. Committed to reinforcing the absolutist state, the Spanish court also coveted the handsome source of income that a stranglehold over spices, precious metals, pearls, and gems from the Orient would provide. In 1492, armed with three caravels, Columbus crossed the Atlantic for the first time in thirty-three days, in search of gold and the Indies. He set foot on land in today's Bahamas. The second expedition, this time with seventeen ships and armed, arrived in 1493 on the island which would be called Hispaniola (modern-day Haiti).

While the goal in Asia was armed trade, conquest and colonization took precedence from the outset in America. After the gold jewelry had been seized, there remained the alluvial gold to collect and wash. Hispaniola had a population of one million. Three years later, it had dwindled to half a million. By 1510, only 100,000 remained. Ninety percent of the population had been decimated by smallpox, famine and ruthless exploitation in forced gold panning. The proportion was higher than in the genocides of the twentieth century. Overexploitation destroyed the workforce, while the island was emptied of its gold. The last Caribs were deported to the island of Dominica in the nineteenth century and assimilated.

In order to make up for the labor shortage, Spanish colonists settled and imported African slaves from Guinea; sugar cane cultivation began as early as 1518. In the hope of finding new veins of gold, some migrated to other Caribbean islands (Puerto Rico, Cuba, and Jamaica), where the same drama unfolded as in Hispaniola, and to Mexico or Venezuela. Columbus made two more voyages and died in 1506, still convinced of having found the Indies.

The amount of gold in the West Indies in the form of items to plunder and nuggets to collect was disappointing. Furthermore, it became clear that the lands discovered were neither India nor Asia. In 1519, a flotilla commanded by Magellan, a Portuguese navigator in the service of Spain, left Seville heading to the spice islands in the East via the south of the new continent. But the Spanish crown, threatened with bankruptcy, sold its claims to the Moluccas for cash and the expedition came to naught. The Philippines, of no interest to the Portuguese rival, were retained, but the Spanish empire would be located in America, despite the disappointment of the early years. The diminishing potential of the Caribbean islands encouraged the search for gold on the continent.

In 1517-1518, a group of settlers landed on the Yucatan peninsula in search of El Dorado and learned that there were gold-bearing regions in the interior. An armed detachment of 500 *conquistadors* set sail from Cuba in 1519 to discover this Aztec Empire covered with gold. What followed was a striking illustration of the devastating consequences of contact between Europe and less powerful civilizations. The image of famished carnivores being unleashed on herbivores is apt. A handful of unscrupulous adventurers, eager for loot and enrichment, trained in a more robust society, brought about the fall of a backward empire, its plunder, the extermination of most of its population, and the enslavement of those who escaped death. Deculturation and conversion completed the process of putting this labor force at the disposal of the conquerors.

Many factors facilitated the aggression. The Aztec Empire had been in decline for a century. The attackers' technological advantage had catastrophic consequences. Although advanced in many respects, the Aztecs did not know iron metallurgy, firearms, the wheel, or

the horse. Their religion included the possible appearance of super-
natural beings, a role that the Spaniards seemed to play to perfection.
Stunned, the Aztecs carried out their orders and allowed themselves
to be intimidated by their violence. The superstitious emperor was
duped and assassinated. The social structure being hierarchical, it
passed into the hands of the invaders. They received help, including fighters, from neighboring populations subjugated by the Aztec
Empire. The natives had no immunity against Old World viruses,
such as smallpox. The result was an appalling massacre, but the goal
was achieved in 1521: the capital Tenochtitlan contained quantities
of gold and treasures beyond the most fertile imagination.

To crush a revolt of the population, the Spaniards sacked the city
and massacred its inhabitants. Soon all of New Spain (Mexico) was
conquered and deposits of gold and silver were spotted. Gold panning
gave way to mining, which began in the 1530s. A major revolt broke
out in 1542 but was put down in bloodshed. From 1545 to 1548, a
third of the population perished in epidemics, but silver mines were
discovered in 1548. By the end of the sixteenth century, only one and
a half million of Mexico's 25 million inhabitants remained.

During the 1530s, the Maya Empire in Central America and the
Inca Empire in Peru suffered the same fate, including the kidnapping,
ransoming, and strangling of the Inca emperor despite the handing
over of the requested gold. Its capital Cuzco was occupied in 1533.
The conquered countries were divided up between the conquerors,
who swooped in on the precious metal mines to which they sent
a conscripted population reduced to forced labor akin to *corvée*.
This was the basis of the *encomienda* (a concession of natives), then
repartimiento, systems. Merciless exploitation and mistreatment
prompted mass suicides. Combined with the vulnerability of populations unprepared for new microbial and viral shocks, this led to
demographic collapse.

In Peru, countless statues and gold objects were stolen, but the
empire's primary wealth lay underground: it turned out to be even
richer in silver than Mexico. Located in modern-day Bolivia, the
Potosi Mountain mines, commissioned in 1545, were a fabulous source
of silver, by far the largest in the world. Silver replaced gold as the
leading export product. The American empire that fell to Spain was
immense. Only Brazil, attributed to Portugal, and the northernmost

part of North America, considered of little value at that time, was outside its bounds.

This empire was based on the silver mines of Mexico and Peru. From 1450 to 1810-1820, 70,000 to 100,000 tons of silver flowed into Europe. From 1564, as part of two armed fleets, galleons set sail to pick up the precious metal and deliver it to Seville, the only port authorized to receive it. The crown reserved 5 percent of the arrivals. Demographic bleeding caused Peru to lose more than a quarter of its population from 1530 to 1660. The population of Central and South America fell from about fifty million around 1500 to about ten million around 1650. The aftereffects of the plundering and bleeding of the New World were no lesser than those of the genocides of the contemporary era.

Even more clearly than for Portugal, the sudden influx of precious metals was of little benefit to Spain and it spent little time there. The country's needs exceeded its productive capacities. The deficiencies of its social structure and the backwardness of its economy weakened it. To pay for its purchases abroad, it irrigated Europe, particularly Northern Europe, with the money it received from the Americas. Ending up in Amsterdam, the cash contributed to the prosperity of this new economic metropolis and to the rise in prices in Europe. The hemorrhage left the Spanish economy bloodless. In addition to imports, there was military spending to bolster the Habsburgs' hegemonic ambitions on the continent.

Spain was in debt and constantly in dire straits. The American windfall did not spare the state from going bankrupt in 1557, 1575, 1596, 1607, 1627, 1647, 1653, and 1680, as expenses soared. Portions of money from the Americas were assigned to creditors or pledged before the galleons carrying it even docked in Spain. Representatives of the Fuggers and Welsers, German bankers, were permanently present in Seville to collect what was owed to them.

At the same time, almost all of Cádiz's commercial freight was carried out by non-Spaniards. The colonies were supplied with products from Northern Europe's factories, which emptied mercantilism of its meaning and placed the Spanish economy in a state of dependence. Even the *asiento*, an exclusive and lucrative contract introduced in 1595 for farming out the sale of slaves in the Spanish colonial empire, passed to foreign hands, French in 1701, then English in 1713. The *asiento*, awarded to the South Sea Company in 1714, enabled the English government to increase its revenues, an obsessive challenge that plagued the states of the period, faced with financing serial wars. Based on this monopoly of the slave trade, it was the trade of Spanish America that opened up to England. The fabulous wealth acquired with little effort from American mines devalued the productive economy and caused the long-lasting rentierist sclerosis of Spain.

For Europe, precious metals from America offset the trade deficit with Asia. The surplus drawn from colonial trade allowed a deficit with foreign countries, on the whole a net contribution to the metropolises using the extra-economic power of colonization. Asia-Europe trade was fundamentally unbalanced. For a long time, European products found no market in the East, with the exception of weapons and metal objects. Even constraint alone was not sufficient. A lubricant was indispensable in the eastern trade. Purchases had to be paid for with ingots, bars, and precious metal coins originating from the Americas.

The exploitation of one imperial possession allowed the exploitation of another and made possible multilateral settlements of trade deficits with Asia. The "providential discovery" of the Americas, their colonization and the control over their precious metals obtained at low cost were a powerful lever in the hands of five Atlantic countries of Europe. It helped them to come out of their position as appendages of Eurasia, to gain the upper hand over the older economic centers, to establish maritime-based mercantilist imperialism, and to colonize Asia.

Through colonization, a link was forged between two oceans and three continents, and the contours of an ever-expanding international economy took shape. With American silver, African gold, and commercial circuits now in the hands of Western Europeans, the Mediterranean zone and the Ottoman world from Anatolia to Africa were permanently drained and reduced to marginality. Venice lost its trump card and the Ottoman Empire was stopped before Vienna in 1529 and 1683; it made no further headway in Europe. At the same time, the desire to limit the drainage of metals, in accordance with mercantilist ideas, led Europeans to engage in Asia-Asia trade with a view to finding local goods to give in exchange.

The Portuguese and Spanish empires marked the advent of economic capture by force, a characteristic of mercantilist imperialism.

They ushered in the era of modern overseas colonization, a natural continuation of trade based on extra-economic factors. The Portuguese imposed domination without direct control on societies that could not (yet) be governed; the Spaniards directly dominated more fragile societies after eliminating obstacles, resistance, and even populations. The Portuguese took the first steps towards economic colonization; the Spanish began large-scale settler colonialism. In the Atlantic islands, both gave rise to the slave-based plantation system. In both cases, the extraction of wealth was the goal and the corollary of the use of force.

CHAPTER 7

Rise to power of the Atlantic world: Netherlands, England, France

It is useful to assess the architecture of the global economy at this point. As the merchants of Europe's Atlantic coast went around Mediterranean positions in the Eastern trade, they were also active in the direction of the New World. Preeminent in trade with both Asia and the Americas, they made the countries of West and Northwest Europe the leading centers of the international economy. The Mediterranean and the Baltic were reduced to the function of regional appendages of an Atlantic area which now encompassed them. International specialization transformed Eastern Europe into a large-scale exporter of wheat, reinforcing vast estates and the subordination of the peasantry ("second serfdom," "feudal reaction"). The Atlantic circuits, connecting points at opposite ends of the world, were set to cover the planet and produce contrasting consequences: development in Western Europe, regression elsewhere.

In addition to land and river routes, goods exchanged between the Mediterranean area and northern Europe passed through ports on the Atlantic seaboard. From Bilbao and Seville, iron, wool, wine, and oil arrived in Antwerp, while wheat and Baltic herring went the other way. During the sixteenth century, cargoes were transported by Venetian and Genoese vessels, then by Dutch ships.

The depletion of wood sources raised the construction costs of Italian ships, reducing their competitiveness. The English, the French and members of the Hanseatic League showed up in the Mediterranean. The Dutch and the English made significant inroads, introducing exports from Northern Europe and undermining Italian merchants and shipowners. With England's trade limited to the export of fabrics from London to Antwerp, the country tried to reduce its dependence on the hub-city of the European economy. Its primary outlet was threatened by the Spanish-Dutch War. The English Levant Company (1581) carried English fabrics and European metals to the Ottoman Empire, and supplied itself directly with silks, skins, wines and raisins. The Ottoman Empire even experienced a commercial upturn during the second half of the eighteenth century, with the English and the French as its main partners. In due course, the services of Italian intermediaries became superfluous.

The latter were already suffering from the repercussions of the opening of the direct route to Asia, via the Cape, a genuine outflanking maneuver. In turn, Eastern and Western traffic was withdrawn from the great Italian traders. Squeezed out of lucrative exchanges, merchants and bankers retreated to large landholdings. The social structure was frozen in the aristocratic mode and rents became the most prized category of income. Commercial activity in the Mediterranean declined for a long time, picking up only after the opening of the Suez Canal in 1869.

The stagnating Mediterranean area ceased to be autonomous. It found itself subordinate to the Atlantic world, which had contributed to the collapse of its supplies in the east and taken control of its trade in the west. A sluggish Mediterranean trade was now in the hands of external players. The shift of the European economic center from the Mediterranean to the Atlantic coast, then to the North Sea, was among the major changes in the modern history of the international economy. It was accompanied by a displacement of primacy within the Atlantic world. At the same time as the countries of the Atlantic seaboard were reducing the Mediterranean area to marginality, a differentiation appeared among them between those of northwestern Europe and the Iberian Peninsula, the latter no longer distinguishing itself from the Mediterranean region.

a. The Netherlands replaces Portugal

In the meantime, Atlantic empires succeeded one another. Monopolistic in nature, the Spanish empire in America and the Portuguese empire in Asia aroused envy. Temporarily sheltered from attacks by other states, they came under a certain pressure from pirates acting on their own account or from privateers commissioned by rival or enemy states unable to act for themselves. However, as the weakening of Portugal became evident, buccaneering ceased to be the only means of challenging its imperial grip. The conflict between Spain and the rebellious Netherlands, which began in 1568, continued to the point of interrupting the transport of goods between Antwerp and Portugal by the Dutch. The port of Antwerp was closed in 1585.

The merchants of Amsterdam then decided to go to the source of the spices themselves. In 1595, they organized an expedition to Java and did so again in 1600 with 40 ships. They took Mauritius from the Portuguese in 1598. The intention to replace them was undisguised. The Dutch took advantage of the resentment the Portuguese aroused in Asia, as much by their commercial practices as by their religious intolerance. They failed to enlist local allies. Their domination was above all naval and it was at sea off the island of Java that their navy was defeated by Dutch ships in 1601. Ousted from Malacca in 1641 and Ceylon in 1658, they were driven from the Indian Ocean by the same methods they had used to settle there a century earlier.

The Dutch had the same monopolistic objectives as the Portuguese and applied the same coercive methods to eliminate European and local competitors. The maritime model of imperialism, dating back to Athens and Venice, was an interdependent combination of trade and war. The commercial model itself replicated age-old practices of eliminating competition. Systematically and wherever possible, rivals were expelled and their networks dismantled. Dutch trade, like that of the Portuguese, was based on monopoly and the use of force, i.e., the application of extra-economic means.

Added to this were other extra-economic methods of creating profit-generating scarcity: the restriction or prohibition of spice cultivation and the destruction of crops. As sole sellers, the new pretenders to hegemony in Asia were also the sole buyers in the face of the Indigenous growers. Monopoly was associated with monopsony. The last level was political. In the territories they governed, they levied tribute on the population and did not hesitate to use forced labor or slaves where population had fallen. Many islands, including the Moluccas and Celebes (Sulawesi), whose inhabitants were also subjected to kidnapping in order to supply Java with labor, were devastated by the intensity of exploitation.

Alongside coercion, the Dutch demonstrated in the Far East the efficiency, ubiquity and entrepreneurial spirit that had made them Europe's indispensable carriers. They did not proselytize but they borrowed heavily from the Portuguese, proving to be more methodical and adding new elements to the recipe book of imperialism. The spearhead of the policy applied in Asia was the East India Company, founded in 1602. The *Vereenigde Oostindische Compagnie* (VOC) was at the same time a large joint-stock company, a privileged chartered company and a quasi-state colonial administration, equipped with private armed forces. Wielding extensive powers, it was authorized to wage war, sign peace agreements, seize foreign ships, establish colonies, build fortifications, place garrisons, and mint coins.

To counter Portuguese claims to a monopoly on the trade of the East Indies and exclusivity in the Indian Ocean, Hugo Grotius, the VOC's legal advisor, published *Mare liberum* (*The Freedom of the Seas*, 1609), a treatise which claimed that the seas were an international territory open to all. The same was not true for land; the Dutch followed in the footsteps of the Portuguese and asserted their monopoly and exclusive rights over the Moluccas. In 1609, the Company's fifteen-year term was transformed into a perpetual monopoly.

The Dutch took the Cape in 1652 to make it a supply station for their ships. As well as establishing bases, forts, arms depots, trading posts, and relay stations on the coast of the Indian subcontinent, the VOC positioned itself by force at the source of the raw material in Java, in the heart of the "spice islands" of Insulindia. In 1611, the first governor-general of the Dutch East Indies arrived. From 1615 onwards, the Company was the predominant colonial power in the commercial empire of Insulindia. Effective territorial control was achieved at the cost of armed conflicts and wars of conquest waged against the sultanates and local principalities until the 1750s. Determined to dislodge the Portuguese, the Company also fought against the intrusion of other rivals. It succeeded in shutting down the Mediterranean circuit which had been revived with the weakening of the Portuguese.

The English, secure since the defeat of Spain's Invincible Armada in 1588, turned to overseas colonial expansion. An East India

Company was formed in 1600, on a more modest scale than the VOC. The EIC practiced illicit trade in the Indian Ocean. In 1618, it sent an armed fleet to protect its trading posts; violent fighting ensued in 1619 with Dutch vessels. The English were ousted from the Insulindia archipelago during the 1620s and the EIC reoriented itself towards India. The share of Indian textiles exported to Europe increased at the expense of spices from Insulindia. A lucrative business, the EIC paid generous dividends (40 percent in 1665, 50 percent in 1682) and saw the price of its shares skyrocket. As with its Venetian, Portuguese, and Dutch predecessors, this was a militarized commerce, based on the interdependence of trade and warfare.

The VOC regularly sent its ships from the Netherlands to Asia for round trips during which they sold goods and picked up cargoes of spices (pepper, nutmeg from Celebes, cloves from the Moluccas, camphor from Borneo, cinnamon from Ceylon) and other products (Indian textiles, tea, coffee, porcelain). From 5,000 to 6,000 tons of pepper were shipped to the United Provinces between 1680 and 1690. Even more important than the Europe-Asia long-distance trade was the Asia-Asia trade. Unlike the Portuguese, the VOC engaged in it and ended up dominating it. In command of the growing regions, the VOC held monopoly power over the supply of spices. It also controlled trade between Japan and the rest of Asia, excluding other Europeans from it. But it had to share Indian and Chinese trade with the EIC and the French East India Company (1664).

The English company began trading regularly with China in 1715 and was soon shipping Chinese tea to Britain, which would become its main import. It established a foothold in Surat between 1611 and 1618, in Madras in 1640, in Bombay in 1661, and in Calcutta in 1690, while the French company did the same in Pondicherry in 1674 and in Chandernagor in 1686. The Europeans acted as intermediaries between Asian importers and exporters. They carved out a place for themselves in the movement of Chinese silks, porcelain and lacquer products to India, and in that of cotton from Gujarat and the Coromandel coast, to which was added opium from Bengal in the second half of the eighteenth century, to China.

The VOC ruled Insulindia from Batavia (now Jakarta), the capital founded in 1619. Located at the heart of the cultivation areas, it was also at the geographical center of the network of trading posts where spices were received. It eclipsed Malacca as the key to Asia's trade routes and took full advantage of its equidistance from India and China. Insulindia was an economic colony; the few Dutch present were merchants, administrators, agents and soldiers of the VOC, rather than settlers or landowners.

As the business consisted of buying at the lowest price in Asia and selling at the highest possible price in Europe, creating abundance here and scarcity there thanks to market control, the VOC was prosperous. It flourished in the seventeenth century. Its turnover tripled. The peak was reached during the 1720s. Profits varied according to the risk incurred: extraordinary at the beginning (300 percent), they stabilized at a high level (30 percent) at the end of the seventeenth century.

From the second half of the seventeenth century, the share of spices gradually diminished in international trading. They ceased to set the pace and lost ground compared to other leading commodities: coffee from Yemen; cotton fabrics (calicoes, indiennes) from India; silks, porcelain, lacquerware and tea from China. The coffee boom in the second half of the eighteenth century made Moka a significant port and revived the transit trade via Suez and Cairo, which had been moribund since the opening of the Cape route.

Due to the declining importance of spices, the eighteenth century was a less prosperous period for the VOC. Forced to diversify its product range, it increasingly focused on new promising products instead of of spices, its specialty. For instance, it introduced the cultivation of Yemeni coffee and Ceylonese tea to Insulindia. As a result, it lost mastery of the market and faced competition from English and French companies in conditions where equilibrium in extra-economic means forced them all to come closer to the rules of ordinary trade.

The VOC was the model of a chartered company. It disappeared in 1798. The EIC lost its commercial monopoly in 1813 and saw its prerogatives and possessions transferred to the British Crown in 1858. As for the French company, its path was bumpier and it was not as powerful as its rivals. Chartered companies were tailor-made for trading in precious goods, which were rare, hard to get at, and of a speculative nature. Even at the end of the eighteenth century, a Europe-Asia round trip via the Cape took around eighteen months.

These companies arose from the shortcomings of the dynastic state, which was forced to delegate part of its sovereignty and power to private individuals. The latter acted at the same time as businesses, state administrations, war-making outfits, and buccaneers. Their prosperity depended on forcibly controlling sources of commodities, prohibiting competition, limiting supply, and maintaining high prices. As much as the growing challenge to their monopoly by merchants from their own country, the fact that luxury goods became more common (increased quantities produced, lower prices) or changes in habits undermined their position. With their accumulated income, hoarded profits and negative trade balance, the Netherlands became a rentier country, the destiny of all empires.

Taking advantage of their maritime specialization, the Netherlands rose to the rank of great power with a population of 2.5 million inhabitants, a position midway between Portugal with its million inhabitants and Spain with its seven million. A federation of provinces on a small territory and a prototype of the modern national state, the Netherlands was also a milestone in the transition from city-states to large national states. These were the new national states, with genuine demographic (England: seven million, France: twenty million), economic, military or geopolitical depth, and committed to mercantilist imperialism, that were to supplant the Netherlands. Capable of producing and trading, they could dispense with intermediaries. As in all cases of transfer of hegemony, the process was achieved by force. The English and French pushed the Dutch out of Asia in the same way as the latter had driven out the Portuguese. Moreover, the Netherlands was attacked and defeated militarily in Europe.

b. England elbows out the Netherlands

Challengers to hegemonic empires at the height of their power were forced to confine themselves to smuggling, harassment, and raids on exposed lines of communication. With the approval of their authorities, English and French privateers attacked Portugal and Spain as early as 1556. Ignoring the Portuguese monopoly, Sir John Hawkins made his first voyage to the coast of Africa in 1562 and visited often during the 1560s and 1570s to capture slaves for sale in the Spanish colonies of America. The slave trade was a highly sought-after business.

The failure of the Invincible Armada in 1588 caused Spain to lose its naval supremacy and its ability to prevent intrusions.

While the East India Company encroached on the Asian domain that the VOC had reserved for itself, England engaged in a struggle in Europe to break the Dutch hold on trade and shipping. These full-scale wars between European powers constituted the transfer or the culmination of overseas rivalries and clashes. The use of force was no longer confined to colonial ventures in distant lands; it permeated relations between powers, the object being to assert dominance through the military defeat of the other. Wars between European states were nothing new. The specificity of the wars fought in the seventeenth and eighteenth centuries was their colonial component. The issue was the consolidation of the colonial empire of the winner, the affirmation of the primacy of its imperialism and the weakening, or the seizure, of the colonial empire of the vanquished.

In the sixteenth century, England's commerce was in the hands of Hanseatic traders. English merchants had them expelled from London in 1597, but they faced the Netherlands. England chafed under Dutch preponderance in Europe. Firstly, the Dutch merchant navy outperformed that of England, taking the lion's share of trade flows, including those of English trade itself. Secondly, the flow of imports and exports so efficiently handled by the Dutch, combined with the superiority of Dutch and continental manufactures, facilitated the sending of English raw materials to the continent and discouraged processing in England. The latter faced the prospect of specializing in the role of supplier of primary products and importer of finished goods. In 1614, with the aim of wresting from the Netherlands the more profitable stage of finishing and dyeing, the export of raw fabrics was prohibited (Cockayne's plan). Three years later, the project was abandoned because English craftsmen lacked the necessary skills to fill the void.

England in the seventeenth century was subject to insurrectionary impulses which resulted in the establishment of a constitutional monarchical regime subject to an oligarchy composed of large landowners associated with financiers and leading merchants. The latter were the main beneficiaries of the "Glorious Revolution" of 1688 which brought the revolutionary cycle to a close. In addition to England's foreign trade, merchants and financiers took a particular interest in colonial expansion.

Every outward push involved the extension of the colonization of Ireland. The massacres by Cromwell's troops in 1649 heralded the aggressive intentions of the new power and set in train the subjugation of the neighboring island. Repression and discrimination against Catholics were official policy. Protestant colonists from England and Scotland settled on land taken from Catholics. They acted as a bulwark for the large Anglo-Irish landowners, who were often absentee. Agriculture, henceforth conducted on a commercial basis, generated rents paid by tenants to landlords. Ireland was a testing ground for English settlement throughout the world.

However, the main action was directed against the Dutch, ubiquitous intermediaries and a major obstacle to English ambitions. The resumption of war with Spain between 1621 and 1648 did not seem to harm the economic activity of the Netherlands. England was invigorated by its revolution and eager to shake off its subordination to this republic of merchant-shipowners and to take its place. Both countries had policies firmly focused on trade, the difference being that England and its merchants were more belligerent. From the seventeenth century onwards, as it began its drive towards hegemony, England was in combat mode. Military spending increased drastically, fueled by a large capacity for tax collection. Foreign trade and the gunboats of the Royal Navy were inseparable, underpinned internally by an economy, a society, and a state representing the most accomplished capitalism of its time.

England practiced mercantilism *avant la lettre*, a militant and unabashed economic nationalism, to shake off the Dutch hold and establish its own. Along with the creation of a Board of Trade in 1650, a shipbuilding program, subsidies, premiums and protective tariffs, came more offensive measures. In 1651, a first Navigation Act reserved England's maritime transport for English ships. The idea was to eliminate Dutch merchants and sailors from trade between England and the rest of the world. The Act was an economic warfare measure that led to the First Anglo-Dutch War in 1652. It was imposed on the Netherlands in the aftermath of that war. A second followed in 1660.

England's multifaceted challenge to Dutch supremacy became increasingly clear. Three naval wars pitted the two rivals against each other (1652-1654, 1664-1667, 1672-1674). Not without difficulty, the English prevailed. The Netherlands lowered its flag and marked time. Confronted by France (1672-1678), the Dutch ended up drawing closer to their late enemy, with William of Orange acceding to the English throne on the occasion of the "Glorious Revolution" of 1688. On land, they succeeded in avoiding a French invasion and escaping the consequences of the customs tariff that Colbert introduced first and foremost against them in 1667.

The War of the Spanish Succession (1701-1713) put an end to the commercial supremacy of the Netherlands, which lost markets. The "golden century" of the Netherlands was over. Amsterdam remained an international financial center, a redistributor of stocks of precious metals and a settlement center for credit instruments until the end of the 1780s. The Fourth War (1780-1784) sealed the fading away of the Netherlands. Part of the capital accumulated in the country was invested in the large public debt and in foreign government bonds, especially British funds. Two recurring realities were reproduced: transfers of hegemony entailed the use of force; the end of hegemony meant the conversion to rentierism. In a negative manner, the Dutch case demonstrated the fact that commercial preeminence presupposed military power to back it up.

Displaying all-out activism, permanent belligerence, and an unrivaled consistency, England was on the path leading to world hegemony. Its progression was continuous, its policy constant from government to government. Its successes were cumulative; except for the independence of the United States, positions acquired were never lost. There were no setbacks. Colonial holdings pointed in only one direction: growth. As so many others, this imperialism made its way by the sword. Its quest for supremacy was undisguised. *"Rule Britannia! Britannia rule the waves,"* the finale of an opera produced in 1740 by the composer Thomas Arne, served as a national anthem.

Relieved of the dynastic, religious or security considerations that encumbered its rivals, it responded solely to economic motivations, a corollary of the preeminence of the interests of the merchant, financial and, later, industrial bourgeoisie. Politics was an extension of economics. England generated the most successful and enduring form of mercantilist, Atlantic and maritime imperialism. At the end of the eighteenth century and in the nineteenth, it would show its ability to set up and dominate the next version of imperialism, that of free trade.

In 1654, England signed a treaty with Portugal by which it replaced the Netherlands as the commercial carrier of the Portuguese empire. The following year, a war against Spain allowed it to annex Jamaica. Penetration of North America accelerated. A Royal West Africa Company was chartered in 1660 to trade slaves between Africa and America, and, in 1713, Britain was granted the *asiento*, the monopoly on the importation of "ebony" in the Spanish colonies of America. It took possession of Gibraltar in 1704 and Minorca in 1708, a prelude to the naval domination of the Mediterranean by a power external to this region. Interest in the overseas world was tangible in France in John Law's monetary and banking system (1716-1720) and in England in the literary sphere with Daniel Defoe's *Robinson Crusoe* (1717) and Jonathan Swift's *Gulliver's Travels* (1726).

Of a different nature, the Anglo-Portuguese Treaty of 1703 (Treaty of Methuen) had lasting structural effects. It opened up Portugal and its Brazilian colony to English exports. Trade in Brazilian ports passed into the hands of English merchants. Setting itself up as Portugal's protector during the War of the Spanish Succession (1701-1713), England obtained commercial privileges which reflected its economic supremacy. This original model, destined to spread as "informal imperialism" in the nineteenth century, exemplified how an international hierarchy was established, whereby a power placed a country (and its colonial domain) under its trusteeship, without loss of its *de jure* sovereignty.

The Treaty of Methuen established a relationship representing economic specialization country by country, initiating the international division of labor of the contemporary period. Portugal was assigned the role of exporter of local wine (port), agricultural products, and Brazilian gold, and England that of supplier of manufactured products (woolens, cotton fabrics, drapery and metal items) for Portugal and Brazil. English products accounted for two-thirds of Portuguese exports to Brazil. In trade between England, Portugal, and Brazil, the balance, always favorable to England, was settled in Brazilian gold. A forerunner of the anticolonial nationalists of the twentieth century, the Marquis of Pombal, Portuguese Prime Minister from 1755 to 1776, deplored this abandonment of manufacturing.

A century earlier, England, itself in a position of exporter of raw materials to the Antwerp factories, escaped the status assigned to Portugal. By 1703, its position had changed. Its merchants even controlled the Portuguese wine trade. The Methuen Treaty was the origin of economist David Ricardo's notion of comparative advantage. It prefigured the division of the world traced in the era of industrial capitalism between a "developed" "North," importer of raw materials and exporter of manufactured products, and an "underdeveloped" "South," supplier of raw materials and recipient of manufactured goods from the "North." While England avoided primary specialization and satellization, a large part of the world after the eighteenth century did not, a process resulting from free trade of which Great Britain itself became the great promoter, especially in the nineteenth century.

England's course was the systematic application of an aggressive policy of using military force to serve economic interests, thwart rivals and acquire a vast colonial empire through a relentless quest for colonies. It was in a state of war for 84 of the 165 years between 1650 and 1815. Internal transformations, begun before the march towards paramountcy, then stimulated by it, continued at an accelerated pace. Industrialization was one of those transformations. After defeating the Netherlands, England took on France, a large state but one whose features were more traditional than its own. England, an island and naval power, focused on trade and colonial expansion, and had few concerns for its security.

It faced a rival whose naval, commercial, and colonial ambitions were less exclusive because they competed with continental ambitions and the necessity of protecting its borders. France could not devote all its resources to colonial expansion, a domain that was incidental to her. France was the last to engage in it. While England was a centralized state strengthened by its revolutions of the seventeenth century, and thus able to concentrate on external affairs, the French state was still in the process of being constituted, unified and centralized. Six wars brought England and France into military confrontation from the end of the seventeenth century to the beginning of the nineteenth: 1688-1697, 1701-1713, 1740-1748, 1756-1763, 1777-1783, 1793-1815. Of these 127 years from 1688 to 1815 ("Second Hundred Years' War"), sixty-nine were devoted to hostilities between England and France. The struggle for economic primacy in the seventeenth century pitted England against the Netherlands. In the eighteenth century, England fought France.

Because they required the mobilization of resources, these wars shaped the English financial system. The Bank of England, established in 1694, was a private and privileged company. While it was an issuing institution, it also discounted commercial bills, made advances and lent the State the cash it needed, in return for charging interest. Its notes had the value of paper money accepted by the state. England emancipated itself from the Bank of Amsterdam, a deposit and exchange bank founded almost a century earlier (1609).

The silver metal of America was king in the sixteenth century, but gold took center stage in the eighteenth century after the discovery in 1697 of the Minas Gerais deposits in central Brazil. Thanks to this gold, which was received as payment under the Treaty of Methuen, but whose volume diminished in the second half of the eighteenth century, London replaced Amsterdam as the financial center of Europe and the Bank of England replaced the Bank of Amsterdam, which ceased to be the regulator of the international financial and monetary system even before the invasion of the Netherlands by French revolutionary troops in 1795. The Brazilian gold that found its way to England also served to balance its commercial accounts deficits in Asia, which had less need of English products than England of Asian ones. Gold took over from the silver used a century earlier. Low-cost precious metals from the Americas made it possible to transfer wealth from Asia to Europe.

c. Franco-English competition

The Americas, more than Asia, were at the center of the colonial rivalry between England and France. In a weak position against Portugal and Spain in the fifteenth and sixteenth centuries, the English and French had to content themselves with buccaneering and the search for less promising northern routes to the "Orient." The voyage of John Cabot (the Italian Giovanni Caboto) on behalf of England took him to Newfoundland in 1497. Overseas motifs extended to the sphere of the imagination. In *Utopia* (1516), Thomas More resurrected the Roman notion of the colony. In 1583, Newfoundland would be the first in the New World. For France, Jacques Cartier made his first journey in North America in 1534.

Having found neither passage to Asia nor precious metals, the French and English were partially compensated by the availability of cod and fur. In the absence of lands overflowing with gold and silver, they had to make do with North America, commercial empires and colonization. Ruthlessly exploited in the Caribbeans, Central America and South America, the natives were fought to the point of extermination in North America, except in New France where the French wanted commerce, not land.

Next came the establishment of settlers and permanent colonies. The French founded Port-Royal (Acadia) in 1605 and sailed up the St. Lawrence to found Quebec City in 1608. The Company of One Hundred Associates (1627-1663) was to populate New France. Beyond, the French penetrated the continent with a view to erecting strongholds and connecting the St. Lawrence and the Mississippi. Under their control, these river axes would encircle the English colonies and contain their westward expansion. The latter were established in Jamestown (Virginia) in 1607, Maryland in 1615, New England (Plymouth 1621, Massachusetts 1629), North and South Carolina in 1663, and Pennsylvania in 1681. Boston was founded in 1630. New Amsterdam was taken from the Dutch in 1664 to be renamed New York.

Based on slavery, the cultivation of sugar cane was undertaken in the Atlantic islands, then in the West Indies. It began on the plantations of northeastern Portuguese Brazil at the end of the sixteenth century. Driven away from Asia, Portugal had refocused its activities in Brazil. With the slowdown in the extraction of silver due to the exhaustion of the mines, sugar took over as a source of enrichment. By the end of the seventeenth century, however, the cultivation of sugar in Brazil was in decline, and attention turned to the islands of the Antilles, which had been sacked and depopulated during the first contacts with Europeans. The rise of the Caribbean islands caused Brazil to lose its markets. Portugal then fell back on Brazilian gold which arrived at just the right time to take over from sugar cane and stave off the crisis. In Brazil, the gold cycle succeeded the sugar cycle.

The Caribbean sugar islands became the western counterpart of the spice islands of Insulindia. England took Bermuda in 1615; Barbados, Saint Kitts, Nevis, and Antigua during the 1620s. The colonization of Barbados began in 1624, and sugar cane was introduced in 1640. Jamaica was added to the group in 1655. Production was slave-based. English planters in Barbados and Jamaica prospered in the seventeenth century but the boom was short-lived because the intensity of cultivation exhausted the soil.

The English islands gave way to Guadeloupe, Martinique, and, above all, Saint-Domingue, which became a French island in 1697. It dominated world sugar production in the eighteenth century. Successively the *Compagnie du Sénégal* (1674), the *Compagnie de Guinée* (1684), and the *Compagnie des Indes occidentales* (1748) supplied it with slaves. The sugar islands of the West Indies ("Islands of America") were the jewels of both empires. In addition to sugar, they produced coffee, cotton, indigo, cocoa, and ginger, and in turn imported manufactured objects, edibles, wines and spirits from their metropolis.

The West Indies, North America, and India were the focal points of international trade and the Anglo-French politico-military confrontation. The wars of the eighteenth century resulted in significant gains for England. As a consequence of the War of the Spanish Succession (1701-1713), it kept Gibraltar and Minorca, wrested from Spain. It took Acadia, Newfoundland, and the Hudson Bay territories from France. Finally, it kept the *asiento*. The War of the Austrian Succession (1740-1748) left the colonial situation unchanged but unsatisfactory for both parties.

The Seven Years' War (1756-1763) resolved the stand-off by confirming the overseas supremacy of Great Britain. Winning on all fronts in North America and Asia, it evicted France. In 1763, it took Quebec and New France away from its rival. Already in a position of strength, Great Britain forced France out of North America. In India, the British and the French tried to transform their trading posts into territorial control. Only the former succeeded. The East India Company established its supremacy through war against the French and local powers, while pitting them against each other. After its military victory in 1757, it became a de facto state power, extended its direct or indirect domination to the entire subcontinent, made acquisitions around India—Singapore in 1819, territories in Burma at the end of wars in 1824 and 1852, Sarawak in 1841, Bhutan in 1865, Nepal in 1867—and retained its prerogatives until India came under the authority of the Crown in 1858.

The French, with their political ambitions annihilated, were left only with trading posts in Pondicherry and Chandernagor. The French East India Company was dissolved between 1769 and 1771. A second was founded in 1785. With France out of the way, there was no longer any counterweight to England. India now belonged to British interests who made it the foundation of their empire in Asia and, after the United States gained independence, in the world. The West Indies were divided: Great Britain retained Saint Vincent, Tobago, Dominica, and Grenada, but it returned Guadeloupe, Martinique, and Saint Lucia to France. In the Americas, France's only remaining foothold was in its Caribbean islands.

However, no sooner had France been disposed of than Britain suffered dissidence, then revolt, from its Thirteen Colonies of North America. France exacted revenge through the American War of Independence (1776-1783), but it was short-lived and yielded it little gain; rather, it swelled its debt. Against all expectations, the United States became an economic partner of Great Britain. Furthermore, politically diverted from North America and having exhausted its sugar islands in the West Indies, Great Britain stepped up its push into Asia from its Indian stronghold. Exploration of Australia and New Zealand prompted three voyages (1768-1780) and, in 1788, the East India Company established itself on the Malay Peninsula.

Military and political control of India made it unnecessary to resort to Brazilian gold, which was in fact in decline. Arrivals ceased. More than ever, extracting economic advantages was a matter of coercion and pressure: commercial transactions under duress, higher sales prices, imposed purchase prices, compulsory deliveries. At the same time, the nature of the East India Company changed; from a company seeking commercial profits, it turned into an organization for direct economic pumping.

The population of the conquered territories was fleeced through a tax system leased to tax farmers bent on enrichment. Taxation proved to be the shortest route to the extraction of maximum revenue from India. Annexing Indian states provided new tax resources. The trading company was succeeded by the territorial empire collecting tribute. With wealth transferred unilaterally by extra-economic means, the drainage of the economy proceeded at an accelerated pace. Indian booty allowed England to pay off its debt to Dutch creditors.

Famines, epidemics, and depopulation were the first consequences. Under the aegis of the East India Company, the famine of 1770 wiped out a third of Bengal's population. Periodic famines were a constant feature in the history of colonized India until the 1940s.

In 1866, a famine claimed a million lives. Another, in 1869, was just as devastating. The calamity of 1876-1877 took five million victims. Two more followed before the end of the century. By 1900, India had lost twenty-six million of its people to hunger. The Bengal famine of 1943, caused by London's decision to export Burma's wheat and rice reserves to the Empire, was the last; three million Indians perished.

To famines were added epidemics, among them the plague which killed five million from 1905 to 1910. The dispossession of the population by the company's personnel was so destructive of the country's substance, the abuses so widespread and the rapid enrichment of these profiteers so ostentatious, that even Parliament in London showed concern. It launched inquiries and some of the most rapacious British "nabobs" were discharged.

The wiping out of India's cotton manufacturing (calicoes, indiennes), due to the dumping of textiles coming from mechanized factories in Britain, began at the end of the eighteenth century. Until then, India's cotton manufacturing was more developed than that of Great Britain, making it a net exporter. The production of muslin and cashmere also suffered. Impoverishment and economic devastation took catastrophic forms among craftsmen, weavers in particular, and many "returned to the land." India lost its status as an exporter of manufactured goods and was relegated to that of a supplier of raw materials (cotton, jute), in other words "underdevelopment." Treaties, such as the one signed with Portugal in 1703, and the elimination of the defenses of foreign economies were the two levers by which Great Britain imposed its hegemony in the eighteenth and nineteenth centuries, and mapped out the international division of labor that made it the "workshop of the world."

d. Sugar and slavery

Long-distance exchanges took place within the framework of triangular circuits designed to ensure maximum rotation of ships and capital. The most sought-after and structured international economic system was located in the Atlantic area. It had sugar as its basic commodity and the African slave trade as its cornerstone, but also its propellant. The circuit linked Western Europe to Africa and to the colonies of the West Indies and North America.

European merchant-shipowners sent weapons, rum, cotton, metal objects, and knick-knacks to the African coast, exchanging them for slaves; the boats left laden with human cargo; the slaves were sold to planters on the West Indian islands and colonial goods (sugar, coffee, tobacco) filled the holds bound for Europe. It was an exclusive circuit, a monopoly reserved for metropolitan merchant-shipowners by the "colonial pact" (between merchant-shipowners and planters), in line with mercantilist doctrine. Its French version, the *Exclusif*, was formally instituted in 1717: all the colonies' trade had to be with the metropolis, and all maritime transport to and from the colonies was to be a monopoly of metropolitan shipowners.

The slave trade, a sordid business from whatever angle it is approached, was one of the major sectors of activity in certain European ports (Bristol, Liverpool, London, Nantes, Bordeaux, Le Havre, Amsterdam). Port industries, such as refineries and shipyards, depended on the colonial system. There are no reliable or generally accepted statistics, but at least ten million Africans were enslaved in appalling conditions and forcibly transported to the Americas. To them should be added the millions who perished before boarding or did not survive the horrors of the Atlantic crossing (the "middle passage") where mortality was staggering. Survivors who made it to their destination were exploited like cattle and lived short lives.

The replacement rate implied a steady supply of slaves. West Africa resembled a slave-hunting ground. In addition to the demographic drain on the continent, kidnappings and raids sowed insecurity and instability. The physical and moral breakdown of African societies was one of the long-term aftereffects of the slave trade. Large parts of the continent, once home to functioning states and empires, regressed to pre-state conditions.

In addition to the millions of Indigenous peoples of America who were exterminated, millions of African captives were worked to death. In France, the Black Code of 1685 conferred legal status on slavery, while attempting to regulate the barbarity, but it was scarcely observed. Like precious metals, slavery was a drain on one continent (Africa) carried out by Atlantic Europe to produce sugar on another continent (the Americas), to be monetized on a third continent (Europe). Mercantilist imperialism structured an international economy that brought continents into forced contact, but always to the benefit of European metropolises.

Two related circuits developed. The prosperity of the Antilles did not leave the merchants of North America indifferent and they turned into unauthorized competitors of those of the European metropolises. Their trade had an illicit and clandestine character because it ran counter to the privileges inherent in the *Exclusif* system which prohibited trade with foreign countries. Planters were involved in smuggling because it provided them with imports cheaper than those offered by metropolitan merchant-shipowners.

A first circuit involved the sale of timber, grain, meat, and cod from North America to the West Indies, and the purchase of sugar and molasses for exchange in Europe against manufactured goods to be sold illegally in the West Indies. A second circuit was based on the sale of rum and various objects in Africa, and the purchase of slaves and their resale in the islands against sugar and molasses to be distilled into rum in New England. Since the end of the seventeenth century, transatlantic trade had no equal in importance and intensity. It reinforced the preponderance of the countries of northwestern Europe and acted as a hub to which the various regional networks were grafted, either as supply channels or as conduits for the redistribution of colonial products.

Retrospect and perspective

Until the middle of the eighteenth century, international trade was driven by the search for a rare or exotic product whose sale in Europe would generate profits for the middleman. Venetian, Genoese, Arab, and Indian merchants acquired spices and carried them across vast spaces on three continents. In addition to precious products, they also traded ordinary goods.

Portugal's expansion in the sixteenth century introduced a new element: the quest for access to sources of supply of the desired item and the elimination of non-European intermediaries from the distribution chain. By settling in Insulindia, in close proximity to the fields where crops were grown, the Dutch were only further pushing the policy inaugurated by their predecessors in Asia. They owned a colony of plantations specializing in coveted products that were integrated into the economy of the metropolis. Coffee, another exotic product, took its place alongside spices in the eighteenth century. In India and China, the British and French found valuable articles, such as cottons and silks, which they redistributed in Europe.

Meanwhile, in the Americas, Europeans took control of scarce products, except fur, most of which had to be obtained from northern natives. The Spanish and Portuguese held the most valuable products of all. Although unwittingly, they acted as re-exporters of American silver and gold to Europe. Soon commercial cultivation took over from plundering and mining.

In Brazil and the West Indies, sugar cane plantations and their slave labor meant prosperity for planters and merchant-shipowners, while the warehouse trade developed in the large ports of the metropolises. Tobacco plantations in the northern colonies made London and Glasgow centers of redistribution in Europe. A third dimension completed expansion in the Americas: the establishment of European settler colonies. These extensions of the metropolises were both sources of supply and outlets reserved for the economy of the State to which they belonged by virtue of the "colonial pact."

For three centuries, the internationalization of the economy took place within the framework of colonial-imperialist expansion of a mercantilist type. Its two vectors were the control of a rare (or artificially rarefied) product for the purpose of re-export and the putting captive overseas economies at the service of the European metropolises. Competing powers strove to reserve high-value products for themselves, to establish settler colonies, or to achieve both goals simultaneously. Re-export and settler colonialism translated into attempts to project European economies beyond their borders.

The relentless quest for a monopoly situation and the desire to exclude competition brought the extra-economic dimension into play. Hence the importance of the military factor, a time-honored means of monopolizing a source of supply for a product or of transferring a monopoly from one metropolis to another. The international economy was understood as static, a zero-sum game in which the gains of one state were tallied at the expense of another, and vice versa. Portugal eliminated Venetians and Arabs. It was in turn driven out of Asia and replaced by the Netherlands, then by England. The latter expelled France from Asia and North America, while benefiting from the abandonment of North America by the Netherlands.

The historical phase of mercantilist imperialism revealed three key facts representing a major evolution of the imperialist phenomenon. First, nascent capitalism took over centuries-old imperialist practices to bend them to the economic needs of merchant and financial capital. The economic interests of states never ceased to be served and extra-economic methods of a military or coercive type for extracting wealth were fully employed. What changed was the double fact that empires had first and foremost an economic purpose, and that the plunder and skimming of wealth from abroad were no longer simple confiscation operations but undertakings for structural integration into the capitalist system taking shape in the metropolises.

Second, a new type of empire, maritime and overseas, appeared. Apart from the Athenian, Carthaginian, and Venetian models, empires had until then been land-based constructs carried out by large states which annexed their neighbors, usually by conquering them militarily but sometimes by incorporating them according to a dynastic logic. The old model of land-based empires was now only found in the Chinese, Russian, and Austrian cases, the last two expanding mainly at the expense of the failing Ottoman Empire.

Mercantilist colonial imperialism was that of maritime powers imposing their hegemony and soon subjugating the old land empires.

The sea got the upper hand over the land and Atlantic Europe over Eurasia. The upheaval in the distribution of power was not insignificant; half a millennium later, it is still operative. Among the new thalassocracies, Great Britain prevailed by military force, first at sea, then on land. If Darwinism had any validity outside the context of nature, it was in that of empires.

Finally, in its own way, mercantilist colonial imperialism laid the foundations for the formation of an international and eventually global economy. The Atlantic powers which projected themselves beyond their territories constituted large economic spaces, spread over more than one continent. These entities were brought into contact with each other, but according to the particular mode of mercantilist imperialism. Europe, America, Africa, and Asia were now linked economically, even if the relationship was not egalitarian or consensual.

If there was a "colonial pact," it was decided by only one of the parties and for its sole benefit. European empires took from the Americas the precious metals that helped them obtain Asian products, and from Africa the slaves who produced the crops in demand in Europe. Since resources of precious metals and slaves were inexpensive, if not virtually free, the net economic contribution to Europe was a pumping of wealth under extra-economic coercion, in other words, the essence of imperialism.

PART III

Appropriation by force: colonial imperialism in the contemporary era

In the era of mercantilist colonial imperialism, the transfer of wealth through bulk handovers of overseas possessions had a transparent character. It was coupled with the ability to use the acquisition of new colonies and the dynamics of re-export to give an impetus to the national economy and lead it toward new activities. Although the Netherlands remained a leading carrier in the eighteenth century, it had relatively few new, specifically Dutch, products to sell to relay the re-exports of spices and coffee from Insulindia. This weakness was more acute in the case of Portugal and Spain, which very early on were reduced to the role of passive sub-metropolises. They were metropolises in name only; their territories in Europe and their American domains were at the disposal of Great Britain.

That left Britain and France. Both were in the running in the eighteenth century because they had productive economies and could field the largest navies. These were *sine qua non* conditions for success in an international economy driven by the search for rare commodities, the quest for reserved economic and settler colonies, as well as the systematic use of military force.

However, these were not sufficient conditions. Societies and their hinterlands, far-reaching in Britain as in France, had to complete what military force had started (upstream and downstream linkages), on pain of losing the economic benefits of territorial conquest, as demonstrated by the experience of Portugal and Spain. Since its revolutions of the seventeenth century, Britain was particularly well-equipped politically, socially, and economically to carry out an ambitious maritime and colonial project abroad, and to promptly adapt its productive system to the needs of the markets it conquered by cannon fire.

CHAPTER 8

Cracks in mercantilist imperialism (1776-1815)

The international economic model engendered by mercantilist imperialism, which had been in vogue since the primacy of the Iberian states, enjoyed brilliant years during the eighteenth century. It was even at its peak. The Atlantic economy was at its most prosperous with colonial products flowing to European ports and no shortage of slaves on the plantations. Then, fissures showed in the edifice and it disintegrated from within. The economic model it embodied was discredited even before the independence of the Thirteen American Colonies and the aftermath of the French Revolution brought it down.

During the middle years of the eighteenth century, mercantilism was a tried and tested set of ideas and practices endorsed by European states and business circles. The portrait was one of compact national or pre-national blocs confronting each other. Its colonies organically welded to it, each metropolis engaged in the struggle to strengthen itself to the detriment of its competitors. Even as the template seemed unchallenged, it reached the limits of its development. Its cohesion was undermined by the escalation of conflicts between Britain and France.

This was even more the case because of the tensions which arose between metropolises seeking to apply the terms of the "colonial pact" and colonies less and less inclined to bear the costs of a one-way preference. What was acceptable at the start of colonization, when the military and economic dependence of the settlers on the metropolis was marked, seemed unbearable once security threats faded and less expensive sources of supply, as well as more profitable markets than those of the home country, became available.

The disarticulation of the mercantilist system began with the take-over of the protective regulations of a beleaguered state by rivals acting in their own interest. Foreign traders and agents flocked to Lisbon and Cádiz and, under Portuguese and Spanish names, elbowed their way into the transatlantic trade, in principle reserved for Iberians. The Treaty of Methuen of 1703 opened up the Portuguese market to England, authorizing it to send one permitted ship per year to Brazil. This limit was not respected, so much so that the Portuguese Empire found itself under the thumb of England. A similar fate awaited Spain after the *asiento* was awarded to England. The "colonial pacts" remained intact but they were subverted and emptied of their substance.

If the mercantilist system was discreetly violated in the French islands of the Antilles, it was in the North American colonies of Great Britain, the beneficiaries of the dispossession of the Iberian states, that it was openly challenged. Destabilization began with the rise of the sugar islands of the West Indies (Saint-Domingue, Guadeloupe, Martinique). This gave rise to a tug-of-war between French planters and merchants from Atlantic coast ports (Bordeaux, Nantes, La Rochelle, Saint-Malo). The former were prohibited from trading with anyone other than the metropolis, by virtue of the "colonial pact" to which the latter had to adhere. *L'Exclusif* (1717) reserved the monopoly of maritime transport for the shipowners of the metropolis. Aware that they could buy cheaper elsewhere than in France, the planters protested. In 1767, they were heard: a milder form of the *Exclusif* opened Saint-Domingue to ships arriving with wood from British North America and leaving with molasses.

a. Clandestine trafficking

The measure was not intended solely to satisfy planters. It took place against the backdrop of growing trade—formally prohibited—between the French West Indies and the Thirteen Colonies, as well as the conflict between France and Great Britain. The Seven Years' War (1756-1763) caused France to lose India and North America. The cession of New France was accompanied by the calculation that the lifting of the French military threat would reinforce the penchant for independence of the Thirteen Colonies vis-à-vis Great Britain. It would be revenge for the setbacks of the Seven Years' War. The easing of the *Exclusif* was intended to encourage trade, in fact clandestine trafficking, between the British colonies of North America and the French islands. The relaxation of the mercantilist restrictions on one side would favor the disorganization of the mercantilist system on the other.

Illicit trafficking had already been developing since the emergence of the French islands as an unrivaled area for growing sugar cane, then coffee. Cod, foodstuffs (flour, grain), tobacco, and naval supplies (wood, tar, pitch, hemp, ropes) from North America penetrated the islands and were exchanged for sugar and molasses. North Americans also exported to the British islands of the West Indies in exchange for cash, which they spent in the French isles for the purchase of sugar to be processed into molasses and rum.

This commerce took on considerable proportions during the Seven Years' War and did not stop after the signing of the Treaty of Paris. In 1788, Saint-Domingue sold more than 40 percent of its coffee outside France. Smuggling was so widespread that it took place in broad daylight and with the knowledge of the authorities. It was even thanks largely to the commercial surplus that they accumulated in trade with the West Indies and to the income from shipping that the Thirteen Colonies erased their trade deficit with Great Britain.

However, the war having been costly, the metropolis increased the taxes and duties owed by the colonies. It tightened mercantilist regulations: in 1763, imported sugar, molasses, rum, and coffee were taxed; in 1765, the Stamp Act imposed prohibitive duties on imports of paper and printed matter from Great Britain, as well as on the circulation of any publication in the Thirteen Colonies. Among other decisions, this stamp law constituted a trigger for the crisis which led to the independence of the North American colonies. The absence of French garrisons on the continent after 1763 removed the threat that kept the colonies within the fold of Great Britain.

b. American War of Independence

In economic terms, the American War of Independence (1776-1783) saw the implosion of the mercantilist system of the first colonial power. The conflict made it possible for clandestine trade to flourish. The

Dutch island of Saint-Eustatius became its hub. The illegal relations forged between the French islands and the northern colonies before the war became legal during the war and expanded after 1783. A genuine triangular trade was established between the French ports on the Atlantic coast, the sugar islands and the United States. In 1784, the *Exclusif* was again relaxed for the benefit of planters and six warehouse ports on the islands were authorized to admit American vessels.

The loss of a protected market of 2.5 million people, almost a third of Britain's population of eight million, should have been a major blow to the British economy. These were the operating rules of the international economic model valid for three centuries. However, nothing of the sort happened, and it is this fact, however surprising for contemporaries, which revealed the obsolescence of the mercantilist system.

The British economy did not undergo a noticeable crisis. Anglo-American trade did not slump, despite the fact that France and the United States had signed a treaty of friendship and commerce in 1778. If imports by Great Britain remained below the prewar levels until the early 1790s, British exports to the United States had exceeded the 1774 amount by 1784. Woolens, metallurgy, and glassware retained their markets. The United States' percentage share of UK imports increased slightly. In exports, it rose significantly, then declined under the effect of the local production of a growing number of manufactured articles. Until the turn of the century, the United States was Britain's best customer.

There was, in addition, a new product that the United States imported in large quantities: cotton fabrics that the mechanized industry of Great Britain was beginning to ship abroad. Traditional trade did not preclude diversification. The former colonies were a vital foreign market for the leading sector of British industrialization at its take-off stage. Their growing demand supported the new industry as it took its first steps.

After the war, Great Britain remained the United States' best export market, albeit with one-third of the total rather than the pre-independence proportion of three-fifths. It received two-thirds of tobacco, the primary export of the United States, even if the value of the arrivals rarely reached the levels of the 1760s and 1770s. Furthermore, freed from the constraints of the Navigation Acts, shipbuilding in the United States made rapid progress, but American trade was conducted at least in part through British shipowners.

While licit and illicit traffic between the United States and the Antilles resumed, France did not succeed in increasing its exports to the new state. This bilateral trade remained in deficit due to tobacco imports. France's costly intervention in the American war failed to produce the commercial benefits sought by the treaty of February 6, 1778.

The breakdown of the "colonial pact" resulted from the tensions it aroused between the stakeholders within each empire. The economic consequences of the independence of the United States demonstrated that there was now salvation outside the framework of a regime of protection. The loss of the Thirteen Colonies harmed neither the prosperity nor the growth of Great Britain. Amputation of the British Empire and its bearable aftereffects came at the right time to illustrate the free trade thesis defended by Adam Smith in *An Inquiry into the Nature and Causes of the Wealth of Nations*, published in 1776, the year of independence in the United States.

The book argued that wealth came from the division of labor and productive activity, not from protectionism. The contrasting history of Portugal and Spain, on the one hand, and England, on the other, was supporting evidence. The author pointed to the futility of bullionism and denounced the propensity to seek monopoly, while reality provided empirical proof of his thesis. If mercantilism and the type of international economy it underpinned were not immediately discredited, there developed a sense that they were not defensible.

c. Physiocracy

The physiocratic school criticized mercantilism from an angle that shifted the focus from trade and colonies to agriculture and land. As early as 1695, in *Le détail de la France*, Pierre Le Pesant de Boisguilbert explained that wealth resided in production and trade, not in cash and precious metals. Despite its title, banker Richard Cantillon's *Essai sur la nature du commerce en général*, published in 1755, argued that land was the foundation of national wealth, which was accumulated through labor. The emphasis shifted from bullionism to agriculture and populationism.

In France, free trade was praised in the spirit of reform of the economy, society and the state. The treatises and writings of Quesnay, Turgot, Du Pont de Nemours, and Mirabeau the elder converged sufficiently to justify their grouping under the name of physiocrats. "Physiocracy" captured the idea of "power of nature." These "economists," as their contemporaries called them, set out to make economics an exact science based on the observation of conditions relating to the creation of wealth, free of deductions deriving from political premises.

In his *Tableau économique* (1758), François Quesnay had the merit of conceiving the economy as an integrated system of flows and interactions discernible as a whole. He aimed to trace the source of a society's wealth. To him, it was based on agriculture, the only productive sector. Industry was considered a sterile activity which did not generate a surplus greater than the cost of production. No less unproductive was trade because, involving only the exchange of equal values, it did not create wealth. Physiocracy was the antithesis of mercantilism, the doctrine of commerce, industry, protection, and bullionism.

Only agriculture produced a surplus ("net product"), which represented society's only supplement of wealth. Reproducible annually, it irrigated the entire economy. Only this additional wealth could be validly subject to a levy. Fundamentally flawed, the current tax system neglected this reality. A new "single tax" on the agricultural surplus was preferable. It followed that measures to support agriculture would simultaneously increase national wealth, the surplus, and Treasury revenues. Agriculture deserved a special effort in order to ensure general prosperity. The state ought to care for it because, among other things, its tax revenues depended on agriculture.

The tax would be on the "net product," not on the land itself. "Net product" was calculated on market value rather than physical product. Consequently, high food prices were desirable, all the more so that they encouraged the extension of cultivation and the quest for productivity gains. Physiocracy emphasized surplus growth, reinvestment, land reclamation, improved farming methods and increased productivity.

The physiocrats believed that raising prices required that trade be liberalized both at home and abroad. It was only when it contributed to the increase of income from the land that commerce ceased to be an accessory activity. In this perspective, physiocracy was at the forefront of an innovative movement advocating free trade. "Laissez faire, laissez passer" ("Let it happen, let it pass") was the recommendation, which became a maxim, of this school of thought. Mercantilism, in this case as a protectionist doctrine, was once again rejected.

> Let us maintain complete freedom of commerce, because the form of internal and foreign policing that is the safest, most accurate and most profitable for the nation and the state is full freedom of competition.
>
> François Quesnay, *Maximes générales*
> *du gouvernement économique d'un royaume*

The arguments of the physiocrats contributed to the creation in France of a climate favorable to free trade. During the French Revolution, physiocratic recommendations were partly adopted. Freedom of internal trade was admitted but that of foreign trade was suspended with the outbreak of war. As a defender of agrarian capitalism and high agricultural prices, physiocracy found little echo in a revolutionary context.

Across the Channel, Adam Smith reached a conclusion similar to that of the physiocrats on free trade, but he did so from the perspective of manufacturing.

> The laudable motive of all these [mercantilist] regulations, is to extend our own manufactures, not by their own improvement, but by the depression of those of all our neighbors, and by putting an end, as much as possible, to the troublesome competition of such odious and disagreeable rivals.
>
> Adam Smith, *The Wealth of Nations*

The market was better suited than protectionism as the means to obtain optimal allocation of an economy's resources, specialization through division of labor, economies of scale, and increase in overall wealth. Specialization required a large market and Britain had already secured it in its immense empire.

Added to the work of theorists was the resumption of Anglo-American relations outside the colonial framework. At the end of the eighteenth century, the notion of liberalizing trade by removing prohibitions and lowering tariff barriers left the domain of scholarly speculation and entered that of practical politics.

d. Trade treaties

The 1780s saw the conclusion of international commercial agreements imbued with a liberal spirit. Trade conventions included the principles of reciprocity between the contracting parties and most favored nation treatment. On September 26, 1786, the two main commercial and belligerent powers of the eighteenth century negotiated a commercial treaty based on the recognition of mutual advantages with a view to promoting trade. Valid for twelve years, it limited import duties to a maximum rate of 10 to 12 percent.

The commitment was made at the end of the conflict in America and enshrined in article 18 of the Treaty of Versailles (1783). Du Pont de Nemours was an advisor to the Minister of Foreign Affairs who approached the negotiations with an outlook far removed from mercantilist conceptions.

> Every nation must necessarily tend towards its greatest prosperity, but this prosperity cannot be exclusive, because it would soon be reduced to naught. We do not enrich ourselves with absolutely poor nations; one must be rich to obtain benefits. Moreover, the field of industry is so vast that there is something for everyone to reap... In laying down this basis, I do not mean to exclude the restrictions that a nation believes it must admit to favor its own industry.
>
> Vergennes, Minister of Foreign affairs, to Rayneval,
> commissioner in London, February 1ˢᵗ, 1783
> (from F. Dumas, *Étude sur le traité de commerce
> de 1786 entre la France et l'Angleterre.*
> Toulouse, É. Privat, 1904, p. 8.)

Practical considerations were certainly not absent: the relative overproduction of wines in France called for outlets; increased trade raised hopes of much-needed customs revenues; lower tariff barriers would bring into legal channels products which were the substance of flourishing smuggling activity between Britain and France; and British industrial exports continued to increase legally, despite high duties.

Added to these motivations was thinking influenced by physiocracy. Meeting on May 21, 1786 to examine the draft treaty, the Conseil d'État heard the negotiator present the principles on which it was based: the most useful trade was that of agricultural products; manufacturing in France what could be manufactured elsewhere would be an error; foreign competition was desirable; an industry whose product would be sold for 5 percent more than the merchandise entered fraudulently did not deserve the support of the State; the interests of the consumer took precedence over those of the manufacturer and the merchant; and protection fostered contraband. For practical and theoretical reasons, the ruling circles, both forced and willing, turned their backs on mercantilism, on the type of imperialism that it represented, and on the model of international economy that it implied. France had signed commercial treaties with Portugal on July 15, 1783 and with the Netherlands on November 8, 1785.

e. Foreign trade of Great Britain and France

The foreign trade of the two signatories to the 1786 treaty had grown considerably in the eighteenth century. That of Great Britain was always in surplus when re-exports of colonial origin were taken into account. Over the course of the century, British imports and exports quadrupled, while re-exports quintupled. For France, re-exports made it possible to achieve a favorable trade balance until 1777. However, they were not enough to maintain it; French trade was in deficit from this date; imports soared from 1784 to 1789, with the Treaty of 1786 contributing to this result. This trend was confirmed over the medium term: imports multiplied by six during the eighteenth century, exports by only four, despite the contribution of re-exported colonial products. Overall, French trade quintupled in current prices and tripled in volume.

The trading structures of Britain and France were both comparable and contrasting. They were similar in terms of the growing share in each of the non-European world. This share reached half for British exports, compared to less than a third for French exports. The key role of colonial trade and the resulting re-exports was due to the upswing in the growth rates of both countries' trade in the second half of the eighteenth century. The difference lay in the nature of the overseas markets. For Great Britain, the major features were the number and diversity of trades. Dynamic markets took turns, so that general growth did not falter or encounter lasting reversals. As soon as the West Indian islands stagnated due to wear and tear of the soil and increased production costs, re-exportable Indian cotton goods took over. Military conquests, particularly those of the Seven Years' War, showed how important they were.

As for exports—of manufactured products, in particular—they benefited from privileged access to the North American colonies, which became the fastest growing market in the second half of the eighteenth century. This trend was clearly confirmed after the independence of the United States. A high proportion of cotton items from the young, mechanized industry also went to North America. Continuity of the trade was ensured by qualitative changes in manufacturing processes. Adaptability, a wide range of options, and a succession of new departures characterized British foreign trade.

On the contrary, the situation of French commerce was problematic, despite its expansion. Greater dependence on Europe made exports more vulnerable to competition from fledgling manufacturers and industries in customer countries. On the colonial front, the ill-fated wars against Britain in the eighteenth century left France with only its Caribbean islands. Saint-Domingue was the most productive sugar territory of the second half of the century, but it was attaining the limits of its development. Cane exhausted the land, as was evidenced by the decline in competitiveness of the British islands, which were cultivated earlier. Added to the phenomena of declining productivity and soil erosion was the increase in the price of slaves now brought from the interior of Africa. The result was rising production costs, sluggish profits, overdue receivables, and longer waiting times for profits to materialize.

Other elements of uncertainty weighed on the sugar economy: price fluctuations and the relative narrowness of the European outlet for a product not yet intended for mass consumption. The interests of planters in increasingly close relations with North America subjected the "colonial pact" to significant pressure. However, it was the slave base of Saint-Domingue which collapsed during the revolt of 1791. Even at the height of their prosperity, the West Indies were a fragile pillar for French trade which lacked the depth and substitute markets available to take over from the sugar economy.

All in all, although the growth rates of British and French trade were similar during the eighteenth century and the merchant tonnage reached in 1786 was comparable—a quarter of the European total was British, a fifth French—the former had the advantage of multiple assets and simultaneous participation in a range of trades in several geographical areas. The 1780s were years of demarcation between two commercial structures: in one, Britain had potential in reserve, supported by revolutionary production methods and a diversified set of markets; in the other, France had reached a maturity based on a mercantilist international economy which was being challenged and dismantled on both sides of the Atlantic.

f. The French Revolution

The free trade moment was merely a truce between two empires confronted with new economic realities. It was immediately called into question by the Revolution which broke out in France and, above all, by the war which lasted almost continuously from 1792 to 1815. They shook the balance between the imperial powers and disrupted the international economy, although, in the final analysis, their result was the accentuation of certain trends already in place before 1789. After a quarter of a century of armed conflict, industrialization, the first advances of which were recorded in the eighteenth century, became the dominant economic and political fact. With industrialization, imperialism was to be reinvented to meet the needs of the new industry.

From the standpoint of imperialism and the international economy, the period had a dual character. On the one hand, the war that broke out on the continent comprised a Franco-British conflict, a new edition of a confrontation dating back to the end of the seventeenth century. On the other hand, despite the appearance of continuity, the war of 1792-1815 was not fought with the same objectives. The model of imperialism and the international economy in place since the sixteenth century was, for all practical purposes, obsolete. The stakes were now defined by Britain's industrialization, its power to penetrate foreign markets and the French attempt to stand up to it by drawing inspiration from its methods.

Britain was in a position to dispense with mercantilist-type protection. If France resorted to it, it was in order to concentrate on one aspect of mercantilist objectives. Whereas the accumulation of precious metals and the development of warehouse trade were dropped, assistance to national manufacturing/industry through the reservation of the national, then European, market was pursued. This refocusing placed the struggle on a more circumscribed and future-oriented terrain.

The record of the French Constituent Assembly was ambiguous. It abolished the monopoly of the East India Company and opened India's trade to other French traders. In a state of bankruptcy, the Company was dissolved in 1795. On the other hand, the Assembly faced a dilemma regarding foreign trade and colonial affairs. Integral liberalism entailed freedom of trade and abolition of the slave trade, eventually of slavery itself, in accordance with the Declaration of the Rights of Man and of the Citizen.

The colonial question was debated in March 1790, but no decision was taken on the subject of the slave trade and the *Exclusif* remained untouched. At first glance, planters and traders won their case. In fact, the *Exclusif* was no longer respected in the West Indies where traffic with Britain and the United States increased irresistibly following the weakening of royal authority since 1789. De facto the "colonial pact" gave way to commercial freedom. On March 15, 1791, the Constituent Assembly adopted a customs tariff which moderately raised tax rates; import duties could not exceed 20 percent.

Undermined by fraudulent trafficking, the colonial system was shaken by the slave revolt which broke out on August 23, 1791 in Saint-Domingue. The prosperity of the sugar economy was over; even if reconquest were to be successful, production and security costs would rule out a return to previous profitability. The planters went back to France or fled to the United States, Jamaica, or Cuba. The colonial system, whose solidity was already doubtful in 1789, experienced the repercussions of the Revolution.

The echo of events in France, much more than a specific decision, undermined a type of colonial relations and imperialism expressed by mercantilist doctrines. While encouraging blacks to fight Britain, the Convention ratified the *fait accompli* by abolishing the slave trade in July 1793 and slavery without redemption by the slaves or compensation to the planters in January 1794.

With the disorganization of transatlantic traffic, port traders seemed to turn towards the European continent. The role of the Gironde fraction was significant in the declaration of war on Habsburg

Austria on April 20, 1792. With its many twists and turns, the conflict lasted twenty-three years. It altered the course of the Revolution and led to a reshaping of international economic relations. British predominance, tangible before 1789, was overwhelming in 1815. The United States expanded into foreign markets thanks to wars in which it did not participate. As for France, it now had a national market freed from domestic legal and customs barriers, but its position in the international economy had crumbled. Deprived of an empire, it found itself on the sidelines of the imperialism of the period, which was linked to the possession of colonies.

The continental war stemmed from the spilling abroad of internal political struggles, fear of invasion, provocations by emigrants, patriotic and revolutionary sentiment, and economic aims. It did not take long to acquire a maritime and colonial dimension when France declared war on Great Britain on February 1, 1793. The contours of this overseas conflict made it part of the eighteenth century clashes between the two rivals.

From July 1793 onwards, Britain implemented its customary peripheral strategy: blockade, naval engagements, operations against the French navy, expansion of the colonial domain, monopolization of trade routes. When France occupied the Netherlands in 1795, Britain took the Cape and Ceylon. When it annexed the Netherlands in 1811, Great Britain seized the Dutch East Indies. At the end of the Napoleonic Wars, it also seized Mauritius and the Seychelles in the Indian Ocean, Tobago and Saint Lucia in the West Indies, Malta and the Ionian Islands in the Mediterranean, and Heligoland in the North Sea.

War with Britain contributed to tipping the Revolution into protectionism. The denunciation on March 1, 1793 of the commercial treaty of 1786 was due to the situation of belligerence, notwithstanding Article 2 which provided for its validity even in the event of a breakdown in relations. Nevertheless, since its coming into force, many chambers of commerce had strongly criticized it on behalf of manufacturers, especially those in the cotton sector, hard hit by competition from British industrial products. Although it was a response to an immediate situation, the protectionist turn also came from a desire to safeguard national production from an exporter whose technical advances were well known.

The prohibition of British imports fell into this vein: textiles in March 1793, all goods in October 1796. French manufacturers enjoyed generalized protection against their most formidable competitor. On September 21, 1793, the Convention promulgated a navigation act establishing privilege of the flag. French goods had to be transported by French ships. The measure was more than just circumstantial. Drawn from the mercantilist arsenal, it corresponded to the kind of laws that earned Britain maritime supremacy. It was also accompanied by a reminder that the principle of freedom was only defensible if everyone subscribed to it.

Despite severe disruption, West Indian trade was not interrupted either in 1791 or after 1793. The British navy prohibited direct relations between France and its colonies, but neutral ships had access to French ports on condition they called at a neutral port. Practicing profitable neutrality, the United States took advantage of the situation by making itself indispensable. Already present in the Antilles, the United States was the first customer and the first foreign supplier of the French islands in 1788, taking 41 percent of their exports and delivering 51 percent of their imports.

After 1789, the United States gave new impetus to these relations. The conflict in Europe allowed it to rise to the rank of leading commercial power in the Antilles. United States merchants contributed to the emergence of Cuba as a producer of sugar and coffee, and as an importer of slaves, in the wake of the Saint-Domingue uprising. From the British islands at the beginning of the eighteenth century to the French isles at its end, the base of sugar production in the world shifted to Cuba in the nineteenth century. United States coffee imports skyrocketed: from 500 tons in 1791 to 17,500 tons in 1794 (3,400 percent). Coffee was resold in the United States or re-exported to Europe following a triangular circuit designed to circumvent the British blockade.

The value of United States exports increased fivefold between 1790 and 1807; the tonnage of the United States navy quintupled between 1790 and 1815. The more the number of countries in a state of war increased, the more the neutral role was valued. Passing through the Cape of Good Hope, United States ships burst into the waters of India and Canton, where their trade exceeded that of their British competitor as early as 1796. The second largest merchant navy in the world was not French but American.

Despite the maintenance of certain commercial flows, French Atlantic ports, port industries (refineries, shipyards), and those in their hinterland (drapery, linen, rope-making, salting) suffered a sharp decline of activity. European products destined for the Antilles and South America were directed to New York. French ports lost their status as colonial goods warehouses, a function which was taken over by Lisbon, where Brazilian cotton was unloaded, and especially by Hamburg. This port had prospered during the Seven Years' War. It became the point of entry for colonial goods and later for British goods smuggled into European markets during the Napoleonic imperial period.

The measures taken by successive revolutionary regimes in France were intended to stiffen and tighten protection. Under the Napoleonic Empire, similar views were held. The attempt to reconquer Saint-Domingue, as well as the reestablishment of the *Exclusif* and slavery in 1802, were backward-looking in nature, but the apparent attachment to mercantilist conceptions should not be misinterpreted. The conflict was an effort to catch up and bring the French economy into line with that of Great Britain, while being for the latter an undertaking to preserve its lead.

Revolutionary and imperial conquests tied the continent's economies to France. A unified market was formed, freed gradually from internal customs and incoherent regulations. The proclamations instituting a continental blockade (Berlin decree of November 21, 1806 and Milan decree of December 17, 1807) were both military decisions and the completion of the series of protective laws enacted since 1793. The maritime blockade tightened by Britain (Orders in Council of May 16, 1806 and November 11, 1807) had already been in place since 1793.

The economic confrontation turned to Great Britain's advantage because French industry proved insufficiently developed to meet the continent's demand. Mechanization was rare outside of the small cotton industry, which had difficulty sourcing cotton. Smuggling, especially in Hamburg, spread to the point of being legitimized by a system of licenses and exemptions granted by the authorities.

Behind the protective wall, the launching of continental industries was encouraged. Cotton spinning, in particular, made progress towards mechanization, both in France and in Central Europe. Benefiting from the same protection against Great Britain, industries competed with each other. Those in central Europe were able to obtain cotton more cheaply thanks to smuggling. In other fields, such as metallurgy, growth and technical improvements were limited. In all, the economic results were not commensurate with the state's efforts to offer incentives.

A quarter of a century of war left profound economic consequences. Centers of activity moved from the Atlantic coast to Paris and the Rhine axis. Atlantic ports declined. Their role became regional, as it had been before the conquest of the Americas. Their dynamism, based on mercantilist imperialism and sugar, was struck a severe blow. Industry, especially cotton, and banking were now concentrated in Paris. The interior replaced the coastal fringe, a consequence as much of the collapse of colonial trade as of the creation of a national market through the removal of internal tariff barriers.

In France, the centuries-old movement which imposed the primacy of the Atlantic space over the continental space, of the sea over the land, was coming to a halt. The war made Great Britain, even more than before, the pivot of international trade, and the United States the second largest trading power in the world. For its part, France recorded a dramatic fall in the volume of its foreign trade: in 1814, it represented only half of what it was in 1788. It was not until 1827 that the level reached in 1789 was regained.

The Franco-British confrontation of the eighteenth century was fueled by the conceptions deriving from the mercantilist model of the economy and of imperialism. The outcome was unfavorable for France. From 1793 to 1815, the conflict took place against the backdrop of the transformation of French society and the spread of industrialization. France did not close the gap that separated it from the most productive economy of the time. Buoyed as it was by the growth of its industry and served at times by the inconsistency *or* the inherent weaknesses of the opposing party, Britain widened it.

Far from closing off its markets, war was the extra-economic lever which allowed it to enter markets whose economic penetration would otherwise have been slower. Imperialism is achieved by force. The French Revolution did not cause the development differential between France and Britain, but it did not erase it. As in the eighteenth century, war was more advantageous to Britain. In terms of the international economy, it led to a relative weakening of France and internal modernization alone was not sufficient to offset it.

CHAPTER 9

Dismantling mercantilist imperialism (1810s-1860s)

The conflict against revolutionary and imperial France was, in two respects, an element of continuity for Great Britain. In military terms, it completed the cycle of wars successfully waged against the rival of the eighteenth century. If the British Empire did not expand as much as it had during the Seven Years' War, France had virtually no colonies left. Its overseas positions were swept away. The conflict even further undermined the Dutch Empire. Britain was a world power in 1763; in 1815, it was the only one worthy of the name. Its navy enjoyed real or potential hegemony on all seas. As for the countries of the Atlantic coast of Europe, taken as a whole, they possessed empires which occupied a third of the earth's surface.

In economic terms, the extra-European orientation of British trade, already noticeable before 1789, became more pronounced. Disruption of relations with the continent, the effects of the continental blockade, the propensity to mobilize the Empire as a reserve in a war context, all these conditions combined to hasten changes in previous commercial circuits. Seen from Britain, the war of 1793-1815, far from being a rupture, played the role of an accelerator of already confirmed trends.

Among the major categories of British foreign trade, re-exports increased their relative share. In 1797-1798, re-exports accounted for two thirds of all exports and included products whose source the buyer attempted to monopolize in order to compress supply, cause scarcity, and raise prices. This was a feature of commerce in the age of mercantilism and mercantilist imperialism. However, Britain was about to cause a decisive transformation in international trade.

Sitting on top of the sole worldwide empire, Britain was also where steam-driven industry was developing. Its international trade involved importing raw materials and exporting finished products. All sources of supply were likely to be tapped. All markets were to serve as outlets. The production capacity of the new machines dictated expansion; otherwise, losses were to be expected. Britain offered itself as the "workshop of the world" and set about creating appropriate commercial conditions.

The first step was to eliminate or marginalize vestiges and obstacles from the mercantilist era, such as the slave trade and slavery: their relatively low productivity compared to wage labor kept import prices high. Then would come the customs disarmament—by treaty or by cannon fire—of the countries to which British manufactured goods would be directed. In this regard, Britain was particularly targeting the non-European world, which was more vulnerable to military threats than Europe. Finally, Britain dismantled its own tariff barriers in 1846 in order to place itself at the center of an international system of imports of raw materials and exports of manufactured articles. A new type of imperialism was taking shape.

a. The abolition of the slave trade and of slavery

First the slave trade and slavery had to be abolished. Consubstantial with the emergence of capitalism, they were generators of wealth and the starting point of racial classifications and stratifications, the substratum of racism. As the cornerstones of merchant capitalism and mercantilist imperialism, the slave trade and slavery deserve special treatment. It was not because experience had demonstrated the accessory nature of the mercantilist system that it became necessary to bring it down. The juxtaposition of old and new is a condition common to all eras.

For action eliminating the old to become necessary, the old must be harmful to the new or a hindrance to it in some way. An established framework is the expression of interests which do not disperse as long as they have reasons to pursue their existence and as long as no new force has reason to challenge them. If change is inevitable, sometimes to the point of being predictable, it cannot be achieved solely on the basis of an awareness that the new is better than the old, the more so when the stakes are high. The element of necessity must intervene so that the step towards the dismantling of an outdated structure is taken. The end of the African slave trade and slavery provides an illustration of this generalization.

The growth of the British sugar colonies was confirmed in the first half of the eighteenth century. During the Seven Years' War (1756-1763), Great Britain occupied Guadeloupe, Martinique, and Cuba. It agreed to return its islands to France by the Treaty of Paris (1763), retained New France, also conquered, and returned Cuba to Spain in exchange for Florida. This decision was due to an understanding of the growing importance of North America as a source of imports and a market for British exports.

But there was more. The annexation of the French islands would have increased the sugar production of the British colonial empire, reduced prices and caused losses to planters in the British islands (Jamaica, Bermuda, Barbados, Windward Islands, etc.). Profitability depended on strict control of supply in a protected market. Ensuring the coherence of the mercantilist system as a whole meant promoting the interests of each of its stakeholders, in this case the planters. Avoiding immediate overproduction, Britain acquired islands with comparatively new soil (Tobago, Grenada, Saint Vincent, the Grenadines, Dominica) whose cultivation could be profitable, gradual, and with little destabilizing effect on the colonial structure.

Following the Seven Years' War, a phenomenon whose warning signs had been apparent since the beginning of the century materialized as declining productivity in the British islands, with falling profits, and increasing indebtedness for planters. In contrast to plantations that were two hundred years old (Barbados) or one hundred years old (Jamaica), those of the French islands had large tracts of fertile land and were entering the phase of maximum profitability. Their production costs were lower, their average yield significantly higher than that of the British islands and their prices much lower. It was known that the competitiveness of sugar from the French islands attracted traders from the Thirteen Colonies and undermined the British colonial system. The war of independence launched from those colonies was a consequence of the British policy of defending mercantilist arrangements.

While the British islands lost their North American market, the French isles experienced unprecedented prosperity. Their production reached a new peak during the 1780s. Saint-Domingue doubled its market from 1783 to 1789. In 1788, it exported twice the volume of Jamaica. The following year, its production alone exceeded that of the entire British West Indies by a third. Sugar from the French islands sold in Europe for half the price of sugar from the British West Indies. Britain's warehouse trade recorded poor sales. The British islands, recently a cumbersome partner of the Thirteen Colonies, were now a burden on Britain itself.

In the meantime, the Indian side of the British Empire, enlarged during the Seven Years' War, weighed on the West Indian situation. The East India Company encouraged cane cultivation in Bengal and results were promising. The first shipments arrived in Great Britain in 1791. Indian sugar was sold at a price one-fifth lower than that of the West Indies. The labor used in cultivation was legally free and salaried (one penny per day). On the basis of experience, free labor proved to be more productive and, on the whole, less costly.

During the eighteenth century, the slave trade and slavery were subjected to criticism by individual authors influenced by the Enlightenment, by non-conformism (dissident currents vis-à-vis the official Anglican Church, in particular the Methodists and the Quakers), and by pro-freedom sentiment expressed during the conflict between the British metropolis and its North American colonies. However, it was in concrete fashion that the question of slavery in Britain arose. The practice of having servants or valets who were slaves spread as planters enriched in the West Indies returned to Britain to adopt an aristocratic lifestyle. They gave slaves as gifts to the gentry, the small nobility they wished to join.

Since the legal status of the slave in Great Britain was determined under a law, Lord Chief Justice Sir John Holt delivered a judgment in 1689 to the effect that all in England, regardless of color or status elsewhere, had the individual rights of native-born Englishmen. This decision fell into oblivion at a time when the extension of the slave trade and the emergence of the British West Indies broadened the foundations of slavery in metropolitan society. In 1729, a ruling was handed down whereby a slave did not change status upon entering Britain. At the end of the eighteenth century, there were some 15,000 slaves in the British Isles.

Incidents occurred when a slave ran away or was sent back against his will to the West Indies. Such a case arose in 1792. Having become interested in the jurisprudence on the subject, an individual by the name of Granville Sharp took legal action to prevent the forced return to the islands of the slave James Somerset. A trial ensued, at the end of which the defendant was released, as the laws on slavery were deemed valid only in the colonies. The Somerset case set a precedent. In France, it was recognized in 1716 that a slave was free as soon as he touched French soil, a decision reaffirmed in 1762.

An anti-slavery campaign was underway in Britain. In 1774, John Wesley, founder of Methodism, published his *Thoughts upon Slavery*. With Adam Smith, argumentation left the moral and religious terrain to settle on economic grounds. *The Wealth of Nations* challenged the value of the colonial system; its corollary, slavery, was condemned due to low productivity. In Britain as in North America, the anti-slavery movement gained momentum; the number of publications of all kinds increased. In 1775, Quakers in the United States created The Society for the Relief of Free Negroes Unlawfully Held in Bondage. In London, the Society for Effecting the Abolition of the Slave Trade was formed in 1787. On the legislative front, the New England states prohibited slavery after independence.

The anti-slavery movement unfolded against a backdrop of growing difficulties in the British sugar colonies, which were caught in a fundamental contradiction: declining productivity led to an increase in slave labor, which became more expensive in relation to the volume produced. While the arrival of human cargo throughout the West Indian islands reached record levels in the 1780s, crisis loomed on the horizon for the British islands. The ballooning of planters' debt caused payment of interest due to fall behind schedule and bankruptcies to increase, resulting in losses for metropolitan lenders. These came in addition to defaults by traders forced to place expensive sugar on European markets. If slavery remained profitable for the planter, it now proved costly for the merchant, the re-exporter, the refiner, and the creditor.

As long as the islands were the jewel in the crown of the colonial system, anti-slavery activity was of an intellectual or religious character, with only limited resonance. It was the work of enlightened, courageous, and justice-loving minds. Influential interests stood in their way. As soon as the islands lost their value and became a burden, the anti-slavery proponents gained a wider audience. Their arguments combined with the turnaround of the situation in the West Indies and produced judicial and, soon thereafter, political outcomes.

In the late 1770s, parliamentary circles took up the issue of the slave trade and slavery. Henceforth, the political process reflected and refracted the alignment of interests in the world of the wealthy, without religious, intellectual, sentimental, or patriotic considerations disappearing from the discourse. The debate pitted representatives of the commercial and financial bourgeoisie, as well as those of landowners, against each other. The planters were not without spokespersons, particularly among the landed aristocracy and among the members of Parliament from the "rotten boroughs," who were aware of the importance of not allowing any privilege to be eroded. However, their support in business circles was dissolving. Many of the latter were bearing the brunt of the West Indies monopoly and setbacks. The situation was serious for planters not because they represented a less profitable sector, but because retaining their positions directly harmed those of well-established interests.

William Wilberforce, a wealthy Wesleyan, was the scion of a family of merchants. It was no coincidence that this MP from Hull, a port more linked to the Baltic than to the West Indies, should lead the anti-slavery campaign in its parliamentary phase. He could count on the support of the East India Company, which was about to market a sugar product competing with that of the West Indies, and of Prime Minister William Pitt himself.

The preferred strategy was to proceed in stages: first the slave trade, then slavery. In May 1789, the Commons debated a resolution on the abolition of the slave trade. After numerous adjournments, the House rejected the bill by 163 votes to 88 in April 1791. The following year, it was adopted by a majority of 145 votes, but the Lords used delaying tactics and postponed their decision, which lost relevance after the outbreak of war against revolutionary France. A wind of conservatism, associated with protectionism, swept across Britain. Pitt parted company with Wilberforce and the abolitionist campaign, especially as Britain attempted to seize the French islands. Under those circumstances, the prohibition of slavery was no longer fashionable in government circles. Wilberforce pursued the campaign, encountering a number of unfavorable votes in Parliament before finally achieving success. On June 10, 1806, both Houses approved the total abolition of the slave trade as of May 1, 1807.

Severe competition from the French islands undoubtedly played no small part in the motivations of politicians at the start of the abolitionist campaign. The opposite would be surprising. At the end of the eighteenth century, Britain was the leading slaveholding power. It supplied the French islands themselves with some of their slave labor. Stopping the trade would hit a rival hard at a time when the West Indies were no more than a liability to powerful interests in Britain.

Events overtook these calculations. The Saint-Domingue uprising and the island's declaration of independence in 1804, the first successful slave revolt in modern times, transformed the situation in the Antilles. The West Indies were not immune to slave revolts; Jamaica was the scene of a dozen rebellions in the eighteenth century. Were slavery to be maintained in the other islands, labor would be even less productive than before. The law of 1806 was in line with the evolving situation.

In the meantime, the British islands proved incapable of significantly increasing their production to fill the void left by the fall in supply from Saint-Domingue since 1791. The price of West Indian sugar and coffee doubled; planters' profits soared. However, in 1799, the depression was deep. Better able to respond to external stimulation, Cuban plantations outperformed those of the British islands. The sugar they produced made a remarkable entry into markets that had eluded the West Indies. The expansion of cane cultivation in Cuba, Louisiana, and Mauritius relegated the British and French West Indies to the margins of sugar production.

In Britain, the concern more than ever was to import tropical products at low prices. This factor outweighed the ulterior motive of causing harm to a more competitive slave-owning rival. Industrial manufacturing required abundant and cheap raw materials. It was estimated that the higher productivity of salaried labor would make it possible to lower the selling price of sugar—the Bengali example illustrated this—to the benefit of importers and manufacturers, even if slave-owning interests suffered.

At the beginning of the nineteenth century, the major trends in the British sugar trade that had been apparent since the end of the eighteenth century became more pronounced. Britain's sugar imports increased steadily, but the aim was no longer re-export, which was stagnant. Rather, it was to refine and sell on the domestic market; average consumption was rising rapidly. The case of sugar showed that, in the nineteenth century, Britain's relationship with the world economy no longer conformed to the model of the previous three centuries.

With British demand far outstripping Indian supply, Britain extended its abolitionist campaign to the rest of the world, albeit with varying degrees of determination. It aimed to get the countries concerned to outlaw the trade and to actively combat it. The first objective was easier to achieve than the second. Approaches were made to Portugal, Spain, and France, accompanied by offers of financial compensation. Britain negotiated the right for its navy to "visit" ships suspected of engaging in trafficking. While testifying to its seriousness, the request was not without ulterior motives: humanitarian and legal justifications could serve as alibis for interventions of all kinds, according to need.

The decline of the West Indies as a source of sugar seemed irreparable. The suppression of the slave trade had no incentive effect on production. In 1833, Britain abolished slavery, with emancipation taking effect on August 1, 1834. The 800,000 slaves in the West Indies and Mauritius had to undergo an apprenticeship period of four to six years. Planters were compensated to the tune of 37 pounds and 10 shillings per slave, a total of around £20 million. Faced with the labor shortage, indentured workers or coolies, poor people originating mainly from India, were introduced. Under the July Monarchy in France, the planters of Saint-Domingue were compensated at the expense of the independent state of Haiti. In 1825, the latter had to take out a large loan of 150 million gold francs from Parisian bankers to indemnify the former colonists, a burden it would carry into the twentieth century. Slavery was abolished in 1793 but reestablished by Napoleon in 1802. It was definitively abolished in France on April 27, 1848, during the revolution.

In 1850-1851, Brazil put an end to the slave trade. The Treaty of Washington of April 1862 provided that United States ships collaborate with those of Britain to suppress traffic to Cuba. The last shipment arrived in 1867. The emancipation of slaves in the United

States on January 31, 1865, and the outlawing of slavery on July 29, 1880 in Cuba—even if an apprenticeship system was in force until 1886—and in 1888 in Brazil did not erase this coercive labor relationship from the international economy. When it is not in competition with more productive relations, it is revived if an abundance of raw materials met a shortage of labor or, conversely, if a plethora of labor was associated with a shortage of raw materials. In the form of forced labor, it manifested itself in the Dutch East Indies from 1832 to 1890, in the Congo of the Belgian King Leopold II (1884-1908), in South Africa, in Liberia, and elsewhere up to the present day.

Even the abolition of slavery failed to increase the volume produced in the British West Indies. Their soil was too exhausted to compete with new countries, regardless of the legal status of their workforce. Demand in Britain continued to rise and the imperial preference for West Indies sugar was lifted in 1846. Entry duties on imported sugar were lowered. By 1847, a fifth of the sugar consumed in Britain was foreign, mainly Brazilian and Cuban; the proportion rose to a quarter in 1851. Deprived of customs protection, Indian sugar did not recover. Officially opposed to slavery, Britain contributed to the maintenance of the slave trade and slavery in Brazil and Cuba.

Whatever the level of productivity of these plantations, Britain needed their sugar since it lacked access to other sources of supply. Britain would also be the foreign support of slavery in the South of the United States because its textile mills demanded the raw material. Industrial capitalism, as the most modern mechanical production, and free trade may be antithetical in principle to primitive forms of social labor, but in fact they coexisted with and benefited from them. Abolitionism was valid only when British interests did not oppose it.

Furthermore, the relative inefficiency of labor under extra-economic constraints was not sufficient reason for its disappearance, insofar as it generated profits, however paltry. It could be maintained as long as its "factors of production" (raw materials, labor, facilities, etc.) were not called for by more productive and profitable forms of work organization. One must therefore be careful not to think that the appearance of new relationships and ideas in a dominant economy automatically or even quickly led to their validation or application throughout the world. In the international economy, new structures arose from old ones and were superimposed on them. Interpenetration and substitution took place according to the particular history of each economic entity.

b. The independence of Latin America

The colonial systems of Spain and Portugal had been empty shells at least since the beginning of the eighteenth century. Although the structures remained in place, the substance of the "colonial pacts" went out of the hands of the Iberian states. Northern traders, ship-owners, and slavers, particularly the British, took advantage of this. The Spanish and Portuguese metropolises were in reality sub-metropolises reduced to a status of economic and military dependence, so much so that they practically acted as transit points and sources of legitimation for formally illicit exchanges between Great Britain and Latin America. As subordinate empires, they found themselves in the paradoxical position of states having to bear the costs of administering their colonies without reaping the benefits.

In fact, Spain and Portugal were metropolises in name only. Their exports to the Americas consisted mainly of agricultural products, such as olive oil, wine, fruit, and flour. Only Barcelona textiles belonged to the industrial sector. All Spanish and Portuguese export-able products were available locally in the Americas or were likely to be, so that supply from Spain or Portugal was in no way essential. Their products, far from providing the colonies with the goods they needed, competed with those they had. The industrial items they received were not of Spanish or Portuguese origin.

Even the slave trade was now in non-Iberian hands. Barely more developed than their colonies, Spain and Portugal were too undeveloped to play the role of metropolises. As indicated by the provenance of the majority of products sent to the Americas—and even by the foreign nationality of the shipping lines serving the transatlantic cir-cuits—the Iberian states appeared as intermediaries or centers for the re-export and redistribution of goods from northern Europe.

Spanish authorities spared no effort to make the link with the Americas less artificial. They strove to reestablish their authority, to centralize controls, to tighten regulations, to reserve for the state a monopoly on a range of products and, above all, to increase its revenues. Like the Thirteen Colonies in North America, the Spanish possessions came under increasing fiscal pressure during the second part of the eighteenth century. Their resistance was just as strong, especially since the Spanish home market was no longer sufficient for the large landowners exporting agricultural products from the colonies.

Tensions between *criollos* (Spaniards born in the Americas) and *peninsulares* (Spaniards born in Spain) flared up, but without any significant impetus being given to an independence movement. Indeed, although they considered themselves more capable than the Iberians to occupy the highest administrative positions, the "great whites" were only too aware of the weakness of their numbers at the top of an informal but real colonial hierarchy, comprising mestizos, Amerindians, freed blacks, mulattoes and slaves. A conflict between Creoles and Peninsulares would risk turning to the advantage of a third party.

The wars unleashed during the French Revolution and the Napoleonic Empire precipitated events. From 1796, Cádiz was blockaded by the Royal Navy, while British exporters supplied South America, bypassing the Spanish relay. Spain's imperial relationship and commercial monopoly were broken. The colonies now traded directly with Britain and the United States. At Trafalgar in 1805, the Spanish Atlantic fleet was sunk, severing the last links with America.

While the colonies looked for outlets for their exports and new sources of supply, Britain faced the continental system established by Napoleon in 1806. Caught in the vise of increased production by machinery and continental markets whose penetration was becoming more complicated, it intensified its extra-European orientation. The offensive on the American markets was particularly strong. Between 1809 and 1811, Latin America accounted for 35 percent of Britain's total exports.

The British were not content with monopolizing South America's trade. Setting out from the Cape of Good Hope, an expeditionary force captured Buenos Aires in June 1806. It had to surrender in August. Another force occupied Montevideo in February 1807 and suffered the same fate. In both cases, local volunteer militias were responsible for repelling the invaders. By default, the defenders were forced to take their destiny into their own hands and act politically and militarily without referring to Spain.

Meanwhile Napoleon ordered Portugal to close its ports to Great Britain. In November 1807, with a French army marching on Lisbon, the court and the administration were transported to Brazil by the British navy. This did not come without a quid pro quo: the secret convention of October 1807 stipulated that British protection would be repaid by the abolition of the Portuguese monopoly on trade in Brazil. From January 28, 1808, Brazilian ports were open to trade for all. Commerce between Portugal and Brazil collapsed. The last traces of the "colonial pact," already taken over by Britain a century earlier, were erased. Lisbon was abandoned; Rio de Janeiro, flooded with British goods, became the entrepot and hub of Britain's trade with South America.

However, London demanded other advantages from a state that could refuse it nothing. In February 1810, a commercial treaty granted British merchants extraterritorial privileges and lowered duties to a maximum tariff of 15 percent *ad valorem* on British imports into Brazil. At that date, this rate was 1 percent lower than that applied to Portuguese products. The ceiling for the latter was reduced to 15 percent in October 1810. The metropolitan monopoly was de facto transferred to Britain.

While the gap widened between the Iberian metropolises and their American possessions, formal political links remained. The process of rupture was triggered by the imposition of Joseph Bonaparte as monarch in Spain in 1808 and the entry of French armies into the country. Based in Cádiz, the central junta (a committee bringing together representatives of the forces of opposition) was sensitive to the needs of trade. Cancellation of the "colonial pact" was not part of its program. In reality, the colonies were once again left to their fate due to the turn of events in Europe. Refusing to recognize Joseph Bonaparte or the body in Cádiz, they remained loyal to the Bourbon Ferdinand VII. The prospect of total control of Spain by French troops led the colonies to break away from the mother country and form autonomous governments in 1810.

Returning to Spain in 1813, Ferdinand VII attempted to reconquer the American colonies by force. In so doing, he transformed autonomist aspirations into a movement for independence. The war, involving a multitude of piecemeal conflicts stretching from Mexico to Peru, lasted more than a decade. In 1826, only Cuba and Puerto

Rico remained in the Spanish fold, while the commercial monopoly of the metropolis was far from watertight.

Since 1808, Great Britain observed a policy of neutrality in this conflict. The war against the Napoleonic Empire, then the isolation of France after 1815, forced it to treat Spain with consideration. But its interests in Spanish America precluded indifference towards insurgents who could soon lead independent states. From this point of view, it was prudent not to let the United States get ahead. Britain did not support repression, but it was in no hurry to recognize the new authorities in America. It only did so against the signing of commercial treaties.

In any case, the opening up of Latin America to British trade proceeded inexorably. British merchants set up permanently in the ports of the continent, and the London financial market granted advances to traders and loans to the new governments. In the early 1820s, Latin America's share of British exports rose from 10 percent to 15 percent of the total. Britain was the leading importer of Latin American products. Foreign Secretary George Canning was not wrong when he wrote "Spanish America is free; and if we do not mismanage our affairs, she is English."

That left Brazil, which had become the true metropolis of the Portuguese Empire since the arrival of the court in 1807. The king only returned to Portugal in 1821, forced by a liberal uprising which threatened him with deposition in the event of refusal. The administration of Brazil was left to his son. Faced with the centralizing intentions of the Cortes of Lisbon, the movement for independence made headway, to such an extent that the prince regent put himself at its head and was proclaimed emperor of Brazil in Rio in September 1822. Britain was the first commercial partner of Brazil, which constituted its third largest foreign market during the 1820s. It intervened to get Portugal to recognize the independence of Brazil in 1825, in return for the latter's signature of a treaty—concluded in 1827—stipulating the maintenance for fifteen years of the privilege of a maximum tariff of 15 percent for British imports.

For Latin America, independence, accompanied by trade treaties, constituted a transfer from the Iberian metropolises to the British metropolis. The Spanish and Portuguese intermediaries, now superfluous, were eliminated from the commercial circuits over which they had gradually lost control. The scope of freedom of trade was circumscribed by British primacy. In Latin America, the outlines of the international economic order of the nineteenth century took shape. In order to export, Britain had to ensure that its potential customers possessed the resources to pay for their imports. These could only originate from their exports to Great Britain, the pivot of the international economy.

It turned out that Latin America did not live up to expectations. Foreign trade only grew moderately: the purchasing power of the majority was too limited to support a significant expansion of markets. Moreover, many mining companies were disappointments and many governments went bankrupt. The free trade arrangement sought by Great Britain and the first independence leaders was fragile. It only lasted for a short time; one by one, the new states adopted measures to protect trade.

c. A major exception: the colonization of Algeria

Though the era of mercantilist imperialism may have been in its twilight, it was far from over. In fact, the occupation of Algeria from 1830 onwards was reminiscent of settler colonialism in the Americas, the main difference being that it took place in the "Old World." The clash with the local population gave rise to a multi-faceted, bloody, and long-lasting conflict. A large-scale armed struggle began upon the arrival of the French and lasted until 1847. It was followed by various acts of resistance, including a major uprising in 1871 and a revolt in the south of Oran from 1881 to 1892.

As for the relationship with France, Algeria was as attached to it as the "American islands" had been to the metropolis. This expansion was akin to a rebirth of the empire that France had just lost in the West Indies. Through Algeria, France began the constitution of its second colonial empire. In Algeria, not only was there no evolution of imperialism towards new forms but, with settler colonization, it was downright backward-looking. While free-trade imperialism spread in the nineteenth century, Algeria remained a possession administered according to the colonial practices of the past. History is not accustomed to the immediate severing of all continuities.

Initially a prestige operation to divert attention and save the monarchy, the Algiers expedition of 1830 turned, at the urging of the merchants of Marseille, into a takeover in 1834. Decided in 1840, total occupation was a ruthless war of conquest waged by a regular army. French, but also Spanish, Maltese, and Sicilian settlers arrived as early as 1830. There were already 110,000 of them by 1848. Land speculators followed, while the administration accompanied colonization by sequestering native lands and converting them into state property. Metropolitan companies, such as the *Société générale algérienne* (1866), were soon at work. All the parameters of settler colonialism were already present: installation of settlers, displacement of Indigenous people, land grabbing, maintenance of the system by armed force.

The model was crude, adorned neither with theoretical subtleties nor with complicated justifications. Two universes lived side by side: while France was moving towards a republican regime, its universal principles applied in reality only to the minority of settlers, with the "Muslim" majority excluded. The colonization of Algeria demonstrated that old forms of domination can endure, and that the evolution of metropolises did not necessarily imply a rethinking or updating of their relationships with their overseas possessions.

Characteristic of the modern and contemporary era, the division of the world between Western Europe, where wealth and power were concentrated, and the rest was operative everywhere and on all levels. Algeria joined America and southern Africa in the category of settler colonies. At the same time, in a similar process, colonies were set up in various parts of Australia and New Zealand. As elsewhere, Indigenous populations bore the cost: Aborigines in Australia and Maoris in New Zealand. In Australia, the first gold rush began in 1851; others followed for a century, resulting in colonization and dislodgement of populations.

CHAPTER 10

Heyday of free-trade imperialism (1830s-1860s)

Mercantilism and mercantilist imperialism were unraveling on all sides. More importantly, Britain gained unprecedented preeminence. Already dominant outside Europe and on all seas in the eighteenth century, it saw its supremacy reinforced by the weakening of its rivals and by the industrial revolution that it alone experienced. There was hardly any area in which it did not have a decided advantage, including in the natural endowment of coal and iron, key substances of industrialization.

Never before had the stars been so well aligned over such a long period for a country, and never before had a country been so successful in reinventing itself by taking advantage of its strengths and the setbacks of others according to circumstances. Long experienced in the business of domination, starting with that of its own population, the British ruling class in all its components—landed, commercial, financial, industrial—and all its political factions had a lucid and shared vision of the priority of the quest for wealth and power in the world. Its international action, a genuine program resting on duration and continuity, maintained its trajectory without interruption from the sixteenth to the twentieth centuries and gave it a preponderance that it exercised to the full.

The British Empire, established through an aggressive policy and the systematic application of force, was also based on a modern capitalist economy that underwent continual and cumulative transformation. In 1815, it remained a mercantilist entity, notwithstanding the loss of the thirteen North American colonies. The replacement of the mercantilist system would take place at the center, in Great Britain, rather than on the overseas periphery. Its successor, free-trade imperialism, was the second form of capitalist imperialism.

a. Free trade

Even if Adam Smith praised laissez-faire and mocked mercantilism, bullionism and protectionism in his 1776 book, this was not enough to bring down the walls of the temple. It would be requisite, on the one hand, for liberal theory to sharpen its arguments in order to pre-scribe precise actions and, on the other hand, for the socio-economic conditions of the early nineteenth century to make the transition unavoidable. Free trade was fashionable at the end of the eighteenth century, as evidenced by the Franco-British treaty of 1786. But, after the hiatus of the revolutionary and imperial wars, everything had to be restarted. At the end of this period, Great Britain was still mer-cantilist; it was surrounded by customs and tariff barriers. The "col-onial pact," moribund because of the importance of trade with the independent United States, had not survived. The Navigation Acts were in force and chartered companies exercised their monopolies. The idea of free trade had to be based on theoretical reasoning and concrete recommendations if it was to be translated into economic policy and legislative measures.

David Ricardo formalized and further developed Smith's theses in *On the Principles of Political Economy and Taxation* (1817). By the "law" of comparative advantages, he postulated that each country should specialize in what it did best, export these products and import what it did less well than others. For Great Britain, the only country in the process of industrialization, the situation was clear: it had to focus on industry, even if it meant sacrificing an agricultural sector that was less productive than that of the others. Both the Physiocrats and Ricardo advocated free trade, but the former were the econo-mists of agriculture, while Ricardo was the economist of industry. Ricardo's demonstrations were arguments in favor of the division of labor and international trade with any foreign partner who could be complementary to the British economy, either as a supplier or as a customer. That went beyond the colonial framework at the heart of mercantilism and led to freedom of trade.

In 1820, London merchants submitted a petition to Parliament supporting principles of free trade, including the following assertion:

"That the maxim of buying in the cheapest market and selling in the dearest, which regulates every merchant in his individual dealings, is strictly applicable as the best rule for the commerce of the whole nation."

However, the transition from theory to practice was subject to the vagaries of economic conditions and the level of resistance of agricultural interests called upon to accept the lowering of customs duties that protected them. In this respect, Britain—and, even more so, other countries—was far from the mark. In 1815, it even passed Corn Laws to further protect its agriculture. It did so again in 1828 with the imposition of a new duty on foreign wheat. Dominant in the House of Lords, powerful in the Commons, the large landowners rejected the withdrawal of these laws in 1838.

The economic crisis of 1836-1842 brought back attention to the question by way of the high cost of bread. Poor harvests were compounded by an industrial slowdown. Unemployment and falling profits hit, respectively, workers and employers. The first supported the Chartist movement for the establishment of universal suffrage, the second began to challenge the protectionist system and embraced its replacement by free trade. For employers, the high price of bread meant they had to pay correspondingly high wages, whereas importing cheaper wheat would enable them to lower wages and prices, and to export more to markets that had revenue from their grain sales which could be used to import British products.

A vast agitation campaign, financed by the employers of the new mechanized industry, was organized and efficiently carried out across the country by the Anti-Corn Law League. British history has the merit of providing political processes in which economic and ideological interests are displayed with uncommon clarity and transparency. In December 1838, the Manchester Chamber of Commerce, home of the industrial revolution, petitioned the Commons to protest against the Corn Laws which kept the price of bread artificially high. British manufacturers were said to be handicapped: their foreign competitors benefited from bread sold at half the price of British bread, raising fears of nothing less than the transfer of national industry to foreign countries.

From 1839 to 1842, Britain was in the throes of an economic depression and the atmosphere was pre-revolutionary. The poor grain harvest in England and the famine in Ireland at the end of 1845 put an end to resistance. Hundreds of duties were eliminated or reduced between 1841 and 1846. The Corn Laws were repealed in 1846. Three years later, in 1849, the Navigation Acts, the cornerstone of the mercantilist edifice, were abolished. The victory of the new industrial bourgeoisie was decisive; henceforth it steered the economic policy of the state and bent its imperialism to its needs. Some of the Tory magnates balked. However, neither for the first nor the last time in British history, the spokesmen of the ruling classes put their differences aside and united to defuse a potentially revolutionary situation. A circumstantial and peculiar junction between the industrial bourgeoisie and the working class was avoided.

The era of free trade was ushered in by Great Britain through unilateral customs disarmament. As the only industrial power, it had nothing to fear from hypothetical competition. Its merchant navy was so dominant that the Navigation Acts had become superfluous. As Prime Minister Robert Peel pointed out, his country's lead over the rest of the world was considerable. In reality, free trade, while to Britain's advantage, was only the last step in the consolidation of its hegemony. It imposed this hegemony within the framework of mercantilism and protectionism, rigorously applied, and not without recourse to monopolies. Once primacy has been achieved, it shed its mercantilist shell to broaden its field of action beyond the colonial sphere. The issue was not so much a choice as a necessity for an industrial apparatus that had to sell in new markets.

These markets were abroad, given the limits of purchasing power in the domestic market. The United Kingdom banked on accelerating its industrialization and made the trade-offs that this choice dictated. Year after year until 1914, Britain exported a quarter to a third of its production, an exceptional proportion. From 1841 to 1870, exports increased by almost 5 percent per year, more than the GDP. There was a doubling of exports and a tripling of imports between 1854 and 1880. At the same time, the United Kingdom imported half of its food requirements, thereby reducing its production costs. The knock-on effect of the British engine of the international economy and the structural consequences on the rest of the world were significant.

Henceforth, at the forefront of British policy was the promotion of free trade everywhere in order to eliminate the protections of other countries, given that the latter were less able to compete. The aim was to transform them, by peaceful or warlike means, into markets for British industrial exports, as well as sources of foodstuffs and raw materials. The application of the "law" of comparative advantages was a powerful means of reconfiguring the international economy according to the interests of its ultimate regulator and beneficiary, Great Britain. The world would depend on it, like the countryside would on a large city. As the "workshop of the world," enjoying a monopoly on industrial production, it would confine others to primary products. Like mercantilist imperialism, free-trade imperialism froze the "periphery" in subordinate roles. Through the effect of external demand and political intervention, it curtailed subsistence or self-consumption agriculture in favor of commercial and export agriculture, while consolidating precapitalist structures.

Portugal (wine) since the eighteenth century, and Argentina (wheat, meat), Chile (copper and nitrates), and Peru (guano) since the nineteenth century, were already in a relationship of complementarity with the British economy, while remaining sovereign countries. With countries having the capacity to resist, trade treaties would be preferred. For those less able to defend themselves, a gunboat policy would force them to comply, open their economies to British interests, and undergo forced specialization. While in the era of mercantilist imperialism, chartered companies had their own private warships, in the era of free-trade imperialism, the vessels were those of the state. In the case of the United States, Great Britain sided with the Confederacy in the American Civil War (1861-1865). Unlike the North, a potential industrial rival, the South was a supplier of cotton to the Lancashire spinning mills. Slavery was not an insurmountable obstacle; economic interest took precedence over anti-slavery tenets.

The corollary of Britain's ascendancy was the prospect of an Anglocentric world economy on which would be superimposed a British-dominated world order ("Pax Britannica"). A man of the Enlightenment, Adam Smith had a reformist conception of free trade as an element of humanity's progress and a factor of world peace. The fact remained, however, that free trade was the credo of the strongest and Britain was in a favorable position. If free trade was antithetical to protectionism and mercantilism, it was in fact their continuator as an instrument of power and updated imperialism. Dependence on Britain will be accomplished by choice or by force.

Such were the foundations of free-trade imperialism. Liberal doctrine advised against the possession of colonies: they were portrayed as a mercantilist anachronism, an unnecessary burden and reserved markets when all markets had to be free. Britain was urged to swap colonial markets for the world market.

In reality, theory and rhetoric notwithstanding, free-trade imperialism was not averse to colonies; their acquisition continued as before (colonization of Australia and New Zealand, occupation of Natal in 1842, protectorate over Lagos in 1853, annexation of the coastal zone of the Gold Coast/Ghana in 1865), and was now complemented by the subordination of countries that remained formally independent and were not part of the British Empire. The Colonial Office was created in 1854 and the India Office in 1858, in the wake of the great anti-British revolt of 1857. In his *Lectures on colonization* (1861), Herman Merivale described countries whose independence was a fiction as "an empire in all but name."

Thus was born the "informal empire" of Great Britain, distinct from the directly controlled "formal empire." This duality was specific to the era of free trade and its type of imperialism. As for the settler colonies (Canada, South Africa, Australia, New Zealand), they were kept as outlets for overpopulation or the periodic gluts of goods or capital that were feared in the metropolis. In general, overseas territories were assigned the function of a safety valve to ward off the dangers of revolution.

The two spokespeople and linchpins of the Anti-Corn Law League, Richard Cobden and John Bright, were cotton company owners and members of Parliament whose worldview combined quasi-utopian idealism with well-understood material interest. As followers of Adam Smith, they considered free trade to be the key to prosperity for all and a guarantee of universal peace.

> "I see in the Free Trade principle that which shall act on the moral world as the principle of gravitation in the universe, drawing men together, thrusting aside the antagonism of race, and creed, and language, and uniting us in the bonds of eternal peace."
>
> Richard Cobden, speech in Manchester, January 15, 1846

In international affairs, Cobden and Bright were advocates of non-intervention. After their success in 1846, they were quickly marginalized by the belligerent current of British liberalism. Prime Minister Lord Palmerston (1855-1858, 1859-1865) was the architect of a foreign policy based on power, interventionism, unilateralism, and aggressive action, and was prone to demonstrations of force. That current was not above bluster aimed at pandering to British chauvinism. A Tory prime minister like Benjamin Disraeli (1868, 1874-1880) could easily continue this type of liberalism.

Borrowing from both idealistic and realistic tendencies, Prime Minister William Gladstone (1868-1874, 1880-1885, 1886, 1892-1894) advocated interventionism, but for reasons he presented as disinterested and based on justice and morality. He preferred the collective action of the concert of European powers to the individual action of Great Britain. As far back as the nineteenth century, the broad outlines of contemporary Western foreign policies emerged in the options that materialized in Britain.

The influence of liberal thought and British economists continued to be dominant. Laissez-faire was held to represent the recommended path to prosperity and rising standards of living. It enjoyed a premium due to its aura of modernity and scientificity. Great Britain's example had imitators in Europe; Austria, Spain, the Netherlands, Belgium, Sweden, Norway, and Denmark liberalized their trade. The French economist Jean-Baptiste Say, the translator of Adam Smith, systematized and disseminated his master's ideas, while Charles Dunoyer and Frédéric Bastiat were more outspoken in their advocacy of laissez-faire.

On the other hand, and unsurprisingly, continental industrialists were less likely to call for free trade, given that it would make them compete with superior British industry. At the same time, procolonial thought was so little appreciated that its defense shifted to the register of racism, as in Arthur de Gobineau's *Essai sur l'inégalité des races humaines* (1853-1855), in which it was made into a guarantee of the dominance of the white race.

On the continent, the initiative belonged to opinion leaders and public authorities. Successor to the Franco-British trade treaty of 1786, the treaty signed in 1860 between the two partners was first and foremost the brainchild of Emperor Napoleon III, who hoped to consolidate his policy of entente with London, stimulate modernization and win over the working class by providing it with basic necessities at low prices, and of Michel Chevalier, a Saint-Simonian keen on bringing peoples closer through trade. The cotton manufacturers of the North were reluctant and the treaty, which removed quantitative barriers and lowered customs duties, was negotiated in secret. The way was paved for European states to sign free trade treaties with each other, including the most favored nation clause. Bilateral liberalization spread to other countries.

Not all continental economists embraced the doctrines emanating from Great Britain. The German Friedrich List believed that classical liberal political economy (the Manchester school), with Adam Smith as its founder, served British interests; it reflected their hegemony and aimed to extend it. Its universalism and cosmopolitanism were judged to be a sham. The emphasis it placed on the individual and on the international dimension obscured the nation and national economies, the true framework of analysis. After having taken advantage of protectionism to strengthen itself and industrialize, Britain sought to deny it to others through generalized free trade in order to keep them in a position of inferiority. A contemporary of List, the American economist Henry Charles Carey, was of the same opinion.

Where free trade was not consented to, it was forced. In Latin America, the signatories of trade treaties with the United Kingdom were more or less willing. British traders and their government inserted themselves into the meshes of the disintegrating "colonial pacts" to speed up the process and take advantage of it. Elsewhere, Britain resorted to coercion to achieve the same ends, in other words, it used extra-economic means to serve economic interests. Such was the case for the penetration of Asian markets. The Southern Hemisphere was an important customer: in 1860, half of all British exports went there.

b. The Ottoman Empire forced to open up its trade

Commercial relations between the Ottoman Empire and European countries were governed by the Capitulations. These conventions, freely granted when the Empire was at the height of its power in the sixteenth and seventeenth centuries, authorized foreign merchants to trade from certain Ottoman ports (the "*Echelles du Levant*") and granted them extraterritorial privileges, such as the privilege of being judged by consular courts in criminal cases and tax exemption. The Capitulations of 1673 set the tax rate at 3 percent *ad valorem* for imports and exports. A 2 percent sales tax was added to imports, but exports were subject to much higher, even prohibitive, duties. As for internal customs, they levied complex and heterogeneous taxes on merchandise circulating within the Empire.

The advent of industrialization in Britain meant that new sources of raw materials had to be found to supply the factories, and foreign markets had to be opened in order to sell the growing quantity of manufactured goods produced. That being the case, the arrangements resulting from the Capitulations were no longer acceptable to Britain. Its merchants complained about the difficulty of accessing raw materials. Ottoman authorities were indeed concerned about supplying craftsmen and, even more, about feeding the urban population prone to revolt. The export of many products was prohibited. Others were subject to high export duties.

Furthermore, British traders were no longer content with the port markets designated by the Capitulations. They brought their goods into the country, where they were subject to internal customs duties. In 1826, the government established a monopoly on the purchase of export products such as wool, opium, olive oil, silk, and cereals. The governor of the Ottoman province of Egypt did the same for all exportable goods. All these practices constituted obstacles to the growth of trade which the British authorities set out to eliminate.

The Anglo-Ottoman customs tariff, established in 1820, expired in 1834. This was the opportunity to obtain a free trade treaty from the Ottoman government. Palmerston was Secretary at the Foreign Office. The project was all the more opportune as the Ottoman Empire was facing two dangers. It suffered defeat in its war against Russia in 1828 and 1829. On its southern flank, it was in a state of armed conflict with the governor of Egypt, who won a military victory at Konya in 1832 and threatened to march on Istanbul. It was then that Russia persuaded the Sultan to sign the Treaty of Unkiar Skelessi (1833) which placed the Ottoman Empire under its military protection, granted it commercial privileges, and conceded it a right to intervene in the internal affairs of the country. The Ottoman Empire was practically a protectorate of Russia, a long-standing enemy. The search for a counterweight on the British side acted in favor of accepting the commercial conditions laid down by the Western "protector."

The Anglo-Ottoman Commercial Convention, concluded on August 16, 1838, was the customs charter of the Empire until 1914. It abolished all monopolies and prohibitions throughout the Empire and granted complete freedom of purchase to foreign importers. Ottoman exports were taxed at 12 percent *ad valorem*, imports at 5 percent, and goods in transit internally at 3 percent. This agreement on total freedom of trade fulfilled the wishes of British commerce: direct access to raw materials and availability of the domestic market. It even gave foreign merchants an advantage over their Ottoman counterparts. Their sales in the Ottoman Empire were subject to a 5 percent tax, while Ottoman exporters paid the equivalent of 12 percent of the value of their sales abroad. Moreover, internal customs barriers were only lowered for imported or exported goods. Production for the Ottoman domestic market was not exempted.

Freedom to export caused grain shortages, followed by periodic returns to the prohibition regime. The most serious consequence was the influx of Lancashire cotton. In total imports, the share of textiles increased from 26.6 percent in 1837-1838 to 63.1 percent in 1855-1857. Ottoman spinning, still at the handicraft stage, was decimated in less than a quarter of a century. The construction of railways facilitated the inflow of imported goods, nipping in the bud the emergence of local manufacturing.

Also penalized was Egypt, an Ottoman province whose governor or pasha, Muhammad Ali, had undertaken a "top-down" modernization program. Egypt had to open its market. Under external coercion, state protection and monopolies in trade and manufacturing were abolished. Incipient industrialization was stifled. In 1840, the military threat from Great Britain, supported by Russia, Austria, and Prussia, completed the offensive. "Liberalized" Egypt was now economically available. In Western North Africa, Morocco signed trade conventions in 1856 that opened its market to British exports. Commercial disarmament was followed up with a loan contracted with City financiers to pay off a huge indemnity imposed by Spain after a war in 1859. Morocco was subordinate to Great Britain until the advent of French and German interests at the end of the nineteenth century.

The preconditions were thus laid for its transformation in the short term into a complement to the "workshop of the world," i.e. an unprotected export market for British products and a source of cotton, the raw material needed by the textile factories of Lancashire. It was the exemplification of the pattern of international specialization specific to the era of free-trade imperialism. Having become the occupying power in Egypt from 1882 onwards, Britain took great care to prevent the emergence of local manufacturing likely to impede British exports.

The 1838 convention was a specimen of the diplomatic instruments designed to force specialization, bring about the international division of labor and reorganize the international economy in line with the requirements of British industry. The Ottoman Empire's status as exporter of raw materials and importer of manufactured goods was reinforced and perpetuated. As such, it did not have an advantageous position, even temporarily, in the new international economy because its exports were likely to be offered by other suppliers. They also came up against customs barriers erected around European agriculture. The difficulty of exporting limited the growth of disposable income and compressed the capacity to import industrial products.

This situation was not unique to the Ottoman Empire; it constituted one of the weaknesses of this international economic order. Government borrowing was called upon to make up the difference between imports and exports, and, more generally, to supplement the chronically strained finances of states committed to free trade. The Treaty of 1838 was more than a commercial agreement; it was a vehicle for the integration of one economy into another, namely that of the new and, for a time, the sole metropolis of an informal empire understood as the destiny of the entire world.

Other European countries were granted the same advantages as Great Britain. For the Ottoman Empire, this generalization weakened it even more because any request for modification on its part was likely to be vetoed by any of the powers invoking the Capitulations. Eager to increase revenues, and aware of the damage suffered by the Ottoman economy, the authorities called for changes. In 1861-1862, complementary treaties raised the import tax rate to 8 percent *ad valorem*

144 • IMPERIALISM: AS RAMPANT TODAY AS IN THE PAST

but provided for the gradual reduction to 1 percent of the export tax. Only the context of the First World War allowed the repeal of the Capitulations and the adoption in 1916 of specific duties better suited to the needs of national production. By comparison, Persia and its market were made available by force. After a first war in 1839-1842, a second in 1856-1857 ended with a trade treaty, among other things.

c. The "opening up" of China

China was a large, virtually self-sufficient country that could do without the international economy and trade with Europe. With regard to it, Great Britain could not confine itself to the role of interested bystander, waiting for a window of opportunity. It took it upon itself to tear down *manu militari* the obstacles standing in the way of its entry into an empire whose immensity was the stuff of dreams for foreign traders and industrialists. The "opening up" of China to Western trade was a textbook example of the violent deployment of free-trade imperialism, itself an extension of the new international economy based on the industrialization of Great Britain, followed by that of Western Europe and the United States. Opium was the agent of penetration into the Chinese Empire.

In China, the East India Company and the British Asian trade faced a challenge similar to the one they had to confront in India. China was a vast country, the largest in the world in terms of demographics, free of any need to trade with the outside world, and showed little interest in European products. On the other hand, Chinese tea, silks, and porcelain were in great demand by English traders for sale in Europe. In Britain, the lowering of import duties on tea in 1784 contributed to the increase in imports.

From the 1770s, India's foreign trade was reoriented from the Near East to Southeast Asia, China, and the Philippines. The British took Singapore in 1819. A chronic imbalance in trade set in. From 1781 to 1793, imported tea alone accounted for six times the value of all British exports to China, namely woolens, cottons, cotton yarns, and metal products. The difference was settled in silver and *carolus* (Spanish silver dollars minted in Mexico), which spread to Southeast Asia from the Philippines.

China presented a difficulty that Europeans no longer encountered in India. The Manchurian Empire was a centralized state with a government whose authority extended over the entire territory. The imperial authorities were well aware that European trading posts, bases, and bridgeheads had led to the conquest of India. They intended to resist encroachments in order to spare China the fate of its neighbor. Christian merchants and missionaries were kept at a distance and closely controlled for reasons that have more to do with caution than contempt.

Since 1757, Western traders had been allowed to reside and do business only in the port of Canton. Their warehouses were located in a district of the port and they traded only with duly designated Chinese houses. On two occasions, in 1793 and 1816, Britain sent embassies to Beijing to obtain the opening of new ports and the reduction of customs tariffs. The mistrust of the Chinese authorities was not overcome.

At the same time, the British sought to stop the outflow of silver metal. Brazilian gold was in short supply and China was no more interested in European exports than India. So the opium grown in India was mobilized by the East India Company to replace gold as a balancer for the British trade deficit, but also to raise land taxes. From the early 1770s, it promoted poppy cultivation in Bengal and opium manufacture in Calcutta. The smuggling of the drug into China began immediately, with Canton as the entry point.

While retaining the monopoly on production, which could be likened to a state monopoly, the Company sold the merchandise to private individuals who were responsible for the infiltration stage in China. The British government benefited through taxation. The first American commercial ship arrived in Canton in 1784. United States traders in turn smuggled opium acquired in Persia and Turkey. When the East India Company's monopoly in Chinese trade was abolished in 1834, British private traders and agency houses established in India took up trafficking.

As the trade was lucrative, shipments increased rapidly. From 2,000 crates (a crate weighed 60 to 72 kg) in 1800, average annual exports reached 35,445 crates between 1830 and 1835. Millions of smokers fell victim to opium addiction. The scourge spread to institutions, the army and all social strata, fostering disease, impoverishment, as well as the disorganization of social life and the functioning of the state. The corruption on which smuggling depended undermined the economy and society; the venality of civil servants jeopardized the authority of the state.

Until 1870, opium represented half of all imports. Public finances and the country's economy were threatened. The amount spent on opium exceeded twice the state's revenues. Such purchases caused a hemorrhage of silver metal and destabilized the monetary system based on the ratio of silver to copper. As the price of silver rose, the state's reserves were depleted, and its revenues fell. China's trade balance was now in deficit, while the flow of silver was reversed.

With the aid of opium, Britain did more than stop the flow of the precious metal; it turned the tide in its favor. Opium was the dissolving substance which unraveled the Chinese Empire, forcing it to react and provide Britain with the occasion for provoking a showdown to extract commercial concessions.

After protracted discussions at court and in the administration, the resistance party prevailed. A new imperial commissioner was appointed in Canton to crack down on trafficking. In March 1839, he ordered foreign traders to hand over the thousands of crates of opium in their possession. The contents were solemnly destroyed on June 3 and 25, while Chinese traffickers and users were arrested, and the narcotics confiscated. As armed incidents between British ships and Chinese patrols increased, London learned on August 5 that opium trafficking had been forbidden.

Preparations for war were underway when China closed the port of Canton to foreign trade in January 1840. Hostilities began in June 1840 and ended in August 1842. Enjoying complete strategic and tactical mobility, as well as superior weaponry, the British were faced with Chinese officials too afraid to put the country on a war footing or to mobilize irregular forces, and divided between conciliatory factions and supporters of firmness. The unbalanced war led to the Treaty of Nanking, the first "unequal treaty" in the contemporary history of China.

Great Britain obtained the payment of an indemnity of 21 million silver *yuan*, the occupation of Hong Kong, the opening of five southern and central ports to foreign trade, the lowering of Chinese customs duties to 5 percent *ad valorem*, the most favored nation clause and the legal privileges of extraterritoriality for its nationals. Foreign warships could freely enter China's territorial waters and all its ports. The Treaty of Nanking undermined China's sovereignty. In 1844, the United States and France obtained the same advantages as Britain. Bit by bit, the consulates transformed various areas of the five ports into "concessions" and gradually withdrew them from imperial authority.

With all obstacles removed, opium smuggling increased at an accelerated rate. It was necessary to balance the accounts of British traders; without opium, China's trading account would still have been clearly favorable. Beyond the port regions, Lancashire cotton fabrics found fewer buyers than expected. Britain and France demanded the opening of the northern ports. The Qing Empire was in a state of dire weakness. In addition to Western pressures, it had been shaken since 1851 by the great uprising of the Taiping, peasants who were overtaxed, among other things, to pay the war indemnity. China's refusal of Anglo-French demands was followed by the Second Opium War in 1856.

During this conflict, the capital fell and was sacked, including the Imperial Palace, by British and French troops. The Treaties of Tientsin and Beijing of 1858-1860 opened eleven new ports, allowed foreign goods, merchants, and missionaries into the country, lowered customs duties, legalized the import of opium, and imposed a heavy war indemnity. Customs had already been headed by an Englishman since 1855 and Shanghai became an international concession in 1863. Constrained and coerced by free-trade imperialism, China was integrated in a subordinate and dependent position into the international economy being drawn up by the industrial countries of Western Europe.

d. India in the era of free trade

India, by far Britain's most important colonial possession, stood as the primary negation of liberal and free trade theses that colonies were undesirable and a burden to be rid of. Under the influence of triumphant political and economic liberalism in Britain, the settler colonies (Canada, Australia, New Zealand) were granted self-government. Liberal notions were so pervasive that even Disraeli, a Tory protectionist and opponent of the repeal of the Corn Laws, described the colonies as "miserable" and "a millstone around our necks."

The idea emerged that Britain possessed an empire without really intending to do so ("reluctant imperialists"), having acquired it in a moment of inattention ("a fit of absence of mind"). This apologetic mythology was reinforced by the awareness that the other European powers were in no position to compete by building empires. Over the course of the nineteenth and twentieth centuries, there was no reluctance to expand the Empire in Africa, Asia, and Oceania. There was never any question of granting self-government to India, let alone of Britain divesting itself of India or any other colony. On the contrary, India was the centerpiece of the Empire, playing a central role in the British economy and its payments system.

India had four functions in its economic relations with Britain. For a long time, it supplied the textiles that the East India Company imported into Britain, some of which it re-exported. This was its traditional role. It also had a financial function as a significant source of tax revenue for British circles interested in the subcontinent. The East India Company was merely a new parasitic power taking over from those it had displaced.

Far from seeking to overturn the Indian economy, the Company was quite content to live with it as it was. The tribute previously paid to local potentates who spent it in India was now paid to the Company which transported it to Britain to transform it into dividends for distribution to its shareholders. The assets of this capitalist enterprise included regal rights as well as the collection of land rent and duties of all kinds, in accordance with the precapitalist practices of its predecessors.

Beyond tax revenues, India provided Britain with a trade surplus, interest on investments, and categories of income linked to political control of the country. Because the costs of British conquests in Asia were borne by India, its public debt swelled to the benefit of loan-issuing banks and creditors in Britain. From £30 million in 1837, it increased sevenfold to £220 million in 1900. Another contributing factor was the hasty construction of railways, stimulated by the guarantee of interest granted to the builders (British, of course) by authorities. Lastly, India carried the weight of the "Home Charges," that is the cost of the occupying army, its purchases in Britain and the civil administration of the country, including the salaries, allowances, and pensions of British civil servants, and the expenditures relating to the India Office in London.

Tax seizure, trade surpluses, public debt servicing, and "Home Charges" raised criticism that Britain was siphoning off India's wealth; hence the notion of "drainage" used by some Indian authors. One economist estimated it at £9200 billion in 2018 value for the period from 1765 to 1938. For comparison's sake, the GDP of the United Kingdom in 2018 was £2100 billion.

Since the second part of the eighteenth century, India established itself as a key axis of Britain's foreign trade. In this respect, it joined North America in the category of foreign mainstays of the British economy. What followed was the reversal of the commercial flow between the metropolis and the subcontinent induced by the industrialization of cotton manufacturing in Britain and the annihilation of Indian manufacturing.

Textile trade between India and Great Britain

	Exports from India to Great Britain	Exports from Great Britain to India
1814	1,266,608 pieces of cotton	818,208 yards of cotton fabrics
1835	306,086 pieces of cotton	51,777,277 yards of cotton fabrics

1 yard = 0.9 meter

Impoverished by mercantilist imperialism, India was then impoverished by free-trade imperialism. In both cases extra-economic means took precedence. With its manufacturing suffocated, it was artificially handicapped. From then on, it was an importer of textiles, so much so that it soon became Lancashire's main foreign outlet. In 1828, cotton goods constituted 50 percent of British exports to India. The latter received 6 percent of British cotton exports at the end of the Napoleonic Wars, 31 percent in 1850, and 50 to 60 percent after 1873. The volume of textiles sold in India by Great Britain increased from 1 million yards in 1815, to 51 million in 1835, 450 million in 1855 and 995 million in 1870. Until 1939, India was the main foreign market for British cotton goods and the safety buffer which helped Britain's economy to weather depressive troughs and the emergence of new competitors in the world.

The corollary was the loss of its external, and soon internal, markets by the Indian textile industry, which faced stiff competition.

Indian handicrafts were ruined, in what many observers described as "deindustrialization." Instead of textiles, India was driven to export raw cotton, agricultural products, and raw materials, according to the international, vertical division of labor imposed by free-trade imperialism. It thus became part of the international economy evolving around Britain. The accelerated laying of railways after 1853 brought rails, rolling stock, and other metallurgical products to India.

While India's imports and its trade deficit with Britain had increased since the beginning of the century, there was a surplus elsewhere and the balance was positive. It could not be otherwise because the Indian economy had to generate the surplus income which found its way to Britain in the form of financial transfers. India absorbed British exports and financed British imports from elsewhere in the world. As a secure market and provider of funding, it was an essential cog in the functioning of the British economy.

From the beginning of the nineteenth century, industrialization considerably broadened the prospects of British manufacturers and traders. They could not leave a market as large as India to the East India Company alone. Private traders and agency houses banded together to obtain the abolition of the Company's monopoly in 1813, followed in 1833 by the withdrawal of its right to engage in trade. India was "open" to all British operators. Commerce became "free."

The relationship between Britain and India was not just bilateral. The Indian subcontinent constituted the junction between Britain and China. Britain's trade in Asia, like its trade in the Atlantic region, was organized on a triangular basis. India's fourth function was to close the commercial, financial, and monetary loop between Britain and China. Indian exports to the Chinese Empire led to a trade deficit for China, siphoned off its money and made it available to Western traders. In 1850, opium still represented 35 percent of the value of Indian exports to China. Other goods, of less value, were raw cotton and indigo.

e. The United States imitates Great Britain

The Portuguese arrived in Japan in 1543 to trade. The unregulated activities of English and Dutch missionaries (1550-1560) led to political and armed unrest involving converts to Christianity. The Tokugawa imperial power closed off the country (*sakoku*), forbade foreign trade, prevented the Japanese from traveling abroad, and kept Westerners at bay. The conquest of India and the Opium Wars against China did little to reassure the court, the shogun (military) authorities who ran the central government, or the provincial lords. After the disappointments of the first opening, only the Dutch were not completely turned away: they had the right to send one boat per year, and only to Nagasaki. Japan refused all Western requests.

Great Britain soon had imitators also eager to "open up" foreign countries by force. The United States was not indifferent to trade with Japan and was as interested in China as the European powers. Between Shanghai, a port "opened" in 1842, and San Francisco, Japan could, like Hawaii, serve as a stopover for resupplying American ships.

In July 1853, a flotilla anchored in Tokyo Bay to present the demands of the US government. The threatening request to trade was accompanied by the promise of a return in 1854 for an answer. Under duress, aware of not having the means to resist, the central government agreed in February 1854 to open two ports for supplies and allowed the installation of a US consulate in Shimoda. Similar concessions were granted to Britain and Russia, but Japan did not agree to the signing of a commercial treaty. Regardless, its self-isolation came to an end.

The presence in the Far East of the British and French navies during the Second Opium War posed a threat to Japan that Western diplomacy exploited for penetration purposes. In 1857, the Netherlands obtained a treaty permitting free trade in two ports, abolishing the monopolies of Japanese traders and setting a 35 percent *ad valorem* duty on imports to Japan.

Russia signed an identical treaty, but the US found it insufficient and demanded the opening of six ports to free trade, a 5 percent tariff, extraterritoriality for its nationals, and the right for the consul to reside in the capital. Once again, under threat, Japan signed the amended commercial treaty with the US in July 1858 and, during the year, granted the same benefits to Britain, Russia, and France.

In Japan as elsewhere, right after the conclusion of these treaties, an awakening occurred and the authorities were accused of capitulation. Unrest, even civil war, spread across the country, destabilized the government and led to a transfer of governance from the Tokugawa shogunate, a military power, to Emperor Meiji. Coming to the throne in 1867, he inaugurated an era of reform based on the strengthening of the state and its modernization ("revolution from above").

The Meiji Restoration abolished the feudal system and promoted the business classes, without removing the military aristocracy (samurai) associated with the shogunate from the upper echelons of the state. This was an extremely rare case of a country successfully reacting to the threat of foreign domination presented by free-trade imperialism. The *diktat* aimed at subjugating it became the starting point for its rise and metamorphosis into a rival to the industrial countries of the West. Its entry into the international economy proceeded on terms very different from those they had in mind.

CHAPTER 11

Neomercantilist imperialism and its implosion (1870-1945)

Imperialism of the capitalist type is marked by a succession of phases. It was first colonial/mercantilist. Several Atlantic empires competed for primacy and colonies in a context of modern state-building. The best placed won over the others, invariably through war. Imperialism being a system of extraction of economic advantages abroad by extra-economic means, the use of force to succeed and to overcome rivals was a constant feature. Empires were equipped with the combat doctrine of mercantilism.

The international system was polycentric, with predominance passing from one metropolis to another better endowed one. Portugal, then Spain, having supplanted Venice, were overtaken by the Netherlands. Too small in the era of large dynastic states, the latter was reduced *manu militari* by England, a more aggressive metropolis with superior economic, demographic, social, political, and military assets.

France remained a major rival but one less focused on overseas expansion. Between Great Britain and France, the confrontation unfolded from the early eighteenth century to the early nineteenth century. It was punctuated by armed conflicts, the most important being the Seven Years' War (1756-1763), which can be considered the first world war. Each of these powers could only grow at the expense of the other. The Seven Years' War was an unqualified success for Britain in Asia, North America, and Europe. As master of the seas and the overseas world, it set itself apart from all the other powers.

The War of Independence of the Thirteen Colonies was a hiccup that was quickly overcome, and the revolutionary and Napoleonic wars ended in the seizure of new colonies and the turning of France into an outcast.

Britain was already by far the first colonial power, and perhaps the leading power altogether, when the industrial revolution, an exclusively British phenomenon, sealed the outcome. From then on, British hegemony was indisputable. As the "workshop of the world," it viewed the universe as its market. The colonial framework was too narrow for the new and only industrial power, leading to the abandonment of mercantilist imperialism and its protectionist corollary.

Specific to commercial capitalism, it was replaced by liberalism and free-trade imperialism, better suited to industrial capitalism and even more to Britain's advantage than mercantilism had been. Britain did not give up any of its colonies and even acquired new ones but, beyond the Empire, its field of action extended to the entire world. As the second phase of capitalist imperialism, colonial/free-trade imperialism structured an Anglocentric international economy and an international system which tended to be less polycentric and increasingly monocentric. For the first three quarters of the nineteenth century, Britain was the only true world power.

The status quo was thrown out of kilter from the 1870s onwards. The rapid industrialization of Germany and the United States, and to a lesser extent that of France and Japan, sounded the death knell for British hegemony. The second industrial revolution and the structural transformations of capitalism strengthened Germany and the United States to the detriment of Great Britain. The last quarter of the nineteenth century began with an economic crisis and a challenge to free-trade imperialism and the British order. The emergence of competitors led to the return of protectionism, a frantic search for colonies, the advent of (neo)mercantilist imperialism and multipolarity in the international system, i.e., the third phase of capitalist imperialism.

For three quarters of a century, until 1945, a state of muted or vociferous antagonism existed between the great powers while a redistribution of positions took place according to the new balance of power. As in the seventeenth and eighteenth centuries, but on a larger scale, the expansion of imperialism pitted states against each other. It was the verdict of arms that determined hegemony. The two world wars, although immeasurably more destructive, were of the same nature as the Seven Years' War. The result would be the collapse of neo-mercantilist imperialism and the transition towards a fourth version of capitalist imperialism and to US hegemony.

With the spread of industrialization and the appearance of rivals to Great Britain, conditions were created for a paradigm shift. Just as liberalism replaced mercantilism in the early nineteenth century, it in turn gave way to the revival of various forms of mercantilism at the end of that century. The period that began in the 1870s was that of stagnant capitalism and neomercantilist imperialism, sparking a craze for empire-building and the constitution of formal empires. At the same time, the international movement of capital, in the form of investment in bonds and shares, was a historical novelty which acquired such importance that it rivaled international commerce in value. After mercantilist imperialism, then free-trade imperialism, neomercantilist imperialism, the third form of capitalist imperialism, took hold, before entering a long crisis leading to its disintegration in the interwar period and its dismantling in the aftermath of the Second World War.

a. The impact of economic conditions

Optimal functioning of the capitalist economy is a sine qua non condition for the success of liberalism: adequate profitability, business opportunities high rate of investment, steady growth, market ensuring competition, and allocation of resources. Liberalism and free-trade imperialism are ultimately based on capitalism in a state of expansion. If the economy slows down or seizes up, the liberal project is rapidly called into question. Its shortcomings are revealed and its virtues are cast into doubt. Its modus operandi based on laissez-faire and free competition loses its luster, as does its extension, free-trade imperialism.

The peak of free-trade imperialism correlated with the economic boom of the 1850s and 1860s. The cycle reversed at the beginning of the 1870s, marked by general sluggishness in business, falling profit rates, and difficulty exporting to foreign markets, themselves clogged and less receptive. The slump raised doubts about the self-regulating qualities of markets and aroused disaffection with free trade and the informal imperialism that went with it. The United Kingdom lost its status as the only great industrial power; France made advances during the 1850s and 1860s; in the last quarter of the nineteenth century, Germany and the United States caught up and overtook the former "workshop of the world."

Each of these countries needed markets for their exports, sources of raw materials for their industry, and tariff barriers to keep out imports. This led to the delimitation of reserved markets by tariffs on foreign imports and the quest for privileged access to raw materials. Behind the protection of tariff barriers, prices on the domestic market were maintained or raised, with the profit allowing exports at reduced prices (dumping).

The economic boom of the 1846-1873 period, and especially of the 1860s, was marked by a sharp increase in investment, a notable rise of the GDP and a significant growth in foreign trade. Although there was a slowdown in France, the years 1866 to 1873 were brilliant for the British economy. Then came the breakdown, more prolonged than any of the cyclical crises which preceded it in 1817, 1825-1829, 1836-1842, 1847-1848, 1857 and 1866. Until the 1870s, after a halt and the devaluation of part of the capital, post-crisis recoveries were vigorous.

The pattern did not apply to the end of the nineteenth century; this was a depression that lasted more than two decades. It was made up of a series of recessions and recoveries over the course of twenty years. What was new about it was the fact that it represented the first capitalist crisis of an international nature, bringing to the fore connections between economies. Prices, interest rates, and profits plummeted. From 1873 to 1896, wholesale prices fell by a third. Bankruptcies and unemployment were on the rise, while growth was sluggish and choppy. The dynamism of the British and French economies was undermined. Confidence in liberalism, laissez-faire, and free trade was shaken.

A speculative frenzy made the prices of railway company shares soar, triggering a crash in Vienna in May 1873 and in the United States in September 1873. Austrian banks collapsed, causing the railway companies they supported to falter and halting their operations. Rail orders fell sharply, prices plunged, bankruptcies multiplied, and unemployment increased. While the aftereffects spread to Berlin through the blow suffered by the steel industry, the Austrian and

American crises had repercussions on Great Britain, which saw its metallurgical exports decline. The rebounds that followed were too short-lived to reverse the secular slowdown. The upturn of 1879 was brought to an abrupt halt in 1882 by a railway and banking crisis in France. A cascade of bankruptcies ensued. In Britain, a recovery began in 1886 but it was short-lived and stagnation prevailed from 1890 to 1895.

For the European economy, the result was two lean decades characterized by business lethargy, squeezed profit margins, and falling interest rates, all of which convinced the business community of the reality of the depression, despite the skepticism of some British economists who cited the resilience of their country's national product and national income. A Royal Commission was appointed in the United Kingdom to inquire into the circumstances of the commercial and industrial depression and propose solutions; the views of the chambers of commerce were reflected in its report submitted in 1886.

The depression of 1873-1895 had many causes. The most obvious at the outset, namely speculation, reflected the widespread diffusion of the mechanisms of capitalism and the accumulation of masses of capital in search of gainful use. The industrialization of Germany, the United States, and Japan, combined with that of Belgium and France, increased the supply of industrial products more quickly than domestic and foreign demand. However, technical progress brought down production costs and prices. The commissioning of more economical steamships and the opening of the Suez Canal in 1869 reduced maritime transport costs.

Cheap wheat from the "new world" was introduced into Europe, competing favorably with the local product and undermining the still-important farming community and its purchasing power. American wheat cost less in France than French wheat. The invention of refrigerated ships did the same for meat from Australia, New Zealand, and Argentina, and dairy products from North America, whose imports grew rapidly. In 1897-1900, American goods arrived in Europe on a massive scale. This reduction in the prices of primary products further lowered costs, including wages, and encouraged the resumption of investment from 1896 onwards.

Capitalism is driven by an internal dynamic geared towards the search for profit and incessant accumulation. It cannot make do with

the stationary state towards which it tends and which occurs periodically. Its short-term or cyclical crises ("recessions")— decennial from
the 1810s to the 1860s—were recurring phases of overproduction
which seized up the mechanism. They were resolved as soon as the
slowdown produced its effects: devaluation of capital and pressure
on the wage bill, which restored the rate of profit. Demand ended
up reducing unsold stocks and absorbing production as it restarted.

Depressions, less frequent but far-reaching, are general crises
which reveal systemic dysfunction. They result in stagnation with no
foreseeable end and challenge capitalism to reshape itself in order to
last. The way out of the depression took two directions: geographic
expansion and deepening of the economic model. The first was extensive, easier, and quicker to execute; it led to the enlargement of the
colonial domain. The second was intensive, less based on voluntarism and less likely to produce results in the short term. It consisted
of embracing the technological and structural changes which were
reconfiguring the productive system and the entire economy.

The period 1873-1914 represented a hiatus between the mature
phase of the lead sectors of the first industrialization (textiles, iron,
coal, metallurgy), still flourishing, and the deployment of the second
industrialization (steel, chemicals, electricity, aluminum, oil, eventually automobiles and airplanes) which took over from them. In this
second phase, standardization and mass production (assembly lines)
compressed production costs and boosted productivity and the profit
rate. It also involved the formation of very large companies capable
of managing a larger production apparatus. Chronologically, overseas
expansion intensified from the 1870s on. The effects of the second
industrial revolution only began to emerge towards the end of the nineteenth century. The two processes, one extensive, the other intensive,
then proceeded synchronously.

The international implications were notable. The expansion of
the geographical area overseas postponed wars in Europe, as long as
there were non-European territories to appropriate. At the end of the
nineteenth century, with the world practically divided, the overseas
valve lost its usefulness. Any enlargement could only be achieved
at the expense of rival powers. At the same time, the effects of the
second industrialization became operative. As the size of companies
grew, the national base was becoming too narrow for the further

deepening of the process. Expansion into neighboring countries and subordination of rivals pointed to armed conflict, in other words war for predominance.

Trade between Europe and the rest of the world grew by 16.1 percent per year between 1830 and 1870, but by only 4.1 percent between 1870 and 1913. The annual growth of British exports was just 2.7 percent from 1881 to 1911, despite the boom of the early twentieth century. The United Kingdom had a diversified customer base; more than a third of its exports went to Europe, less than a third to the empire, more than a tenth to the United States, less than a third to the rest of the world. The colonial surplus covered the European deficit. But Britain was no longer the only manufacturer, less and less the "workshop of the world" and even losing momentum.

Per capita productivity was lower there than in Germany and the United States. British production continued to grow, but less rapidly than German and US production, which integrated new technologies and processes more easily than did their British counterpart. Its lack of presence in the new industries was the price it paid for its concentration on the old industries it pioneered and which ensured its success.

However, demand was plateauing for the old industries, whereas it was vigorous for new ones. In 1913, Germany produced twice as much steel as the United Kingdom. The German and American rise was spectacular in terms of industrial production and national income, among other things. As early as 1859, oil was being extracted in Pennsylvania and the United States became the first user of this new source of energy. As for electrical and chemical production, it was dominated by Germany, with a significant presence of the United States.

The United Kingdom's supremacy was now contested, a new historical fact heralding a future of competition from which it had been spared. Explicit titles expressed concern. *Made in Germany*, a best-selling book published in 1896, sounded the alarm. The gaze turned westward with the publication in 1902 of *The American Invaders: their Plans, Tactics and Progress*. Industrial production in Germany and the United States each exceeded that of the UK. From a third in 1870, its share of world industrial production fell to a fifth in 1900 and to 13 percent in 1913. By comparison, that of the United States, the world's leading industrial power, reached a third in 1914. Germany, in second place, was home to 15 percent of global industry. French and Belgian production was not negligible, and Italy and Russia were industrializing.

Great Britain, however, remained the greatest financial, colonial, and commercial power, even if Germany had quadrupled its trade since 1875 and exported almost as much in 1913. The City of London was the leading financial center in the world and the pound sterling the international currency, accepted as the equivalent of gold. The franc, the mark, and the dollar, also appreciated and stable, circulated on a smaller scale internationally. Representing a third of the world's tonnage, Britain's ocean-going merchant marine carried half of the world's maritime trade. Freight revenue amounted to 5 percent of national income. Added to it were brokerage fees and premiums for maritime, fire, life, and other insurance.

The prosperity of the years 1896-1913 ended up compensating for the mediocre results of the depressive years 1873-1895, so that the average annual GDP growth rate in Western Europe and in the "new countries" over the entire period 1870-1913 (2.8 percent) was higher than that of the period 1820-1870 (2.3 percent). In Europe, the picture varied: 1.6 percent in France, 2.2 percent in Great Britain, 2.9 percent in Germany. At 4.3 percent, the United States rate was the highest. French national income doubled over the four decades from 1870 to 1914. The crisis was resolved and the depression overcome. The cyclical crisis of 1900-1903 was short-lived; the stock market-induced crisis of 1907 remained contained, despite its initial severity.

Although the recovery of 1896-1913 was vigorous, it led to a rise in prices that hampered the sale of industrial products on domestic markets whose purchasing power remained limited by low wages. Recovery from the depression of the 1870s was achieved by the classic route of raising the rate of profit by means of the destruction of part of the capital stock, but also by resorting to various counter-cyclical measures: protectionism, corporate concentration, capital exports, and colonial expansion.

b. Protectionism and corporate concentration

Shrinking markets trigger the reflex to protect through tariffs. It is remarkable how little liberal ideology, the *mythos* and quasi-religion of the nineteenth century, resisted the imperative of the search for outlets; concrete needs overrode theory. One by one, European countries once again erected the customs barriers that they had lowered under the influence of the Manchester school of economics. Germany was the first in 1879. It was followed by Austria-Hungary, France, Italy, and Russia; in 1882 Europe was bristling with fences, obstructing the international trade which had flourished in the nineteenth century.

The free trade treaties of the 1860s were repudiated. Revision after revision, duties were extended and strengthened. Switzerland, Spain, Portugal, Romania, and Greece joined the forerunners. Trade wars, made more bitter by the prevailing nationalism, broke out in Europe during the 1880s and 1890s. In the United States, the McKinley tariff (1890) imposed entry duties of 50 percent *ad valorem* on industrial products. The optimistic age of free trade was over.

Even the United Kingdom, the temple and bastion of free trade, was not immune to the winds of protectionism. A Fair Trade League, founded in 1881, campaigned for "equitable" commerce for Britain. In 1903, a Tariff Reform League, echoing the demands of the hard-pressed metallurgical industry of the Midlands, advocated protection and its extension to the Empire ("imperial preference"). These organizations, reverse images of the Anti-Corn Law League, were not to be successful because the industrial, commercial and financial fabric was closely woven into the international economy. Furthermore, protectionism, while of no help to exports, would raise the price of imports of essential goods, possibly kindling social unrest. Finally, the Empire only accounted for a third of British exports and less than a quarter of British imports, not enough to replace the world-scale commercial architecture in place since 1846.

Economic crises tend to bring down the most fragile companies first. The typical nineteenth-century company was family-owned, small, self-financed, and independent of both the stock market and the banks. The depression of the end of the century hit it directly. All businesses experienced a decline in their rate of profit. For all of them, a short-term reaction to the market instability was to organize and share markets by forming cartels (also called groups, counters, syndicates, trusts, Konzerns, etc.) to limit supply (agreed production for each member), demand (sales quotas allowed to each member, market sharing, joint marketing organization) and prices, while lowering costs.

The next stage was the formation of the large oligopolistic enterprise. In both cases, the restriction of competition produced situational rent or surplus profits. By shielding the national economy from outside competition, protectionism facilitated this process of concentration, to which competition itself led. In each sector, a small number of operators accounted for a significant share of total activity. Free competition remained the credo of the age but, in reality, it was undermined.

More sustainable, the merger of companies made it possible to reduce costs by benefiting from economies of scale. Vertical integration placed various stages of production under a single management. Horizontal integration of companies engaged in the same activity was an antidote to competition. Conglomerates brought together diversified companies to reduce risks by pooling operations or results. Control was sometimes exercised through a holding company which owned shares in several companies.

The phenomenon was more widespread in Germany and the United States than in Great Britain and France, and more characteristic of the industries of the second industrialization than of the first. Concentration also affected banks. In Germany, very large industrial companies were intertwined with very large banks, which had become shareholders, members of their clients' boards of directors, and providers of financing. This "organic" interpenetration was new, both for banks and for non-banking companies.

The depression of 1873-1895 was the crucible of the concentration of businesses and the emergence of the first forms of a capitalism driven by large groups wielding colossal masses of capital and by large production units. Once again capitalism was reinventing itself: the transition from free competition to protectionism and oligopolistic competition was of the same order as the transition from mercantilism to free competition.

c. Export of capital

One of the most striking phenomena of the period 1870-1914 was the scale of the movement of capital crossing borders to be employed in foreign countries. Its growth rate came to exceed that of international trade. Unlike the latter, the movement of capital was a historical novelty. Although foreign trade had long been regulated by states to ensure customs revenues or to assist the economy, the movement of capital was entirely free until the First World War. There were no formal limitations, no barriers to exit, and no obstacles to the repatriation of earnings (interest and dividends).

In its early form, foreign investment was a marginal phenomenon, with financiers and bankers, such as Jacques Cœur, the Fuggers, the Welsers, and the Rothschilds lending their own resources to the Pope or to needy sovereigns. At the beginning of the nineteenth century, bankers became intermediaries for foreign states wishing to raise funds by issuing bonds on the London financial market. The securities issued were quickly sold to the public by the banks and bankers guaranteeing the operation. The borrowers were the United States and the newly independent countries of South America. At the time, Britain was, to all intents and purposes, the only source of capital.

Past the 1850s, other exporters joined in without ever reaching the same level. The financial center of Paris attracted capital that was invested in railroads in Spain and Italy. The Mediterranean area imported capital from France, but also from Britain. The reasons were diverse: military difficulties undermining fragile countries which had to turn to Europe because of internal deficiencies and defense imperatives (the Ottoman Empire after the Crimean War), payment of war indemnities (Morocco after 1862), participation in the capital of the Suez Canal project (Egypt), or quest for economic development (Tunisia).

Industrialization in Europe in a liberal and free trade context induced the non-European world to engage in international specialization as a supplier of primary products (foodstuffs and raw materials). The prerequisite was the establishment of the infrastructure necessary for the transport and exit of goods to the outside world: railways, port facilities, telegraph lines. To pay for them, borrowing in Europe was resorted to, in the form of bond issues whose interest and repayment depended on the export of primary products.

Sooner or later, overindebtedness in relation to income led to default and bankruptcy (Tunisia in 1869, Peru in 1871, Ottoman Empire in 1875) or near bankruptcy (Egypt in 1875). Once debt reorganization was complete, capital export flows resumed. For borrowing countries, the risks of going bankrupt were not the only ones they faced. Failure to meet commitments could have political consequences. Foreign creditors turned to their governments, which sent out gunboats (Mexico 1863, Egypt 1882, Venezuela 1902-1903), imposed international commissions whose purpose was to take control of the revenues of defaulting countries, the first step in the direction of trusteeship over the state (Ottoman Empire, Greece, Serbia) and, sometimes, military occupation (Tunisia, Egypt).

After the late 1880s, investors turned away from the Mediterranean, the Middle East, and Central Europe. For France, Russia became the primary destination, accounting for 27 percent of the total, followed by the United States (20 percent), the Middle East (Ottoman Empire-Egypt, 9 percent) and the colonial empire (9 percent). Economic development, railway construction, and military needs called for resources that it's new Russian ally did not possess.

The amount of capital directed abroad increased rapidly from 1870 to 1914, with a peak from 1906 to 1913, synchronous with the economic recovery which began in 1896. From 7 percent of world GDP in 1870, foreign assets approached 20 percent in 1914, a level which would not be reached again before the 1980s. They fell to 8 percent in 1930, 5 percent in 1945, and 6 percent in 1960. The latest version of globalization brought a vigorous recovery: 25 percent in 1980, 49 percent in 1990, and 92 percent in 2000. The annual outflow of European capital tripled between 1870 and 1913. From 1900 onwards, the rate rose from 2-2.5 percent per year to 4.5 percent per year.

Increasingly, private bankers gave way to incorporated banks with a strong capacity to gather savings. Large deposit banks, capital-rich investment companies, and merchant banks connected to the markets handled considerable amounts of capital, part of which was channeled into financial operations abroad.

As in all other domains, Europe was the master of international capital movements. At the beginning of the nineteenth century, this activity was the prerogative of Great Britain. France began to participate mid-century. Its stock of capital placed abroad tripled between 1880 and 1914, going from 7 percent to 15 percent of its domestic investments. Joining the two leaders after the 1880s, but more modestly, were Germany, Belgium, the Netherlands, Switzerland, and the United States. In 1914, these seven countries accounted for 95 percent of exported capital. The main holders of the global stock of expatriate capital were as follows: United Kingdom 42 percent, France 20 percent, Germany 13 percent, Belgium-Netherlands-Switzerland 12 percent, and United States 8 percent. The dynamic German and American economies absorbed more capital, leaving less to export. A special feature of the United States economy was the fact that it also remained an importer of capital, as it had been since the beginning of the nineteenth century.

Embedded in the international economy, the United Kingdom invested up to a third of its national wealth abroad. From 1870 to 1914, it devoted 4 percent per year of its GDP, on average, to foreign investments, an exceptional rate. In 1914, they represented 17 percent of its total investments. During these forty-four years, its foreign assets grew faster than its domestic investments. One-tenth of Britain's national income was generated by lending and investing abroad. These external revenues were of great importance for a country with a negative trade balance.

With interest and dividends drawn from abroad, as well as income yielded by shipping, insurance, and financial services ("invisibles"), Britain erased its trade deficit and generated a positive balance of accounts. This surplus multiplied fourfold between the years 1890 and 1911-1913. A formula summed up Britain's economic profile: its GNP (annual production of wealth domestically and abroad) supported its GDP (annual production of wealth at home).

After a productive phase which propelled it to the pinnacle of the world economy in the first half of the twentieth century, Britain settled into the status of a rentier country, consuming more than it produced thanks to accumulated capital and to the growth of the tertiary sector relative to the primary and secondary sectors. The picture for France was similar: income from loans and investments abroad, amounting to 5 percent of national income, was sufficient to offset the trade deficit, without even adding income from services and tourism. The typical course of imperial powers could again be observed. In contrast, for a not yet "mature" country like the United States, the trade balance was in surplus since the 1870s.

Much has been written about the export of capital and the causes of the phenomenon. These include the slowdown of European economies, the brake on the expansion of the domestic market represented by low wages and purchasing power (underconsumption), the unequal distribution of income, the accumulation of capital in search of profitable investment (surplus capital), and the falling profit rate, making it imperative to find an external outlet. None of these explanations enjoys unanimous acceptance. What can be observed is the fact that capital left Europe independently of the cyclical situation. The volume was not solely a function of poor conditions in Europe since it was higher in the growth phase (1896-1913) than in the slowdown phase (1873-1895).

Even if capital accumulated, the process was less one of expulsion from the home country (push) than of attraction by the outside (pull) due to the existence of a differential. Money placed abroad earned more than money used domestically. The 3 percent interest paid in Paris tripled or quadrupled in Constantinople or Cairo, because demand far outstripped supply. The relative abundance of capital in the "mature" markets of London and Paris weighed on rates, while the relative scarcity in foreign countries translated into higher profitability. The economies of capital-exporting countries continued to generate returns but it was more profitable to invest savings elsewhere. For Britain, investment at home grew by 80 percent between 1875 and 1914, but by 165 percent abroad.

External demand was stronger in developing foreign economies than in the colonial world where profit rates were higher but where the size of the economies limited investments. This explains why the volumes of capital destined for foreign countries exceeded those directed towards the colonial world. Europe was the recipient of three fifths of French capital exports (especially Russia) and half of German capital (Balkans, Ottoman Empire). Their colonial empires received 8.9 percent and 2.6 percent, respectively, of the total. The British Empire was entitled to half of the capital exported from Great Britain (about equally divided between India and the "white" colonies of Canada, Australia, and New Zealand), the United States, and Latin America to one fifth each. The United States invested mainly in Mexico, Cuba, and South America.

d. A great colonial surge (1870-1914)

Colonial expansion was the most spectacular international phenomenon of the period 1870-1914. The empires established since the end of the fifteenth century fell apart from the end of the eighteenth century to the beginning of the nineteenth century during a "decolonization" *avant la lettre*. The French Empire was almost no more, the Spanish and Portuguese lost their American bases, and the Dutch only survived in Insulindia because Britain had no direct interest in it. As the leading colonial power from the eighteenth century onwards, Britain easily overcame the loss of the Thirteen Colonies in North America and took advantage of the setbacks suffered by its continental rivals during the revolutionary and Napoleonic wars to take away their overseas possessions and enlarge its own, as it always did during conflicts.

The expansion of its Empire was uninterrupted, notwithstanding the liberal/free trade doctrine. Consolidating its hold on India and expanding its area, it engaged in informal imperialism that put the world, particularly South America, at its disposal. For all practical purposes, Britain was the sole imperial power for three-quarters of the nineteenth century. France's thrust into Algeria (1830), New Caledonia (1853), Senegal (1854-1865) and Indochina (1863)—likewise the expeditions to Lebanon (1860) and Mexico (1861-1867)—were limited in scope, even if the expansionist impulse and the desire to reconstitute an empire were palpable.

All changed in the last quarter of the nineteenth century, when a new colonial push began. Due to the economic depression of 1873-1895, the search for sources of raw materials and markets was much more pressing than it had been before. Industrialization progressed rapidly, requiring ever more raw materials and markets to absorb increasing production. This industrialization occurred against a backdrop of competition between national economies. More and more countries were industrializing.

Lastly, the economic cycle stimulated colonial expansion: in the depressive phase (1873-1895), the fear of markets drying up gave impetus to the idea of reserving overseas outlets; in the growth phase (1896-1914), new markets had to be found for the increased production generated by prosperity. In both cases, the privileged markets of the colonies exerted an attraction. Moreover, investing in the colonies was not without interest in the light of the bankruptcies in the Mediterranean world and the contraction in demand for capital in Europe and the United States.

The economic depression of 1873-1895 was synchronous with the return to a global configuration characterized by several colonial empires. If the old Spanish, Portuguese, and Dutch empires languished, France, constituting its second colonial empire, and newcomers, such as Italy, Germany, the King of the Belgians, and, later, the United States and Japan entered the scene. At the same time, Great Britain increased its formal possessions, which were already enormous compared to those of the others. From 23 million km^2 in 1881, the empire had 29 million in 1914. The French empire went from 0.9 million to 12 in the same time frame.

Direct control of one part of the world and indirect control of the other by a handful of great powers, mainly European, was one of the most remarkable facts of the end of the nineteenth century. The world was divided up between them. An exceptional expansionist drive brought Africa and what remained independent in Asia under the direct control of eight European and two non-European countries. In 1914, the eight countries, representing 1.5 percent of the earth's surface, had colonial empires covering a third of it.

With a population of forty-five million, the United Kingdom occupied 0.05 percent of the earth's surface. It alone governed a quarter of the world's population and a fifth of its landmass—some 400 million people, including 315 million Indians (a fifth of the world's population). A third of its surface area and a fifth of its population were added between 1870 and 1898. The Empire had ninety-seven times the size area of the UK and eight-and-a-half times its population. It was administered by eighty-seven colonial jurisdictions. As the basis of British power, resulting from four centuries of continuous growth, it was the largest empire in history, on which, the saying went, the sun never set. Second largest in the world, the French Empire had fifty million inhabitants and covered a third of the surface area of its British counterpart. Lands and seas were, to all intents and purposes, in the hands of ten countries, in reality two (Great Britain, France), with four determined to snatch their share (Germany, United States, Japan, Italy).

Leaders of the great powers went on an acquisitions spree. It was at its height from the 1870s to 1914. All observers were struck by it. The lure of gain, the quest for power, the thirst for prestige, and bouts of chauvinism all came together to fuel the race for colonies, footholds, bargaining chips, and square kilometers. Measuring the comparative size of empires and comparing colors on the world map turned into an obsession, so much so that even the imperialist Lord Salisbury himself exclaimed that maps drove men mad. The size of empires became the yardstick by which powers were assessed and their respective ranks established. This informal but widely-used standard of measurement would only become obsolete with decolonization after 1945. It was replaced by the possession of nuclear weapons.

The idea took root that prestige imperatively required having a colonial empire, preferably as extensive as possible. It also led to the use of ideological references and justifications: proselytizing for one's religious faith, the blossoming of national "genius," social Darwinism, the "civilizing mission" of the "superior races" vis-à-vis the "inferior races" ("white man's burden" by Rudyard Kipling, an "altruistic" variant of Gobineau's ideas). The baton passed from the missionary zeal of the sixteenth and seventeenth centuries, to the fight against slavery in the nineteenth century, and on to the mobilization of freedom, human rights, and democracy in the twentieth and twenty- first centuries. .

The power gap and the abuse of the force differential called for legitimization and camouflage. The dissemination of an imperialist "popular culture" glorifying the colonial epic made it possible to build fellowship collectively in a unitarian impulse and to create a consensus, smoothing out class divisions and providing a diversion from socioeconomic tensions. Last but not least, it should not be overlooked that colonization offered an opportunity for social and psychological advancement to people of modest status, enjoying little consideration in their home country but propelled to the status of masters and lords in the fundamentally unequal society of a colony.

Colonial issues came to occupy a prominent place in international relations, in diplomatic dealings, and in *fin de siècle* conflicts. The dynamic was reminiscent of the mercantilist seventeenth and eighteenth centuries, as was the return to protectionism under the effect of the economic depression. Without informal imperialism, associated with free trade, being repudiated, a neomercantilist imperialism took shape and gradually supplanted it. Playing on all fronts thanks to the importance of its assets, Britain practiced both forms of imperialism. Its latecomer rivals tended towards neomercantilist imperialism, with protectionism and direct control, even if France also practiced informal imperialism in the nineteenth century.

Economic motives of various kinds were hardly concealed. The search for markets was proclaimed by Jules Ferry ("colonial policy is the offspring of industrial policy"), by Jules Méline (the colonies must "fulfill willingly or unwillingly their natural role as outlets reserved, by privilege, for metropolitan industry"), by Joseph Chamberlain ("Empire is trade"). Most of the capital exported went outside colonial empires, where capacity for absorption was greater than in the colonies. Nonetheless, colonial possessions provided additional investment opportunities, offering higher rates of profit and less foreign competition, which was not the case in independent countries. While colonies may not have represented the greatest demand for capital, they were de facto the reserved domain of metropolitan nationals.

Moreover, there was a widespread demographic argument, a sort of incipient *lebensraum*: colonies made possible the dumping of a poor, landless, and jobless population that the metropolis was unable to support ("overflow"), thus avoiding social unrest and revolution. Imperialist businessman Cecil Rhodes put that argument bluntly. Even if emigration was mainly directed towards the "new countries" of the Americas, the colonies were considered destinations. Underlying the enterprise of colonial aggrandizement was the ambient context of economic difficulties in Europe and the need to remedy them.

Escaping the influence of liberalism, free trade, classical political economy and their anti-colonial rhetoric, as far removed as it may have been from reality, was essential to further colonial expansionism and revive protectionism with mercantilist overtones. But in addition to the economic imperatives created by the depression, minds had to be prepared for the great turnaround. In 1872, former Prime Minister Disraeli enunciated an imperialist program. Back in office in 1874, he decided on the purchase by the British government of the Khedive of Egypt's shares in the Suez Canal Company, an unusual entry by a state into the capital of a private company and a step towards taking control of the finances of Egypt, then of Egypt itself. In 1877, he crowned Queen Victoria Empress of India with fanfare and, the following year, secured the cession of the island of Cyprus to Great Britain. In France, Prime Ministers Léon Gambetta and Jules Ferry were committed to a policy of overseas expansion.

A number of books, several times republished, were landmarks in the reversal of attitudes. As early as 1868, Charles Dilke praised the virtues of the Empire and advocated new conquests in *Greater Britain*. John Seeley with *The Expansion of England* (1883) and James Froude with *Oceana, or England and her Colonies* (1886) did likewise. According to Seeley, expansion was an obligation for Great Britain, its territory being too small for its growing population. Froude extolled the merits of the Empire as a reliable buyer of the metropolis' exports, since free trade and the world market no longer offered sufficient guarantees. Paeans in praise of the Empire followed one after another. In *The Origin and Destiny of Imperial Britain* (1900), J. A. Cramb presented the British Empire as the apex of the earlier phases of world history and its terminal point, nine decades before another devotee of another empire announced the "end of history."

The page was turned on the Little Englanders, who were wary of overseas adventures; Cobden and Bright were a thing of the past. In France, the economist Paul Leroy-Beaulieu, hitherto a staunch liberal, went against an article of the faith of the Manchester school by publishing in 1874 the resounding *De la colonisation chez les peuples modernes*, an economically motivated argument and manifesto for an activity discredited by the liberals. With *Principes de colonisation et de législation coloniale* (1895), Arthur Girault provided the textbook for training colonial administrators and jurists. In the United States, Captain Alfred Mahan's work, *The Influence of Sea Power upon History, 1660-1783* (1890), highlighted the role of the navy in the formation of the British Empire, leaving no doubt about his country's interest in following the same path.

Supported by chambers of commerce and business circles, colonial lobbies proliferated: Colonial Society (1868) which became Royal Colonial Institute (1882), Imperial Federation League (1883), Primrose League (1885), United Empire Trade League (1891), *Kolonialverein* (1882), *Deutsche Kolonialgesellschaft* (1888), *Alldeutscher Verband* (Pan-Germanist League, 1891), *Comité de l'Afrique française* (1890), *Union coloniale* (1893), *Comité de l'Asie française* (1901), Italian Colonial Institute (1906). Whipped up by internal pressure and international competition, the lukewarm enthusiasm of political leaders towards colonial expansion turned into an ardent conversion to the acquisition of any land available and within reach.

Delay in "planting the flag" would run the risk of leaving it to more enterprising rivals ("steeplechase"). Setting aside coveted regions for later exploitation counted as much as their immediate value.

The bulimia of territorial conquests, combined with the fierce competition between powers on various points of the globe, resembled the transfer outside of Europe of antagonisms between European countries since the Italian and German unifications established a new geopolitical balance and stabilized the map of the continent. Having become aggressive in the era of Realpolitik, nationalism seemed to be moving overseas, projecting itself onto the colonies. But it was not only political, notwithstanding outbursts of national pride and even bellicose chauvinism. Nationalism was not enough to explain the colonial expansion at the end of the century. In this case, nationalism covered an undisguised search for wealth available outside Europe and for substitute markets for those which were contracting in Europe. Economic factors and political context combined to give impetus to a swift takeover of most of the planet.

The partition of Africa and the occupation of Indochina proceeded simultaneously in the last quarter of the nineteenth century. Prior to this period, Europeans had no possessions in Africa, apart from Algeria and small trading-post territories on the coast (Senegal, Gambia, Sierra Leone, Rio de Oro, the Portuguese colonies [Portuguese Guinea, Angola, Mozambique], the Cape Colony). The interior of the continent was practically unknown to them. What was new at the end of the nineteenth century was their desire to penetrate the hinterland in search of precious metals, raw materials, and markets. The pretext invoked was the application of the abolitionist recommendation to replace slavery with legitimate commerce.

During the 1870s, Equatorial Africa attracted the attention of Leopold II, King of the Belgians but above all a businessman acting on his own behalf, and of France. Britain was concerned about the possibility of seeing its trade excluded from the region. In order to create a buffer zone between the possessions of the great powers, the Berlin Conference (1884-1885) handed over to Leopold II the "independent" state of the Congo, with the obligation to maintain neutrality and commercial freedom in the Congo basin and its tributaries (the "conventional basin"). This state became a colony of Belgium in 1908, with a surface area seventy-six times that of its metropolis.

The conference attempted to regulate acquisitions where conflict was anticipated in order to prevent clashes between European countries. Typical of all negotiations of this era, these arrangements between European powers were unilateral and took no account of the populations concerned. The French moved upstream on the Ogooué during the 1870s and, in 1886, made Gabon a colony from which the French Congo (Brazzaville) was born in 1898. Federated with Chad, it gave birth to French Equatorial Africa (AEF, 1910).

In North Africa, from its base in Algeria, France occupied Tunisia in 1881 and imposed a protectorate in 1883. Under the pretext of defending the route to India and the Suez Canal, which were threatened by no one, Britain occupied Egypt in 1882 for the purpose of restoring the absolutist power of the viceroy, quelling the liberal-nationalist movement which had defeated him and preventing Egypt from regaining control of its finances, calling into question the bondage created by debt and escaping the grip of the powers. In 1883, Sudan rose up against Anglo-Egyptian administration; the reconquest lasted until 1896. France completed its control of the Maghreb by establishing its protectorate over Morocco in 1912, following the international crisis in Agadir.

In West Africa, the British and the French had an identical agenda: to rush inland to establish their authority and drain trade towards their trading posts on the coast. The British, starting from strongholds on the Gold Coast and the Niger Delta (a region rich in palm oil), moved up the Niger River towards the interior. The French made Senegal their starting point and took the Senegal River. Conflict was latent but it was avoided. West Africa was divided: Senegal, Guinea, Ivory Coast, and Dahomey to France; Gambia, Sierra Leone, the Gold Coast, and Nigeria to Britain. The Royal Niger Company, founded by George Goldie and chartered in 1886, incorporated Nigeria into the British Empire. France continued its expansion into the heart of the Sahel and Sahara and brought together its conquests in French West Africa (AOF, 1895).

In southern Africa, a unique conflict pitted Britain against the Boers (or Afrikaners), Dutch Calvinist settlers, farmers, and breeders. Turning their backs on the British, they founded the republics of Orange and Transvaal in the interior, north of Natal and the Cape Colony, which were British territories with an expansionist bent. A first attempt to control the Transvaal in 1877, not unrelated to the discovery of diamonds in 1867, ended in a defeat for the British in 1881.

The discovery in 1886 of the richest gold deposit in the world attracted large numbers of prospectors, researchers and adventurers of all hues, mostly British (Uitlanders). In 1888, Cecil Rhodes founded the De Beers Consolidated Company and, the following year, the British South Africa Company, a chartered company whose area of action became Rhodesia, in 1898. As Prime Minister of the Cape Colony in 1890, his aim was to expand British territories northwards. Only the two Boer republics stood in the way of total control of southern Africa, from Cape Town to Rhodesia, including Bechuanaland (Botswana), which had been a protectorate since 1885.

The traditionalist and puritanical society of the Boers took a dim view of these new and restless settlers. Relations became strained and friction increased. The Uitlanders appealed to the British government which provoked a war against the Boers (1899-1902), mobilizing 450,000 soldiers from all over the Empire against 30,000 Boers. Britain won the war but not without difficulty, and with recourse to the burning of villages and the internment of their inhabitants in concentration camps. In 1910, it annexed the two republics and united the four territories into a Union of South Africa (1910). To the east of Rhodesia, it established its protectorate over Nyasaland. These two territories prevented the Boers from expanding to the north. For its part, France established its protectorate on the Comoros Islands in 1887 and on the large island of Madagascar in 1895. The following year, it annexed Madagascar.

East Africa was the scene of a three-way division. Italy entered Somalia in 1885 and Eritrea in 1890. Italy's attempt to seize Abyssinia ended in military defeat at Adwa (1896), the first setback for a European power in the face of a non-European army. In 1884, Germany took possession of three African countries: Togo, South West Africa (Namibia), and German East Africa (Tanganyika and Ruanda-Urundi). Karl Peters founded the *Deutsche Ostafrikanische Gesellschaft*, a chartered company, in 1885. Three years later, William Mackinnon obtained a charter for the Imperial British East African Company. Its territories were handed over to the Crown to form the protectorates of Uganda (1894) and Kenya (1895). In 1895, Britain settled on the island of Zanzibar.

Needless to say, the process was fraught with violence. The uprising of the Hereros and Namas of Namibia which broke out in 1904 was ferociously suppressed. The survivors of what was the first genocide of the twentieth century, recognized by the German government in 2021, were deported. The practice of scorched earth, causing famine, put an end to the Maji-Maji revolt which spread in Tanganyika (German East Africa) from 1905 to 1907. In less than four decades, the African continent was carved up and divided between European countries. With Italy who occupied Tripolitania (Libya) in 1912, only two African countries remained independent: Ethiopia and Liberia.

In Asia, Great Britain enlarged the Indian Empire with protectorates in Malaysia during the 1870s and the annexation of Burma in 1886. In Insulindia, the British North Borneo Company, a chartered company, made it possible to expand the British protectorate over Sarawak to the northern part of Borneo in 1888. France had occupied Cochinchina and Cambodia since 1858-1863. From 1873, it attempted to extend its control to Annam and Tonkin. After setbacks in 1873 and 1882, it succeeded in 1885 but only at the cost of a war against China, overlord of Tonkin, and against strong Vietnamese resistance.

In 1893, under the pressure of a war and a blockade, Siam (Thailand) ceded Laos to France. The colony of Cochinchina and the four protectorates (Tonkin, Annam, Laos, Cambodia) were united in the Indochinese Union, formed in 1887. Opposition to the French presence continued unabated; the Can Vuong movement did not die out until 1896. Among other things, from 1901 to 1936, the population of the Bolaven Plateau in southern Laos waged a prolonged guerrilla war. Siam remained a buffer state between French and British possessions.

A Korean uprising against Japanese encroachments led to a Sino-Japanese war in 1894-1895. Following China's defeat, Japan seized Korea and Taiwan and opened Chinese ports to its trade. China was forced to pay an indemnity amounting to three times the state's annual revenue; this induced her to take out loans in Europe. As in the case of the Ottoman Empire and Morocco, the war was the forerunner of the entry of finance onto the scene. Modernizing and industrializing in less than thirty years, Japan achieved the status of regional and colonial power.

After its defeat, China was carved up, like the rest of the non-European world. From 1895 to 1900, European powers allocated themselves zones of influence within which they had territories on long-term lease. The scramble was Anglo-Franco-German. Japan and the United States were not invited, the latter calling for an "open door" policy throughout China. The essentially peasant movement led by the Boxer Society was repressed in 1900-1901 by an armed intervention by eight "interested" foreign powers (United Kingdom, France, Germany, Russia, Italy, Austria-Hungary, Japan, United States), which ransacked the capital Beijing.

Among the penalties, China had to remit a new indemnity, payable in thirty-nine years. Railways, businesses, and mines were now owned by foreigners. Like the Ottoman Empire in 1908, China underwent a revolution in 1911 and it was indebted and destined to be dismembered in the near future. As for Persia, it was partitioned between Britain and Russia in 1907. A year before, it had carried out a liberal-constitutional revolution. With the Netherlands still in the Dutch East Indies (Indonesia), Asia, like Africa, was entirely divided. Continuing its expansion southward, the Russian Empire had already annexed territories in the Caucasus and Central Asia.

The United States entered the race for colonies by way of a war against Spain (1898) which brought it the Philippines, Cuba, and Puerto Rico. An independent Philippine republic declared in 1899 was suppressed by the United States in a bloody war. The United States had purchased Alaska in 1867. In Hawaii, after the Dole fruit company (pineapple) and American marines overthrew the native monarchy in a coup d'état in 1894, the United States established its protectorate over Hawaii, then annexed it in 1898, making the archipelago a strategic springboard towards China. After a "revolution" in Colombia detached the territory of Panama and allowed the founding of an "independent" state in 1903, the United States leased the intercontinental canal. It practiced "dollar diplomacy" combined with the "big stick." In 1904, it took control of the finances of the Dominican Republic and, in 1912, occupied Nicaragua. These manifestations of formal imperialism went hand in hand with the fact that Latin America was mainly subject to informal American and British imperialism.

The maritime empires of the Atlantic, which had prevailed since the sixteenth century, and the Japanese Empire had possessions which were overseas colonies of exploitation or settler colonies geographically separated from the metropolises. The Russian Empire stood apart from this model in that it was a land-based entity practicing expansion into neighboring countries, then incorporating them into its territory. It had a traditional profile, similar to that of the formation of Western states such as Great Britain, France or the United States, and to that, dating back to Antiquity, of states which conquered their neighbors to absorb them or amputate parts of their territory. After the consolidation of Muscovy, territorial extension began in Siberia from the seventeenth century, towards the Black Sea in the eighteenth century, in the Caucasus and in Central Asia in the eighteenth century. This continental type of expansionism involved "internal" colonialism, but it led to the addition of new acquisitions to the national domain.

Russia was part of the old military empires of ancient times, in the same way as the Ottoman Empire and the Habsburg Empire. It was no coincidence that all three collapsed due to the ordeal of the First World War. Russia also shared another characteristic with the Ottoman Empire: it was preponderant in its geographical area and at the same time subordinate to Western imperialism. It was dominated economically, while the Ottoman Empire was dominated in every respect. Although it exercised its ascendancy over the Ottoman Empire, Japan inflicted a major defeat on Russia in the war of 1904-1905, a momentous setback by a European power against a non-European adversary.

Since the sixteenth century, colonial expansion had consisted in acquiring overseas territories, usually by force, and using them for the benefit of metropolitan interests. Extra-economic action brought economic advantages that were beyond the reach of economic activity alone, or over and above what economic activity could provide. It was the premium or surplus value which lay at the root of imperialism and constituted its ultimate purpose.

Following the phase of free trade and informal imperialism, an era of neomercantilist imperialism ensued, borrowing features from the original mercantilism: formal territorial acquisitions, forced integration of colonial economies in the international division of labor, the "colonial pact" which imposed primary specialization on them (single-crop agriculture, extraction of a natural resource or collection of a raw product for export purposes) with a ban on processing on site in order to favor the sale of finished products from the metropolis, exclusive right on the colonies for the benefit of "their" metropolis, and privileged companies (chartered, concessionary). The "development" of overseas possessions meant turning them into specialized annexes (i.e., rubber in Malaysia and Katanga, copper in Rhodesia, cocoa in Brazil) of the imperial economy limited to selling raw materials to the metropolises and buying their exports, often more expensive than those they could acquire elsewhere.

The portrait held as much for Great Britain, whose Empire supplied a quarter of imports and took two-fifths of exports in 1914, as for France (9.4 percent and 13 percent). In 1870, these proportions were only one-fifth and one quarter for Britain. Linked to the home country, the French Empire was its trading partner, surpassed only by the United Kingdom and Germany. Overall, the two empires were put in tow of their metropolises. With their increasingly negative trade balance vis-à-vis the metropolis, they were more buyers than sellers, under constraint in both cases. In 1900, India was the largest market for British exports. The Empire in general, and India in particular, played a key role in Britain's trading system: the surpluses it generated alleviated the deficits it recorded with Europe and the United States.

In Africa, the archaic commercial economy based on rudimentary pumping out of raw materials was perpetuated, with merchants and trading houses exchanging overvalued European goods for undervalued African products. The surplus profit generated was an illustration to the point of caricature of the extra-economic factor at the core of imperialism. In all the colonies, the economy was configured to ensure the production and export of raw materials, and the inflow of imports. Hence the emphasis on infrastructure such as railway and telegraph lines, roads, waterways, port facilities, and, where appropriate, dams for agriculture.

These islands of capitalism coexisted with economies and social structures that, on the whole, remained precapitalist. That was all economic development boiled down to. The costs of construction were borne by the population through taxation and borrowing on European financial markets; the servicing of the debts ultimately depended on taxation. The colonies were expected to be financially self-sufficient. They had to assume their expenses and balance their accounts, in addition to the trade deficit. India was responsible for sovereignty expenditures decided by London (costs of the metropolitan army, security, and colonial administration).

The intention was to draw peasants away from their plots of land or small family farms, from self-sufficiency and subsistence farming, and to bring them into the circuits of export and monetization. In this regard, colonial political power played its role of supporting metropolitan interests; it required that taxes be paid in cash, forcing the population to cultivate products likely to be marketed or to turn to low-paid wage labor. The levying of taxes gave rise to numerous abuses. Another type of exploitation was contract or unpaid labor in the form of forced labor or *corvée* on plantations. Practices went back to a sort of disguised slavery to provide labor.

The concessionary companies were notorious for using forced labor, combined with various forms of abuse and cruelty, even atrocities (scandal of severed hands), for the collection of ivory and then rubber in the Congo, methods which contributed to a demographic collapse. Established during the 1880s in the French Empire, the *régime de l'indigénat* was a system of penal and fiscal coercion which gave sanction, among other things, to forced labor. Condemned by the International Labor Office in 1930, forced labor persisted in the colonies. It was not abolished by France until April 11, 1946.

The abandonment of food crops and self-sufficiency was a direct cause of famines and depopulation (India, Java) and an indirect cause of epidemics (India). In settler colonies, taking possession of communal lands and those of the "natives" to hand them over to settlers was the prerequisite for putting them under cultivation. Expropriation, expulsion, confinement, and confiscation of "vacant" land by the state administration were the usual procedures. Both proletarianization and dispossession resulted in the impoverishment and the "hoboization" of uprooted and idle populations, typical of "underdeveloped" societies.

Around 10 percent of Africa was under European trusteeship in 1876; the proportion was more than 90 percent in 1900. By 1914, there were no more "free" territories left to conquer in the world. In a period of four decades, the great powers had taken over the planet. Even the North Pole was claimed by the United States in 1908 and the South Pole by Norway in 1911. The world was essentially divided into half a dozen blocs, differentiated by size and power, composed each of a metropolis and its empire, and in conflict-ridden relations with each other.

An observer would have noted a situation where realities of distinct natures intermingled. An economic depression beginning in the 1870s spurred protectionism, business concentration, the export of capital, and the quest for new colonies. Neomercantilist imperialism appeared to have two dimensions: a maturation of capitalism and a craze for the acquisition of colonies. The latter was more visible than the former, so much so that it was easy to consider imperialism as primarily colonial or interchangeable with colonial empires—which, incidentally, was the case with mercantilist imperialism.

However, the informal imperialism which succeeded mercantilist imperialism broadened the notion of imperialism, extending it beyond colonial possessions. Furthermore, the concentration of businesses and the export of capital had a scope that did not coincide perfectly with the colonial framework, even if they did overlap. On the one hand, the colonial surge began during the 1870s, at the same time as the advance of protectionism. On the other hand, the world was partitioned before the proliferation of giant oligopolistic companies. Some (Unilever, Cadbury, Dunlop, Michelin) invested in an already existing colonial domain. Others (Shell, United Fruit Company, British American Tobacco Company) were present in both formal and informal empires. Finally, some (Nestlé) were based in countries that had no colonies. All would be stakeholders in a possible redivision of the world, inevitably by means of war.

By its tangible, even spectacular, character, the colonial phenomenon came to overshadow all others. Contemporaries were engrossed with an optical effect. Imperialism tended to take on a colonial envelope which masked the relative and historically delimited nature of colonization. Intense scientific, ideological, and political debates have been ongoing since the end of the century about the essence of imperialism, its wellspring and its consequences. Chapter 12 examines these issues in order to untangle a complex web.

e. Zenith and end of course of neomercantilist imperialism (1914-1945)

In a state of permanent tension since 1870, international relations took on a bellicose tone at the start of the twentieth century. Buoyed by its economic growth, Germany made claims to compete with Great Britain, the hegemonic power of the nineteenth century. The desire to go beyond Europe to play a global role (*Weltpolitik*) and the construction of a navy capable of combat on the high seas (*Kriegsmarine*) put the two powers on a collision course. The scenario was comparable to those that Europe had experienced since the sixteenth century, but on a larger scale; from the Seven Years' War to the First World War, the value of international trade increased fiftyfold. The dispute covered everything from colonial ambitions to the quest for primacy in all markets and fields of investment, regardless of the political status of the targeted countries.

The beginning of the twentieth century was marked by a succession of international crises, interspersed with truces and provisional agreements. Whenever armed conflict loomed, the primary authority was political and military. Once the economy created the conditions for belligerence, diplomacy and armies took over. Military preparations, alliance-building, support of allies and weakening of the opposing alliance became the main activities. The maintenance of peace or the tipping into war, whether circumscribed or general, hung on circumstantial factors, random developments, or incidents seemingly exogenous to the Anglo-German tug-of-war.

Fearing encirclement by Britain, France, and Russia, Germany had to support its only ally, Austria-Hungary, which was struggling with pan-Slavic nationalism and the threat of its breakup. All it took was the assassination by a Serbo-Bosnian nationalist of the Austro-Hungarian Archduke in Sarajevo on June 28, 1914 to set the tinderbox ablaze. The local Austro-Serbian war turned into a general war pitting the great powers against each other. All disputes came together: between France and Germany over Alsace and Lorraine, between Russia and Austria-Hungary over predominance in the Balkans, between Austria-Hungary and the Slavic world. The most fundamental, the one with the most far-reaching consequences, was the escalating competition between Britain and Germany for world hegemony.

The period of 1914-1945 was a crisis of neomercantilist imperialism leading to two clashes of paroxysmal intensity: total war on a global scale, separated by two decades of pause. Both involved Germany's aspiration to wrest global hegemony from the established powers. The First World War brought the German enterprise to a halt and the Second put an end to it. However, for the victorious powers, it was a Pyrrhic victory which exhausted and diminished them in favor of their American ally that had been biding its time since the end of the nineteenth century.

After its collapse during the First World War, Russia, which became the Soviet Union, recovered, industrialized, and strengthened itself. It broke with the imperial goals of pre-revolutionary Russia. As the main anti-German force during the Second World War, it emerged victorious but was bled dry. The result of internal tensions within neomercantilist imperialism, the two world wars brought this third phase of capitalist imperialism to its conclusion, paving the way to the fourth, that of postcolonial planetary imperialism under the aegis of the United States.

During the First World War, the destruction of productive capacities at a time of growing needs led to lasting results. It reinforced one of the pre-war trends, accelerating corporate concentration in the name of efficiency. The share of oligopolies in the economies of the belligerent countries grew. It was more convenient for the state to deal with them than with small businesses, so much so that it encouraged cartelization and mergers.

A novelty unknown in the pre-war period was the extent of state intervention in the economy. Under the influence of necessity, it established a fixed exchange rate for banknotes (suspension of convertibility into gold) and foreign exchange controls. It then had to manage shortages by requisitioning, rationing, allocating raw materials, setting prices and wages, awarding contracts and orders, and granting credit to manufacturers, particularly large companies whose growth was encouraged.

Departures from liberal conceptions multiplied, reflecting the reconversion of the state from liberalism to *dirigisme*. It became the main economic actor, rendering the "laws" of the market obsolete. Neither planned nor theorized, the abandonment of the liberal economy was nonetheless spectacular and no less instructive in that it demonstrated the feasibility of state intervention in the economy, a heresy in liberal doctrine. Although the experiment was considered temporary and the return to liberal practices was the watchword after 1918, the episode would not be forgotten.

In one respect, the situation changed completely: from being a net creditor, Western Europe was now a net debtor, in this case vis-à-vis the United States, while the American position vis-à-vis Europe was also reversed but in the opposite direction. European assets abroad were liquidated during the war or canceled by host countries; the basis of neomercantilist imperialism was shaken. In addition to its indebtedness, Europe depended on American capital. The transformation of the financial relationship between the United States and Europe illustrated the new balance of power and the redistribution of cards within neomercantilist imperialism.

New York competed with the City of London for the status of the world's financial center, while Paris had difficulty resisting the weakening of the franc. United States supremacy was established; the world's leading bankers were no longer British and French, but American. For France, the victory of 1918 was no happier than the defeat of 1871: it fell back in the ranking of world powers. Europe, dominant until recently, was now diminished. It found itself in a position of subordination vis-à-vis the United States, similar to that of the world vis-à-vis Europe before 1914. Conversely, Britain and France established a more favorable balance of power towards Germany.

Wars are the crucible of decisive shifts in the distribution of power. Extra-economic instruments par excellence, they result in a transfer of advantages, notably economic ones, from the vanquished to the victors. The reparations imposed on Germany, the restitution of Alsace and Lorraine, the eviction from Eastern Europe, the loss of 10 percent of its territory as well as its overseas possessions and positions, the confiscation of the remainder of its fleet and of its external assets, not to mention the loss of three quarters of its iron ore resources, represented the tribute demanded by the victors.

The years 1918-1939 saw a vain attempt to revive the pre-1914 foundations and take advantage of Germany's temporary eclipse. The war ended abruptly, without an indisputable verdict. The German army was not defeated militarily; it requested an armistice because it knew it could not win, its resources being insufficient. Germany's overall strengths were intact, its industrial capacities superior to those of Britain or France. Its recovery was beyond doubt and a war of revenge was expected within twenty to twenty-five years. All the efforts of the victors would be focused on the measures to keep Germany in the status of vanquished for as long as possible, to postpone the expected rematch, and to design a framework to contain the adversary. In fact, the armistice of 1918 and the peace of 1919 were not more than a ceasefire.

Despite the incantations and the policies adopted, "return to [the pre-1914] normal" after the cataclysm proved arduous and costly to achieve. In the immediate aftermath of the war, one of its legacies revealed its harmfulness. Unknown since the beginning of the nineteenth century, inflation was now a permanent fact. As a consequence of the enormous expenditure and the swelling of the money supply during the four years of conflict, hyperinflation was rampant in several countries, reaching stratospheric levels in Germany. In 1923, the monthly rate there was 1000 percent. The wholesale price index rose from 1 in 1913, to 12.6 in 1920, to 36.7 in 1922. In 1923, it skyrocketed from 2,785 in January, to 74,787 in July, to 750,000,000,000 in November.

The currency collapsed: $1 was worth 4.2 Marks in July 1914, but 4,200,000,000,000 Marks in November 1923. Everywhere imports became more expensive, prices soared, currencies depreciated. Their convertibility into gold at a fixed rate belonged to the past; they floated, and their exchange rate was determined by the market. Parities became highly unstable. These fluctuations dried up long-term investment flows, which were unsustainable in the absence of predictability, and encouraged short-term ("floating") capital movements, which were volatile and often speculative.

All currencies were affected, apart from the United States dollar, while the pound sterling had to be defended by the Bank of England. Britain was determined to return to the gold convertibility of the pound at its 1913 parity and to restore its eminent pre-war status. In 1925, the pound was reevaluated. However, this revaluation made it an overvalued currency. The old industries to which Britain owed its power and prosperity were hard hit.

Losing competitiveness since the end of the nineteenth century, these countries lost their markets in Asia to new competitors, such as

Japan, an exporter of cotton fabrics. The return to the gold standard was a painful policy which diminished the attractiveness of exports, weighed down on economic activity, and threatened employment. At the same time, the United Kingdom consolidated its status as a rentier country; income from its overseas investments was at an all-time high. Neither for the first nor the last time, the financial sector of "mature" economies decoupled from the real economy.

Defending the pound sterling implied a deflationary policy with all its attendant consequences: rising interest rates ("dear money"), less investment, slower economic activity, reduction in public spending, and compression of wages. Foreshadowing its policy of the 1980s, the United Kingdom strengthened its currency and the City of London at the expense of its economy. At the very least, it succeeded in putting the City on the same level as Wall Street; the two markets shared global financial supremacy during the interwar period. Anglo-American financial, naval, and oil rivalry was so palpable in the early 1920s that armed conflict did not appear unthinkable. At the opposite end of the spectrum from the galloping inflation that was eating away at many economies, deflation also had an exorbitant economic cost. Monetary disorder alone sufficed as evidence that the economic system was at an impasse.

In fact, whole economies underwent an upheaval from which they were struggling to recover. Old and new imbalances combined to sap recovery efforts. Added to this was a two-pronged dispute which weighed on economies and poisoned international relations in the 1920s: the payment of reparations demanded from Germany and the insistence of the United States on obtaining repayment of the loans it had granted France during the war. Pleading an inability to pay, Germany and France dragged their heels. From the Dawes Plan of 1924, followed by the Young Plan (1930), the United States demonstrated its new preeminence by advancing Germany the credits it needed to pay reparations, enabling France to carry out payments on its debt. "Dollar diplomacy," experimented in Latin America, was extended to Europe.

The United States economy was the most productive in the world and the best equipped for mass production. Its large companies adopted the latest technical processes to obtain the best yields, benefit from economies of scale, and lower costs. They also applied

Taylorism, a more efficient organization of production, including the advanced division of tasks, "rationalization," product standardization and work on "assembly lines." The outcome was the homogenization of consumption patterns. They also introduced Fordism, i.e., wage increases, to create markets. The United States made the most of the second industrial revolution. It replaced the United Kingdom as the world's leading exporter.

Exports at current prices
millions of dollars, at current exchange rates

	1870	1913	1929
United Kingdom	971	2550	3550
France	541	1328	1965
Germany	424	2454	3212
United States	403	2380	5157

From 22 percent in 1913, the United States' share of exports from industrialized countries rose to 28 percent by 1928. Its trade surpluses ensured a positive balance of payments. With the surpluses accrued, Americans became the world's leading lenders, surpassing Great Britain. From $2 billion in 1919, the amount of their long-term credits in Europe rose to $4.6 billion in 1929. Their worldwide portfolio increased from $6.5 billion to $15.4 billion. In 1929, they held 60 percent of the world's gold stock.

The arrival of United States dollars in Europe was both a sign of the passing of the baton in terms of global hegemony and an indicator that the stabilization and recovery of the European economy depended on American credits. In addition to loans and bonds, a new kind of capital export had been occurring since the end of the nineteenth century. It was driven by the United States and it progressed during the 1920s. Foreign direct investment (FDI) took the form of subsidiaries of American companies or of controlling shares in foreign companies. It had a bright future ahead of it; its growth took off after 1945 with the expansion of American multinational firms.

A pyramid of debt was created on both sides of the Atlantic, with American banks and finance companies at its apex. The euphoric growth of the years 1924 to 1929 was based on credit. So was the Wall

Street stock market bubble; credit fueled the overvaluation of listed securities and speculation. This lasted until the Wall Street crash of October 24, 1929. When the collapse occurred, stocks lost half their value and holders found themselves saddled with debts that were impossible to pay off. Banks wrote off the sums lent to speculators, saw the value of the shares—accepted as collateral for advances or included in their assets—melt away, and suffered a run from depositors. Many small banks went out of business. The stock market crisis morphed into an economic crisis. With credit drying up, production slowed down, while mass unemployment became a scourge. As economic activity waned, the US GNP contracted sharply, falling by a third.

The impact of the collapse of the credit structure in the United States was transmitted beyond its borders, with repercussions on sensitive points of the international economy. Only the Soviet economy escaped this capitalist crisis. Restored with difficulty after the war, the architecture of international economic relations was shaken. Ties which had barely been reestablished were broken. Vital for the reactivation of the European economy, the flow of dollars to Europe turned into repatriation. The latent imbalances in the European economy and its dependence on inflow of funds from the United States were highlighted. Financing for economic activity dried up. Businesses were stifled and debts held by German and Austrian banks became unrecoverable, precipitating their collapse.

The Wall Street meltdown had a domino effect, shattering the fragile foundations of the international economy and transforming a stock market crash and severe deflation into the worst depression in the history of capitalism. The United States was the epicenter of the crisis which spread to all industrial countries except the Soviet Union. As in the United States, production plummeted and mass unemployment reached calamitous levels, particularly in Germany. Currencies felt the impact of the stock market shock. Capital withdrew from the London market, causing the abandonment of the gold standard and the devaluation of the pound in September 1931. Twenty-five countries also let their currencies float. The gold standard ceased to be in force in June 1932.

At the same time, mirroring the economic slowdown, the dislocation of the world economy and protectionist measures, international trade fell to a third of what it had been in 1929. Sluggish since the war, export industries were devastated. After the devaluation of the pound, the adoption by the United Kingdom of a partial customs tariff in November 1931 and a general tariff in February 1932, in other words the abandonment of free trade in its birthplace, was another bombshell. The pivotal power of the era of free-trade imperialism and the first pillar of the era of neomercantilist imperialism was no longer in a position to exercise a regulatory function in the world economy. Furthermore, during the 1930s, Great Britain's balance of accounts moved into the deficit zone: income from foreign investments, freight, and insurance ceased to cover the deficit in the trade of trade. Even the rentier status was reaching its limits.

From the end of the nineteenth century, a hegemonic succession was on the horizon. However, against a backdrop of general disorganization, the United States was not in a position to move forward. Despite the size of its economy in the world, it was less internationally integrated than Britain and less accustomed to playing a global role. On the European continent, Germany had not said its last word since the failure of its attempt at imperial replacement in 1914. The severity of the depression in Germany provoked radical responses: strict *dirigisme* with a military orientation, protectionism to the point of self-sufficiency. However, autarky required resources that its territory did not have, foreshadowing wars of conquest and territorial enlargement. Since the beginning of the twentieth century, the candidates to succeed Britain as the hegemonic power were the same: the United States and Germany. Industrial capacity was the most telling indicator.

Distribution of industry worldwide
Percent

	United States	Germany	Great Britain	France	Russia/ USSR	Italy	Japan
1870	23.3	13.2	31.8	10.3	3.7	2.4	
1896-1900	30.1	16.6	19.5	7.1	5.0	2.7	0.6
1913	35.8	15.7	14.0	6.4	5.5	2.7	1.2
1926-1929	42.2	11.6	9.4	6.6	4.3	3.3	2.5
1936-1938	32.2	10.7	9.2	4.5	18.5	2.7	3.5

The First World War was a moment of maximum intensity for a number of issues: recovery of Alsace and Lorraine for France, nationalism of the Slavic peoples, Russia's need to overcome its internal difficulties and to halt the erosion of its position abroad, the Ottoman Empire's headlong flight into war to avoid disintegration. However, the main and most structuring conflict was Anglo-German; it pitted the dominant thalassocracy of the nineteenth century against the continental power that aspired to replace it. It was about the maintenance or the transfer of hegemony within neomercantilist imperialism. Britain got the upper hand but at the cost of the entry on the scene of the new American competitor and a loss of substance on the part of its French ally. The fact remained that victory gave rise to the traditional sharing of spoils: war indemnities, amputations of territories, disarmament, and so on. As a lever of imperialism, war was an opportunity to reap economic benefits through the use of extra-economic means.

The First World War led to a reshuffle in the power relationship of the metropolises within the neomercantilist imperialism. The system was shaken, revealing dysfunctions and flaws, including the collapse of ancient empires—Austro-Hungarian, Russian, Ottoman—and, above all, the birth of a counter-system embodied by the Soviet Union. There remained the colonial aspect. The British and French Empires were called upon to contribute to the war effort. Soldiers and supplies were rushed to the metropolises and battlefronts.

The colonies were redistributed in favor of the winners. As in the seventeenth and eighteenth centuries, the defeated powers were dispossessed of their empires. All German colonies passed into the hands of the victors: Britain and France shared Togo and Cameroon, Britain and Belgium took German East Africa, and South West Africa (Namibia) fell to the Union of South Africa, therefore to Britain. The German sphere of influence in China was transferred to Japan. Possessions in the Pacific were awarded to new beneficiaries: Samoa to New Zealand (British), the German part of New Guinea to Australia (British), and the Marshall and Mariana Islands to Japan. Many German trading companies were sequestered and bought out by French or British interests, formerly competitors.

By the Sykes-Picot agreement of May 16, 1916, Great Britain and France divided up the Arab territories of the Ottoman Empire, behind the backs of their Arab allies to whom independence had been promised. The result was an expansion of the victors' overseas possessions, in the form of colonies or mandates from the League of Nations. The British and French Empires were larger than ever before, even as their rejection by colonized peoples gained momentum and was expressed in increasingly articulate terms.

Cut off from their metropolises during the wars, the colonies revealed their state of dependence, particularly in industrial terms. Attempts to manufacture on site remained embryonic. The restoration of peace meant the return of industrial imports from the metropolises and the reaffirmation of the "colonial pact." Despite the presence overseas of a few processing activities, industry was reserved for the metropolises, with the colonies confined to the role of suppliers of raw materials and reserved markets.

The colonial contribution to Great Britain and France during the war drew the attention of the metropolises to these reserves and to the advantage of developing them. During the 1920s, overseas production and better use of it were on the agenda. A major effort was made to make empires popular with metropolitan populations, hitherto considered indifferent. In April 1921, the French Minister of Colonies, Albert Sarraut, announced a program to renovate infrastructures and public works, involving planning under the aegis of the state which would guarantee borrowing by the colonies and contribute to reducing their budgetary deficits. However, the metropolis being in straitened circumstances, the plan was only partly implemented and remained largely at the draft stage. In the absence of planned development, the Empire and the protectorates were nevertheless a construction site for infrastructures, utilities, and public works (railroads, ports, hydraulic and hydroelectric assets, civil engineering works, sanitation, water supply, etc.).

Tightening commercial relations between metropolis and empire was part of the quest for economic, political, and demographic size that the war had made more pressing. This was reflected in the promotion of the notion of a "greater France," comprising the metropolis and the colonies in a single entity welded together by close links. France was moving towards a customs union, an application to the neomercantilist framework of a well-known formula for economic integration. In 1928, a protectionist customs law united France and its colonies under a common tariff system with a view to promoting intra-imperial self-sufficiency through exchange between the parties, at the expense of trade with foreign countries. Great Britain did likewise by creating the Empire Marketing Board in 1926 to encourage the importation of colonial products into the British Isles, as well as trade between the metropolis and its colonies. The Colonial Development Act of 1929 was intended to extend grants and loans for investments in various projects but the fund was modest and not fully utilized.

The depression shook imperial relations but accentuated trends towards self-sufficiency and protectionism. For the metropolises, the closure of markets was a spur to find substitutes by turning to colonial outlets, even if their absorption capacity was dented by the fall in the prices of tropical products. The fallback on the Empire and a policy of imperial preference were indicative of the search for salvation in the overseas possessions, although these were in dire straits. In 1932, in order to concentrate and coordinate efforts, France adopted a voluntarist colonial policy ("managed economy") which, among other things, strengthened commercial ties with metropolitan France, imposed duties on foreign imports, and supported the price of colonial products.

An Economic Conference of Metropolitan and Overseas France, held in 1934, promoted the tooling of overseas possessions. Great Britain introduced imperial preference in 1932, with the main measure being the lowering of customs duties between the metropolis and the Empire (colonies, dominions, protectorates). The center and the periphery granted each other tariff privileges, foreshadowing the formation of an imperial economic bloc. The demands of the Tariff Reform League bore fruit three decades later, putting an end to the free trade era of which Great Britain was the pioneer and guarantor.

Empires played a greater role in the ailing economies of the metropolises, if only because of the economic slowdown and the decline in the share of their relations with the rest of the world due to protectionism, quotas, and prohibitions. Already in 1930, the Empire accounted for 42 percent of British exports. The colonies were the destination of 14.5 percent of French exports in 1920-1922, and 29.5 percent in 1936-1938. Even before the depression, the Empire was France's leading trading partner. Never before had the neomercantilist, or even the classic mercantilist, model reached such fullness. Emerging with the depression of 1873-1895, neomercantilism triumphed three decades later with the depression of the 1930s.

As much as the metropolises tried to bring overseas possessions closer to their economies, the latter tried to distance themselves politically. The "European civil war" of 1914-1918 having shaken the arrogance of the colonial powers and punctured the myth of their invincibility, autonomist, or nationalist tendencies, already evident before 1914, benefited from a fresh impetus. But representatives of the colonized were, for all practical purposes, given short shrift at the Versailles conference. National rights and the principle of self-determination applied to Europe, but not to the colonies. The colonial status quo was confirmed, subject to a purely formal alteration: the new acquisitions (because overseas possessions increased after 1918) were called "mandates" of the League of Nations. Nevertheless, during the interwar period, empires were openly contested. By definition an opponent of the capitalist world order, the Soviet Union reinforced, if only by virtue of its existence, a nationalist trend which took various forms depending on local conditions.

Being settler colonies, the Dominions (Canada, South Africa, Australia, New Zealand) detached themselves gradually from Great Britain, without rupture. In 1926, the Commonwealth was created to unite the United Kingdom and the Dominions within the British Empire. The Statute of Westminster of 1931 ratified the accession of the Dominions to autonomy, subject to maintaining the link to the Crown. In the British and French colonies, protectorates, and mandates, all demands for autonomy, reform, or self-government came up against the firm resolve of the metropolises to hold on to their control. There were countless revolts, breaking out in Nigeria (1918), Egypt (1919), India (1919, 1920-1922, 1930), Iraq (1920), Palestine (1921, 1929, 1936), Tunisia (1920-1922, 1938), Syria and Morocco (1925, 1930), China (1922-1923), and Indochina (1930).

Preceded by the Indian National Congress and the African National Congress (South Africa), founded respectively in 1885 and 1912, nationalist anti-colonialist political parties emerged in the overseas possessions: National Congress of British West Africa (1918), Wafd in Egypt (1919), Vietnamese National Party (1927), Destour (1919) then Neo-Destour (1934) in Tunisia, Indonesian National Party (1927). In addition to political independence, or as an integral part of the quest for political independence, economic demands were formulated, such as an end to land grabbing and the development of industry.

On-site processing was hampered by the absence of tariff protection, in keeping with the "colonial pact" which was at the heart of the neomercantilist system, as it had been of the mercantilist system which preceded it. The hardships of the depression in the imperial possessions mobilized broad social strata in support of nationalist demands, transforming parties of notables into mass parties. On the eve of the Second World War, the overseas universe retained its outdated appearance as an extension of the metropolises where, however, increased resistance and signs of decomposition were evident.

The Second World War continued the first, even if the entry into war took on an unusual character. Essentially it was a resumption of the conflict for hegemony within neomercantilist imperialism. The First War did not provide a lasting answer to this question. The contender to replace British primacy was still Germany. Hardly defeated in 1914-1918, forced to pay but not subdued during the interwar period, it took up arms again under new conditions. On the one hand, because of the war, the United States positioned itself to take over from Great Britain. On the other hand, in the East, emerged a state that was breaking with capitalism.

Implemented by the Nazis, German strategy differed from that of 1914. While Germany still laid claim to its lost colonies, the focus was now on Europe. In order to avoid confronting all enemies at the same time and waging war on two fronts, it planned to conduct limited campaigns to annex countries one by one under the guise of revising the iniquitous Treaty of Versailles. The conflict in the west would be postponed until Germany strengthened itself through successive annexations. The aim was to gain control over the Soviet Union, a source of raw materials and a territory for German settlers. Settler colonialism was the essence of the Nazi imperialist project. In this, it did not differ from what other European countries had done on other continents. German imperialism planned to colonize in Europe in the same way that European powers had colonized the non-European world.

Western enemies were to be mollified by the representation of the *Drang nach Osten* (drive to the East) as an ideological struggle of European civilization against Asiatic and barbaric Bolshevism. As an unsophisticated plan of predation, it embodied a crude system of plunder, enslavement, atrocities, and settler colonialism, with "racial" pretensions serving as justification. Combining Neanderthal impulses and modern techniques, and pushing colonialism to its limits, Nazi expansionism demonstrated that neither advanced capitalism nor a modern society precluded the systematic reliance on plunder and savagery.

Events did not unfold as expected. Conciliatory Western powers practiced appeasement until 1939, when they realized that Germany would become too powerful; hence their initiative to launch the war. Germany then fought the West which it had not envisaged to do at such an early date. The results were mixed: France was defeated, but not Britain. Stopping on its Western front, Germany returned to its original plan of attacking the USSR. The European war took place mainly in the East, where Germany was, against all odds, defeated between 1942 and 1944. The Western front was then activated in 1944, with the entry of the United States on the scene, as in 1917. This time, the European powers were more exhausted than after the First World War and the United States was the undisputed master in Western Europe. However, Eastern Europe was out of its reach, with the USSR keeping a watchful eye on areas which had been corridors for the invasion of its territory.

The Second World War left neomercantilist imperialism in tatters, even though the overseas expansion following the First World War had brought it to its peak. It sank with the European powers that had been its architects, trustees, and beneficiaries. A system imploded under the effect of hegemonic struggles within it. In waiting since the turn of the century, the United States could pick up the pieces and put them back together according to its views and interests. With the metropolises enfeebled and prostrate in Europe, it remained to determine the future of the colonies and other overseas possessions. Having lasted three quarters of a century, the neomercantilist phase of imperialism came to an end. A new phase began.

CHAPTER 12

Theories, theorization, and theorists of imperialism

Colonial bulimia, economic transformations, and dangers of war provoked profound reflection on the question of imperialism. The end of the nineteenth century and the beginning of the twentieth century were the founding moments for the analysis of this phenomenon. The interpretations that emerged would mark the ground and exert a powerful influence for a long time to come. It is appropriate to address them at this stage of the study, given the information available to the theorists and the context in which they found themselves. The aim is to pause briefly in order to survey the corpus of these pioneering approaches and to draw up a critical assessment. Three main currents expressed views on imperialism: liberalism, reformism, and Marxism. All were critical but they started from distinct premises, had different approaches and carried out analyses which led to divergent conclusions.

a. Liberalism considers imperialism to be a non-economic phenomenon

The liberal movement, a sworn opponent of mercantilism, had a position on imperialism since the end of the eighteenth century. Its conceptions crystallized in the doctrines of classical political economy which constituted the backbone of liberal principles. For liberalism and classical political economy, economics and politics were distinct, and imperialism was a non-economic phenomenon. Synonymous with colonialism, it was seen as an archaic vestige, an a-economic offshoot, or a fundamentally anti-economic transplant. Time and enlightenment would sooner or later put an end to this theoretically indefensible and practically regrettable state of affairs.

The doctrine of the Manchester school, built on the refutation of the teachings of mercantilism, was anti-colonialist. Free trading and anti-monopolist, it earnestly denounced the "old colonial system," tainted by privileges, hemmed in by restrictions and regulations, embalmed in a shroud of protective measures. Adam Smith criticized it as early as 1776. Following in his footsteps, the Philosophical Radicals, from Jeremy Bentham to James Mill, constantly denounced the possession of colonies as a source of wars, a prop for corrupt governments and a reserve of sinecures for a parasitic aristocracy.

The "economic harmonies" (as per Frédéric Bastiat) of free competition, confidence in markets to ensure growth, the optimal allocation of resources and the division of labor, and the hope that the mobility of "factors of production" would lead to a global specialization beneficial to everyone by virtue of the principle of comparative advantage, were all achievements but were not, however, the alpha and omega of economic liberalism. Behind the certainty that long-ignored truths were now being revealed, there was anxiety; behind the equanimity, doubt.

The profit rate being the regulator of activity in the capitalist economy, its maintenance constituted the *sine qua non* condition for the continuation of accumulation. But this index tended not only to equalize in all sectors of the economy, but also to decline in general. A steady and unchecked fall could only result in a halt to investment, a "stationary state" and stagnation. Could the downward pressure on the average rate of social capital be attributed to competition between individual capitals constantly moving from low-profit activities to those with higher rates, inevitably depressing the latter? Adam Smith thought so.

For David Ricardo, the threat to the rate of profit came from diminishing returns on land. The rise in food prices would cause wages and land rents to move in the same direction. The share of profit, the third element in overall income according to the Ricardian model, could only fall, to the point of stifling any stimulus to investment and, consequently, to accumulation and growth.

The compression of wages was, in Ricardo's opinion, the way to sustain the rate of profit and investment. Its prerequisite was the importation of cheaper foodstuffs, and therefore the removal of protections surrounding cereal prices (the Corn Laws). At the same time, opening up the British market to foreign wheat exporters would provide them with the means to purchase the products of British industry.

The classical economists were too attached to the idea of a fundamental equilibrium between production and consumption to worry about the possibility of a crisis of general underconsumption or over-production. Production would create its market since the sellers of certain goods were the buyers of other goods, and the labor force which manufactured them must provide for its maintenance. Convinced that global income would be spent entirely on consumer and capital goods, they did not consider hoarding to be a real problem. Jean-Baptiste Say, a disciple of Adam Smith, put the proposition tersely: one can only sell if buyers have means provided by their production, so that it is production itself which opens up markets for goods.

Thus, on a general level, supply would generate demand and the "plethoras," "bottlenecks," and "congestions" which haunted knowledgeable minds would be resolved naturally thanks to the self-regulating mechanisms of the market. They could not become general and permanent. It was with products, for which money was only a form of mediation, that other products were bought. If one commodity was not sold— "overabundant"—it was because others were not produced in sufficient quantities. More production would open outlets. A certain commodity may be produced in excess of needs, but what favored the flow of one commodity was the production of another.

The theory of spontaneous equilibrium, the cornerstone of classical political economy, translated into the "law of outlets" or "Say's law." As markets, colonies were superfluous since the extension of free trade easily compensated for the renunciation of reserved overseas territories. The classical economists did not see colonies as playing a significant role in raising the rate of profit. Being self-sufficient and independent of exogenous variables, the economic systems they built dispensed with a theory of colonialism.

The abolition of the Corn Laws, the holy ark of free trade, consecrated the preeminence of liberal doctrine. Economists, historians, publicists, and politicians adhered to it for a long time, notwithstanding economic crises likely to shake their faith. The credit attached to colonialism was devalued in the era of the new consensus. Did not the Tory Disraeli famously explain in 1852 that the colonies would be independent in a few years and constituted millstones hanging around Britain's neck? Only European settler colonies (Canada, Australia, New Zealand) were concerned by these remarks.

The practical effect of anticolonial unanimity was more the slowing down of the expansion of empires than any conversion to decolonization. In the real world, the anti-colonial current coexisted with the maintenance of colonies. The enlargement of empires towards the end of the nineteenth century met with undoubtedly sincere objections on the part of proponents of liberalism. John Bright resigned from the British cabinet in July 1882, the day after the bombing of Alexandria. Gladstone, the Prime Minister, only reluctantly turned his back on Cobden's ideas and only in practice; he continued to talk like a liberal but did the opposite in fact. Later, others, like Joseph Chamberlain, would not only participate in the race for colonies; they would discard whole swaths of classical political economy, such as free trade and anticolonialism.

The realization that the market was not a transparent and self-correcting mechanism, like a set of mathematical equations, only took hold slowly, even after the depression of the end of the nineteenth century set in. For a long time, no disorder was recognized that the market could not smooth over unaided. While classical doctrine proclaimed the uselessness of colonies, Europe embarked on the path of their acquisition, a phenomenon justified here and there by the need to free itself from economic imbalances whose permanence was not admitted by economic theory, at least until the advent of the Keynesian synthesis. This example was indicative of the gap between thought and the real world.

If classical economic doctrine faltered in the aftermath of the collapse of the great boom of the mid-nineteenth century, it was not necessarily debunked. In France, the *Journal des économistes* defended with sententious dignity the purity of an orthodoxy that could not be altered by heresies such as state interference in laws of the market, protectionism and colonialism. Opposition to colonial policy could certainly be explained by the reasoning that France ought to turn inwards in order to reestablish its position in Europe, but it was also based on an economic argument drawn from classical political economy. What were protected colonies worth, with modest purchasing power, compared to free trade treaties with states providing vast markets? Why divert to the Empire men and capital that France so desperately needed? How could the ruinous expenses incurred by the metropolitan state for the conquest, defense and maintenance of regions of such mediocre economic interest be justified? It would be better to let the development of society follow its natural course than to try to force it through military adventures and an arsenal of regulations which, in any case, could only produce results contrary to those expected.

The conviction that the colonial enterprise constituted a bottomless pit of wasted funds, a misapprehension, a mirage, even a swindle, contrary to the calculable, rational, and well-understood interest of the metropolis will live on, backed by the liberal vision of a flawless capitalism, considered to be a source of harmony, good understanding, and material benefits for all stakeholders. A deplorable loss of direction in economic terms, colonial expansion also generated unfortunate conflicts between imperial powers. The fact remained that it occurred and that it required explanations, if only to demonstrate its folly. The main characteristic of liberal thought on the subject of imperialism and colonialism was not the rejection that they were the deeds of capitalist societies but the assertion that they were not inherent to capitalism nor part of its nature. They stemmed from causes that were foreign to the mainspring of the capitalist economy and even contributed to disrupting its normal functioning.

The successors of liberal economists, such as Charles Gide, Gustave de Molinari, and Yves Guyot, were followed by authors from a wide variety of backgrounds. Karl Kautsky, one of the leaders of German social democracy and the Second International, believed in peaceful expansion, preferable to that based on violence. He drew the wrath of Lenin, for whom this sort of thinking was just an intellectual exercise, out of touch with the reality of international relations. Kautsky's attitude was, in his eyes, nothing more than an apology for capitalism and an attempt to suggest that it would be enough to wait for the leaders of the combatant states to listen to reason and for imperialism and colonial expansion to cease.

In his famous article published in *Die Neue Zeit* on September 11, 1914, a few weeks after the outbreak of war, Kautsky summed up his thoughts. Capitalist production required the maintenance of a fair proportionality between the various sectors, particularly between industry and agriculture. In the event of a rupture, periodic crises restored it. The tendency of industrial countries to expand the agricultural areas that trade with them took two forms: free trade and imperialism. The international division of labor between Great Britain, the world's workshop, and other countries, its agrarian zone, did not last long: the latter took the path of industrialization and sought to seize the parts of the world that remained "free." This was the beginning of imperialism.

Capitalism could continue to develop as long as the growing industry of the capitalist countries succeeded in bringing about a corresponding increase in agricultural production. This was becoming increasingly difficult, but it did not lead to economic collapse if agriculture kept pace. On the other hand, contradictions between capitalist states undermined the economy. The arms race and the expenses incurred for colonial expansion threatened the pace of capital accumulation, hence the export of capital, the basis of imperialism. The latter would be its own gravedigger. From a means of developing capitalism, it would become an obstacle. Premature bankruptcy would result from the continuation of this policy.

However, change remained possible if imperialism represented only one mode of expansion among others. By imperialism, Kautsky meant the tendency of each large capitalist state to enlarge its colonial empire at the expense of other empires. From an exclusively economic point of view, a new stage, ultra-imperialism, was not inconceivable. It would have to be fought, as imperialism was fought, but the danger it would pose would no longer be in the arms race or the threat to world peace. The more the war dragged on and exhausted the participants, the closer it brought them to an alliance of imperialists, however distant this solution may have seemed.

Kautsky adhered to an anachronistic conception of capitalism and imperialism. His point of reference seemed to be mercantilism and its colonial system, to which he opposed laissez-faire and free trade. More than a century after the classical economists, he took up their struggle within identical parameters. Furthermore, in his view, capitalism was structured around the binary industry-agriculture, not on other features, such as private ownership of the means of production, individual appropriation of the fruits of production, the generalization of wage labor, and the process of reinvestment on an ever-increasing scale of a part of the profit made. Periodic crises more closely resembled what Ernest Labrousse described as "crises of the Ancien Régime" than capitalist crises, due to the very nature of the process of reproduction of capital.

The upshot was an interpretation of imperialism focused solely on the penetration of less developed or agrarian areas, achieved either through free trade or grabbing of territory. This latter path constituted imperialism, understood as synonymous with colonialism. In addition, the nature of the link between industrial and agricultural countries was ambiguous, sometimes commercial, sometimes based on the export of capital. As for war, it was strictly a phenomenon of colonial rivalries. For Kautsky, imperialism—understood as colonialism—and war did not seem unrelated to capitalism, but they were not intrinsic to it. They simply represented one option, valid only up to the point beyond which they became a hindrance to capitalism. But how could competition between capitalist states driven, according to the author, by the quest for agrarian zones for their industries, fall within the realm of choice? Was it not consubstantial with capitalism?

Kautsky took for granted what needed to be demonstrated, namely that colonialism, military spending, and war were economically harmful to capitalism. That they could result in military disasters, destabilize belligerent states socially, and provoke challenges to political authorities was hardly doubtful. However, the economy, mobilized in favor of military production, could benefit from situations of war, provided military, social, and political conditions allowed it to break out and continue. What did it matter from the point of view of capital accumulation whether the profits were of civilian or military origin? If, as so happened, colonial powers entered into agreements with each other, should it be presumed that they were responding to economic imperatives? The military, social, and political risks of an armed conflict may well have appeared disproportionate to the hypothetical economic benefits.

This is to say that the way Kautsky posed the problem could be completely inverted: the capitalist economy and the competition that distinguished it led to conflict, but extra-economic considerations may sometimes have been a brake. Far from being propelled off its trajectory towards war, a situation deemed unnatural, the economy would then seem to be subjected to conditions of peace. One could rightly search for the causes of the maintenance of peace with as much interest as those of commitment to war. Lenin sharply rebuked Kautsky because the German social democrat recommended peaceful behavior to societies that remained capitalist.

Buried deep in Kautsky's conception was the good seed of Cobdenism, nurtured by confidence in the peaceful essence of liberal and free trade capitalism. Economic competition would not necessarily lead to conflict. Armed expansion and war would even be antithetical to capitalism, although, for a gamut of reasons, they were present within it. In this respect, Kautsky's line of thinking was linked to the liberal analysis which separated capitalism's deep-rooted or permanent mechanisms and the dross, considered as transient and destined to disappear.

Joseph Schumpeter, a firm believer in an ideal and Cobdenian capitalism, a faithful image of its period of free trade, anti-monopoly and pacifist virginity, also considered imperialism and colonial expansion to be absolutely contrary to its nature, an atavism, a warlike relic of a bygone era. Imperialism was an irrational and impulsive policy, hence the negation of the spirit and the true interest of capitalism. It was to be understood as the disposition, even if devoid of objectives, of a state to practice expansion by force beyond any definable limit. A complete aberration, its driving forces did not belong to the present but derived from values that outlasted the precapitalist social structures in which they originated. Over time, the evolution of the modern world tended to cast them aside. No one pleaded better than Schumpeter for the recognition of a radical antinomy between, on the one hand, capitalism as he conceived it and, on the other hand, imperialism and colonization.

Schumpeter shifted the doctrines of classical political economy. Taking his cue from the Manchester school, he borrowed its opposition to mercantilist colonialism and applied it to his era. However, beyond criticizing the old colonial system, the classics were not at all forthcoming on the question of the colonies of their own time. For them, it was an incidental element to their analyses. Schumpeter saw their indifference as reason enough to conclude that there was a fundamental contradiction between capitalism and imperialism.

Although he was not the first to emphasize the sociological, political, and ideological aspects of imperialism, Schumpeter presented one of the clearest versions of this type of interpretation. Without insisting on the influence of precapitalist periods, his epigones pursued the search for the causes of the colonial movement outside the capitalist economy. Raymond Aron, while confining imperialism to the political sphere, detached it from its concrete historical references. Viewed as a millennial manifestation of the nature of men and states, it became a timeless and ahistorical entity. Imperialism was defined as the diplomatic-strategic conduct of a political unit that built an empire by subjugating foreign populations to its rule.

Classical political economy remained the theoretical foundation of the liberal interpretation of imperialism and colonial expansion, especially since neoclassical economics did not deal with the issue. As remnants of mercantilist policy, colonies were said to belong to the past, to be pruned away as complete free trade and international specialization were established for the benefit of all.

At the core of the liberal interpretation lay the general proposition postulating the absence of a direct relationship between capitalism, as a mode of production or a system of economic organization of society, and the process of imposing a multiplicity of servitudes on the international level. It was acknowledged that coercive methods were employed, but they did not derive from any particular economic necessity or logic.

At most there may have been the hope, no less illusory because of its tenacity, for considerable wealth to be accumulated by methods alien to economic science, or even to simple common sense. Forces external to the economy—old-fashioned mentalities, the crowds whipped into a frenzy by nationalists, competition from rivals, Bismarck's freezing of the European geopolitical system, non-collaboration of colonial elites, strategic imperatives, etc.—forced political leaders to abandon or put on hold their principles and to give in to expansionist calls that had no economic basis.

The idea that some economic benefits could have been obtained from imperialism and colonial expansion was by no means certain, but not inconceivable: sometimes a tribute paid by the colonized for their development and modernization, sometimes regrettable concessions to greed. Whatever the case may be, the idea of governing distant lands did not stem from the economies of the metropolises. The aim was not to find in the colonies some way out of a structural impasse from which capitalism suffered. Even if economic attraction might have had a part in a particular acquisition, capitalism was foreign to the phenomenon.

Basically, the liberal conception took for granted that the internationalization of the capitalist economy was an essentially harmonious, peaceful, and beneficial development for all. That having been said, it was up to historians to explain why and how imperialism and colonial expansion disturbed this assessment. In the liberal sense, imperialism had a circumscribed political meaning, namely the action of a metropolitan state leading to the formal subjection of a colonial state, and more precisely, to the constitution of empires (colonization and colonialism). Nothing else and certainly nothing economic.

For liberals, imperialism and colonialism were synonymous. Imperialism was the act of seizing territories by force and ruling them against the will of their inhabitants. Economic expansion as such was not imperialist and did not involve coercive action on the part of the state. Exceptionally, politics may have lent a hand to economics, but only if unforeseen obstacles stood in the way of the smooth running of the latter. Even then, this pairing took place with many reservations and on a strictly occasional basis, given that the state was by its nature foreign to economic activity.

The merit of the liberal conception of imperialism lies in its reminder that the expansion of capitalism is an ancient and continuous historical process, independent of the creation of colonial empires and predating the colonial surge of the end of the nineteenth century. It also postdates it. The reformist and Marxist currents consider that capitalism is first and foremost national and that its internationalization is a novelty to be put down to hitherto unknown internal or structural defects, the definition of which is a matter of controversy. They challenge the generous portrait painted by liberal authors of a capitalism without major flaws, or of an international division of labor established in the best interest of all.

They also refute the cheerful idea that internationalization is usually accomplished in a peaceful manner, with imperialism and colonial expansion being merely an interlude due to the interference of non-economic considerations, and destined to end in an eventual return to the intrinsic logic of capitalism. If, for others, internationalization only occurs at specific moments in history, a phenomenon that calls for explanations, for liberals, only imperialism, understood as colonialism, would need to be explained, and only by political motivations, since internationalization itself is a permanent and non-conflictual dimension of capitalism.

b. Reformism, underconsumptionism, and colonial therapeutics

Even if the demonstrations of the classics, echoed by historians, publicists, and politicians, gave liberalism lasting luster, their anticolonialism never eliminated arguments in favor of acquiring colonies. India, for example, was excluded from British anticolonialist discourse, which in practice was limited to European settler colonies. A de facto colony, Ireland was treated as an integral part of the United Kingdom.

At the same time as classical political economy, a heterodox current was born, less serene, preoccupied by the fear of stagnation or a breakdown of the economic system, perhaps generating social revolution. Although it accepted free trade, it did not consider this doctrine to be a fetish and did not swear by its efficiency. In the eyes of underconsumptionist economists, industrial capitalism suffered from chronic distortions, deriving from the weakness of consumption in relation to production, and materialized in the overabundance of goods for which there was no effective or solvent demand.

Two propositions characterize any underconsumptionist theory of the capitalist economy: first, a state of depression is conceived, not as a phase of the industrial cycle or a temporary conjunction of circumstances, but as a condition towards which the economy tends by its very nature, in the absence of counter-tendencies; secondly, the state of depression is understood as the result of a persistent propensity towards insufficient demand for consumer goods. The fall in the rate of profit is just as predictable as it is for the classics and for Marx, but its cause would be located in the sphere of commodity circulation ("realization") rather than at the stage of production, i.e., of capital itself.

From the rejection of one of the foundations of classical political economy, underconsumptionists ended up revising its corollary, namely the anticolonial or colony-indifferent position. Capitalism being unable to regulate itself—"the invisible hand" —it would find itself prey to serious complications. Colonial expansion was seen as a remedy to alleviate the dysfunction of capitalism and to postpone the crises that accompany its evolution. In this regard, paradoxical similarities emerged. Advocates of colonization, such as Paul Leroy-Beaulieu, Jules Ferry, Joseph Chamberlain, and Cecil Rhodes, put forward the same arguments and were on the same page as the critics of capitalism, in fact relaying them.

Following in the footsteps of Bernard Mandeville, Simonde de Sismondi expressed the theoretical and practical concerns of underconsumptionists who located the cause of economic crises in the unequal distribution of income and the poverty of the working class. He maintained that only increased consumption could lead to increased production, and that in turn consumption could only be regulated by consumer income. Whereas the classics admitted the possibility of transitory overproduction that would always end up being absorbed, Sismondi confronted the classical theory of reproduction with the possibility of lasting overproduction. Whereas classical political economy relied on theory to interpret overproduction/underconsumption as a simple accident, underconsumptionism drew from an undeniable empirical fact the guiding principle of a theory.

Fearing the violent crises caused by capitalist industrialization, Sismondi took issue with productivism, which was harmful both to the producer burdened with unsold goods and to the consumers unable to meet their needs due to lack of purchasing power. An increase in production was only desirable if it was followed by corresponding consumption. In a typical declaration, mingled with the aroma of corporate regulations of yesteryear, Sismondi asserted that he did not ask for products to be scarce, but for them to be scarce enough, compared to demand, so that whoever brought them to the market would make a legitimate profit from selling them. The multiplication of products was desirable when they were demanded, paid for, and consumed; when they were not demanded, the producer could only take a consumer away from a rival's products. Sismondi's perspective and moral judgments earned him the title of outraged economist of small-scale producers battered by the ruthless competition and unlimited accumulation inherent in capitalist-type industrialization.

Malthus also dissented from classical political economy. While Sismondi deplored the unequal distribution of income, the English underconsumptionist worried about contraction in demand resulting from an excessive increase in savings by the wealthy. This was also the concern of his fellow countrymen, such as Lord Lauderdale and William Spence. They rejected the notion of equilibrium assumed by the "law of outlets": the accumulation of capital would only compress total demand in relation to total supply.

Malthus came to advocate for the consumption of non-essential goods by the well-off social classes. The sale of these goods to the only customers capable of acquiring them would be considered socially beneficial waste. The remedy would be all the more appropriate as the state of crisis was always imminent. Indeed, in his vision, the collapse of profits and the rate of return would result from demographic growth, which would lead to a shortage of foodstuffs, higher prices of basic commodities, and, sooner or later, higher wages.

Sismondi and Malthus posed the problem of demand in all its scope, but neither proposed a colonial solution to resolve it. It fell to Robert Torrens, R. J. Wilmot-Horton, Edward Gibbon Wakefield, and other "Colonial Reformers" of the early nineteenth century to advocate colonization to relieve the metropolis of unsaleable goods, overabundant capital, and " redundant" or surplus inhabitants. Colonies would absorb the surpluses that threatened to take society from a depressive condition to a "stationary state," or even to calamitous crisis or social revolution. Gluts and colonies, stagnation and empire, congestion and outlets were now linked in binaries headed toward a promising ideological, political, and historiographical future.

Unlike anti-industry economists, the "Colonial Reformers" did not yearn for the preservation of a precapitalist world threatened with disappearance. They embraced capitalism, accommodated the advent of industrial society, and accepted policies that fostered its prosperity, including free trade—Torrens was an exception on this point —and the abolition of the Corn Laws. Furthermore, while they advocated colonization, being free traders they could not identify with the privileges, prohibitions, and protections of the mercantilist colonial system.

With the "Colonial Reformers," underconsumptionism shifted from a blanket rejection of capitalism to a search for measures to help it out of its predicament. Since social and political transformations were not envisaged, colonization was called upon to make up for the shortcomings of the new society. With its critical extensions excised, underconsumptionism was now primed for use by politicians and business circles.

The "Colonial Reformers" were practical men rather than theoreticians and not exempt of a primary "overpopulationism." Furthermore, their diagnosis of the conditions likely to cause the decline in the rate of profit and stagnation put them at odds with the orthodoxy of the classics, given that they professed the heterodox doctrines of underconsumption, generalized plethora, and surplus capital. Torrens remarked with irony that the school of political economists attributed to capital the hidden quality of creating its field of use and adjusting demand to supply.

The economic difficulties in Great Britain, following the boom which accompanied the Napoleonic wars, the crisis of 1825, unemployment, social unrest, the jacqueries, and intensifying conflicts around demands for reform of the political system, conferred urgency to the search for remedies to the ills of the economy. Hence the appeal of emigration as a way of reducing poverty. Without seriously undermining the Olympian serenity of the classical economists, distress and social unrest ("the condition of England question") at least allowed supporters of colonization to escape marginality and gain a foothold in society.

Wilmot-Horton, under-Secretary of State for the Colonies in 1821, advocated a program of "systematic emigration." He gladly turned to public authorities. With the aim of reducing the number of poor people and the economic burden they represented, the state would lend to parishes by taking their social assistance budget (poor laws) as collateral. The proceeds of these loans would be used for the acquisition of colonial lands by emigrants, who would reimburse the parishes. However, the Wilmot-Horton project was quickly eclipsed by that of Wakefield.

A flamboyant personality, as well as a tireless and unscrupulous publicist, he published *A Letter from Sydney* in 1829 to describe Australia and draw attention to its assets. Wakefield established himself as the leader of a school of thought, rallying to his views Torrens, Bentham, and eminent representatives of political economy, notably John Stuart Mill. His program of "systematic colonization" was surely the most ambitious and the one promoted with the most consistency. Businesses, trades, and professions were clogged; the multitude of unemployed people was a burden on the community. This overflow of population ought to be directed to the colonies to relieve the metropolis. But these migrations had to be "systematic" if they were to succeed and if the metropolis was to derive any benefit from them.

Wakefield himself was methodical in *England and America*, published in 1833. In a chapter on "the art of colonization," he endeavored to argue for his plan. From the point of view of the metropolis, colonization served three purposes: the extension of the market in order to sell surplus goods, the reduction of excessive population, and the enlargement of the "field of employment" of capital. Commercially speaking, importers of industrial products from the metropolis and exporters of foodstuffs would be brought together, which was not always the case in a non-colonial context. As for "overpopulation," Wakefield rejected the objections that classical political economy raised against emigration.

Devotees of a religion all their own, the classical economists worshipped capital. For them, the employment of labor being proportional to capital, and emigration being costly, the latter would reduce capital and, as a consequence, hiring. Wakefield replied that it was not true that all capital employed labor, before adding that idle capital could very well finance emigration without negatively influencing employment. Finally, capital accumulated without finding a sufficiently profitable "field of production" in the metropolises.

It was all the more necessary for colonization to be systematic in that it faced a difficulty that reduced its usefulness. The abundance and cheapness of land in the colonies enabled emigrants to become freeholders. As obstacles to the creation of a working class, they would maintain a shortage of labor, keep wages high and, consequently, discourage the arrival of capital from the metropolis. Moreover, the dispersion and autonomy of the population did not favor the division of labor and economic progress; thus they compressed the demand for industrial products from the metropolis. Since slavery was hardly a practical political or economic solution, Wakefield proposed in *A view of the art of colonization* (1849) the centerpiece of the program of "systematic colonization," namely the theory of "sufficient price."

Raising the sale price of crown land would prevent settler-agricultural workers on relatively long-term contracts from becoming owners too quickly. Private companies would be authorized by Parliament to make sales at floor prices. On the other hand, the sums they accumulated would be used to pay for the passage of new immigrant farm workers. This was Wakefield's "system," one he devoted his life to promoting and applying.

The differences between "systematic colonization" and "systematic emigration" fueled an intense feud between Wakefield and Wilmot-Horton. The former relied on private enterprise to pay for colonization and colonial development, while the latter called on the authorities. Politically, Wakefield would grant self-government to settler colonies; Wilmot-Horton, less sure of retaining their markets, leaned towards a Zollverein of Britain and its possessions with common customs tariffs. Wakefield envisioned colonization as a means of building a society from scratch; hence the emphasis on the selection of young childless couples from all social classes. Wilmot-Horton saw it rather as an ad hoc measure to combat pauperism. His proposal was to make the family with children the basic unit of emigration, an idea which his rival ridiculed as a mere shoveling out of paupers from Britain.

Wakefield clearly intended to reproduce in the colonies the unequal social structure of the mother country, namely the large landholdings worked by a hired workforce. Did this not mean perpetuating overseas the causes of pauperism that had to be fought in Britain? Wakefield was not concerned. Marx would outline in broad terms the methods used to tailor-make a working class. Wilmot-Horton was more inclined to encourage the creation of a layer of independent peasant-owners. This dispute was reminiscent of the debate between Hamilton and Jefferson in the United States.

These proposals reveal the plurality of policies that flowed from underconsumptionist analyses in the nineteenth century. The "Colonial Reformers" would probably not have come out of the fringes if the guardians of the classical creed had not agreed to give them a place, albeit a secondary one, in the world of political economy. Provided that the heretical connotations of the presuppositions of the "colonizers" were removed or silenced, Ricardian doctrine could admit colonization as an accessory process, but not a necessary one, to the maintenance of fundamental equilibria and the pursuit of capital accumulation. If McCulloch remained inflexible, other economists were less so.

In a series of lectures delivered at the University of Oxford in 1839, 1840, and 1841, Herman Merivale in turn endorsed colonization. On several occasions, he addressed the worries of classical political economy regarding the harmful effects of such a movement. Emigration was not to be feared because where Britain established a colony, it established a country of customers. The export of capital would be perfectly bearable. The sums devoted to colonization would remain insignificant and would have no appreciable effect on the prosperity of the metropolis, even if it was admitted that the arguments of the "Ricardian school" were in all respects correct. In any case, this capital would not be wasted since it would be used to create new markets. It had also to be remembered, explained the speaker, showing his classical affinities, that the withdrawal of capital from industry could temporarily be the most effective way of preventing a drop in profits and stimulating accumulation.

Classical political economy was not a definitive doctrine, impervious to surrounding influences. The evolution of John Stuart Mill was significant in this regard. In 1844, he showed himself to be a firm supporter of the "law of outlets" and did not admit the possibility of a general or total halt of sales. Sellers and buyers for the totality of goods had to be in balance. If there were more sellers than buyers for one good, there had to be more buyers than sellers for another. Overproduction was ruled out in terms that Say would not object to: it was production that created the market for production and any increase in production created its own demand. The absence of a permanent surplus of production did not rule out the possibility of a temporary surplus of a particular item or of commodities in general, but the cause would be a lack of commercial confidence and not overproduction.

However, as a witness to the Chartist movement and labor unrest, Mill was less sure than his predecessors of the virtues of laissez-faire policy, state abstentionism, and unlimited accumulation. In 1848, in *Principles of Political Economy*, his main treatise, he laid out the fundamental elements of classical political economy, but accepted that, in order to slow the erosion of the average rate of profit, part of savings be directed abroad, thus helping capital to continue its reproduction. Chapter IV of Book IV dealt with the causes of the tendency of profits to decline towards the minimum. Mill adopted Wakefield's theories on the limits that the narrowness of the "field of employment" placed on the production and accumulation of capital.

Colonization appeared to him to be both a means of redistributing labor, thus relieving one market while meeting the needs of another, and a policy favorable to production, since it led to more efficient use of the world's resources. It had therefore to be understood as a path likely to slow the fall in profits. Colonization would be the best business that the capital of an old and rich country could do.

The economic prosperity of the 1850s and 1860s took the urgency out of thinking about colonization. It was undoubtedly no coincidence that the economic crisis of 1873, the relaunch of the weekly *L'économiste français*, and the publication in 1874 of the famous study-manifesto by Paul Leroy-Beaulieu were simultaneous. A defense of colonization, the book was also a polemic against opinions, deemed too superficial and facile for understanding the usefulness of colonies from an economic point of view. The liberal economist and journalist went along with Merivale and Mill as classical thought evolved towards the approval of colonization. Here was a disciple of the Ricardian-Cobdenian seraglio who did not seem to mind the outflow of metropolitan labor, who gave some credence to the hypothesis of a state of general underconsumption, and who praised privileged markets and reserved jobs in the colonies, ideas which reeked of mercantilist sulfur.

If he did not encourage mass emigration, it was because it could not be a population regulator or a sure cure for pauperism. Natural and spontaneous emigration was no less beneficial to gifted emigrants and to the mother country which relieved itself of disruptive elements. It provided a guaranteed customer base abroad, extended the prestige and the market of the metropolis, opened lucrative careers, and facilitated the gradual increase of the population. Around the world, it led to better use of human resources and took them where they could be most productive.

While agreeing with Say's rejection of the idea of a general congestion or a universal plethora of capital, Leroy-Beaulieu feared that international specialization would make it possible. In that case, the fall in profits would be a very real evil and the stationary state a frightening prospect. By raising interest and profits, the emigration of capital could create new demand and help reduce the danger. While the emigration of capital could take place without colonization, it was better to export capital to one's own colonies than to foreign countries.

Although a doctrinaire liberal, Leroy-Beaulieu did not recoil at the idea of state intervention if it was in favor of colonization. On the contrary, he took an accusatory tone, expressing surprise that those who wished to extend state action internally neglected the colonizing duty of the modern state. Even if Leroy-Beaulieu's book was permeated by heterodox conceptions, it nevertheless retained ties with classical economics. As the depression deepened, it was reissued several times.

Leroy-Beaulieu did not dispel the anticolonial prejudices of liberal economists: witness the loyalty of Frédéric Passy, Gustave de Molinari, and Yves Guyot—the latter two were directors of the *Journal des économistes*, the organ of classical political economy—to the principle of opposition to colonies. Among economists, only Charles Gide yielded to the colonial siren song. On the other hand, outside the profession, there emerged a body of economic beliefs whose links with the work of the classics was very tenuous. It originated mainly with journalists and practitioners, businessmen and politicians, who were increasingly distancing themselves from classical political economy without rejecting it outright.

It all looked as if practice or deeper thinking in economic matters came into contradiction with theory. Had not Sismondi congratulated himself—no doubt prematurely—on the fact that most economists had adopted the analyses of Say and Ricardo but that almost all businessmen acted according to the principles set out by Malthus and himself? Nearly seventy years later, business circles and politicians, faced with the difficulties of the depression, sensed the flaws in capitalism and questioned the economic doctrines which extolled its self-regulating qualities.

Jules Ferry made a famous speech on colonial expansion during the debate of July 28, 1885, in the Chamber of Deputies on the affairs of Madagascar. An apology for its author's policies, it was also a charter of colonialism, albeit without theoretical originality, featuring a set of arguments framed to counteract the influence of classical political economy among his colleagues. Ferry based colonial policy on three foundations. From an economic point of view, the colonies were called upon to correct the well-known underconsumptionist distortions of capitalism. The speaker eloquently enumerated the remedies: asylum for population overflow, investment for excess capital, outlet for surplus goods.

Ferry did not feel the need to demonstrate the structural character of these defects—an effort in no way sanctioned by classical doctrine—as if the reality of the consequences of the economic depression dispensed him from doing so. The burden was on him to explain why their solution should be colonial, this kind of medicine not being part of the pharmacopoeia of the classics. Ferry acknowledged that economists saw the real opportunities in trade treaties but, he observed, Germany surrounded itself with protective barriers and the United States practiced excessive protectionism. The speaker then made a significant connection: where there was political predominance, there was also economic predominance.

The generalization/trivialization of this type of reasoning at the end of the century should not obscure the fact that it was the antithesis of the prescriptions and hopes of the classics, who were still respected in matters of doctrine. From the "humanitarian and civilizing" point of view, Ferry dwelled on the "right" and the "duty" that the "superior races" had towards the "inferior races," a vein destined to enjoy a prosperous future in the arguments for imperialism. Finally, he evoked political considerations such as the need for way stations for the navy and the necessity for France to stand out and maintain its rank in the world.

Observing the general scramble for colonies, Ferry asked in the preface to his *Tonkin et la mère-patrie* (1890)—his mind already made up—if the phenomenon was only a whim, false conceptions such as classical liberal interpretations or, on the contrary, the compelling manifestation of an economic state common to the whole of Europe. Then followed the memorable passage on colonial policy being the daughter of industrial policy. In the presence of abundant capital and accumulating goods, exports were essential and the "field of employment of capital"—a Wakefieldian expression—as well as the demand for labor, were determined by the extent of foreign markets.

By expressing his regret that a methodical and rational "division of industrial labor" could not be established between European producing countries, Ferry delivered in his own way a funeral oration for the Ricardian theory of comparative advantage and its expectations of the advent of an international division of labor beneficial to all. The treaties of 1860 tended towards the ideal that Europe would not have to look for markets beyond itself. But one after another, European countries took the path of industrialization.

It was not enough to raise tariff barriers to defend oneself. Ferry invoked Torrens who argued that the growth in industrial production—"an increase in manufacturing capital"—had to be accompanied by a "proportional extension of outlets abroad," the absence of which would cause a general fall in prices, profits, and wages. The protective system, because it boosted the production of industrial goods, while eliminating outlets, would be a steam engine without a safety valve if it did not have as its corrective and complement a colonial policy worthy of the name.

When Ferry stressed that the decline in profits and the stagnation of wages, due, according to him, to the plethora of capital involved in industry, were not an abstract law but a concrete evil whose consequences were not confined to the economy, one can only presume he was speaking to classical political economy and its followers. Influenced by the underconsumptionists, Ferry was inhabited, like them, by the same catastrophic forebodings.

Social peace appeared to be a question of markets. The economic crisis, which had created unease in society, coincided with a decrease in exports. European consumption was saturated; without new markets abroad, society ran the risk of going bankrupt and setting the stage for a social cataclysm at the start of the twentieth century. Switching gears, Ferry concluded with a vibrant appeal to the pride, taste for competition, and missionary spirit of the French.

If the standard plea of underconsumptionist colonialism reached its finished form with Ferry, it was Joseph Chamberlain, aided by his political longevity, who gave it the widest and most sustained dissemination. The historian James Froude had already made the transition in Britain from the sentimental outpourings of Charles Dilke and the moralistic history of John Seeley to the association of colonial expansion and the economic needs of the mother country. He claimed to be astounded by the indifference of economists towards settler colonies. For them, they were superfluous since free trade had made the whole world Britain's market.

Froude intended to disabuse them because he was convinced that commerce followed the flag—an idea that the classics would have considered heretical. According to him, statistics showed that, in proportion to their populations, the colonies bought three times more British products than foreign countries. Furthermore, faced with its new rivals, the United Kingdom could no longer rely entirely on free trade to retain its markets. It could no longer bet everything on its ability to sell more cheaply than anyone else. It therefore needed secure colonial markets, and a customer base whose rivalry it would not fear.

Chamberlain gave these themes an unparalleled resonance, aided in his task by the deepening of the depression and the intensification of international competition that Britain no longer believed it could sustain with the same ease as in the past. Well before his appointment in 1895 as Secretary of State for the Colonies, Chamberlain was resolutely in favor of expanding the colonial domain. In 1903, he advocated a preferential tariff regime for the Empire.

His arguments are grounded in bona fide underconsumptionism, although his attention was specifically devoted to commercial challenges, such as safeguarding the national market and defending external outlets. Chamberlain added to them an ethnic pride which he displayed unreservedly and not without military intonations. In his countless speeches, increased trade was associated with the multiplication of colonies, combative protectionism and plain bellicosity.

On October 7, 1903, he complained that foreign states were subjecting British exports to exorbitant tariffs, while Britain's markets were being flooded with their products. The latter had to imitate their policy since it ensured prosperity. The object of their protective regime was first to consolidate national industry, then to invade other countries, in particular the United Kingdom which was left defenseless against these economic assaults.

Cobden's hopes could not be better parodied and classical political economy less kindly ridiculed. Everything that the Manchester school disapproved of was praised to the skies by the former Birmingham industrialist. The key to increased trade became the acquisition of reserved markets rather than the abolition of tariff restrictions. It would be up to British politicians to promote trade with the Empire's colonies, even if commercial relations with foreign countries suffered. With irony, Chamberlain noted that the Americans had not acted according to Cobden's assumption that, with the adoption of free trade, they would abandon industry to devote themselves to agriculture, thus meeting Britain's needs.

A historical phenomenon, the agitation led by Chamberlain for the extension of the Empire and tariff reform was distinguished more by its political scope than by its theoretical content. The speaker offered little in the way of an explicit interpretation of capitalism, his concern being to demonstrate the vanity of free trade and of confidence in the doctrine of the automatically optimal distribution of wealth. He repeatedly said that Britain would happily slow down the pace of its colonial acquisitions and refrain from erecting tariff barriers, provided all its rivals did the same.

In other words, it was enough for some to reject the recommendations of classical political economy for them to be invalidated in the eyes of all. The observation that the flow of goods constituted a problem to be solved in capitalist economies permeated all his speeches. The movement driven by Chamberlain nonetheless remained dependent on the economic situation: presented as a way out of the economic depression, the program of unbridled colonial expansion evolved into a program of protectionist tariff reform at a time when the resumption of economic growth removed any sense of urgency. Hence its rejection by the electorate in 1906. More fundamentally, a protectionist program was hampered by the fact that capital invested outside the Empire would suffer the consequences of the raising of tariff barriers against the countries that had received them.

Chamberlain's campaign represented the culmination of a process of integration of underconsumptionist conceptions into elite discourse. Since the inflection given by the "Colonial Reformers," a theory of capitalist imperialism had taken shape. Its proponents were not confined to Europe. In the United States, the fear of plethora had made its way into business circles, which were clamoring in the financial press, notably Boston's *US Investor*, for a consistent policy of imperialist expansion. The development of trusts was claimed to have made the plethora of capital and goods more critical, and the need for outlets more pressing. State power was explicitly called upon to get to work beyond borders to advance reputedly national interests and garner advantages for them. In true underconsumptionist style, the argument put at the service of capitalism reasoning borrowed from its detractors of yore.

An essential reference for the underconsumptionist interpretation, John Hobson's work stood at one of the major crossroads in its history. No one had done more than this author to elucidate the economic motivations behind foreign expansion. The takeover of underconsumptionism that had occurred since the time of the "Colonial Reformers" for the benefit of the defenders of capitalism ended with Hobson, who reappropriated, on behalf of the reforming movement, a theoretical corpus endowed with obvious dissenting properties.

Although it reconnected with the original, Hobson's underconsumptionism did not lead, as did Sismondi's, to the rejection of capitalism. Hobson intervened rather as a nostalgic advocate of free trade liberalism and as a healer of a capitalism afflicted with the underconsumptionist disease. Far from contradicting the Cobdenian theses, openly or in a roundabout manner, as his predecessors did, he regretted that they were discarded and hoped for reforms that would revitalize them. With Hobson, underconsumptionism found its most lucid analyst because he was at the same time a critic determined to render it obsolete.

Too imbued with the liberal faith to accept a magic solution based on colonies, Hobson intended to go to the root of the capitalist disease to prescribe a new treatment against underconsumption. In his book *Imperialism: A Study* (1902), the first general theory of imperialism, diagnosis and cure went hand in hand. From the "Colonial Reformers" to Chamberlain, underconsumptionists believed that capitalism suffered from permanent and generalized structural defects, the mitigation of which depended on the acquisition of colonies. Convinced, on the contrary, that these troubles were temporary and localized, Hobson initiated a shift which set the underconsumptionist school on an anti-colonial course.

The critic turned out to be more forbearing towards capitalism than the apologists. Harking back to the missionary tone of Cobdenism, he replaced the panacea of empire with social reform and income redistribution, medicine all the more beneficial in that it had democratic features. More optimistic than the early underconsumptionists, Hobson saw capitalism as capable of overcoming its deficiencies through a reallocation of income between wages and profits, without having to rely on the false solution of colonial expansion.

From the outset, Hobson drew a clear distinction between colonialism and imperialism. The first was said to be healthy, the second harmful. By colonialism, he meant settler colonies, a natural overflow of the nation. The term "imperialism" was reserved for colonies of exploitation, where no "white" colonization was envisaged. The contrast with colonialism would be fundamental because the subjugation and annexation of inhabited territories entailed a progressive decline in freedom within the empire as a result of the increase in the proportion of subjects deprived of the power of self-government. The enlightened citizen and liberal thinker in Hobson railed against the threat posed by imperialism politically.

The main criticism, however, related less to the political consequences of imperialism than to the economic sources behind its appearance. The imperialist phenomenon referred to the use of state power by private interests for economic gain outside their country. Hobson believed that the commercial benefit of imperialism was minimal. The most significant increase in Britain's foreign trade was recorded with rival industrial countries whose political enmity risked being aroused by the policy of expansion. They were France, Germany, Russia, and the United States.

This behavior was all the more incomprehensible as the commercial value of new territorial acquisitions remained negligible. Imperialism added tropical and subtropical regions to the empire with which trade was weak, precarious, and stagnant. An irrational policy if ever there was one, it was flawed by the fact that the military and administrative expenses incurred by the state outweighed the economic benefits derived. For Hobson, as for the liberals, colonies were a bottomless pit.

Hobson wondered what could have induced Britain to embark on such a deleterious enterprise. The only possible answer was that the economic interests of the country were subordinated to those of certain sectoral interests which usurped control of national resources and employed them for private gain. Even if imperialism had proved to be a bad deal for the country, it was a good deal for certain social categories and national industries. His chapter was titled "Economic Parasites of Imperialism." It was from this angle that the rationality of imperialism emerged, a burden for the nation, but a boon for the minority which fattened on the public windfall.

And Hobson went on to list the individuals who were fleecing society, monopolizing the state, and turning the Treasury into a trough for their own use, namely large companies of all stripes seeking public orders, exporters to annexed countries, shipowners, young men from the aristocracy and the bourgeoisie in search of careers in the armed forces or the civil service, and, above all, financiers behind lending and investments abroad whose growing cosmopolitanism constituted the greatest economic change of recent generations. A product of both intuition and observation, this line of thinking made Hobson the founder of the current which, generally speaking, saw imperialism as a gain for the few and a loss for the nation.

The most important economic factor in imperialism was the migration of capital. Hobson's attention to finance was undoubtedly his main contribution to understanding the phenomenon of imperialism. Income in the form of interest deriving from foreign investments would far exceed profits made from import-export, and grow at a faster rate. As for the United Kingdom's recent foreign policy, it was for him, above all, a struggle to wrest remunerative fields of investment. The country's dependence on overseas tribute would increase and the beneficiaries would not fail to resort to state action to preserve and extend their investments.

Financiers, more dangerous than savers (or rentiers) in Hobson's eyes, enslaved the state. This ubiquitous crowd of speculators, stock market tycoons, bankers, brokers, discounters, syndicators, and promoters formed "the central node of international capitalism." Finance was able to manipulate and direct patriotic sentiment thanks to the influence it exercised on the press and, through it, on public opinion.

What remained to be elucidated were the causes of the cross-border capital rush. Corporate concentration maximized profits by stifling competition: compressed volume of products and high prices translated into increased profits. When these profits sought reemployment as capital, outlets were insufficient because the monopolistic practices of the trusts restricted the need for fresh capital. As savings piled up, the concentration that accelerated their accumulation also deprived them of profitable investment opportunities. Hence the anguished search for an external outlet to absorb the resources that the national economy could not.

Overproduction of goods and surplus capital underpinned the policy of expansion abroad. The "economic taproot" of imperialism was there in its entirety: excessive production not matched by consumption, and plethoric capital in need of advantageous employment. By putting forward this underconsumptionist explanation, even from a critical point of view, Hobson found himself side by side with the business community which used an identical analysis to plead for the necessity of imperialism, touted as the only corrective to an imperfection in the capitalist mechanism.

However, Hobson considered imperialism avoidable, provided the appropriate measures were taken to cure capitalism of its ills. The surpluses of goods and capital that led industrialists and financiers to clamor for imperialism would disappear as soon as purchasing power was raised. Supporting consumption would create demand for industrial products and stimulate investment. Ultimately, redistribution of national income through social reform and political action would be the antidote to imperialism. There was no need to open new foreign markets; national markets were capable of infinite expansion.

Originating in the Cobdenian matrix, Hobson's interpretation seemed tailor-made to satisfy the theoretical thirst of social-democratic groups, the Labor Party, and trade unions. There would be no shortage of means to carry out social reform: higher wages would be accompanied by the return home of surplus goods and migrating capital. Foreign loans were just a way of preserving the unequal distribution of national income. However, this distribution was not irreversible and imperialism was merely a tendency, in no way a universal law.

If Hobson judged capitalism capable of doing without imperialism, Rosa Luxemburg considered imperialist aggrandizement essential to its survival. It was thanks to this expansionism that the capitalist mode of production, riddled with contradictions, managed to perpetuate itself and postpone the moment of rupture preordained by its internal inconsistencies. Luxemburg combined the rejection of capitalism of the early underconsumptionists and the conviction of the pro-capitalist underconsumptionists that the system could not, by its own means, correct its defects. Although a Marxist and a revolutionary, Luxemburg belonged to the underconsumptionist school.

In fact, imperialism was not her initial problem. Her essay published in 1913, *The Accumulation of Capital*, was set in the context of the struggle against Eduard Bernstein's revisionism underway within German social democracy since the end of the nineteenth century. The fact that capitalism had not collapsed and that real wages had increased, led some to revise Marx's analyses on impoverishment in particular, and on the lifespan of capitalism in general. The support that the revisionists gave to the policies of colonial expansion and to imperialism were all the more reason for the revolutionary current to see in the aid of the outside world the salvation plank which had rescued capitalism.

From the outset Luxemburg placed herself on the terrain of theory. She directed her criticism against the proposition that capitalism evolved by its own motion and could, therefore, develop indefinitely. In her view, Marx's schemes of reproduction of social capital were based on an error. How, in a society composed exclusively of capitalists and workers—such was Marx's premise—could the accumulation of capital continue when workers' wages did not allow them to buy the goods they produced and profits were higher than the products that the owners of capital intended to acquire, both for their own consumption and for the replacement of worn out means of production? In the absence of demand for surplus products, investment would dry up, accumulation would end, and capitalism would enter a terminal phase. Since the disposal of the surplus was not possible within the framework of a capitalist society, only recourse to external outlets postponed disaster.

Foreign markets must also be located in non-capitalist regions, otherwise the ills of the exporting society would be encountered again. Luxemburg sought to demonstrate the dependence of capitalism throughout its history on the precapitalist world. This necessary relationship was at the source of the rivalry between capitalist states. Imperialism was therefore the political expression of the process of capitalist accumulation manifested by competition between capitalists for the last non-capitalist territories still available. The continuation of the accumulation process required the integration of new areas. However, as capitalism transformed the universe in its own image and, in doing so, shrank the non-capitalist sphere, it deprived itself of escape avenues and brought closer the time of reckoning, one where no external entity could throw it a lifeline. Then capitalism, having become a closed system plagued by its internal defects, would sink, as socialist thinkers predicted.

A radical underconsumptionist, Luxemburg gave priority to the "realization" of surplus value. The export of capital was, from this perspective, only a means of encouraging the receiving country to order goods from the creditor country. Regarding the problem of markets, critics did not fail to criticize Luxemburg for the narrow bases of her argument. She seemed to overlook the fact that part of surplus value was reinvested in expanding the means of production. Furthermore, the undeniable conjunctures of overproduction only took on apocalyptic overtones if the process of capital accumulation was treated statically. Recognition of its dynamic and continuous character showed that the surpluses of one moment were absorbed in the next in a constant, if not harmonious, movement.

At the root of Luxemburg's misunderstanding lay her attachment, within the framework of Marx's theory, to the model of the simple reproduction of capital. She ignored expanded reproduction through investment in capital goods, one of the specificities of capitalism. Excluding from the outset the possibility of the expansion of the stock of fixed capital led to a predictable conclusion that accumulation, or even capitalism itself, could not continue. And yet they did. Hence the appeal to an external factor to explain a development that ran counter to logic.

In the end, it would be justified to ask why, in the terms of her theory, increased foreign trade should not have the same effect as imperialism. The definition of the latter was severely limiting. Not only was it reduced to the acquisition of colonies, but it postulated their non-capitalist nature. Regions where capitalism predominated were automatically excluded, a choice based on a preference for foreign markets spared from the plethora of capitalist society, therefore likely to act as shock absorbers for its imbalances. Beyond underconsumptionism, the distinctive feature of Luxemburg's interpretation was the affirmation of the absolute necessity of the colonial contribution to the smooth running of capitalism, even if this was only temporary. Were capitalism to impose itself undividedly throughout the world, it would cease to be viable.

Whether underconsumptionism led to a reformist (Hobson) or cataclysmic (Luxemburg) conclusion, it limited demand to the acquisition of consumer goods. It was not until the findings of John Maynard Keynes, published in 1936 but applied after 1945, that a new theory of effective demand was formulated. It is discussed in Chapter 13.

Between liberals who denied the economic interest of colonial imperialism and underconsumptionists who emphasized its economic essence, there was at the turn of the century a nebula of socialists and anarchists representing their respective political or doctrinal currents. In *Le colonialisme* (1905), the Frenchman Paul Louis deplored the search for outlets and fields of investment, but he did not examine the sources of the connection between capitalism and colonial expansion. Some admitted the merits of European expansion in the non-European world with comments that Jules Ferry would have endorsed, although they denounced its consequences. They would have preferred colonization to be peaceful and benevolent, rather than violent.

Most, like Jean Jaurès, Gustave Hervé, or Paul Vigné d'Octon, were detractors of imperialism but, whether they saw it as a manifestation of economic greed or not, their opposition was not based on economic reasoning. They condemned it above all for its dehumanizing brutality and acts of plunder, as well as for the deleterious effect it could have on the political mores of the metropolis, among other things, the strengthening of the influence of the military. None invoked the collective rights of colonized peoples, even though all denounced the mistreatment and abuses to which the colonizer subjected them. In the final analysis, it was a political or moral critique, with no economic foundations and no conceptualization of imperialism.

c. Marxism and imperialism

The influence of Marxist conceptions of imperialism has been so great that their treatment poses a problem. As the obligatory reference point for any discussion on imperialism, especially its economic core, they have dominated the theoretical and historiographical landscape to such an extent that the key ideas which give them their specificity can be assumed to be known. It would be inconceivable, however, to refrain from examining the positions of the current that made the subject a specialty, even an exclusive one. The dissection of a complex and highly developed organism, with ancient antecedents and numerous offspring, is necessary.

Heuristic ambition and concern for the historical framework give explanatory power to the Marxist problematic. Liberals traced back their origins to Smith and Ricardo, underconsumptionists to Sismondi and Malthus. Marxist conceptions are distinguished by the inclusion of imperialism in the very course of the evolution of capitalism. Of a theoretical and historical character, they do not regard as abnormal a phenomenon which appears to liberals to be an unfortunate outgrowth liable to excision, and to underconsumptionists as a birth defect to be tolerated or corrected by a remedy designed to reform the unequal distribution of income. Marxists attempt more than a conceptualization of imperialism; they make it the indispensable analytical grid of the economy, society, and politics of a capitalism fully into the global phase of its history.

Finally, there is the formation of Marxist thought on imperialism. It is constituted by successive additions, because of the need for an understanding of social reality as a whole. Initially, all roads led to Lenin; all revisions were structured in relation to Lenin. Then, after the Second World War, a period of diversity, dispersion, and trial and error began in the face of the evolution of capitalism. From the 1980s, the Marxist conception and the very notion of imperialism faded away in the face of the apparent triumph of capitalism, its transformations, and its globalization.

Marxist conception? Marx had no theory of imperialism. The term is not found in his writings. In the first book of *Capital*, he noted the role of the colonial system in the genesis of capitalism—"primitive accumulation"—and commented harshly on Wakefield's colonizing projects. He wrote detailed articles on the non-European world and on Ireland. Nowhere was there any elucidation or in-depth research into the causes of colonial expansion. Colonization was attributed by Engels in 1895 to stockjobbers for whom the European powers divided Africa and France conquered Tunis and Tonkin.

Like the classical economists and the underconsumptionists, Marx, in the third section of Volume III of *Capital*, detected a downward trend in the average rate of profit. For him, this resulted from the very nature of capital, in particular its "organic composition," rather than from market disorders or the mismatch between overall production and overall consumption. Capital's hidden defect was in its normal movement. In Marxian terminology, the increase in constant capital (the part of capital intended for the acquisition of the means of production) led to a decrease in the rate of profit, with variable capital (the part of capital used to provide the means of subsistence for workers) representing the sole source for the extraction of surplus value (surplus product).

Profit rate = surplus value ÷ constant capital + variable capital

A steady, unchecked downward trend in the rate of profit could only lead to a cessation of economic activity ("the stationary state") and stagnation, for the classical economists; to crisis, for Marxists. Capital would be at a halt, producing no profit. A crisis occurs when there is a surplus of means of production relative to labor power. Then it is no longer possible to generate surplus value at a remunerative rate.

When Volume III mentioned the profitability of capital in the colonies, it did so as an observation. Capital yielded higher rates of profit in the colonies because their lesser development generally translated into higher rates and because the exploitation of labor through slavery or the coolie system was more intense. It was this differential which explained investment abroad, not the impossibility of employing capital in the metropolis.

In a section of Volume III on "surplus capital" and "overproduction of capital," Marx argued that, if capital was exported, it was not because of an absolute impossibility of using it domestically. But investment abroad earned a higher rate of profit. As for foreign trade, it served to lower the price of constant capital (raw materials) or variable capital (means of subsistence), thereby raising the rate of profit (ratio of surplus value to constant capital and variable capital).

The absence of an irresistible pressure to internationalize was notable. Riddled with tension and contradiction, capitalism did not seem, in theory, obliged to allay them by going abroad. Links with the outside world were a fact of life, a reality, rather than the effect of an absolute need of the metropolis. Was it the absence of constraint that explains why Marx left only scattered observations and no theory on the subject? It was clear that, at the level of abstraction where he placed his analysis, capitalism would, conceptually speaking, be able to overcome its economic difficulties all by itself, although at the cost of drastic cures such as crises.

The rise of protectionism, the formation of trusts and cartels, concentration (predominance of large companies), and centralization (mergers of companies) led the Austrian social democrat Rudolf Hilferding to postulate the emergence of "financial capital," the title of his book published in 1910. By this concept he meant bank capital, capital in the form of money, transformed into industrial capital when placed in industry. As concentration required the mobilization of enormous amounts of capital, the role of banks changed. Little by little, they took control of industrial companies, seized production channels, and contributed to the formation of trusts.

From simple intermediaries, they transformed themselves into industrial enterprises, as their assets were immobilized in the productive sector. Having become industrial capital, bank capital gave birth to financial capital, understood by Hilferding as capital at the disposal of banks and employed by industrialists. Financial capital resulted from the banks' takeover of the industry. Compatible with the German model of its time, where four large banks dominated the economy, the concept was less valid elsewhere, either because the merger process was embryonic, or because the large industries were not always under the control of the banks. There was no doubt that large companies multiplied in the United States, Great Britain, and France at the turn of the century, but their capital was of an industrial or banking nature, not "financial."

Monopolization slowed down the decline in the rate of profit. Hilferding believed that it mitigated imbalances and crises within the national economy by introducing an element of planning. In doing so, it transferred tensions to the international level. Sources of raw materials and outlets for goods and capital became the object of intense rivalry between monopolies backed by their respective states. Transposed onto the international stage, competition between national firms translated into competition between states. An aggressive tariff policy, applying combative protectionism, made it possible to raise domestic prices and use surplus profits to subsidize exports and sell on foreign markets at prices below production costs. International agreements could only be truces, given that participants resumed the struggle as soon as they seized an advantage.

The internal consistency of Hilferding's paradigm seemed to have been achieved at the expense of its usefulness as an explanation of the real world. Firstly, it was excessive, and certainly premature, to extrapolate from the amalgamation of capital the coming of organized capitalism. Monopolization did not put an end to tensions, crises, and competition on the national level, as mutations of all kinds brought with them latent threats to acquired positions. Monopoly contained competition, and competition monopoly. On the other hand, shocks between large companies could be cushioned and transferred to smaller companies and independent producers, less able to bear the brunt of crises.

Second, the identification of protectionism and financial capital accentuated Hilferding's penchant for erasing the existence of non-financial capital. Did protectionist policy respond to the wishes and interests of trusts, cartels, and consortia alone? Third, international economic rivalries and the intervention of states to assist their nationals predated the process of monopolization. Furthermore, even after the advent of concentration, non-monopolist capital, as well as banking and industrial capital, still circulated on the international scene and they were not deprived of state support.

Did the association, combination, or union of various types of capital change Marx's analysis and call for the creation of a new concept to complete the categories defined by him? This question must remain at the forefront of any critical presentation of the Marxist conception of imperialism. Hilferding bequeathed, to those of his followers who were not careful, the habit of considering potentialities or trends as accomplished and definitive facts, and as a prism for understanding the present.

The pitfall for Hilferding as an activist was that of exaggerating the pace of change deemed favorable to his cause. Was it not desirable for finance capital to take hold, since it socialized production and paved the way for the abolition of capitalism? Finance capital created conditions for socialism and made the transition easier. It was a short step from there to downplaying or ignoring the competition continuing within the very framework of concentration. Still, Hilferding's attempt to give concentration a theoretical status based on an original type of capital broke new ground and, without providing a concept of imperialism, laid the foundations of the Marxist analysis of the phenomenon.

If Hilferding placed himself on the terrain of the national economy, Nikolai Bukharin turned his attention to the international economy in his pamphlet entitled *Imperialism and World Economy* (written in 1915, published in 1918). More precisely, Bukharin was concerned with the articulation between the global economy and national economies, following the constitution of finance capital. Two parallel processes were at work: on the one hand, capital was internationalizing and spreading throughout the world; on the other, it was nationalized and organized on a national level. This antinomy summed up Bukharin's line of investigation.

The unit of analysis was the world economy, a concept designed to capture the international division of labor and the system of production and exchange relations on a global scale as a coherent whole. This original approach showed the accelerated growth—extensive and intensive—of the world economy, the prodigious increase in production, the rising productivity of social labor, the multiplication of transportation networks, the growth of trade, human migrations, and the circulation of capital across borders.

The formidable development of heavy industry gave particular urgency to the search for raw materials and markets. Exported as interest capital and profit capital, capital took five forms: public loans, equity in companies (purchase of shares or bonds), direct financing of companies abroad, credit facilities, and purchase of foreign shares for resale.

According to Bukharin, the anarchic characteristic of the world economy stemmed from the monopolistic structure of national economies. The internationalization process appeared to be the counterpart of the nationalization process. This was so because the stifling of competition at the national level and the agglomeration of capital, under the aegis of monopolies formed within a national framework, raised competition to an international level. Imperialist policy represented a special case of capitalist competition, namely competition in the era of finance capital.

It was no longer a question of competition between private companies for markets, but of political and military confrontations between groups of national capital on a global scale. National capitalist trusts with colossal resources and the support of their respective states were engaged in an unprecedentedly ferocious struggle to secure raw materials, markets, and spheres of investment. These economic clashes translated into geopolitical conflicts. Expanding economic territory implied subjugating foreign rivals.

Imperialism was the policy of conquest of finance capital. It could have no other policy. An economic structure based on trusts was linked to a specific policy: imperialism. On the one hand, finance capital could not refrain from a policy of conquest and a series of wars was inevitable. On the other hand, this policy of conquest that was imperialism constituted a historically-defined category specific to finance capital.

As the two authors belonged to the same school of thought, the criticisms leveled at Hilferding also apply to Bukharin. The latter's pamphlet, by broadening the main framework of the analysis to a global scale, raised the problem of the causes of the international-ization of capital and that of its consequences. Why was capital exported? Two responses could be gathered from Bukharin's study: the deterioration of the conditions of profitability in the country of origin, and the quest for surplus profits abroad. A drop in the rate of profit and a relative overabundance of capital produced a sort of out-flow of unused masses of capital. The more developed a country, the lower the profit rate, the more intense the "reproduction" of capital, the more powerful was the process of elimination abroad. Conversely, the higher the profit rate, the lower the "organic" composition of cap-ital, the higher the demand for capital, the greater was the retention.

It should be noted in passing that an explanation based on the profit rate differential implied that capital would flow only towards less developed countries, where, in accordance with Marx's analysis, the low organic composition of capital allowed high profit rates. Bukharin rejected this conclusion in his critique of Luxemburg: monopolistic links with developed countries were also a source of profits.

Alongside the thesis of the expulsion of capital abroad coexisted that of the natural movement of capital. Capitalism displayed a con-stant tendency to expand and move beyond its national boundaries. This was part of its essence. Bukharin quoted Marx on the incessant revolutions in the methods of production, the constant depreciation of capital, competition and the necessity, for the sake of conserva-tion and on pain of ruin, to constantly perfect and extend produc-tion. However, spillover across borders should not be understood as an absolute necessity. It was a matter of surplus profit generated by exchange between countries with different economic structures. Plethora was not an immutable limit. The driving force of capitalism was not the impossibility of doing business at home but the pursuit of a higher rate of profit.

The dilemma remained: did capital emigrate out of desperation for profits or in pursuit of additional profits? Bukharin offered a nuanced response. While referring to overproduction and overaccumulation of capital, he recognized, following Marx, that it was above all a search for a higher rate of profit. The export of capital occurred almost throughout the evolution of capitalism, but it acquired an unprecedented importance in his time. Finance capital was the most penetrating form of capital, in need of investing in all parts of the world, provided that profit flowed in sufficient quantity. But, it might be objected, since its inception was this not the very nature of capital?

There remained the question of the consequences of the internationalization of capital. If imperialism was the expanded reproduction of capitalist competition, should the same process of concentration and centralization be expected to take place on a global level as it did within national economies? A single worldwide cartel, the foundation of the peaceful super-imperialism or ultra-imperialism in which Kautsky believed, would be an abstract economic possibility. But, agreeing with Hilferding, Bukharin dismissed it in practice because political and social factors would stand in the way of the very formation of this universal trust.

The trend toward internationalization would eventually gain the upper hand, but only after a long period of bitter struggle between national capitalist trusts. Although conceivable from a theoretical point of view, super-imperialism was unlikely to take shape. Developments did tend towards the constitution of a single, universal trust, encompassing all companies and all states, but so many conflicts and upheavals would arise that capitalism would give way to socialism before that happened.

It is remarkable that a debate with such far-reaching political consequences can be based on something left unsaid. Would the clash between Kautsky and Hilferding-Bukharin-Lenin over the possibility of organized world capitalism have taken place if the two sides did not roughly share a common starting point, namely the conviction that a nationally organized capitalism was a reality? Monopolization must be deemed absolutely antithetical to competition for the theme of universal trust to be accepted as relevant. Confronted with the logical but unrealistic conclusions that derive from this line of reasoning, Bukharin and Lenin drew a distinction between the possible and the achievable. The national economy, which the long march towards monopolization did not transform overnight into a mass of concentrated and centralized capital, deserves the same finesse. The clustering of capitals on a national basis and their clinging to state power do not necessarily mean their fusion.

While Lenin integrated, synthesized, and systematized Hilferding's ideas on finance capital, as it was constituted in Germany, and Hobson's on the export of capital by Great Britain, he reworked and modified them, so much so that his conception of imperialism stood apart, both in terms of content and impact. It was set out in the brochure entitled *Imperialism, the Highest Stage of Capitalism*, published in 1917. Like Bukharin, Lenin wrote his manuscript during the Great War—in 1915 for the first, 1916 for the second. More than Bukharin, Lenin was primarily concerned with the significance of the conflict and the collapse of the Second International. He strove to demonstrate that the war was imperialist—not one of national defense—and that it was determined by the structure of the economy. He argued that economic conditions rendered aspirations of peace illusory, leaving only revolution as the means to end imperialism, which was responsible for the war. The booklet was an intervention in a political context, not an abstract study.

Tsarist censorship forced him to avoid overtly political analysis. However, the economic causes of the war and its political consequences were detailed with such clarity that the political conclusions were compelling. Rather than a scholarly treatise, Lenin produced a "popularized essay" intended to enlighten and influence socialists and workers whom he considered misled by their representatives. The economic statement underpinned an intervention bearing on the politics of the European socialist movement. The target was those—in particular Kautsky and the representatives of the late Second International—who relied on pacifism by diverting attention as much from the structural character of imperialism as from the revolutionary path to defeat it.

In the first four sections, Lenin arranged the empirical data he collected on the economy into an explanatory framework that Hilferding would have approved of. The development of industry and the concentration of production gave rise to monopolies. It was "a general and fundamental law of the present stage of development of capitalism." Lenin put forward a date for this structural change. For Europe, it was at the beginning of the twentieth century that the new capitalism definitively replaced the old.

Inaugurated during the depression of 1873-1895, cartelization took off after the crisis of 1900-1903. With cartels becoming one of

the bases of economic life, capitalism was transformed into imperialism. Unlike Hilferding and Bukharin, Lenin did not seem to believe
that monopolization extinguished competition. Far from eliminating crises, the monopoly created in certain industries increased and
worsened the chaos inherent in capitalist production as a whole. In
fact, the issue was less about monopolies than about oligopolies. The
penchant for the term "monopoly" was due to the desire to conceive of
the economy and of production as already organized, even socialized,
therefore ready for the advent of socialism. While it prolonged the life
of capitalism, imperialism was a terminal and pre-revolutionary stage.

Given that imperialism was not a conjunctural policy but a stage of
capitalism, the elimination of imperialism required the end of capitalism. At the same time, the political strategy took shape: imperialism
led to war, which is the antechamber of revolution. As with the other
theorist-activists of his time, the topics Lenin addressed and analyzed
were always imbued with politics and led to practical conclusions.

Banking concentration was complemented by close links between
banks and industries. The outcome was merger or interpenetration
of banking capital and industrial capital, and the constitution of
finance capital. Hilferding's definition failed to satisfy Lenin because
it overlooked the fact that concentration gave rise to monopolies.
The accumulation of capital having reached immense proportions,
its export ensued. Capitalisms had distinctive features: the old one,
where free enterprise reigned, exported goods; the new, where monopolies dominated, exported capital. The export of capital began in
the middle years of the nineteenth century, before the emergence of
finance capital and monopolies, but its preeminence since the end of
the century was well established.

Lenin assigned a central role to concentration and echoed
Hobson's analysis on the multiplication of monopolies which leave
few opportunities for investment and the surpluses of capital in search
of employment which went abroad. Monopolies, capital exports, and
colonial expansion were linked. Clearly aware of the possible consequences of this interpretation, he anticipated reformist solutions, such
as income redistribution. He declared the modernization of agriculture and the improvement of living standards for the masses to be
inconceivable under capitalism. Contrary to all expectations, Lenin
leaned towards underconsumptionism since he excluded investment

and implied the generalization of stagnation ("overripeness"). This was the only time Lenin put forward a cause for the export of capital. Nothing in the previous writings of this implacable critic of Russian populists foreshadowed this tangent.

Nevertheless, the use of the plethora explanation necessarily led to the underconsumptionist camp. This drift did not invalidate the thesis on the permanence of capital exports: migratory flows continued even after the Keynesian-inspired transformations and the establishment of measures to support effective demand. No causal link appeared to exist between national living standards and international capital exports.

For Lenin, the emphasis on monopolies was intended to demonstrate that revolution would be the solution to imperialism and war, rather than the ultra-imperialism (or super-imperialism) of Kautsky which left open the possibility of reconciliation and good understanding between capitalists. The confrontation between national capitals ceased to be a circumstantial phenomenon and became inescapable if it was anchored in a new stage of capitalism, that of monopolies. The latter took possession of the production in their respective countries and divided up the world.

The world economy was undergoing divisions and redistributions according to the clashes and truces that arose between the giant companies that entered the fray. Any idea of stable and lasting agreement, the basis of Kautsky's ultra-imperialism, had to be discarded because finance capital and trusts did not lessen the differences between the pace of development of the various elements of the world economy; rather, they widened them. Besides, a monopoly could never completely suppress competition on the world market for a long time.

Lenin drew a parallel between the economic division of the world by capitalist groups and its territorial partition by the great powers. World colonial policy was going through an original epoch, closely linked to the most recent stage of capitalist development, that of finance capital. This far-reaching postulate called for a close demonstration. Lenin suggested that finance capital was at the origin of colonial conquests because it emerged at the same time as the acquisition fever of the end of the nineteenth century. The role of non-cartel companies, trading companies, and non-financial capital is not taken into account. The transition of capitalism to its monopoly stage, that of finance capital, was said to be linked to the intensification of the struggle for the partition of the world. As the world was already divided up before the beginning of the twentieth century, the date Lenin proposed as the beginning of the era of monopolies, the issue was now one of redistribution and it would reach its climax with the First World War.

His deduction was based on the widespread idea that free competition and anti-colonialism went hand in hand; a colonial thrust could only be the manifestation of the establishment of monopolies. The criticism addressed to Lenin to the effect that capital did not go to the colonies in large quantities or that the flows were not in harmony with the territorial divisions is not very convincing insofar as (conflictual) redistributions brought political situations into line with ever-changing economic realities. A metropolis that neglected its colonies would soon lose them to more enterprising rivals.

The definition of imperialism as a monopoly stage of capitalism is well known: monopolies play a decisive role, financial capital is born, the export of capital takes on particular importance, international monopolies share the world, and the great powers divide the globe between them. Equipped with these notions, Lenin vilified ultra-imperialism and Kautsky's hopes of seeing understanding between the belligerents and a new capitalist but peaceful stage, which would adjourn the prospects of revolution. He attributed the workers' patriotism to the harmful influence of a higher stratum corrupted by the excess profits of the monopolies. Under his pen, imperialism appeared as an inevitable and final phase in the evolution of capitalism, the prelude to a revolution seen as imminent.

It is striking to note how often clear-cut statements were immediately qualified. The impression is one of a balancing act between an understanding of the complexity of reality and an awareness of the inadequacy of the theoretical instruments available. Was imperialism historically determined? Lenin recognized the absurdity of quibbling over dates. Did monopolies take over? Yet they did not eliminate competition. Was the export of capital a feature of finance capital? Lenin took into account all types of capital in his totals. Was capital exported to the colonies, where profit rates were higher? He knew that large companies also moved it from one developed country to another. Did imperialism breed rot, parasitism, and stagnation? That did not rule out rapid, albeit uneven, growth. Was the "labor aristocracy" bribed by imperialism, a new stage of capitalism? Lenin quoted Engels evoking the same phenomenon of co-optation in 1858.

In other words, the effort to link international behavior to domestic causality is a delicate undertaking, fraught with the risk of rigidity and univocity. Lenin countered this by multiplying reservations and pointing out counter-tendencies. Intending to rest his demonstration on an unshakeable footing and to convince, against Kautsky, that the war was imperialist (not in defense of the homeland) and that imperialism was a necessity and not a choice, a contingency, or an epiphenomenon, he linked it to a new type of capital. Was finance capital so different from non-financial capital that it deserved a distinct theoretical status? Given that it was observable only in Germany, was it justified to extrapolate from a specific case, however illustrative it may have been, and to set it up as a general model? Had it transformed capitalism to such an extent that it was necessary to define a new stage of development? Did the structures of capitalism have to be altered for foreign expansion, economic appropriation and war to occur?

If contemporary socialists were convinced of this, it was because they subscribed to a surprisingly charitable assessment of early nineteenth-century capitalism. Respectful of free competition, it was believed to have been peaceful and anti-colonialist. The aura of classical political economy and the influence of the speeches of political leaders were palpable. However, the facts belied these received truths. Although the great powers avoided a general European war, they clashed militarily in 1853-1856, 1859, 1866, 1870 and almost did so in 1827 and 1840. Peace had less to do with the intrinsically peaceful nature of free trade than with the international geopolitical configuration.

The intensification of rivalries, the rise of tensions, and the multiplication of confrontations between the powers at the end of the nineteenth century challenged the socialists. Did they result from a change in the structure of capitalism or from capitalism itself? The war of 1914 involved more participants, more industrialized economies, larger businesses, mass armies, and heightened warmongering. But was it due to a new stage of capitalism and the intervention of a new type of capital—finance capital, in this case—or to the fact that the expansion of national capitalisms could only be achieved through the subjugation of others? The First World War was inseparable from capitalism, but capitalism was not solely financial.

As for colonization, it had been uninterrupted since the fifteenth century. Reflecting the official discourse, socialists of the early twentieth century did not distinguish between British settler colonies and colonies of economic exploitation. They pointed out that at the zenith of free competition, between 1840 and 1870, British political leaders were hostile to the extension of colonial policy and saw the detachment of the colonies as useful and inevitable. They omit that there was never any question of letting go of the economic colonies already held or of granting them self-government, an arrangement reserved only for settler colonies. As the end of the century was marked by a fever for the acquisition of colonies, they reasoned that expansionism was the action of a new kind of capital embodied in imperialism, not of capitalism per se.

Basically, socialists all too easily accepted the claims of the ideologues of liberalism, then of imperialism, and, in concert with them, conflated historical circumstances and deep nature, opportunity and essence. If, as Bukharin wrote, liberalism was the policy of industrial capital, then imperialism had to proceed from another type of capital. From the moment a precise conduct, rather than an orientation, was inferred from structures, it became difficult to avoid theorizing new structures to understand each turn in the course of events.

Socialists paid a heavy price for letting themselves be influenced by official ideology. Lenin had to deal with an atmosphere or a general state of mind that tended towards reductionism, even if the nuances and reservations followed to refine categorical assertions. Since free trade, conceived as a peaceful program, was accepted as the modus operandi of capitalism, international clashes could only represent a qualitatively new phase, completely at odds with the previous one. The pairing of industrial capital and competition, synonymous with free enterprise, was succeeded by the pairing of finance capital and monopoly, an inverted image of the other. In a way, each type of capital would have its own nature: industrial capital would be considered non-confrontational; financial capital would be inclined towards domination. Territorial expansion and armed competition had to be considered incompatible with industrial, banking or commercial capital—a surprising but implicit acquittal—to make them a specific trait of finance capital.

In the debate between them, Lenin and Kautsky shared the same a priori view on the diametrically opposed stages of competition and monopoly. Given that a structural break was postulated between a peaceful era and a warlike era, the disagreement boiled down to the possibility (for Kautsky) or the impossibility (for Lenin) of returning to this lost era of peace. In search of what never existed, Kautsky's ultra-imperialism created a new phase of imperialism inspired by the supposedly harmonious past. Lenin ruled out any new phase of imperialism but admitted periodic truces and agreements. However, these could be for extended periods. In a peculiar twist of history, the revolution and the Soviet state in which Lenin was more than a spectator contributed not a little to this result.

What should be retained from Lenin's interpretation? More than the criticism of certain points would suggest. The effort to take into account in a single model, among other things, the internationalization of capital, the increased interweaving of national economies, the rooting of imperialism in the mechanisms of the capitalist economy, the relationship between political and economic action on the international scene, confrontations between imperialist powers, and colonial expansion was a tour de force. His brochure was a reminder of the interrelations between phenomena, regardless of the divergences which may arise with the author's assessments. As a Marxist, Lenin's global vision and quest for coherence led him to look beyond appearances and to extend his gaze to the imperialist process as a whole.

A political leader as well as a theoretician, he was the first to link opposition to imperialism on the part of the peoples who endured it with opposition to capitalism in capitalist countries. What seemed self-evident after him and because of him was not so for dominant opinion, on the right and on the left of the political spectrum, which believed that imperialist expansion was beneficial wherever it was deployed. Whatever its limits and the non-generalizable or outdated nature of some of the situations described, Lenin's pamphlet remains the essential reference, the one which sets the standard for the treatment of the subject, and the most powerful analysis of imperialism ever produced, because it combines comprehensiveness and conciseness in a text where the theoretical and historical dimensions, the abstract and the concrete, mutually support each other. All themes relating to imperialism were taken into account.

Three elements are worth highlighting. A decisive contribution of Lenin is the understanding of imperialism as a phenomenon going beyond colonialism and empires. Even if, in his time and sometimes in his pamphlet, the two realities were mixed, the difference was clear, insofar as imperialism subjugated countries that may be formally independent. This conceptual advance would take on its full meaning after the decolonization of the second half of the twentieth century. Secondly, the recognition of the precedence of the export of capital over the export of goods is a major and indispensable contribution to the study of imperialism. Hobson's inspiration is unmistakable, but the observation of this novelty on a world scale and the attempt to embrace all the facts relating to it, are Lenin's.

Finally, one fragile aspect of his thesis is nevertheless fruitful. Lenin formulated a severely restrictive definition of imperialism—a stage of capitalism dominated by finance capital, as Hilferding understood it—leaving many historical and contemporary situations uncovered. If exported capital was non-financial, the concept would lose its relevance for more than one case of domination. However, the emergence of finance capital was indeed a novelty, as was the fact that the export of capital of all kinds was irreversibly overtaking the export of commodities.

Retrospect and perspective

Neomercantilist imperialism led to two world wars, the ancestor of which was the Seven Years' War (1756-1763). The First World War shook the system, the Second brought it down. These two conflagrations put an end to the primacy of European metropolises and to the colonial imperialism—mercantilist, free trade then neomercantilist— that they engendered, and which has been part of their history since the end of the fifteenth century. They ruined each other, making it impossible for all of them to maintain their individual or collective supremacy. As it took away their empires, post-1945 decolonization sealed the fate of this type of capitalist imperialism active for more than half a millennium. It consisted of the acquisition of as many overseas territories as possible to make them a reserved domain and a springboard for further acquisitions. The world was divided into empires warring to expand and weaken others by amputating their territories and colonies. This was so because the growth of some could only be achieved at the expense of others.

Primacy went to the power which imposed itself through a process of natural selection, in accordance with a sort of international Darwinism. Everything was decided within the Atlantic world. From Portugal to Spain, from the Netherlands to England, hegemony belonged to the power which won by its economic capabilities, by the wealth of its colonial empire, and by the verdict of arms. After a period of commercial efficiency or economic productivity in its early youth, each entered a phase of "maturity" or rentierism, during which it took advantage of situational rents and lived beyond its means thanks to external inputs.

Last in line, England had to overcome the Netherlands and France by military means. Dominant since the eighteenth century, Britain established its primacy thanks to its navy and the industrial revolution. If the world was fragmented into imperial blocs, their expansion and the development of capitalism broadened the scale of the international economy. In the nineteenth century, Britain was the first power in a position to lay the foundations of a world market and an international economy centered around itself.

However, although it had the means to integrate less developed countries, especially non-European ones, into its economy, it could not place rival metropolises in a position of subordination and incorporate their economies into its own. Its capitalism was neither concentrated nor multinationalized enough to link up with others and assume the role of center of globalized production. European economies remained national, and none was yet capable of rising sufficiently above the others to establish and govern a global capitalism. The international system was multipolar, even in the era of British preponderance.

Great Britain exercised an ascendancy, not tutelage, over the others. If, in the past, European powers suffered defeats, they retained their autonomy even after territorial losses, colonial relinquishments, or the payment of indemnities. The novelty of the 1945 context lay in the fact that metropolises were now in a position similar to that of overseas possessions and could be integrated into a more encompassing imperialism, emanating from a more evolved capitalism. Such preconditions were conducive to the advent of a global economy and universal imperialism without colonies, formal empire or imperial bloc, as well as their political corollary, unipolarity.

PART IV

Forced incorporation: postcolonial imperialism in the present

The Second World War, as much for imperialism as for other issues, was a more important historical turning point than the First. While the German challenge was repulsed in 1914-1918, British primacy was not consolidated. Left in abeyance, the duel resumed two decades later. The Anglo-German confrontation of the two world wars unfolded within the framework of neomercantilist imperialism, pitting two powers of equivalent size against each other. By force, each tried to gain control and reserve for itself as much territory as possible, in Europe and overseas, while compressing the space ruled by the other.

The French, Dutch, Belgian, Spanish, Portuguese, and Japanese empires also had a colonial base. This had been the case since the fifteenth century. The United States was proportionally the least colonial of the lot. None of these empires were global, however extensive their possessions. Each could only grow at the expense of the others. The logic was neomercantilist, similar to that which prompted inter-European wars for more than four centuries, notably the Seven Years' War (1756-1763).

The Second World War marked a turning point in the history of imperialism and capitalism. In the clash between Great Britain and Germany, the winner was neither one nor the other. There were two, the United States and the Soviet Union, and these "superpowers" were of an entirely different dimension. Each was distinguished by its orientation. The United States had been a contender for global primacy since the late nineteenth century. Even before its entry into the Second World War, the influential press magnate Henry Luce titled the February 17, 1941 editorial in the mass circulation magazine *Life*, "The American Century." The United States took advantage of the exhaustion of European powers in two world wars to rise to the top. Its assets allowed it to go beyond neomercantilism, a system territorially defined with a metropolis and overseas possessions, and to encompass the entire world in a new type of imperial project.

Unlike the European powers, whose means were more modest, the United States embarked on the path of controlling the colonized regions as well as Europe and Japan. It did not limit itself to the old practice of taking colonies from the vanquished; it added control over the vanquished themselves, hence the originality of this historical phase. An imperialism with a planetary vocation took shape. The conditions were in place for the establishment of a world empire.

With the exception of the limited case of the Anglo-Portuguese relationship of the eighteenth century and the short-lived Napoleonic Empire, no great power had subordinated other powers with a view to integrating them permanently in its economic or military system. The aim was not to weaken or bully them, as had been done for a long time, but rather, in the long term, to bring about the interpenetration of their economies with its own. For the first time in the history of capitalism, one power was in a position to command others in every respect. Of course, forms had to be observed and an overly heavy-handed domination avoided, all the more so as the USSR set itself up as a counter-model and a counterweight.

The other "superpower" was a fundamentally atypical state, from its birth in 1917 to its victory in 1945, including its history during the intervening decades. The socialist revolution was expected where capitalism and the industrial proletariat were strongest, in Germany, and secondarily in Great Britain or France. As this did not happen, Lenin innovated by analyzing world capitalism as a chain that can be broken at its weakest point. The socialist revolution would begin in Russia, a country where capitalism was lagging behind and the proletariat was a minority, but with a change in the strategy: the proletariat would have the peasantry as its ally. This revolution would only be the trigger for the socialist revolution in the most advanced capitalisms, which would pull the new Russia in its wake. The socialist revolution was always understood as being worldwide. Here appeared the first voluntarist act.

History contradicted expectations and the revolution in industrial Europe did not occur. This would have a major consequence for everything that followed in Russia, China, and elsewhere: wherever revolutions succeeded, the first task would not be the establishment of socialism but development, catching up, and modernization, i.e., the prerequisites and elementary conditions to the establishment of socialism. Russia was isolated, exhausted, and in ruins after the First World War, a civil war, and the intervention by fourteen foreign armies to bring down the Bolshevik regime. Against all odds, Soviet Russia was victorious. Second act of voluntarism. The country was still isolated and its future bleak. The strategic decision to build social-ism in Russia alone meant industrializing an immense agricultural country, a titanic undertaking carried out in a short period of time and at very great cost. Third voluntarist act.

The Nazi threat loomed, more deadly than the previous foreign intervention. The USSR won. Fourth act of voluntarism. It was the unexpected winner of the Second World War. Nothing could have suggested that this country, born of a backward Russia shattered by the First World War and the civil war, industrialized belatedly and by forced marches during the 1930s, would manage to avoid subjugation to Germany and prevail against a seemingly invincible war machine. As of 1942, despite the loss of vast territories, it was producing twice as many tanks as Germany and one and a half times as many aircraft. Since 1917, the USSR, a singular entity in a world that did not resemble it and which barely tolerated it, had been the result of daring, even desperate, bets, because conditions were fundamentally unfavorable to it.

The triumph of the USSR, at the cost of untold sacrifices and destruction, did not make it a competitor for world hegemony. It had neither the means nor the ambition to go in that direction, its logic being territorial, classic, and confined to what directly affected it. But it was able to exclude itself and Eastern Europe from the globalist aims of the United States, putting a third of the planet beyond the latter's reach. Taking the USSR head-on militarily would have entailed enormous cost, with no clear prospect of success. The presence of the USSR made the goal of a world organized according to the operating rules of capitalism headed by the United States unattainable. It also contributed to the detachment of colonial possessions from the European powers.

Their demotion in the wake of the two world wars was coupled in short order with the dissolution of their colonial empires. The overseas nationalists who opposed them since the nineteenth century witnessed them being undermined by the European "civil wars" of 1914-1918 and 1939-1945, resulting in the defeat and the downfall of several European metropolises. After the Second World War, these metropolises faced a new type of resistance organization, based on mass movements and broad social coalitions, supported by combatants practicing guerrilla warfare. The emancipatory essence of the anti-Nazi war in Europe blew a wind of rejection of domination everywhere.

The old pride in flaunting colonial assets gave way to an embarrassment at having colonies under one's supervision. Underdevelopment, the low standard of living, and the poor record in health and education made it necessary to justify one's presence overseas to world opinion. Added to this were the natural opposition of the socialist USSR to capitalist colonialism and the reservations of the United States with regard to the obstacles posed by European possessions to the advent of a world market open to all, particularly itself.

In the South as in the North, what was at stake was the establishment of capitalism or socialism, as well as political regimes in line with one or the other. Most overseas dependencies, whatever their legal status, wrested their independence in the two decades following the Second World War. Decolonization was one of the major trends of the postwar period. Control will then become indirect and informal, without territorial acquisition, neocolonial according to its critics. The postcolonial era began and that of neomercantilism came to an end. For the first time since the establishment of the Portuguese and Spanish empires in the sixteenth century, colonies were neither the basis nor the dominant feature of imperialism.

Palestine remains a glaring exception to decolonization. There are two remarkable features pertaining to Zionist-Israeli colonialism: first, the anachronism of its emergence at the very historical juncture when colonialism was losing whatever acceptability it had and entering its terminal phase; second, the fact that it was the crudest form of colonization, namely settler colonialism, implying the dismemberment, displacement, and replacement of a native population. Settler colonialism reared its head at the very time decolonization was getting underway. Its persistence and the full-fledged sponsorship, support, and armament by Western states underscore the fact that advanced capitalism and present-day postcolonial imperialism are compatible with the most primitive species of colonization, enforced as it is by everything from segregation/apartheid to ethnic cleansing, collective punishment, mass bombing of civilians, war crimes, crimes against humanity and genocide. Their predecessors, mercantilist and neomercantilist imperialism, showed the way, presiding over extermination in the Americas and in Namibia, slavery in the Atlantic economy, forced labor in the Dutch East Indies and the Belgian Congo, massacres in India and Sudan, collective punishment and concentration camps in South Africa and Kenya, and more. Uninhibited violence has historically been the lifeblood of settler colonialism since its objective is more to dispossess and disperse a subject population than to just exploit it. The colonization of Palestine is a vivid reminder that modern imperialism can be in a symbiotic relationship with primal colonialism. Given that interests converge, Western-style liberalism is capable of partnering with systems that negate the principles it claims to profess, all of which requires constant exertion to paper over or draw attention away from the contradictions.

Before 1945, imperialism was embodied in a few powers subject to a hierarchy that had the handful of the most industrialized countries at the top. After 1945, the gap between the United States and the others was such that the alignment changed. Only one power reigned supreme over imperialism, the others being reduced to the rank of regional sub-imperialisms headed by the United States (Great Britain, France), or even downgraded outright (Italy, Netherlands, Belgium, Spain, Portugal). The vanquished, Germany and Japan, were under United States tutelage. There was a transition from several specimens of imperialism to a single one, *e pluribus unum*, one might say.

The history of post-1945 imperialism was that of the quest for hegemony over the entire globe, an objective beyond the means of neomercantilist imperialism. Although close, it has, however, not been reached. Opponents of different stature as well as the project's inner deficiencies stood in the way. Soviet power, unexpectedly generated by the Second World War, became the primary obstacle to overcome. It obliged the United States to lift up its German and Japanese enemies

and to spare the British and French allies whom it intended to supplant. The presence of the USSR was one of the factors that helped
prevent total subjugation of Western Europe and Japan and favor a
rise in living standards in the West as a way of warding off the possibility of revolution. A united "free world" had first to be stabilized
against the internal ferments of socio-political unrest, to be able to
confront "communism."

Various reasons excluded wars between Western powers: American
superiority was overwhelming on all levels; wars of great magnitude
generated revolutions; the United States needed its allies as much as
its former enemies to confront the USSR, a top priority; the West
faced the emergence of a Third World up in arms against imperialism
and, later on, independent. The global scale of United States capitalism, the integration of competing capitalisms, the Cold War, and
decolonization welded the countries of the transatlantic bloc. The
standardization of their elites, who became stakeholders in the same
framework, facilitated coordination.

Initially successful, the operation came up against the fact that the
economic system was running out of steam in the early 1970s. Getting
it back on track was the new priority. As it turned out, the crisis in
the "communist world" was even more serious and it was dismantled.
With the path finally clear, the march towards the globalization of
imperialism could resume and be accelerated. New obstacles then
arose: economic crises in globalized capitalism, that of 2008 being a
major one, and the re-emergence of states resistant to Americentric
globalism. Russia rose from the ashes of 1990-1991 and China, now a
"workshop of the world," dared to act on its own behalf. In the name
of national sovereignty, Russia and China contested United States
unipolarity, unilateralism, and exceptionalism, in other words the
universal imperialism to which the United States aspired.

CHAPTER 13

Imperialism during the thirty-year economic boom (1945-1973): hegemonic relay and decolonization

In the aftermath of the war, the international landscape was full of contrasts: absolute primacy of the United States in the Western camp, but appearance of a socialist camp beyond American control, and effervescence in the colonial world. In all three cases, the situation was unprecedented. The establishment of United States world hegemony required that all tasks be carried out simultaneously and they were, in general, interrelated. Confronting the USSR went hand in hand with the anti-communist struggle in Western Europe. Policies to prevent Western countries from tipping over to socialism were a prerequisite for their integration into the American sphere. The deployment of the United States variant of imperialism highlighted its particular features and the weight of new circumstances arising from a world divided along ideological lines.

a. A new hegemon

A simple survey revealed the privileged situation of the United States. Its GDP more than doubled between 1939 and 1945, despite, or rather because of, the war. It increased its production of aircraft from 6,000 in 1939 to 100,000 in 1944. By the end of the conflict, its supremacy was complete; the imbalance was outrageous. It was clearly in the lead in all areas of the economy: industry, agriculture, finance. It dominated the most advanced industrial sectors. Its companies were the largest, most modern, most productive, best organized, and best suited to mass production. It succeeded where interwar European capitalism failed: combining mass consumption (Fordism) with mass production of standardized, mass-produced products (Taylorism).

In 1946, the United States accounted for half of the world's GDP and three-fifths (two-fifths in 1939) of the world's industrial and mining production: steel, aluminum, ships, planes, automobiles, oil, coal, synthetic rubber, textiles. It held two-thirds of the world's gold stock. The dollar was the only true international currency. The United States was the only country with goods to export, and therefore the only one able to trade internationally. Two-thirds of the world's merchant fleet was American.

The United States was the belligerent that had suffered no material damage on its territory. The Second World War was a boon to its economy. In the eyes of a world ravaged by war and poverty, the "consumer society" (or "affluent society") and the American way of life looked like a paradise on earth. Relatively high standards of living, prosperity, spacious houses, consumer durable goods (automobiles, stoves, refrigerators, electrical household appliances, televisions, telephones), and ordinary consumer goods were the stuff of dreams in the rest of the world.

To mass production and consumption, the United States added mass culture, an object of fascination in Europe and elsewhere, so astonishing in its strangeness, its accessibility, its simplicity, and its liveliness. Culture was part of consumerism. The United States authorities did not hesitate to impose the importation of Hollywood films as tools to impregnate minds with an attractive and desirable model, while hoping to rally support for the Cold War. Inspired by advertising and marketing for commercial purposes, propaganda through seduction contrasted with the old, hectoring, assertive, and overbearing style. More than ever, cultural imperialism in the form of "winning hearts and minds" was a component of imperialism itself. Naturally the cultivation of pro-Americanism had as a predictable consequence the correlative extension of anti-Americanism.

In Europe, the picture was very different. To be sure, a surprising proportion of productive equipment escaped destruction and bombing, and overall production did not collapse everywhere.

GDP indices
(1913 = 100)

	Germany	France	Britain	Italy	United States
1939	166.2	139.0	133.8	161.8	166.8
1945	134.2	70.7	154.5	91.5	317.9

Nonetheless, the fact remained that material losses (factories, infrastructure, buildings, dwellings) were considerable. Coal, fuel, basic necessities, and everyday consumer goods were lacking. Food shortages affected a population that was poorly housed, poorly heated, and poorly clothed. Prices soared, inflation spiraled out of control, and currencies lost value. The USSR was even more tested. In addition to the loss of twenty-seven million of its inhabitants (250,000 for the United States), it suffered enormous destruction, as much as all the other belligerents combined. Japan, set on fire by the incendiary bombs of the US air force, devastated by atomic weapons, was a heap of rubble and devastation, like Europe. In the short term, United States food aid kept the European population alive.

Dealing with the most pressing needs and laying the foundations of the new imperial order had to proceed simultaneously. Any delay was damaging for capitalism, now competing with a rival system. There was urgency because the deprivation of the population of Europe gave rise to fears of increased adherence to revolutionary programs and solutions, reinforced by the existence of an alternative model in the east. By its mere presence, the USSR played a passive and indirect role in all postwar developments ("contagion"). However, capitalism was less threatened by the USSR than by its own internal workings and malfunctions, painfully demonstrated by the depression and the war, and by a new crisis forecast for the immediate postwar period.

The overriding priority was to rescue it in order to save it from itself. The United States was in the best position to take on this task, even if it meant postponing the particular benefits it intended to derive from its supremacy. The leniency, generosity, and consideration shown towards its adversaries and rivals of yesterday, and later their rehabilitation—practices little known in the past—were due to the necessity of putting the capitalist system back on its feet. Failing that, no imperialism, American, or other, was conceivable. To rally their populations and keep them away from protest or revolt, the triple program of peace, stability, and growth was an indispensable prerequisite. The new globalized imperialism was in the making, but its inauguration could not be immediate.

Furthermore, the United States did not have to fear competition from other Western countries, because the power differential was so great; interimperialist conflicts were put on the back burner. A moment of historical transition, the first postwar years were a specific phase following a deep crisis dating back to 1929. During those years, a system had to be restarted and a new imperial mode of operation put in place. The civilian non-military productive apparatus, both for capital and for consumer goods, had to be renewed, a task that had not been undertaken after the crisis of 1929-1933.

b. An Americentric international economy

Planning the international economic order began during the war, even before victory was assured. A reconfiguration of capitalism was the order of the day. Decision-makers were driven by the need to correct and prevent the dysfunctions that accompanied the depression of the 1930s: protectionism, closed monetary zones, exchange controls, absence of fixed parities. The Gold Exchange Standard was based on convertible currencies. It had had its day when, in September 1931, the gold convertibility of the pound sterling was suspended, leading to its depreciation. The devaluation of the dollar in January 1934 sealed the outcome. Rival currency zones formed around the pound, the dollar, the mark, the franc, the yen. This fragmentation had to be overcome if currency wars were to be avoided and trade facilitated.

As early as 1942, senior American and British officials were preparing projects for international monetary reorganization. An international conference attended by delegations from forty-five states was inaugurated on July 1, 1944 in Bretton Woods, New Hampshire. A return to the gold standard system was out of the question because it would cause monetary restriction and deflation, a disaster for the world economy. All delegations agreed on the need to stabilize exchange rates through fixed parities and to create an international organization that would lend to countries with balance of payments deficits.

By what mechanism would fixed parities be defended? The British delegation proposed the creation of a world clearing house (a sort of international central bank) with the power to issue liquidity, in other words a new monetary unit not linked to gold. The intent was to put the dollar on the same level as other currencies, in particular the pound sterling, and to prevent it from becoming the world's currency. On the strength of its currency convertible into gold, of which the United States held the lion's share of the world stock, and usable to purchase American products, the United States delegation rejected the idea of a new currency and called for the recognition of the dollar's privileged role.

The dollar was convertible at the rate of $35 per ounce of fine gold. Each country would define the value of its currency in gold and dollars and abide by a defined parity relative to gold or the dollar. If a currency deviated by more than 1 percent from the official parity, each central bank was required to intervene in the foreign exchange markets. A new gold exchange standard appeared but the basis of the international monetary system was, in reality, the dollar, as long as the rate of $35 per fine ounce of gold was respected.

The United States currency gained the status of de facto international transaction and reserve currency. It was held in central bank reserves as much as, if not more than, gold. International settlements were denominated in dollars and oil benchmarks, such as Brent and West Texas Intermediate, were pegged to the dollar. A national currency became an international currency. For so long the pivotal currency of the international economy, the pound sterling was dethroned, as was Britain itself. The Bretton Woods agreements were a marker of the transition of hegemony in the world economy. The fixed exchange rate system being binding, an International Monetary Fund (IMF) was created in 1945 to enforce it, ensure the free convertibility of currencies between each other, and grant credits (drawing rights) to countries in difficulty. A World Bank granted long-term loans for reconstruction and development.

The primacy of the United States was confirmed, with the onus on it to maintain the gold backing of the money it issued. In fact, economic conditions meant that only the dollar could be freely converted into gold. In 1947, in a final attempt to recover the pound sterling's standing, its convertibility into gold was restored. The Bank of England had to sacrifice so much currency that the measure was abandoned and exchange controls reintroduced. Coupled with a precarious balance of payments, the episode signaled the end of the sterling era and of British claims to an eminent status in the world economy. The Bretton Woods system was monetary but it also had a commercial purpose. The new monetary system facilitated trade liberalization. In 1947, the General Agreement on Tariffs and Trade (GATT) oversaw this process by promoting the lowering of customs barriers, the prohibition of discriminatory practices, and the generalization of the most favored nation clause.

The United States took charge of the economic destiny of Europe and its integration into an Americentric system of international trade. For the restoration of capitalism, the flagship project was the European recovery program (Marshall Plan). It followed on the United Nations emergency aid (United Nations relief and rehabilitation administration) and the loans the United States granted to Great Britain and France in 1945 and 1946. These relief plans proved to be insufficient. Although demand for American exports was strong around the world, it was insolvent because of lack of financial resources. Potential buyers had to be provided with the liquidity they needed. Nearly $13 billion in grants and loans enabled the sixteen recipient countries in Western Europe to import United States products. An Organization for European Economic Cooperation (OEEC) was founded in 1948 to distribute the funds and achieve coordinated development of European economies.

The reaction of the USSR came as no surprise: it declined invitations to take part in this relaunch of capitalism under United States supervision and, in 1949, formed with the other countries of Eastern Europe the Council for Mutual Economic Assistance (COMECON). The Soviet model reigned there, with nationalizations, centralized planning, agrarian reform, and collectivization. The economies were integrated on the basis of complementarity, which was difficult to achieve, and of production specialization, which gave an unusual character to the whole: the USSR was often in the unexpected position of being the supplier of raw materials and the customer of its partners' industries, notably East Germany and Czechoslovakia. It was instructive to note that the USSR applied a flexible policy towards its COMECON partners, similar to that of the United States in the West, in order to stabilize and restart their economies. The fact remained that the Cold War was now also economic, and Europe was split into a Sovietized eastern flank and an Americanized or "Marshallized" western flank.

c. Multinational corporations and foreign direct investment

The most striking aspect of the United States economy was its sheer size, as was the case with every other dimension of American life compared to the rest of the world. The same applied to American companies. As oligopolies, they stood out in many respects: capitalization, assets, turnover, productivity, competitiveness, innovation, technological advance, management, multidivisional departmentalized structure, research and development, subcontracting and, eventually, outsourcing of certain functions. In each sector, one (i.e., IBM) or a few (i.e., General Motors, Ford) were dominant, an indicator of the degree of concentration of the economy. They controlled the various stages of their production, from upstream to downstream, from raw materials to sales (vertical integration), and sometimes similar companies (horizontal integration).

In the conglomerate form, headed by a holding company (parent company of a group), they absorbed the most diverse firms and operated in business lines sometimes unrelated to each other. Embodying the process of rationalization of economic activity, concentration and centralization of capital, they spearheaded the expansion of the United States abroad. Some "multinationals" began their internationalization at the end of the nineteenth century. These were mainly trading subsidiaries set up to penetrate new markets because they enjoyed an advantage, or raw materials extraction companies. Few industrial companies manufactured all or part of a product outside the borders of the United States. In this respect, they did not differ from the large European firms.

The novelty in the post-1945 era was the proliferation of American subsidiaries processing abroad components of the goods they produced. Production was multinational, combining parts from the parent company and parts from one or more external subsidiaries. The label "Made in ...," lost meaning and was less and less common. A significant proportion of the total turnover was generated from activity abroad. In many sectors, the value of these companies' production abroad exceeded the value of their exports from the United States. Not only did they manufacture outside their home market, which radically altered the classic model whereby metropolises reserved industrial activity to themselves, but they also produced capital-intensive high value-added goods abroad. They tended to dominate nerve centers of host economies, leading edge sectors where technology counted, basic industries and large markets.

Their industrial character prompted them to expand preferably in developed countries (the "center"), unlike older companies which operated internationally, normally in the primary sector (i.e., the United Fruit Company in Central America) but also in the telephone sector (ITT in Europe and South America). When the host countries were less developed (the "periphery"), "multinationals" concentrated in the traditional extraction of raw materials (i.e., oil companies).

United States foreign direct investment (FDI) in 1952
percent of total

	Western Europe and Canada	Other regions
Extractive activities	23	60
Industry and commerce	60	20
Public utilities	6	17
Miscellaneous	11	3

During the 1980s, the 600 largest multinational firms, American and other, controlled a quarter of world production. The internal trade of these companies (intra-firm) accounted for a third of world trade.

Financial markets had been shrouded in mistrust since the crash of 1929. The Bretton Woods agreements aimed to create a stable monetary framework to promote international trade, not the movement of capital around the world. At half-mast since the 1930s, international investment began to rise after the war, becoming a dominant feature of the world economy. Foreign direct investment (FDI), involving control of businesses by non-residents, was less common than "portfolio" investment, except for the United States. The share of FDI increased during the interwar period, with the United States and Great Britain being the main sources.

The pace accelerated after the war, with the United States becoming the leading foreign investor in many countries. In international flows, the volume of FDI clearly outweighed the volume of "portfolio" investment. "Multinationals" were the drivers of FDI. They gave it unprecedented importance and launched the phenomenon of relocations and global "value chains."

Fueled by private capital, "multinationals" took over in Europe from the public capital of the Marshall Plan. For many products, sales by subsidiaries exceeded exports from the United States. These subsidiaries also served as platforms for exporting to other countries, sometimes to the United States itself. They inserted themselves into the economic fabric of their host countries and self-financed by reinvesting their profits or turning to local capital markets, without significant recourse to the export of capital from the United States. Part of their shareholder base was local, and nationals could sit on the board of directors of the subsidiary and manage it. Working conditions—remuneration, training, promotion—were often better than in national companies, which helped them attract talent.

In many ways, United States companies became the standard in their field and helped to homogenize Western ruling classes. They reproduced abroad the practices developed on a continental scale in the United States. Their cost had already been amortized in the United States or was likely to be amortized more quickly thanks to cross-border expansion. They had one or more advantages over foreign competitors. Their strategy was one of "oligopolistic competition," meaning that, in a long-term perspective, horizontal concentration to maintain or increase market share, marginalization or elimination of local competition, and erection of economic barriers to entry of new competitors on the market could be as important as short-term profits, even if the latter were not disdained. It was a matter of applying abroad the process of concentration, the methods, and the technical and/or organizational advances that led to their expansion in the United States.

In this case, imperialism consisted in stifling or preventing competition, enabling the extraction of monopoly profits once the market

Stock of FDI by country of origin
billions of current $ and percentage

	1914		1938		1960		1971		1978	
	$	%	$	%	$	%	$	%	$	%
United States	2.7	18.5	7.3	27.7	32.8	49.2	82.8	48.1	167.7	41.4
Canada	0.2	1.0	0.7	2.7	2.5	3.8	6.5	3.8	13.6	3.5
Great Britain	6.5	45.5	10.5	39.8	10.8	16.2	23.7	13.8	50.7	12.9
Germany	1.5	10.5	0.4	1.3	0.8	1.2	7.3	4.2	28.6	7.3
France	1.8	12.2	2.5	9.5	4.1	6.1	7.3	4.2	14.9	3.8
Belgium	-	-	-	-	1.3	1.9	2.4	1.4	5.4	1.4
Netherlands	-	-	-	-	7.0	10.5	13.8	8.0	28.4	7.2
Switzerland	-	-	-	-	2.0	3.0	9.5	5.5	27.8	7.1
Japan	-	-	0.8	2.8	0.5	0.7	4.4	2.6	26.8	6.8
All countries	14.3		26.4		66.7		172.1		392.8	

Stock of FDI of US origin
billions of current $

	1929	1946	1957	1967	1980
Destination					
Canada	2.0	2.5	8.6	18.0	44.6
Latin America	3.5	3.1	8.1	10.2	26.0
Europe	1.4	1.0	4.1	17.9	95.7
Other countries	0.6	0.6	4.4	13.2	47.2
Total	**7.5**	**7.2**	**25.2**	**59.3**	**213.5**
Sectors					
Industry	1.8	2.4	8.0	24.1	89.1
Oil	1.1	1.4	9.0	17.4	46.9
Mines and metallurgy	1.2	0.8	2.4	4.8	6.5
Other sectors	3.4	2.6	5.8	13.0	71.0
Total	**7.5**	**7.2**	**25.2**	**59.3**	**59.3**

was under control. Imperialist strategy borrowed from the operating mode of capitalism at the national level. As an instrument of an economic integration which crossed state borders, and a symbol of an Americentric internationalization of the economy, the phenomenon of multinational (or transnational) firms fascinated some observers and worried others, sparking innumerable analyses during the 1960s.

A final institutional recomposition directly influenced FDI, among other consequences. The construction of a European entity was an idea promoted by the United States since the end of the 1940s. The intention was to bring European countries together to restore their economies and make a more coordinated military contribution to the Cold War against the USSR, thus reducing the cost for the United States. But asking old nations, barely emerging from a bloody conflict, to work together was unrealistic. The approach had to be gradual and long term. It was resolved to proceed step by step. As far as the military angle was concerned, the coalition that emerged was not European. The North Atlantic Treaty Organization (NATO, 1949) was an alliance led by the United States. It put an end to interimperialist military conflicts, united members against a common enemy and forced them to cooperate under the command of the strongest among them.

In the European context, the economy was the area of rapprochement. In 1951, the European Coal and Steel Community (ECSC) grouped six countries around the metallurgical sector. In 1957, the six created the European Economic Community (EEC), both a common market and a framework for developing common policies. The removal of internal barriers to trade did not benefit Europeans alone. United States companies also called for the unification and standardization of European markets. The elimination of obstacles and specific local conditions facilitated the movement of goods exported from the United States or produced by subsidiaries of "multinationals" established in Europe, whose number was increasing thanks to the common market.

Although less ambitious, the European Free Trade Association, formed in 1960 on the initiative of Great Britain, was also a step in the direction of opening up borders to trade. The CEE and EFTA justified increased FDI, encouraged by new growth prospects in the host and neighboring countries. The United States was a supporter of European integration, especially since the condition of postwar Europe did not make it a competitor. Canada and Europe were the main recipients of United States industrial FDI. The CEE effect could be seen in the increase in Europe's share. This trend would be confirmed with the creation of the European Union. In 2000, 46.1 percent of United States FDI was in Europe, 10.2 percent in Canada, and 4.5 percent in Japan.

US industrial FDI
millions of current $ and percentage

	1950		1966	
	Millions of	$ Percent	Millions of	$ Percent
All countries	3381	100	22,050	100
Canada	1897	49.5	7674	34.8
Europe	932	24.3	8879	40.3
Brazil	285	7.4	846	3.8
Argentina	161	4.2	652	3.0
Mexico	133	3.5	797	3.6

With the completion of reconstruction, the conditions for growth were in place. It was triggered by the Korean War; there was fear it would ignite a third world war. In order to build up stocks, governments placed massive orders, bringing production to a peak and keeping factories and subcontractor workshops running at full capacity. The pace continued for two decades. The thirty-year economic boom (1945-1975) was the strongest and longest phase of growth, without a major crisis, in the history of capitalism. The average annual rate of expansion of international trade reached 7 percent, inducing GDP to rise by around 5 percent. These rates were lower in the United States where the stimulating effect of catching up did not come into play.

If national performances differed, the gap was modest. Investment rates (gross fixed capital formation) in relation to GDP were high, unemployment rates low. Finally, slowdowns and "recessions" were short-lived; they did not spread to all countries at the same time and were quickly overcome by the regularizing action of public authorities, in accordance with Keynesian prescriptions. The atmosphere was such that growth could be taken for granted and seem permanent.

In Japan, the picture was even more pronounced: large-scale reconstruction, very high investment rates, competitive industry, skilled and inexpensive labor, a protected market of 100 million consumers, annual GDP growth rates of around 10 percent, higher than in any other country in the world. Added to this was the absence of competition from the United States and the accessibility to its market, concessions it made to the economies —including the Japanese, Taiwanese, and South Korean—that it had to rehabilitate if it wanted to strengthen the bonds of loyalty in the Cold War. In the postwar phase and for special geopolitical reasons relating to the struggle between the superpowers, extra-economic means were used to relieve the partners, rather than to overwhelm them. As in Western Europe, the "Asian miracle" occurred in exceptional circumstances where political considerations took precedence. Paradoxically, the USSR had an indirect role in the recovery of capitalist economies and post-1945 growth.

There were many reasons for the growth which spanned three decades: demographic dynamism (baby boom), rise in total factor productivity, corresponding rise in real incomes, fall in relative prices, industrialization and transformation of agriculture into agrobusiness, expansion of international trade, cheapness of oil and other raw materials, sustained demand, and significant state intervention in the economy according to the recommendations of Keynesian theory. As a redistributor of income, the state supported demand, smoothed out cyclical fluctuations, financed infrastructure and provided public services, including education and healthcare. Thus, a virtuous circle was established: mass production met a solvent market and sustained growth. While United States "multinationals" contributed to the boom, they were also driven by it. Their entry onto the scene in Europe could, in fact, be explained by their interest in positioning themselves to take advantage of growth.

d. Imperialism without colonies

The economic upturn in the North was synchronous with a historic transformation in the South, bringing the neomercantilist/colonial phase of imperialism to a close. Decolonization was a major turning point in the evolution of imperialism. It ushered in its postcolonial phase during which the direct and formal control of less developed or precapitalist countries was replaced by indirect and informal control, similar to that exercised by Europe since the nineteenth century over legally independent but weaker countries, such as the Ottoman Empire. The era of imperialism without colonies took shape after 1945. The informal imperialism that had appeared a century earlier became the main form of imperialism.

If the First World War gave birth to the USSR, it also marked the victory of imperialism, which perpetuated itself. The redistribution of power between the victors and the vanquished left the Western powers (Great Britain and France) with larger territories than before the war. While imperialism was shaken overall, it emerged stronger in colonial terms, with new possessions sometimes referred to as protectorates or mandates.

The same cannot be said for the Second World War. The authority of the great powers in the colonial world was undermined. France, the Netherlands, and Belgium were defeated and occupied. Great Britain was damaged and exhausted. The French imperial domain in Asia was occupied by Japan, and those in North Africa and Syria-Lebanon trampled underfoot by German, Anglo-American, and British armies. The Dutch East Indies came under Japanese control. Hong Kong fell to Japanese forces; its British governor was taken prisoner. The fear that a dominant power seeks to impose, namely the impression of omnipotence and invincibility so necessary for the colonizer to overawe and govern vast territories, was dissipated.

The current created by the struggle against Nazi oppression was genuinely liberating; it was the antithesis of the colonial spirit for which domination was a natural or positive fact. To this trend must be added Japan's self-interested action in the form of agitation against "white" colonialism. In a speech delivered in 1960, British Prime Minister Harold Macmillan acknowledged this "wind of change." Finally, the military legacy of the Second World War was not to the advantage of colonialism. The notion of resistance, praised in its anti-Nazi version, was susceptible to orientation in an anti-colonial direction. Military action in Europe legitimated the concept of armed struggle and protracted guerilla warfare against an overseas colonial power. People's war was a component of many "national liberation movements," representing coalitions of social strata and political tendencies, which multiplied after 1945. Here again analogies could be drawn with European interclass and multiparty resistance movements.

From Asia (Syria, Lebanon, India, Pakistan, Indonesia, Vietnam, and others) to Africa, both north and south of the Sahara, decolonization unfolded. Each process of independence reinforced another, sometimes through armed confrontation followed by negotiations, sometimes through negotiation alone. The tasks facing the new countries were immense, with development being first and foremost. The quest for growth in the North had its counterpart in the quest for development in the South. Development was conceivable only with the uprooting of the legacy of colonization. For decades, sometimes centuries, it had structured overseas dependencies around the extraction of a raw material, the harvesting of a tropical product, or the monoculture of a profitable agricultural product for export.

Import-export dominated other economic activities, each evolving with little connection between them. The result was underdevelopment, a dual and unbalanced socioeconomic structure: modern, commercial and oversized for the export sector alone; backward or even at subsistence level for the rest of the economy. An enclave capitalism, an extension of metropolitan capitalism rather than a local phenomenon, coexisted with a precapitalist economy subjected to the enclave and providing it with primary sector products to be drained off to the outside in a raw state.

Underdevelopment affected three-quarters of humanity. Its corollaries included, among other things, anarchic urbanization, a proliferating informal sector, poverty, short life expectancy, malnutrition, illiteracy, and the elementary nature of health services. Social spending was superfluous for economies specialized in skimming off raw materials. Putting an end to underdevelopment had been discussed in United Nations agencies since its creation. A developmentalist consensus emerged, which made the reduction of external dependence and the local processing of raw materials the foundations of economic policy in the Third World. Put beyond the reach of these countries by mercantilism and neomercantilism, industrialization was seen as the basis of any modernization project and the guarantee of independence. The goal was to use their raw materials to manufacture locally the industrial goods that had been imported under mercantilist and neomercantilist regulations.

The period had a contradictory effect. On international markets, commodity prices were falling. The terms of trade were changing to the detriment of the South and in favor of the North, whose labor productivity was higher and whose prices were rising rapidly; hence the concept of "unequal exchange." Industrial products traded above their value, raw materials below. Trade by the group optimistically called "developing countries" played an increasingly minor role in international commerce, mainly happening between the countries of the North and involving industrial products. Two-thirds of world trade was carried out by the United States-Western Europe-Japan triad. The situation called for industrialization. However, importing the costly capital goods necessary for this purpose required foreign exchange earned from the export of raw materials and primary products, the prices of which were falling.

Because of the absence of factors indispensable to industry or resistance from private interests or both, industrialization could only be undertaken through the agency of the state. The Soviet model of industrialization, crowned by victory in 1945, was surrounded by the prestige of success. As a result, nationalizations and some planning were commonplace. The former were justified by the argument that companies had siphoned profits out of the country and would continue to do so; the second by the need to make them contribute to national development. This did not prevent foreign companies from offering their services and states from using them.

While the Northern states were interventionist, those of the South practiced assertive *dirigisme*. Once industrialization had restored economic equilibrium, development would be "inward-looking" rather than "extroverted." From Europe (excluding pioneer Britain) to the United States, industrialization required the defense of infant industries against external competition. Customs protection therefore succeeded the liberalism of the colonial period in the new countries. As the playbook of development programs, import substitution industrialization (ISI) had an honorable past, that of virtually all previous industrializations, except that of Great Britain.

Achievements were modest and fragile in Algeria, India, and Egypt. All relied on the export of raw materials to pay for the import of capital goods. There was no exit from the global market; neocol-onization was not ruled out. In China, industrialization by a five-year plan following the Soviet precedent failed; the collectivization of agriculture in order to generate surpluses to be used for industrializa-tion ended in disaster. With its older manufacturing base, Japan was the laboratory of a growth model built on industries whose output replaced imports and, in an original twist, was destined for export, the new engine of growth. At the opposite end of the spectrum from the "inward-looking" strategy, export-led growth implied integration into the world market. South Korea, Taiwan, Hong Kong, and Singapore were the first "newly industrialized countries" (NICs) or "Asian tigers" to follow Japan. Next in line came the Philippines, Thailand, and especially China. The only similarity was that both paths were based on strong state involvement in the economy.

e. Imperialism on hold

The post-Second World War period was original in the history of capitalism. Growth took place in a geopolitical framework with-out parallel in the past. First, the capitalist sphere was faced with a counter-system advocating modernity and capable of defending itself—which distinguished it from the traditional societies that Europe had toppled since the fifteenth century. Against this rival, cohesion and unity were the watchwords; dissension was condemned. Second, the configuration of the West was unprecedented. One power so dominated the others in all respects and the latter were in such a state of need that their relationship was one of subordination. Interimperialist confrontation and wars were out of the question. With regard to its European competitors, Great Britain formerly exercised primacy. It did not have the means to impose a hegemony that would make any resistance illusory.

At the time of the thirty-year boom, without any of its foundations being modified, imperialism took a back seat to the major work of overhauling the structures of national economies, rebuilding the cap-italist sphere of the international economy, and competing by seduc-tion with the Soviet system. With the United States in control of the capitalist world and the knowledge that the two world wars turned to the benefit of socialism, a period of peace opened between the capitalist countries. Interimperialist wars, central to the Hilferding-Bukharin-Lenin theory, seemed relegated to oblivion. Coordination replaced them. Rivalries for preeminence visibly gave way to the determination, under the aegis of the United States, to prevent the extension of the socialist sphere.

The mothballing of armed conflicts between capitalist powers, and the collaboration displayed between them, modified the situation which prevailed between 1870 and 1945 from the point of view of the analysis of imperialism. In the North, the relaunching of capitalism and the lull in interimperialist relations due to the absolute superiority of one of the powers focused attention on the mode of operation of the restored economies and United States penetration into the countries of the capitalist camp. In the South, a new era in the history of capitalism began. More than five centuries after having acquired them, the West no longer possessed most of the colonies that were the foundation of mercantilist and neomercantilist imperialism.

The historical page of colonial imperialism had been turned, that of imperialism without colonies was being written. Consecrating the advent of postcolonial imperialism, decolonization shifted attention towards neocolonialism and the continued dependence of new countries towards former imperial metropolises. As for the West/East and capitalism/socialism oppositions, they are so self-explanatory that they require no scholarly elucidation.

f. Theorizing: successes and limits of Keynesianism

During this period, the history of the theory of imperialism took a new turn calling for separate treatment. Coming to the fore in the postwar period, the Keynesian approach was adopted by the authorities of all political hues, from left to right, that governed Western countries. Keynesianism was the new idiom they spoke. As a theory of effective demand, it reintegrated investment in capital goods—a fact not ignored by classical political economy—and, for the first time, took into account government spending. Thus modified, underconsumptionism could rise from the purgatory of nonconformity to the paradise of accepted ideas. Keynes influenced the underconsumptionist trend without actually being part of it; he was concerned with demand that was not confined to consumer goods.

To be sure, the First World War had already introduced society to large-scale intervention by the state in economic activity. Undoubtedly the depression of the 1930s provided a striking demonstration of the drying up of investment and the lack of coordination between production and consumption. Keynes' theoretical endorsement of underconsumptionism was nonetheless necessary to grant it the legitimacy it had hitherto been denied.

With a profoundly original approach, the British economist made a double break: with classical political economy and Say's law of outlets to the effect that income would be invested or spent automatically and in its entirety; with the neoclassical marginalism of the Austrian school and the primacy attributed to the individual and the firm. Henceforth, investment would depend on overall demand, in the broad sense, and the analysis would be carried out at the level of national aggregates.

Keynes' silence on the subject of imperialism followed logically from the model he established of the functioning of the economy. If effective demand was maintained and investment continued, surpluses of goods and capital would be absorbed, and, with them, the substance of imperialist expansionism. It was through a detour that Keynesianism encountered the problem of imperialism. Strongly influenced by Keynes, the economists Paul Baran and Paul Sweezy considered themselves followers of Marx and regretted the theoretical void in which the monopolistic stage of capitalism had been left, since *Capital* only dealt with the competitive phase. Although open to question, the distinction dated back to socialist analyses of the beginning of the twentieth century.

Baran and Sweezy's theory of monopoly capital (*Monopoly capital*, 1966) was based on a concept coined by them: economic surplus, defined as the difference between what a society produced and the costs of production. The fundamental law governing monopoly capitalism was the tendency for surplus to increase constantly in relation to total output. This was so because monopoly eliminated price competition characteristic of competitive capitalism. Absorbing these inexorably accumulating surpluses would constitute an affliction specific to the monopoly stage.

There were three possibilities of absorbing surplus: consumption, investment, and waste. From an underconsumptionist point of view, the first was always insufficient. As for investment, it was not up to the task. Propping the rate of profit required underutilization of productive capacity. The tendency towards stagnation resulting from underconsumption was then reinforced by the contraction of investment to a hopelessly low volume. If investment were to increase, it would only accelerate growth, hence the accumulation of the surplus. State spending helped support demand and encouraged investment without absorbing the surplus. The first two options offered no way out.

There remained waste in the form of advertising costs—which served, admittedly, to increase consumption, however indefensible— or state spending on the military, considered to be by far the most important. As for the export of capital, it offered little relief since, in short order, it siphoned off from abroad revenues greater than the amounts committed and caused more surplus to flow back to the metropolis. As a result, monopoly capitalism was entangled in a depressive logic, periodically mitigated by resort to countermeasures.

Produced during the postwar boom, Baran and Sweezy's theory had the merit of challenging the spirit of complacency and self-congratulation that pervaded economics as it celebrated its mastery of the secrets of smooth growth. The two authors therefore gained a wide following in opposition circles, particularly the "new left." Although methodical, their analysis was nevertheless vulnerable to criticism.

Baran and Sweezy intended to follow in the footsteps of Marx. However, the latter's analysis of capitalism was anchored in the realm of production, while theirs, which was underconsumptionist, was rooted in the circulation of goods, that is to say, markets. The specific features of Marx's theory were absent: the distinction between constant capital and variable capital, the concept of surplus value, and the theory of value. For them, the source of profit was not surplus value but the high selling prices that the monopolies could charge. The pressure exerted by an ever-increasing surplus bore little relation to the pressure caused by a falling rate of profit, the result of the increase in constant capital in relation to variable capital in the "organic composition" of capital. For Baran and Sweezy, the tendency was for the surplus to swell, not for the rate of profit to fall.

Finally, there was the stagnationist interpretation given to the evolution of capitalism: were it not for exogenous stimuli, a sort of doping, capitalism would not be able to extricate itself from the stationary state. Marx placed at the center of his analysis the dynamic character of the process of reproduction, expansion, and accumulation of capital, with crises being merely a pause necessary to reestablish the conditions of profitability and prepare a new advance. In effect, Baran and Sweezy's interpretation was more akin to Keynes' than to Marx's. Both underconsumptionist and Keynesian, it clearly highlighted the fact that the *General Theory* did not make capitalism immune to difficulties.

Furthermore, the usefulness, even the validity, of the concept of economic surplus remained problematic. What was specific to capitalism in the identification of a difference between what a society produced and the costs of production? What elements should be included in the current surplus? How was the potential surplus that could be generated by a society reorganized to end the irrationality of capitalism to be measured? Was it empirically verifiable that the current surplus increased, given the constant rise in production costs, particularly fixed capital? Should it be accepted that price competition had disappeared during the so-called monopolistic stage?

All in all, the theory of Baran and Sweezy was a reminder, Keynes notwithstanding, of the persistence of the conditions which gave rise to underconsumptionist conceptions. The redistribution of national income, the strengthening of demand, and the incentive to invest did not overcome the evil believed to be chronic to capitalism, the one on which all the others were grafted, namely the weakness of consumption in relation to production. Nor did they smooth out the rough edges of a capital accumulation process that remained bumpy and unbalanced. It was as if the advent of monopolies cancelled out the beneficial effect of Keynesianism and the emphasis it put on effective demand. In the meantime, capital was exported continuously.

With the theory of Baran and Sweezy, underconsumptionism reached the end of its evolution. An enduring phenomenon, the deficit of demand in relation to production resisted the remedies recommended by Hobson and Keynes. In the underconsumptionist scheme, demand generated supply. If more resources were to be transferred towards increasing demand, the result would be inflation and increased production, with more profits being added to the capital put away while waiting for gainful employment. If the path to reform now seemed a dead end, so was the outward expansion stressed by the catastrophist current running from the "Colonial Reformers" to Luxemburg, since the repatriated gains (dividends, interest, and commissions) swelled the stock of capital reduced to idleness.

Although a powerful remedy, Keynesianism had not cured capitalism. In this respect, the latter seemed irreformable. The crisis that broke out from 1973-1974 supported the assertions of Baran and Sweezy. The regime appeared to be characterized by a recurring overproduction of commodities, capital goods, and money capital, even after the implementation of investment and spending measures designed to absorb surpluses. It was a durable condition, with distortions laying at the very heart of the production process. Even if they could be postponed, crises of overproduction/underconsumption or ones resulting from the fall in the rate of profit could not be averted. As in the past, they would periodically act to clear the way for the restoration of profitability thresholds and the resumption of accumulation.

Did the classical and neoclassical theorists who took stability as the normal state of the economy misunderstand the importance of consumption? In reality, while the classics, working at a high level of abstraction, relativized the uneven nature of the real production process, underconsumptionism identified an undeniable fact and made it the guiding principle of a theory. It thus placed itself on the same ground as the currents it was criticizing, namely faith in equilibrium, impaired by the existence of an unconsumed surplus product and its consequences.

Underconsumptionism was an awkward notion. Compelling from a theoretical point of view, it had a tenuous relationship with concrete realities. Both conceptually and in reality, underconsumption was a permanent and insurmountable fact of life, because everything invested was, as a result, withdrawn from immediate consumption. It was the traveling companion of any accumulation process. As added value was not fully consumed, the domestic market always remained too narrow in relation to national productive capacities. Whatever the extent of markets opened, spheres of investment conquered, or improvements in living standards, underconsumption would persist, unless growth (or "expanded reproduction") was abandoned. Its disappearance would presuppose the stoppage of accumulation.

Historically, the Keynesian experiment showed that supporting effective demand—by expanding the market for consumer and capital goods—did not put an end to surpluses. It did prove that impoverish-ment, absolute or relative, was not inevitable: real wages (the standard of living) could increase in the long term on condition that their share in national income did not have a negative effect on the profitability of capital and as long as productivity increased. Not only were the social reforms advocated by the Hobsonian current implemented, but they were combined with investment-favorable policies legitim-ized by Keynesian theory. The curative qualities of these measures proved effective, but only within the limits set by the economic model ("accumulation regime").

All in all, the notion of underconsumption pointed to a permanent feature in economies governed by the growth imperative (or "expanded reproduction") rather than an irregularity contrary to their nature. Policies that promoted consumption or redistributed investment did not resolve underconsumption. Concluding that the economy was pre-carious and improperly organized maintained the hope of purging it of underconsumption, a property which was part of its nature. Reformist underconsumptionists, with Hobson in the lead, held up redistribu-tion of income as a remedy for underconsumption and an alternative to foreign expansion. However, the application of measures to support effective domestic demand did not put an end to outward flows.

A particular firm or private interest could unburden itself of excess goods or idle capital by turning to an external outlet. At the micro level (the company or the individual), internationalization made possible the absorption of surpluses and the loosening of the grip of underconsumption. But at the macro level (the economy), it did not eliminate it. On the one hand, exports of goods and capital did not slow down—they even accelerated—during periods of growth, that is to say when the increased use of productive capacities tended to absorb surpluses. On the other hand, the safety valves abroad included societies congested with surplus, just like the exporting economy.

Rather, the role of internationalization was to smooth out the distortions and imbalances resulting from differences in the pace of development of the various branches of the economy. These growth gaps made it difficult, sometimes for one sector (or firm), sometimes for another, to find outlets in branches that had temporarily fallen behind. Hence the incessant extension of the limits of economic activity, even in developed economies also suffering from surpluses.

g. Theorizing: rise and decline of the dependency school

With decolonization all but complete, Third World countries faced the risk of an essentially economic form of domination. Imperialism did not disappear; it took on a new meaning. From a struggle for hegemony between great powers, the concept increasingly referred to neocolonialism or the economic subjugation of Africa, Asia, and Latin America by the collective imperialism of the former colonial powers. Independence appeared to be nothing more than an artificial paradise. Facts seemed to have caught up with theory: Kautsky's ultra-imperialism emerged from the shadows and looked all the more credible in that multinational or transnational corporations bypassed state borders and seemed to be on the verge of creating a global bourgeoisie composed of citizens of their respective firms.

Many authors considered that the proletariat of developed countries had exhausted its revolutionary potential and turned their attention to the peoples of the Third World and "developing" countries. This was where the most active front or the "main contradiction" in the world could now be found, an assessment shared in official circles in both the capitalist and the socialist camps.

While Lenin always elicited respect, current ideas borrowed little from his approach. Of all the prewar theorists, only Rosa Luxemburg would have found heirs, generally indirect, among the neo-Marxists of the dependency school. Underconsumption, capitalism, and imperialism defined by market relations, expansion towards less developed regions (precapitalist for Luxemburg), necessity of imperialism (colonialism for Luxemburg) for the existence of capitalism, exploitation of the Third World as the foundation of imperialism, such were their points of convergence.

In fact, dependency theory was not born within the Marxist fold. It was a current of opposition to the modernization paradigm prevalent among development economists attached to universities and international organizations. It took for granted that less developed countries had to follow the same steps as advanced countries to achieve transformation and growth. The modernization toolbox included the Ricardian theory of comparative advantage, specialization, international division of labor, and free trade. No doubt informed by the beginnings of industrialization on their continent during the 1930s and the war, Latin American economists criticized the neoclassical theory of international trade as antithetical to development.

From the late 1940s onwards, they promoted the strategy of industrialization through import substitution, based on active state intervention in the economy, protectionism, and some planning. This would be the only way to break out of the straitjacket of an economy based mainly on the export of raw materials and subject to the vagaries of the international market. Called for by nationalists in Africa and Asia even before decolonization, this program, with all its variants, would be adopted by many states after their accession to independence and would provide the economic framework of Third-Worldism.

Economists and sociologists of dependency were numerous and critical of the Western model of modernization. They represented its most articulate wing and came close to Marxism in their use of some of its concepts and their questioning of capitalism as a whole. The object of their contribution was twofold: to explain why Third World countries had not experienced satisfactory economic development, particularly industrialization; and to make proposals for remedying the situation. Confronted with the theory of modernization, the "dependentists," rejected analyses that attributed backwardness or underdevelopment to the obstacles and constraints that Third World societies placed in the way of progress. On the contrary, they saw these as an inevitable outcome of their insertion into global capitalism. As soon as they fell in its snare, their fate was sealed for a long time and decolonization, a token achievement, changed nothing. They remained "dependent."

Before serving in the context of monopoly capitalism, the concept of economic surplus was used by Baran to describe the draining of Third World resources by advanced countries. The expropriation of surplus was the main, but not the only, mode of exploitation of the periphery by the metropolis, and the mechanism for creating underdevelopment. Baran thus laid the foundations of the theory of dependence. Far from fostering the emergence of local capitalism and contributing to growth, the influence of global capitalism was exerted in the direction of backwardness and impoverishment. All development therefore required breaking the bonds of dependence.

The economist Andre Gunder Frank (*Capitalism and underdevelopment in Latin America*, 1969) sharpened the ideas put forward by

Baran by providing them with historical support and inserting them into a general vision of the world economy. Frank argued that the development of capitalism in the center and the underdevelopment of the periphery represented two faces of the same reality. On the one hand, surplus extracted from the periphery proved essential to the birth and growth of capitalism; on the other, underdevelopment became an inevitable consequence of the participation of dominated countries in global capitalism. Rather than lateness, underdevelopment designated a social structure specific to countries reduced to vassalization. Parallel to the rise of capitalism at the center was the "development of underdevelopment" on the periphery.

By capitalism, Frank meant a system of commodity production that had been global since its beginnings in the fifteenth century. Any country integrated into it became capitalist. A monist conception, it subjected the part to the whole and postulated the existence of a single system encompassing the entire world from the outset. It gave rise to the world-system perspective, a model associated with the idea of a "world economy." No development could be expected without withdrawal from global capitalism, a thesis that supported the strategy of disengagement and "relying on one's own strength" developed during the 1960s in the Third World. This withdrawal was a mission that the bourgeoisie could not accomplish. It required socialism, an objective on the agenda, with no intermediate stage, since the dependent countries were already considered capitalist.

The notion of surplus and the undifferentiated definition of capitalism were subjected to intense criticism. Plunder was as old as the history of human societies; it was not specified in what way capitalism innovated. As for the definition of capitalism, it applied to any individual or collective entity producing goods for sale on a market. The distinctive features of capitalism—such as wage labor and capital accumulation—disappeared, making the qualifier capitalist fitting for any society, from Babylon to the French Fifth Republic. Finally, it was difficult to accept that production for the world market transformed a periphery into a capitalist society. This ignored concrete social structures which could take on very diverse forms. The approach also overlooked the fact that some societies could be integrated in the world market while remaining precapitalist, or that production for the world market could even be a factor in consolidating their traditional character.

Samir Amin, a prolific economist of Marxist orientation, undertook the most ambitious work of the "dependency" group *(Accumulation on a World Scale*, 1970; *Imperialism and Unequal Development*, 1976). He set out to elucidate both the causes and the consequences of the expansion of capitalism. Among the former, underconsumption, the tendency of the rate of profit to fall, the absorption of economic surplus, and unequal exchange played, separately or jointly, an initiating role. Born from the process of expanded reproduction of capital, they led to the spread of capitalism throughout the world.

The emphasis on capital accumulation and the taking into account of social relations distanced Amin from the idea that surplus was pumped out of satellite countries. Rather, the underdevelopment of the periphery resulted from the "disarticulation" of its economy. Unlike that of the center, it was characterized by the existence of more than one mode of production within the same social formation. Integrated into world capitalism to meet the needs of the center, it experienced "extroverted" accumulation, the opposite of the "self-centered" accumulation that led to the development of advanced countries. Peripheral capitalism suffered from distortions of all kinds and a chronic blockage of development as a consequence of the diversion abroad of factors of progress likely to confer dynamism and coherence to the whole.

All "dependentists" subscribed to the idea of exploitation of the Third World through unequal exchange. The theory of comparative advantage, according to which international trade and specialization worked to the advantage of all, was declared null and void. The terms of trade remained unfavorable to the countries on the periphery because the average unit value of their imports was greater than the average unit value of their exports, and the gap continued to widen to their detriment.

The economist Arghiri Emmanuel provided the theoretical demonstration in *Unequal Exchange: A Study of the Imperialism of Trade* (1972). Starting from a few propositions, including that which considered the price of labor power as an independent variable, he deduced the transfer of value from low-wage to high-wage countries. Highly paid labor obtained goods of greater value from world trade than those it gave up. The draining of the surplus was replaced by an extortion inscribed in the very process of international exchange and harmful to accumulation and growth in the periphery.

It was a rigorous construct based entirely on the hypothesis that wages were autonomous. Yet critics did not fail to point out that it was the level of economic and social development that determined wages, not the other way around. Wages were set in the sphere of production and could only rise if production was transformed. Barring extra-economic intervention, goods were exchanged at their value, including that of labor power. Confined to the commercial sphere, Emmanuel's analysis rested on a presupposition that weakened it.

With the theory of dependency, the class struggle gave way to that of the oppressed nations. Thanks to decolonization and the prevailing Third-Worldism, it exerted great influence. Its apogee, in all its forms, was closely associated with the general conditions of the postwar period, especially decolonization, but also the lull in interimperialist relations. During the 1960s, its audience was at its peak; it set the tone for research, gave it direction, concepts, and vocabulary. However, it was to be expected that changes in the real world would be accompanied by a reevaluation in the world of ideas. The erosion of United States primacy at the beginning of the 1970s and the rise of Europe and Japan signaled that the international cohesion of capitalism could no longer be considered an immutable given. Bukharin's and Lenin's theses on interimperialist rivalries had to be dusted off. The same went for those of cycles and crises, because the economic boom was running out of steam.

As for the Third World, results there hardly conformed to the prescriptions of the "dependentists." On the one hand, the newly industrialized countries (NICs) embarked on "export-oriented industrialization" without first "disconnecting" from global capitalism. They even connected more in order to sell their manufactured products in developed countries and opened the door to foreign investments, a departure from the policy applied in the South since decolonization. The Third World bourgeoisie, considered "comprador," was proving capable of achieving development under certain conditions. On the other hand, a number of newly independent countries that had taken the direction of disengagement and followed policies inspired by the dependency school reversed course in the face of unsatisfactory results. At the same time, failures and setbacks—with multiple causes—fueled anti-Third-Worldism during the 1980s.

The dependency theory lost its luster. Its weaknesses came to light. An adequate description of various aspects of the global situation, it seemed of limited use for understanding the deeper mechanisms of capitalism and its extension on an international scale. Its conception of imperialism was insensitive to the evolution of capitalism as well as restrictive; it appeared unchanged since the great explorations and involved only relations with the non-European world.

As an ideological support for voluntarism, populism, and Third World nationalism, the dependency school was said to have accepted, in an inverted form, the main lines of the modernization theorists' approach. In response to the idea that traditional society was responsible for underdevelopment and the international market the path to salvation, its proponents made the opposite assertion. Did they not share with their adversaries the static notion of a "normal" capitalism, namely that of Western countries? Was not the only difference in the means to achieve it?

The dependency school had the immense merit of removing from scientific discourse the opinion to the effect that exogenous influence was uniformly beneficial to Third World countries. The analysis of development could no longer be conducted without reference to the consequences of the historical process of insertion into a specific structure of economic relations on a world scale. The criticisms that rained down on the school during the 1970s did not detract from this achievement. But the weakening of the "dependency" current was unmistakable.

CHAPTER 14

Globalization, financialization, rentierism: imperialism today

The order built after 1945 was that of a regulated and structured capitalism in the form of a pyramid-like hierarchy, with the United States at the summit, the rest of the West (Western Europe, Canada, Japan, Oceania) at a lower level, and the newly independent Third World at the bottom. Alongside and outside of this configuration was the socialist sphere, i.e., a third of the world. The old imperialist rivals were reduced to cooperating but this was not due to the discovery of the virtues of felicitous relations between national capitalisms envisaged by Kautsky. The interimperialist hostilities that punctuated the history of capitalism were muted because American superiority rendered them obsolete, while the confrontation with the Soviet bloc served to impose cohesion.

Far surpassing all other Western countries, the United States assumed the role of supporter and quasi-fiduciary guarantor of the stability of the whole. Replacing the pound sterling, its dollar was the de facto international reserve currency, indexed to gold and playing, to all intents and purposes, its role as the ultimate hedge for all currencies. This was beneficial to its multinational firms and to foreign direct investments (FDI), the main vector of imperialism in its new post-neomercantilist and postcolonial phase. All Western countries resorted to Keynesianism to generate economic growth and turn the page on the torments of the depression. The result was an era of unprecedented prosperity and the smooth functioning of capitalism, to the point of making economic crises seem like a thing of the past.

a. The privilege of the dollar

Prosperity in the North and the first steps towards development in the South showed signs of dysfunction at the end of the 1960s, in the form of monetary disorders. The dollar came under attack on the markets in 1960. Although this had no lasting effects, it did reveal a sensitive point in the postwar economic model. Tensions surrounding the dollar put pressure on the international monetary system. Fixed exchange rates depended on the stability of the United States currency. However, the US trade surplus dwindled, and its balance of payments became negative from the 1950s to the 1970s, thus weakening the dollar. The balance of payments deficits widened from the 1980s onwards.

Proving to be lax, the United States failed to observe the discipline required of a pillar of the international monetary system by issuing currency to meet its needs. It paid for its purchases by means of what amounted to printed paper churned out by the "money printing press," a process destined to expand phenomenally in the future. Its enormous military expenditure, notably for the war in Vietnam, and external investments, in particular FDI from multinational firms which had increased more than sixfold in two decades, showered the world with liquidity and fueled inflation. Dollars proliferated.

The gold standard of the nineteenth century and that of the Bretton Woods gold exchange standard were fixed exchange rate regimes. One of their functions was to set limits on accumulated deficits in the balance of trade or the balance of payments, and on the expansion of the money supply. All countries were subject to a common discipline, but the United States exempted itself and financed its deficits by issuing currency through which it acquired goods and services. European banks too issued dollars ("Eurodollars") for interbank markets, then for lending. As for foreign central banks, they also held dollars.

Inflation in the United States spread to its partners, while the value of their dollar reserves declined. The quantity of dollars put into circulation came to exceed the stock of gold supposed to guarantee them under the Bretton Woods agreements. The convertibility into gold, the basis of the international status of the dollar, became dubious and devaluation predictable, prompting requests from dollar holders for precautionary conversion to gold. Even American companies preferred to hold hard currencies (Deutsche Mark, Swiss Franc).

Confidence in the dollar eroded. It was subjected to speculative assaults forcing the United States to draw on the meager metal stocks to defend it. It became a depreciated currency considered destined for devaluation. During the 1960s, the dollar-based international monetary system was destabilized. The dual role of national currency and international standard was too heavy a burden for the dollar to bear. Taking advantage of its privileged status, the United States prioritized its national imperatives, disregarding its international obligations. The ultimate guarantor of the international monetary system was the one who flouted it.

De Gaulle deplored the "exorbitant privilege" enjoyed by a country that could create money to finance its deficits, free from all constraints. While France called for a return to the gold standard, episodes of speculation multiplied at the end of the 1960s, affecting other currencies as well, such as the pound sterling which was devalued in November 1967.

The United States' balance of payments was in deficit. In 1971, for the first time since 1893, the country also recorded a deficit in its trade balance. The symbolism was powerful, even if the gap was insignificant compared to the yawning chasm that would widen in subsequent decades. The time had come to give undivided priority to US national interests, even if it meant dismantling the web of international arrangements put in place by the Bretton Woods agreements.

The United States' offensive was primarily monetary, and it targeted its partners. On August 15, 1971, two unilateral measures were announced: a 10 percent surtax was imposed on imports to the United States, until foreign currencies were revalued; the convertibility of the dollar into gold was suspended, as had been that of sterling in 1931. The second attempt to make a national currency the official pivot of the international monetary system was abandoned. Calculated in terms of economic growth or unemployment, maintaining the currency at a fixed parity had too high a cost; the discipline that this implied was too restrictive. The United States spent more than it earned and military outlays were an aggravating factor in the weakening of the dollar.

In December 1971, the dollar was devalued (last devaluation: 1934) to give a boost to American exports, and the mark and the yen were revalued to curb German and Japanese exports, which had become too competitive. The Bretton Woods system broke down.

Detached from gold, currencies were no longer anchored, as they traded at daily rates on the foreign exchange market. With the United States trade balance still in poor shape, a further devaluation of the dollar in January 1973 caused monetary disruptions, so much so that all currencies began to float, a novelty ratified in 1976. Flexible exchange rates replaced fixed parities and rates were set on day-to-day markets, definitively putting an end to the Bretton Woods system. Demonetized and stripped of the role of standard, gold was now a commodity like any other. The break was clear: the three decades of Bretton Woods gave way to the post-Bretton Woods era.

In the absence of a *de jure* standard, the international monetary system was now de facto based on the dollar. The aura of Bretton Woods and the size of the United States economy preserved its place as a transaction and reserve currency. Half of the world's trade was denominated in dollars, and so were foreign debts. Oil, the lifeblood of the world economy, was priced and paid for in dollars. Decoupled from gold, the parity of the dollar plummeted, accentuating its official devaluation. But if this temporary downgrading was costly to self-esteem, it was a small price to pay in return for the privilege of having the dollar as the international standard.

For the United States, the end of the dollar's convertibility amounted to a green light to widen the budget deficit, worsen the balance of payments deficit, and expand the money supply by issuing dollars without the safeguard of the relationship with gold. It flooded the market with Treasury Bills. At around $20 billion in the early 1970s, the budget deficit ballooned to $200 billion a decade later. The mass of dollars flowing abroad could increase exponentially, as the United States made use of means of payment that could be expanded at will and cost it nothing.

b. The era of economic deceleration

As their industrial production lost momentum, the United States entered a familiar phase in the history of imperialist powers, that of the transition from productivism to rentierism, from the real economy to the "fictitious" economy of monetary signs and intangible assets. The blockage of the mainspring of profitability in the productive economy induced a headlong rush into an overblown financial sector. Formally, the dollar had no special status; it was a currency like any other. All these currencies had no value other than the market price decided by supply and demand. But the United States profited from the memory of Bretton Woods, the size of its economy, and its issuing power to give the dollar the role of a universal means of payment that could be used to acquire goods anywhere. The enjoyment of an intangible advantage allowing wealth and value to be pumped from outside is the quintessential, purest and most transparent form of imperialism. Financialization and rentierism are symbiotically linked.

Monetary instability was a corollary of dysfunctions in the productive system and changes in the global economy. It reflected the entry into crisis of the postwar economic model. In the advanced capitalist countries, growth rates, which had recorded 4 percent from 1950 to 1973, struggled to reach the 2 percent mark. The finely tuned mechanism showed signs of wear and tear. The engines of expansion were becoming anemic. After being responsible for growth, productivity gains slowed down, lowering growth rates and eventually profitability. They stalled at a time when more investment was needed and wage earners, dogged by stubborn inflation, demanded regular increases in their purchasing power. Wages acquired through combative unionism during periods of rising productivity weighed on companies when the trend reversed. There was less to divide between profits and wages.

Productive investment was lacking because the capital-intensive solution of acquiring more equipment was costly relative to what would be produced, while undermining profitability. If capital stock were to increase, its marginal product would decline. A valuation crisis loomed behind the falling rate of profit. Raising prices was a short-term expedient but its consequence was "creeping" or "galloping" inflation. The market for durable goods, the flagship products of the thirty-year economic boom, reached saturation, putting companies in a state of overcapacity. The speed of assembly lines on which Taylorism ("scientific organization of work") was based found their limits in human physiology. Outside of production, the tertiary sector (administration, services, commerce, finance) was the only one expanding, but productivity gains and added value were modest, certainly less than in the secondary sector. As for the productivist ideology of the "consumer society," it increasingly came to be seen as an alienating way of life and aroused less support.

There was one final factor that explained both the disruption of the growth phase and the United States trade deficit: distribution of wealth in the imperial order was becoming less lopsided. The American share in world GDP, close to 50 percent in 1945, declined to 40 percent in 1960 and, despite fluctuations, to 35 percent in 1975. Europe and Japan, which the United States had accompanied with benevolence in order to restore the Western economy, were now emerging as competitors, their growth rates being higher than that of the United States economy. Capitalism is dynamic and, however regulated and monitored it may be, it is never stationary. The diversity and inequality of growth rates mean that rankings of companies and states alike are constantly called into question.

During the 1960s, the revitalized industries of West Germany and Japan became serious competitors to those of the United States, especially for capital goods. The secondary (industrial) sector represented 26 percent of US GDP in 1966, but only 12 percent in 2016. German and Japanese exports took markets away from the United States and even penetrated North America. While West Germany and Japan raked in surpluses, the United States struggled to maintain a positive trade balance. In 1971, it ran a deficit and has been registering ever-mounting shortfalls since that year.

The rise of the two former defeated adversaries of the Second World War did not mean a return to national capitalisms and the traditional interimperialist conflicts that ensued from it, but it did serve as a reminder that the recent harmony between capitalist powers and current ranking in the international hierarchy were not immutable. Competition was sufficiently intense for coordinating bodies to emerge between mainly Western countries in a transnational and multilateral perspective. The Mont Pelerin Society had been created in 1947, while the Bilderberg group existed since 1954. In 1971, the World Economic Forum appeared, bringing together heads of the world's largest companies and political leaders in Davos. The US Council of Foreign Relations sponsored a Trilateral Commission formed in 1973 to promote collective management of the world economy by the United States, Western Europe, and Japan. From 1975 onwards, another framework, the Group of Seven (G7), brought together the heads of state and government of the largest capitalist economies on an annual basis.

Share in world exports of industrial products
percent

	1953	1959	1971
United States	29.4	18.7	13.4
Western Europe	49.0	54.7	54.7
Japan	2.8	4.2	10.0

Share in total world exports
percent

	1950	1970
United States	36.7	15.3
United Kingdom	11.3	6.8
FRG	3.5	12.1
France	2.2	6.2
Japan	1.5	6.8

Currency realignments and dollar devaluations worsened infla-tion. Paid in dollars, oil producers saw their revenues melt away. At $2-3 per barrel, prices were already low. In fact, the cheapness of all commodities contributed to Western growth during the thirty-year economic boom. The further fall in prices from 1971 onwards pro-voked a reaction from the exporting countries, who sought to raise them to compensate for their losses. They formed the Organization of the Petroleum Exporting Countries (OPEC) in 1960. Two years of tensions and negotiations followed the 1971 United States decisions, culminating in a quadrupling of prices during the Arab-Israeli war of October 1973. Other producers of raw materials demanded an appro-priate increase in the price of their exports and a New International Economic Order, less disadvantageous for the South.

The "oil shock" was one aspect of the disintegration of a Western economy already disrupted by endogenous causes. Still, it completed the process of plunging it into a crisis phase, which began in 1975. The page of the thirty-year economic boom was turned: years of steady growth in GDP and international trade volumes were followed by a double dip. High during the 1960s, the ratio of investment to GDP collapsed and remained at low levels for a decade.

A historical dynamic spanning three decades broke down; an "accumulation regime" got clogged. Contraction set in and unemployment began to rise inexorably, becoming structural. In addition to the unprofitable sectors of the previous decade, such as textiles and coal mining, branches that used larger amounts of fixed capital—for example, steel and automobiles—were now in dire straits.

This was a peculiar crisis because it did not result in deflation and general collapse, as in the 1930s, but in inflation, slowdown in activity, and sluggish growth. An unusual situation, it ran counter to conditions observed in the past and contradicted the postulates of economic science because it combined inflation and unemployment, two realities considered incompatible. Both resisted efforts to reduce them. The simultaneity of inflation and stagnation—described by the neologism "stagflation," for want of an explanation—constituted the distinguishing feature of the crisis of the 1970s.

The crumbling of the previous growth model marked the end of a dynamic era and the beginning of an era of painfully slow progress and chronic stasis. Peaks of activity occurred but they did not have the character of firm trends. The United States, the FRG, and Japan achieved respectable growth rates in the second half of the 1970s, and international trade was buoyant. In February 1979, the revolution in Iran caused a doubling of oil prices. If the Western economy experienced uncertainty rather than crisis, the industrializing countries of the South, like South Korea, suffered a blow.

c. The indebtedness of the South

One of the drivers of international trade and economic recovery is credit expansion. The monetary creation triggered by the breakdown of the dollar-gold link caused prices to rise, including those of raw materials, whose exporters became solvent borrowers. Now over-liquid and loaded with Eurodollars, banks turned to do business in the South. Private capital made a comeback in the non-European world it had crisscrossed from the nineteenth century to the interwar period. This movement had been interrupted by the collapse of commodity prices during the depression and had not resumed after 1945.

In an atmosphere of euphoria, loans to the Third World multiplied from 1972-1973 onwards. After 1974, new revenues from oil-exporting countries ("petrodollars") were used for four purposes: to acquire United States assets, thus underpinning the dollar and its function as a de facto reserve currency; develop infrastructure through construction companies, mainly Western; to purchase weapons systems to support Western military industries; to increase cash assets of Western banks.

Together with other financial resources held by these banks, these dollars were recycled in the form of sovereign loans to states and commercial loans to companies. A mass of capital was available for use in financial set-ups, and banks zealously canvassed customers. They took over from Western governments and the World Bank which had been the main source of flows (loans at "concessional" rates, aid) to the South since the Second World War. By 1977, the ten largest United States banks derived more than half of their revenues from foreign operations.

Overriding Third World distrust of foreign capital, a legacy of the colonial period, many countries of the South borrowed to purchase equipment from countries in the North. Within a decade, the total debt increased tenfold. The curtain fell on the short-lived "self-centered" growth policies of the previous decade and development gains were reversed; "extroversion" echoed the prevailing neoliberalism. Instead of "disconnecting" from the international economy, it was now a matter of integrating into it as best as possible. Purchases of "turnkey" factories and major contracts for infrastructure, public works, and construction constituted the most common activities in this original field of North-South economic relations.

Having slowed down since the end of the 1960s, the economies of the North found new opportunities. For those in the South, the consequences were mixed: alongside an undoubted modernization, a heavy debt was amassed, with all the attendant risks. Many of these projects were based on the expectation that export revenues would be sufficient to service the debt. If these were to fall, borrowers would be unable to meet their commitments or to refinance. A suspension of payments would trigger a financial crisis.

The time of reckoning came at the beginning of the 1980s. In the United States, inflation depreciated the assets of the wealthiest and reduced their share in national wealth. In October 1979, a decision was taken to compress the growth of the money supply by applying a restrictive policy. Against a backdrop of austerity and redistribution to the wealthiest categories, interest rates on the interbank market skyrocketed, exceeding the threshold of 20 percent in March 1980. As other economies dried up, foreign money poured into the dollar to benefit from attractive rates: $11.6 billion in 1982, $36.6 billion in 1983, $100.2 billion in 1984. Treasury bills sold easily, the value of the dollar soared, and the revaluation achieved one of its aims: to attract foreign money to finance United States deficits, a phenomenon destined to be lasting. The more colossal the deficits, the greater the inflow of foreign resources.

From 1985 onwards, the United States became a net debtor. At the same time as it championed a militant neoliberalism, supposed to correct the misdeeds of Keynesianism, it was the most indebted country in the world. Between 1978 and 1984, its balance of payments deficit increased sevenfold to reach $102 billion. Its trade balance deficit rose from $148 billion in 1984 to $171 billion in 1987. This compared with $2.7 billion in 1971, the initial year of foreign trade imbalances. The surplus in the services account was not enough to make up for the huge deficit in the merchandise account.

Elsewhere, such an alarming assessment would trigger a major devaluation of the currency or a serious crisis, both acting as deterrents to foreign capital. In the case of the United States, it no longer had any consequences. This rule applied to them in 1971 and 1973, when the dollar was devalued to rebalance foreign trade. The United States adopted measures, such as the International Multifiber Arrangement in 1973 and the Trade Act of 1974, and the 17 percent depreciation of the dollar between 1973 and 1979 boosted exports. But the currency was the focus of their attention.

Since its detachment from gold, the dollar had also decoupled from the real, physical economy. The anomaly had an explanation that was not economic. By making the dollar a safe-haven asset, the United States exploited a non-economic advantage, namely its geopolitically dominant position, for economic purposes. Contemporary imperialism revealed itself unmistakably. The mystique of the dollar was called upon to become the fulcrum of imperialism in its current version.

Deflationary policy reduced inflation but the sharp hike in interest rates had a depressive effect on the global economy. It fell into a severe recession which reached its lowest point in 1982. More than during the 1970s, bankruptcies and business closures became widespread, while unemployment verged on a social crisis and consumption contracted. It was with the slump of 1982 that the reality of the end of the thirty-year economic boom began to sink in. Average wages stagnated and inequalities widened.

The tightening in the United States had repercussions for indebted Third World countries. Their debts were denominated in dollars and these became more expensive to acquire for debt servicing. As these loans had variable rates, their renewal was subject to increased rates. Third World sources of income were also affected. They found themselves in a critical situation because of the combination of sluggish demand for their products, a drop in their export revenues, barriers to the entry of their products into Northern markets, the difficulty of competing with subsidized European agriculture, prospects of borrowing at high rates, and constraints to repay their debts in over-valued dollars. Declarations of insolvency and cessations of payment were foreseeable. A century after the bankruptcies that followed the economic crisis of 1873, a new series of defaults was at hand. Postcolonial imperialism harked back to the beginnings of neomercantilist imperialism.

Following the rise in oil prices in 1974, a spike in commodity prices between 1976 and 1978 set the stage for a new peak in loans to the Third World. The long-term debt of the countries of the South increased from $66 billion in 1970 to $173 billion in 1975 to $781 billion. Representing 73 percent of export earnings in 1975, debt servicing exceeded 159 percent in 1985. Three South American borrowers—Mexico, Brazil and Argentina—accounted for 40 percent of Third World loans.

Even an oil exporting country like Mexico was forced to announce, in August 1982, its inability to meet its deadlines. Following the shock of October 1979 (the tightening of United States monetary policy) which made the dollar more expensive, it had trouble refinancing itself. Some 120 banks had opened representative offices in Mexico during the boom years and their canvassing had been insistent. Many large American, Canadian, and European lending banks had committed the equivalent of two or three times their capital in loans to the Third World.

The risk of serial bankruptcies posed a threat to the international financial system. Twenty other debtor countries were reduced to requesting moratoria or renegotiations of their debts in 1982; the number had risen to more than thirty in 1983. Banks shifted their focus from the South to OECD countries, preferring bond issues to bank credit and "syndicated" loans. The devastated Third World ceased to demand products from the North, especially as the prices of raw materials and commodities plummeted between 1985 and 1993.

To "restore the credit" of Mexico, a settlement mechanism was put in place and it served in other cases. The IMF, the World Bank, and the United States Treasury intervened with a macroeconomic program that was usable in practically all circumstances (later called "structural adjustment" or "Washington consensus"). It involved conversion of debts into negotiable instruments, debt restructuring and rescheduling, new financing to service old debts—with the imposition of austerity programs as a counterpart— cutting back of public spending, reduction of demand and consumption, slowing down the economy, raising the price of commodities, privatizing public enterprises to make them available to foreign capital, opening up the economy to foreign capital, liberalizing trade, increasing exports, and abolishing import and exchange controls, in other words, the neutering of the instruments of the import substitution policy.

Such conditions ensured that the targeted countries would always be in difficulty, forced to request new loans, and, inevitably, compelled to suspend debt payments. Latin America's foreign debt did not plateau. It continued to swell from $68.5 billion in 1975 to $318.4 billion in 1982, and reached $392.9 billion in 1986.

The measures devised by the IMF were designed to free up the sums needed to service the debt, inviting comparison with the post-bankruptcy policies of the previous century. Forced to maximize their exports, debtors were driven back to their former specialization in primary products and raw materials, at a time when stagnation in the North lowered prices. As the volume exported had to continually increase to bring in the same income, the terms of trade deteriorated for the countries of the South. Not only did their annual GDP stop growing, it declined. The contraction of national wealth meant a drop in the average standard of living. The South was in recession and regression. Banks and the international monetary system were rescued and, for ten years, net transfers changed direction, now going from South to North.

At the same time, the amount of public and private debts owed by the Third World continued to surge. Standing at $610 billion in 1980, it rose to $1,510 billion in 1992 and reached $2,400 billion in 2001. Between 1970 and 2002, Africa borrowed $540 billion and repaid $550 billion in principal and interest, but it still owed $295 billion. New loans to "serve" old ones ensured that it would not get out of debt. Sub-Saharan Africa received $294 billion, repaid $268 billion, but continued to have an outstanding debt of $210 billion. This drainage system gave the notion of imperialism a concrete usurious meaning.

As in the nineteenth century, debt was the catalyst. Once countries got caught in the spiral, they would not be able to escape. Medium or long-term loans were contracted during periods of economic boom and available liquidity, such as in the 1860s and 1970s. They were framed with a view to exports whose revenues would make it possible to service the debt by paying interest, thus regularly amortizing the principal and repaying the balance at maturity. When an economic crisis hit, the whole scaffolding collapsed; there was difficulty to export to markets where demand weakened, falling revenues, insufficient income to meet debt payments, and pre-bankruptcy or bankruptcy.

In the nineteenth century, public debt "boards" or "administrations" were imposed on debtor countries by the countries representing the creditors' cartel. They took control of the finances of defaulting countries to extract the amounts required to service the debt. What followed was political takeover or military occupation, as in Tunisia, Egypt or the Ottoman Empire, and policies favoring the export of products most likely to bring in revenue. This led to specialization in a particular crop, primary product or raw material, in sum, the most direct path towards underdevelopment as an appendage to the world, or more precisely European, market. It also pointed to more borrowing to pursue the policy of specialization or to ensure the service, the "consolidation," the conversion, the staggering or the renewal of old loans.

The immediate impasse of bankruptcy was overcome at the cost of perpetuating the relationship with creditors. Henceforth, debtors were intertwined in a mode of operation governed by indebtedness. Considered as one-off operations, to be unwound at maturity, the first loans led to a permanent system of indebtedness and dependence on foreign lenders, the providers of a flow of capital that had become indispensable. Even when scrupulously "serviced," the debt was never extinguished. The twentieth century model corresponded to that of the nineteenth, with the IMF substituting for trusteeship bodies and military occupations.

A crisis in the productive system hit the North during the 1970s, and a debt crisis flared up in the South the following decade. In both North and South, the 1980s were a period of economic slowdown, even impoverishment. The role of the dollar was crucial. It had appreciated by 40 percent since 1980. At a stratospheric level compared to other currencies, it stifled debtor countries and economic activity in general. United States exporters eventually suffered the consequences. In September 1985, the decision was taken to stop overvaluing the currency in order to facilitate credit and let oxygen into the Western economy.

However, what followed was the collapse of dollar-denominated oil prices ("oil countershock") and the paralysis of oil-exporting countries as international economic players. Fewer "petrodollars" became available for recycling. The debt crisis had already reduced the "exposure" of banks in the North to countries in the South, now the disaster zone of the global economy, subject to IMF structural adjustment plans. Increasing famine, social unrest, and the break-up of states were the most visible symptoms. The high hopes of the era of decolonization and plans for development through import substitution faded into memory. Return to dependence and "recolonization" were the order of the day.

d. Eastern Europe in the doldrums

While Latin America and Africa struggled in the meshes of debt imperialism, Eastern Europe took out loans from Western banks. Being indebted to capitalism is an anomaly for socialist countries, given the dangers of losing independence to creditors, a phenomenon observed time and again in the nineteenth and twentieth centuries. A socialist economy can trade with the capitalist world but becoming a debtor is a risky option.

From the 1970s onwards, the countries of Eastern Europe moved in this direction, due to failure to resolve the problems plaguing their economies. These included stagnating productivity, lack of dynamism, the difficulties of centralized management of complex production systems, and inefficient use of production factors, all of which had been weighing on them and worsening since the 1960s. Structural reform projects proved ineffective or were not carried through. Importing Western technology then appeared to be a solution and a substitute for the changes that were necessary.

Borrowing was the way to acquire the desired equipment and Western banks had plenty of liquidity. Loans underpinned increased trade with Western Europe, expected to boost Eastern European economies. In 1976, the Soviet bloc's debt to Western banks stood at $38 billion ($6 billion owed by Poland). However, recourse to Western Europe coincided with the slowdown that followed the thirty-year economic boom and trade was not sufficient to make up for the deficiencies in Eastern Europe. During the 1980s, the burden of debt servicing grew heavier, while governments made it their duty to honor the deadlines, albeit at the cost of sacrifices on the part of the population. To this end, one of the leaders, Nicolae Ceausescu, was pressuring Romanians on the eve of his overthrow in 1989.

Economic dependence on the West coincided with a Western offensive against the ailing Soviet system. It primarily targeted countries linked to the USSR. Since the Helsinki Conference of 1975, Western policy had highlighted human rights in the Soviet bloc. In the liberal tradition, the aim was to promote individual rights without reference to collective rights and, in doing so, weaken societies and political systems. This campaign differed from the ideological struggle waged by the West from the Second World War until the 1960s. Marked by the theme of freedom against totalitarian tyranny, it focused on the broadcasts of *Voice of America* and *Radio Free Europe*, with little direct intervention in the political life of the targeted countries. Thus, during the uprisings in East Germany in 1953, in Poland and Hungary in 1956, and in Czechoslovakia in 1968, the West denounced the USSR but refrained from interfering, because the logic of geopolitical blocs remained operative. Westerners did not dispute that these countries were part of the Soviet sphere of influence.

This was no longer the case from the 1970s onwards, as the West took the measure of the difficulties of the Soviet world. Intervention was no longer excluded; protesters in the East had the West on their side. The new strategy was evident in the revolts in Poland during that decade. The election to the papacy of the Archbishop of Krakow in 1978 stirred up Catholic feeling in the country. Western support for the Solidarnosc trade union, in conflict with the Polish authorities, was clearly displayed. In 1989, all Eastern European countries were affected, and a new development was the approval of the leaders of the USSR who loosened ties with their Eastern European allies, a prelude to the dismantling of the USSR itself.

e. The awakening of Asia

Far from Europe, East Asia followed an original course, whose significance would become apparent in the medium term. Breaking with the approach based on indebtedness, the emergence of New Industrialized Countries (NICs) in the South was a phenomenon of great historical importance because it rendered obsolete the centuries-old dichotomy between metropolises reserving manufacturing for themselves, and overseas dependencies confined to primary products. The result was astonishing for it succeeded where Western liberalism open to the market and foreign capital, as well as statism guaranteeing endogenous development based on the domestic market, had failed.

Neither the Western theory of modernization and growth by stages or by diffusion, nor the theory of "disconnection," nor the Soviet theory of the non-capitalist development path led to development. As programs tinged with liberal, Third World, or socialist ideologies failed to produce the desired results, the exit from underdevelopment and into development was achieved empirically.

Pragmatic and eclectic, the development strategies employed in East Asia borrowed from socialism and capitalism. Based on internal savings and the domestic market, they combined import substitution and export-led growth. Under the aegis of the state, they brought together a large public sector comprising large national companies and private ownership of the means of production in a synthesis that could be described as state capitalism. A hybrid set comprising a variable mix between the private and public sectors, the model applied as much to China which considered itself socialist as to the other countries of East Asia which considered themselves capitalist. In Japan, the private sector clearly prevailed over the public sector. Without any universal ideological or timeless theoretical pretensions, the strategy attracted attention because of its success. However, the fact remained that, corresponding to specific conditions, it was an exception, and its reproducibility elsewhere has not been proven.

The evolution of East Asia appeared first and foremost as that of a subcontracting annex of the Western economy, all the more so as the conflict with Soviet and/or Chinese socialism took precedence in the Americans' motivations and explained the concessions they made to their allies, such as the possibility of protecting their market and access to the United States market. The export by Japan, Taiwan, and Hong Kong of manufactured objects of low added value at low prices during the 1950s appeared to be a simple process of imitation, even counterfeiting, which did not alter the international division of labor and international economic relations. East Asia's dependence was not called into question. Growth and development were expected from the two known programs only: the liberal laissez-faire approach based on private enterprise and openness to the international market advocated by the West, or the statism and planning preferred by the Eastern bloc and by the Third World. Neither had succeeded in pulling the South out of underdevelopment and moving it towards development.

In East Asia, a third path emerged, borrowing from both programs and adding innovations to produce an unprecedented syncretism. The NICs practiced state intervention, planning, freedom of enterprise, protectionism, awareness of technical advances in the world, market regulation, development of the domestic market, and exports as an engine of growth. Their experience was a salutary reminder of the virtues of empiricism and of the fact that application of theory had to take reality into account.

Japan played the role of forerunner of the Asian growth model. After the Second World War, it went through the stages that others would follow: substitution of imports by national production, growth and protection of the domestic market, high savings rate, intensive investment of national origin, virtual absence of foreign capital, major role of conglomerates (*keiretsus*, formerly *zaibatsus*) interconnected and supported by the large banks from which they borrowed, leading role of the state through the Ministry of International Trade and Industry (MITI), passage from imitation foreign products to innovation, improvement in productivity, emphasis on the export of consumer goods and light industry products, then moving up the production chain towards heavy industry (capital goods, more complex manufacturing, such as automobiles and electronics). Like Europe, Japan was treated kindly by the United States for geopolitical reasons. Initially no fear was felt in the face of this "miracle," as the advance and size of the United States protected its hegemony. But capitalism is dynamic, and the pace of its evolution cannot be decreed.

At the end of the 1960s, the growth of Japan and West Germany began to worry the United States. It was one of the factors which disrupted the postwar economic model. Japan had carved out a large place for itself in shipbuilding and steel industries since the 1960s. Its share of industrial exports increased at the expense of those of the EEC and the United States during the 1970s and 1980s. Even more than West Germany, it flooded the American market with automobiles during these two decades, undermining the major American manufacturers, pivots of the economy, and symbols of its power. To exports were added automobiles manufactured locally in the United States. Japanese brands became as familiar as American ones. By 1980, Japan had overtaken the United States as the world's leading automobile exporter. Then, during the 1980s, came exports of household electronic appliances and semiconductors to the United States and Europe.

Japan was the prime beneficiary of United States policies of budgetary, trade, and payments deficits, as well as debt-driven (over)consumption. It was against Japan that voices calling for protectionism were raised. Its trade balance was constantly favorable and its surpluses structural, so much so that Japanese banks, flush with revenues, dislodged their American counterparts from the top ranks of the world's largest banks in 1985. Already the second or third economic power in the world (depending on the ranking of the Soviet Union), Japan seemed destined to rise to the summit.

As dazzling as it had been, Japan's rise faltered during its most brilliant decade. The United States imposed "voluntary" restrictions on its exports. The 1985 decision to let the dollar slip was accompanied by revaluation under pressure of the mark and the yen. The aim was to boost American exports and reduce the huge surpluses in the German and Japanese trade balances. The operation was so successful that it helped tip Japan into deflation and recession, and soon into stagnation and relative decline. Japanese capital was hastily repatriated from the United States as the value of the dollar plummeted, while the financial bubble formed on the Japanese stock market and real estate market deflated in 1990.

From the 1990s onwards, with its momentum lost, the Japanese economy was mired in lasting stagnation, while state debt exceeded twice the GDP, the highest level in developed countries. Abandoning industry, banks took a financial turn, lending more and more for operations on the money and stock markets. Even businesses could not resist the lure of financial activities. As a bubble formed, they found themselves weakened by masses of debts that proved irrecoverable for banking institutions. Huge losses and closures ensued. A long cure was unavoidable.

Japan was embedded in its region as an importer of raw materials and as an industrial center drawing on the labor of neighbors, such as South Korea, Taiwan, and Hong Kong, for subcontracting purposes. Japanese FDI in Asia laid the foundations for integrated international production. The further up the industrial and production chain Japan moved, the more profitable it became to relocate certain labor-intensive activities abroad. With due allowances for scale, Japanese companies were internationalizing production like the United States pioneers. A process of diffusion was underway in East Asia. Exchanges between the countries of East Asia multiplied in a movement which was reminiscent of the interactions between the various regions of Europe since the end of the Middle Ages.

In fact, the outcome of this densification of relations had a fundamentally historic character: at the beginning of the twenty-first century, the Asia-Pacific zone overtook the Europe-Atlantic zone to become the world's leading economic pole and its new center of gravity. A global redistribution of economic power was taking place. In reality, it was a reestablishment of the old equilibrium: until the beginning of the nineteenth century, Asia accounted for more than half of world GDP. The combined effect of industrialization, which strengthened Europe and imperialism which weakened Asia, was coming to an end. It was as if, after profound transformations to overcome underdevelopment, Asia regained its former status.

It could be argued that Japan was a long-standing industrial power that was just recovering its position. Such was not the case for neighbors who followed suit. The Korean War and, later, the United States war in Vietnam, were powerful accelerators of the regional economy, represented by the "Four Dragons" (South Korea, Taiwan, Hong Kong, Singapore), then the "Four Tigers" (Thailand, Malaysia, Indonesia, Philippines). Japan, South Korea, and Taiwan did not allow foreign direct investment in key sectors of their economies. Foreign capital was not the source of growth; when it came, the intent was to participate in an ongoing process.

Only South Korea borrowed from abroad, but moderately, with debt service remaining far below the value of exports. In South Korea, as in Japan, state-backed conglomerates (*chaebols*) spearheaded the strategy; in Taiwan, a network of small and medium enterprises was the source of the exports. All three industrialized by adopting the strategy of export-led growth and moved up the industrial value chain towards high value-added products. South Korea exported goods worth $33 million in 1960; the total was $51 billion in 1988, making it the tenth merchandise exporter in the world. It became a powerhouse in the steel, shipbuilding, automotive, and electronics industries.

Most East Asian countries recorded annual growth rates exceeding 5.5 percent, even 10 percent for some. Fueled by high profit margins and savings rates, their investment-to-GDP ratios were at record levels. All protected their internal markets, outlets as important as their external markets; one supported the other. Domestic demand was the springboard to exports; export earnings expanded domestic markets. East Asia's share of world trade, 6 percent in 1970, doubled in two decades. Hong Kong, Taiwan, South Korea, and Singapore accounted for 1.4 percent of the world's industrial exports in 1965, rising to 9.2 percent in 1992. The improvement in the standard of living was reflected in the increase in per capita income. In South Korea, it rose from $157 in 1960 to $3,300 in 1988; in Taiwan, from $145 in 1951 to $10,000 in 1993. Recently an economy of scarcity, East Asia was now in the era of mass consumption.

f. China on the road to global economic primacy

China was the latest addition to the NIC group. Its case was both ordinary and singular. It stood out for its size but not for its strategy, which was similar to that of the others. It even intensified the features of the strategy through a ruling party that provided a framework for the state, determined broad orientations, ensured their implementation, and watched over the cohesion of the whole. The model followed by China resembled that of the "Dragons" and "Tigers," all calling on foreign capital. But China delimited its field of action, retained its autonomy, experienced dazzling growth, and achieved the status of world economic power. Such a development would have been considered unthinkable barely a quarter of a century ago.

The uniqueness of China's position stemmed from its past. The era of neomercantilist imperialism left it destitute. Since the birth of the People's Republic in 1949, it had been striving to overcome the poverty afflicting the world's most populated country and to achieve development. Tried and tested socialist formulas did not produce the desired results. The Soviet form of industrialization based on heavy industry proved either inapplicable or was poorly applied. As for the Maoist program of collectivization of agriculture (Great Leap Forward, 1958-1960), the basis of possible rural industrialization, it ended in disaster. During the 1960s and 1970s, the ensuing struggle for power within the Communist Party paralyzed the country (Cultural Revolution, 1966-1976).

It was towards the end of the 1970s and in desperation that China adopted the pragmatic formula of the neighboring NICs. The material needs of its population had to be met. Uplifting the country with the utmost urgency took precedence over ideological considerations in the choice of means. The overarching obligation—and the yardstick of legitimation—was to turn the page on a century of underdevelopment by taking nearly a billion Chinese out of poverty, raising their standard of living, and ensuring growth. At the same time, national recovery after a century of humiliation helped to reinforce consensus. Success was measurable, even if the eradication of poverty is not complete (2 percent remained in 2020). The rate of investment in the productive economy, particularly in major works, infrastructure, and industry, was the highest in the world.

Drawing on an extraordinary national savings rate, the source of an exceptional investment effort, and an enormous pool of low-cost labor from the countryside, it moved from the stage of workshop-country producing everyday consumer goods to being an exporter of higher value-added industrial goods. Leveraging its investments in education and engineering training, it climbed the value chain and entered high-tech in cutting-edge sectors (digital, 5G telecommunications, advanced robotics, big data, artificial intelligence, blockchain technologies), as envisaged in the *Made in China 2025* ten-year plan adopted in 2015.

The annual growth rate of its GDP exceeded 10 percent from the 1980s and for almost three decades, a record in the history of capitalism. It hovered around 7 percent after 2008, at a time when the global economy experienced several phases of slowdown. China came through the Asian crisis of 1997 unscathed. During the United States crisis of 2008 and the coronavirus crisis of 2020, it was the only country to post positive results, with growth at 4.9 percent as early as the third quarter of 2020. Its share in world trade increased from 1 percent in 1978 to 3 percent in 1995 to 12.4 percent in 2018. It joined the World Trade Organization in 2001 and increased its exports tenfold.

Since 2010, it has been the world's largest exporter of goods, outperforming Germany, whose exports benefited from the euro being undervalued compared to a theoretical German currency. In 2018, it was still the world's leading exporter and the second largest importer after the United States. China accounted for 25 percent of global industrial production in 2016, the United States for 19 percent. The obstacles that the United States has been trying to throw in its path for the past decade have had no tangible effect on a seemingly inexorable march. The 2020 pandemic revealed the world's dependence on China for electronics, medical equipment, medicines, and even procedural masks.

The rise of China was one of the highlights of the late twentieth century-early twenty-first century. It demonstrated to perfection the historical constant of economies developing at different rates and primacy passing from one to the other. Having become the "workshop of the world" for a wide range of products, and replacing the United States as the locomotive of the world economy, it saw its GDP skyrocket.

China represented 30 percent of world GDP in 1820, before a century of humiliation reduced it to penury. From 1 percent of world GDP at the end of the 1970s, then around 7 percent in 2000, Chinese GDP was at 15 percent in 2020, on a par with that of the United States. Its economy grew fourfold since the late 1970s. Its GDP surpassed Japan's as second largest in the world in 2010 and, since 2021, it was on the verge of ranking first in the world. At purchasing power parity, China has been in first place since 2017 and still retained that position in 2023. In 2009, it became the world's leading market for the number of automobiles sold; in 2011, for personal computers.

In the 2020 *Fortune Global 500* ranking of the largest companies by revenue, there were, for the first time, more Chinese companies than United States companies, although the latter dominated in the group of the largest companies. Remarkably, China emerged as the beneficiary of a globalization supposed to favor its American initiators. The result is a singular dispute pitting China, champion of multilateralism and open borders, against the United States, which is erecting tariff barriers and railing against the globalization it so recently celebrated.

From being a marginal participant in international trade in the late 1970s, China became the world's leading trader three decades later. Like the other NICs, it is a firm supporter of free trade and the decompartmentalization of markets, a position which contrasts with the traditional protectionism of the Third World, or even of any country in the process of industrialization.

A market economy, economically liberal and open to the world economy, China is, however, no less than the other NICs, administered by a state and a party with broad powers. Five-year planning guides public investments. Currency and banks are under the control of the state, which emphasizes productive investment. The state is centralized, heir to the imperial bureaucratic tradition and socialist *dirigisme*. A state capitalism and a "socialist market economy," pragmatic and unclassifiable, its system aims at socioeconomic development and national recovery, rather than ideological coherence.

China stands out for having used the institutions and practices of socialism, blended with capitalism, to develop and raise living standards in the country with the largest population in the world. It illustrates the worldwide historical record of socialism, mutating from a movement for the emancipation of workers in industrial-capitalist societies in the nineteenth century to a program for the transformation of backward societies from the twentieth century onwards. In one generation, China exchanged its status as an underdeveloped country for that of a world power, on the way to becoming the world leader.

The state is the true driving force of the economy and the guardian of national cohesion. Firms, the market, and billionaires are subordinate to it. Its mastermind is the Communist Party, which has proved to be an adaptable institution. From an organ for the construction of socialism, it turned into a directing center for the establishment of developmentalist state capitalism. From a party of workers and peasants, it transformed into a multiclass party. Because it is structured, it acts as the instrument to counteract ferments of instability inherent in capitalism and the risks, political and other, posed by the opening of the national economy to the world market.

China considers that it is laying the material foundations for the establishment of socialism in 2049, one hundred years after the proclamation of the People's Republic. Reviled during the Cultural Revolution of the late 1960s but consistent with Marxism, the idea that the development of productive forces is a prerequisite for the transformation of social relations is back. Its economy is not a subordinate entity composed of foreign branch plants or dependent on nomadic foreign capital, as the experience of the "Asian Tigers" might have suggested. If openness to foreign capital contributed to globalization, it turned it to its advantage rather than allowing itself to be "normalized," co-opted, and absorbed by it, as could have been anticipated.

This appropriation of the process of its internationalization and its transformation into a factor enhancing autonomy, rather than dependence, constitutes a unique phenomenon. The postwar recovery of Europe and Japan was that of already industrialized countries and did not call into question United States hegemony. The NICs succeeded in industrializing, but they conformed to the US-led international order and were integrated into it economically, politically, and militarily. This is not the case with China. Until recently, it was a developing country which, instead of becoming a simple workshop state, rose to the rank of industrial power through an Americentric globalization to which it opened up but did not sacrifice its independence. Integration into the global market remained under state control.

In China, the key companies in all strategic areas are national or even state-owned, and they account for a third of total production in a mixed economy. FDI and foreign "multinationals" are permitted—China is one of the leading recipients in the world— but they are circumscribed and represent a minor part of GDP. They contribute mainly to stimulate research and innovation in Chinese companies. They are required to join forces with local partners and transfer technology. Like Chinese entrepreneurs, they have the right to make profits but not to escape state control, still less to dictate policy. Foreign capital is supervised by a state which remains in charge and holds the levers of the economy.

The ratio of foreign debt to GDP is kept low, so as not to endanger the country's independence. Memories of a century of subjugation of China by European, American, and Japanese imperialism (symbolized, among other things, by the Opium Wars, the sacking of Beijing, unequal treaties, the Nanking massacre, extraterritorial enclaves), as well as the chaos, famines, and extreme misery for the population, are still vivid.

China is the first country subjected to imperialism to become a great power, while remaining a developing country. It has in common with all less developed ("emerging") countries the primacy it gives to economic development, coverage of basic needs, political stability, and national independence—objectives of a collective nature anchored in their historical experience—over political liberalization and individual freedoms. This baffles and irritates Western rivals for whom collective needs have long since been met.

As for the Chinese desire to assert its sovereignty, it is matched by the means to exercise it. After decades of effort, China has resolved the problems of development, security, and independence that have plagued all countries of the South since decolonization. Moreover, integrated into the international market, it can, because of its size, be the center of a globalization which would replace Americentric globalization, or be self-sufficient because its immense domestic market continues to develop and its savings rate is high. Being self-propelled, it is capable of generating its own sources of growth.

The Japanese "miracle" and its abrupt end illustrated the acceleration of rebalancing in the global economy. In turn, the emergence of China, even more than that of the NICs, demonstrated again the fact that neither history nor capitalism were immutable and that positions acquired were rarely held for long. Such a rapid rise, self-sustaining growth, the impenetrability of its institutional shell by foreign interests, the will and means to be master at home, and the overall mass of the entity had repercussions beyond the economic sphere. For the United States, the dominant power, issues of geopolitics and hegemony became topical.

The opening of China and the dismantling of the Soviet bloc made globalization possible ("new world order"). Now that a universal economy and imperialism, sketched out during the Second World War but left unfinished as long as these obstacles existed, were finally within reach of the "sole superpower," the recovery of Russia and the appearance of an ever-stronger China pushed the horizon back again. Incidentally, the United States had become relatively weaker economically than it was in 1945.

Just as Germany emerged at the end of the nineteenth century to defy British hegemony, China followed a century later to challenge that of the United States. The questioning of the hierarchy and modus operandi of the latest version of the imperialist system, defined after the Second World War, came from the most unexpected quarters, a country recently classified as "developing," then "emerging," that improvised by using a variety of methods to develop itself.

Equally original was the newcomer's projection outside its own borders to outline a globalization with the potential to replace neoliberal and Americentric globalization. China needs raw materials and is ready to invest in transporting them by land routes safe from threats from the American competitor. A gigantic undertaking, the Belt and Road Initiative (BRI), also called "New Silk Roads," was launched in 2013. It provided for hundreds of thousands of kilometers of highways, railways, intermodal platforms, ports, and airports in dozens of countries eager to participate in this "community of destiny." In September 2023, a Western-backed India-Middle East-Europe Economic Corridor, including Israel and Saudi Arabia, was announced in order to counter BRI. But the resurgence of the Palestine question in October 2023, the impossibility of collaborating with Israel while Palestinians are slaughtered and their rights are denied, as well as Israeli efforts to ignite a regional war ruled it out.

Thousands of BRI projects are underway in more than 130 countries. The plan addresses 60 percent of the world's population on three continents in the form of a partnership of mutual interest opposed to unilateralism. China holds a trump card that sets it apart from the West: it does not interfere in the internal affairs of other countries, and does not sponsor "regime changes"; nor does it portray itself as a universal standard, lecturing others and imposing on them models or conditions, such as the "Washington consensus." Supported by the Asian Infrastructure Investment Bank (AIIB), created in 2016 and bringing together fifty-seven founding countries, the BRI would become the economic backbone of Eurasia, welding it together and making China the economic center of the world.

Ultimately, the United States would be confined to North America. Reconnecting with the past, the Old World would regain its primacy interrupted since the sixteenth century by the rise of the maritime economy centered on the North Atlantic. Despite many differences, one being the absence of the threat of force, the situation is reminiscent of the *Weltpolitik* of the early twentieth century by which Germany implicitly questioned British primacy. It is even more historic because it involves the shift of the world's center of gravity not just within Europe but from the West to Asia. After half a millennium of domination by Euro-Atlantic thalassocracies, it would be a shift towards the land powers of Eurasia. What long-term effect the rupture between Europe and Russia, due to United States pressure in relation to the conflict in Ukraine, will have on the Eurasia project remains to be seen. It goes without saying that the United States opposes the BRI which would mark the end of its preponderance. The economic dispute extends to the geopolitical and military spheres. As momentous as the US-Russia conflict, and possibly more so, the US-China contest has the potential to determine the future of imperialism, of the global economy, and of the world order.

g. The globalized neoliberal model

Beyond regional developments, major global transformations were taking shape in the structure of capitalism. The end of the postwar boom seemed to be the prelude to the crisis that Marxist currents have long predicted, even during the years of growth. Paradoxically, at the moment when history proved them right, their analytical and strategic deficiencies, as well as their fragmentation into small groups, factions, and tendencies at loggerheads with each other reduced them to impotence and kept them on the margins. Less forthcoming about an economy in the throes of historic transformation, their successors turned to culture, representations, and identities, as if economic matters had become unintelligible.

The beneficiary of the decline of Keynesianism and social democracy that held sway since the Second World War was the liberal current. Discredited by the memory of the depression, it had been pushed to the political and intellectual periphery after the Second World War. It found itself reduced to the role of powerless protester against state interventionism, at a time when the latter went from strength to strength. The exhaustion of the thirty-year economic boom offered it the opportunity to emerge from the shadows, get the ear of decision-makers and launch an offensive to reconquer its lost ideological hegemony, which it did during the 1980s.

The end of the era of almost uninterrupted growth called for a reassessment of the Keynesian model and the establishment of new conditions of profitability for capital. Liberalism has standard proposals based on neoclassical economic theory: disengagement of the state, neutralization of its postwar "redistributive" character, primacy of the market, priority of supply over demand, free trade, freedom of capital movements, and transfers of public property to private interests. The foreseeable widening of inequalities was to be mitigated by a "trickle down" of wealth. Substituting for the exhausted model, globalization presented a lifeline. It was about globalizing capital, goods, and services, not labor, because, if the wage differential was not maintained, the relocation (offshoring, outsourcing) of companies to the South would be of little interest. Some migration into developed countries was to be favored as a way of easing labor shortages and putting downward pressure on wages. As a byproduct, stirred-up xenophobia could be used to sow discord in society.

The remedy for the attrition of the economic model of the thirty-year economic boom was sought, not in investment in technologies which would lower costs, but in the displacement of production to the South, where it was less expensive. This represented a historic upheaval in the structure of the world economy which hitherto reserved manufacturing for the North alone. It began in special zones where workshops, such as *maquiladoras* or sweatshops, imported parts from the North, assembled them, and exported the products to Northern markets.

Of another nature, following oligopolistic strategies, the relocations of the 1950s and 1960s concerned only the industrial countries of the North. If globalization was a reality dating back to the beginnings of capitalism and intrinsic to it, this latest push was characterized by internationalized production, as well as by sustained pressure to subject states and their legislation to the imperatives of market standardization and the free movement of capital. Contributing to this was an intense promotion of the advantages of neoliberal globalization by means of globalism, understood as an ideology and integral vision of the world and society. The aim was a general restructuring with a view to establishing an operating model that would restore profitability and prevent malfunctioning of the system.

Globalization stemmed from the end of the thirty-year economic boom, from the quest for new markets and, even more, new fields for the employment of capital. Saturated and mature, the United States and European economies no longer generated the expected profit rates and volumes. The gainful investment of productive capital was more difficult. Capital had to be able to extend its sphere to the South, to Eastern Europe and elsewhere, in other words it had to globalize and the conditions for its globalization had to be put in place.

It so happened that Eastern Europe was an open territory since the end of planned economies and the South was available as well. Whereas, during the post-independence years, foreign investment was viewed with suspicion due to the aftereffects of colonization, to aspirations to development and to the desire to build "self-centered" national economies, two decades later, its absence was regretted since autonomist projects were discreetly abandoned.

In full swing, computing, digital processes, information technologies, robotization, and high tech were likely to boost productivity, but not enough to restore the profitability of the productive sector and counteract the shift towards financial activity (next section). In addition to financialization, the way out of the erosion of productivity and profitability called for a redeployment of an extensive nature. This involved the migration of productive capacities to the countries of the South where production costs, especially the price of labor, and social security contributions were those of less developed economies.

Manufactured at ridiculously low costs in the South, despite equivalent productivity, goods were sold at the higher prices of Northern countries, leaving large profit margins for foreign investors. One of the defining features of imperialism today is this kind of extraction and transfer of value, in this case to the detriment of the South and to the benefit of the North.

Like indebtedness, cheaper imports from the South helped to offset the devaluation of labor, the rise in the cost of living, the fall in real incomes, and the weakening of consumption in developed countries, following the end of the thirty-year economic boom. Globalization was the corollary of the closure of this era, and FDI was at the heart of globalization. By moving production across borders, it deindustrialized the North and contributed to industrializing the South, the opposite of what the "colonial pact" was about. Four-fifths of the world's production took place in the South and four-fifths of industrial workers were located there. Gone were the days when manufacturing was the prerogative of the Euro-Atlantic zone.

Contributing to this was the immaterial (intangible) economy, as reflected in the activities of non-financial companies in countries undergoing deindustrialization. The largest of these companies produced nothing but they captured value, enjoyed staggering capitalizations, and were at the top of the stock market. They were digital platforms that dominated retailing by eliminating small distributors, merchants, and middlemen, and placing suppliers at their mercy; that connected customers and service providers (taxis, hotels, etc.); that offered technological services (search engines, virtual communication forums, virtual advertising spaces, data processing, collection and sale of information).

Even those that produced computer or telecommunications equipment, sporting goods or "designer" clothing split their operations: administration and coordination of activities by the parent company in the "metropolises" of the North, but manufacturing was moved to their subsidiaries or subcontracted in Southern countries. In the post-Taylor era, assembly lines manufacturing an entire product became rare. In the new value chains, work was decentralized, fragmented, made flexible, insecure, "networked," outsourced, and dispersed nationally and globally, although control, decision-making, and management were still centralized. Both raw materials and intermediate inputs were sourced from different parts of the world.

h. The financialization of the economy

The internationalization of the production process was coupled with liberalization and financial integration, giving capital unprecedented mobility. The financial sphere expanded and fed on itself, thereby acquiring increased importance and broad autonomy in relation to the productive sphere. The financialization of the economy, a situation in which money accumulates through financial operations without passing through the productive sphere, is a fundamental feature of contemporary capitalism. Accumulated financial wealth exceeds the size of the material economy. Financialization and globalization provided capitalism with a rebound following the disintegration of the parameters of the thirty-year economic boom. They enabled it to escape from the impasse, to reinvent itself, and to widen its scope of action.

The obsolescence of Keynesianism could be measured by the incapacity of the productive sector to generate profits as it once did, and by the absence of prospects of this changing. Falling real incomes weighed on consumption and deterred investment, jeopardizing the future. At the national level, the solution to the problem was financial; the facilitating element was credit, in other words, the deferral to the future of the cost of consumption in the present. As the economy was sluggish, it was driven by debt, that is to say, by doping to shore up purchasing power. Individuals, households, businesses and governments took on debt at unprecedented levels, with total indebtedness exceeding GDP. Demand and maintenance of the standard of living came to be more and more debt-based, with even basic needs requiring borrowing. The financial sector boomed, as debt peonage became widespread. The "consumer economy" turned into the debt economy. To revitalize economic activity, the money supply expanded and the financial sphere underwent phenomenal growth. The real economy gave way to the economy of monetary signs. At the same level as world GDP in 1980, financial assets represented four times that in 2007.

To the commodification of everything, specific to capitalism, was added the financialization of everything. "Financial products" multiplied *ad infinitum*. The omnipresence of finance translated into unbridled speculation and a craze for "leveraged buyouts," futures operations, "derivatives" created on the basis of other securities or financial instruments whose prices fluctuated, exchange contracts (swaps) —including ones relating to payment defaults (credit default swaps)—pledges of assets for borrowing purposes ("collateralization," "collateralized debt bonds"), transformation of loans and other financial or non-financial assets into negotiable and transferable values ("securitization"), "structured products," arbitrage, and stock market transactions.

Creative but opaque and perilous financial engineering ("wizardry") in the service of speculative investments was celebrated. Abandoning productive sectors of the economy as unpromising, shunning investments that only paid off in the medium or long term, money capital poured into financial operations and short-term profits. Listed companies had their gaze fixed on share prices and these bore no relation to their revenues or operating performance. Everything was based on the anticipation of an indefinite rise in the indices. From being a simple intermediary in the service of economic activity, the social stratum of money handlers ensconced itself at the pinnacle of capitalism.

In the background, financial bubbles (asset bubbles) repeatedly occurred, providing opportunities for exceptional profits to be made thanks to a knock-on effect and runaway excitement generated by the prevailing euphoria. All bubbles deflated, leaving behind a trail of damage, often including revelations of fraud, such as insider trading and false accounting, fictitious assets, raiding of pension funds, credit and stock manipulations. The series of bubbles spoke for itself: junk bonds, mergers and acquisitions boom, hostile takeovers, purchases by borrowing (leveraged buyouts) and often for restructuring, asset-stripping, and carve-up purposes, during the 1980s; overinvestment in real estate by savings and loan banks, with deregulation allowing loans without guarantees, during the same decade; the "new economy" based on computing, telecommunications, information technologies, high tech, the Internet (dot.com) at the end of the 1990s; debauchery of high-rate and high-risk mortgage loans (subprimes) transformed into collateral for new negotiable instruments, split up, multiplied infinitely and usable for speculation, during the 2000s. The philosophy was stated bluntly: "Greed is good."

All bubbles involved excessive credit expansion. Acquisitions of companies by corporate raiders were operations for financial or purely speculative purposes. In leveraged purchases, the debt incurred to carry out the transaction was placed on the liabilities side of the balance sheet of the purchased company. To clear the debt, newly acquired companies were dismembered and parts amputated and resold at a profit, which reduced or eliminated the productive base. Even for non-financial companies, stock price profits took precedence over operating profits. Improving short-term performance on the stock market replaced obtaining long-term results in the firm's official business. More and more income came from financial investments, speculation on currency markets, and stock market operations, often for the repurchase of their own shares in order to boost the price of company stock. CEO remuneration was indexed to the company's valuation.

Having gained the upper hand over the patrimonial-family model of the firm in the twentieth century, the managerial model was now challenged by the financial-stock market model. A study showed that the 500 companies making up the Standard & Poor 500 stock market index devoted more than half of their profits to repurchases of their shares between 2003 and 2013, thereby raising share prices. This practice has intensified. Money passed less and less through the productive cycle. The economic activity constituting the core business of companies was unprofitable and becoming even less so as resources used for financial purposes were withdrawn from investment.

Immense "fictitious" paper wealth accumulated in record time, far from the production circuit. Non-existent in 1990, the "derivatives" market alone was estimated at ten times global GDP in 2020 (it was double in 1995). This colossal volume of funds kept active countless operators, a mosaic of traditional banks, mutual funds, pension funds, speculative "hedge" funds, "vulture" funds, unregulated quasi-banks ("shadow banks"), trust companies, private equity firms, institutional investors, and asset, wealth or portfolio managers handling phenomenal sums on the financial markets. Even individually, some represented the largest concentrations of money capital in the world.

The agitation on the United States financial markets attracted liquidity from abroad, which strengthened the dollar and consolidated its international status. At the same time, fueled by an overabundance of credit, finance was becoming autonomous, multiplying and reproducing itself far from the productive sphere (real economy). Subprimes illustrated the modus operandi. Once the mortgage had been signed by the buyer committed beyond his means, intermediaries took charge of the metamorphosis of the document into a financial instrument, repeatedly transformed, split up, revalued, and resold. This multiplication of loaves was lucrative. The more it changed hands, the more its price rose, brought in fees and commissions, and spread toxicity in the financial system. The real economy came back into the picture later, when buyers proved unable to meet their monthly payments, defaulted and were dispossessed of their hard-won homes. The real estate market plunged, and the scaffolding of credit and financial conversion-reconversions collapsed like a house of cards.

The bursting of each financial bubble triggered a crisis. The Internet bubble was followed by the resounding bankruptcies of Enron and WorldCom in 2001-2002. If the Wall Street stock market crash of October 1987 was a warning about speculative financial investments and if the 2000-2001 debacle on technological stocks led to a recession, the major subprimes crisis which broke out in 2008 was worse than that of the Savings & Loans bankruptcies which predated it by two decades and was facilitated by deregulation. It was the first crisis of the globalized capitalist economy, emanating from the very heart of the system and not from a country in the South. Overflowing the United States, it was externalized and spread like a wave to all corners of a financial system that was vulnerable to the harmfulness of subprime mortgages.

Its ramifications were global because many large non-US banks, attracted by speculation on these new kinds of "derivative" instruments, were loaded with worthless paper and on the verge of insolvency. Their fall would have meant an economic collapse on a scale not seen since the 1930s. This 2008 crisis called into question the post-thirty-year economic boom of neoliberalism, deregulation, "casino economy," financialization, and financial globalization. It put an end to neoliberal and globalist triumphalism. Suddenly the idea of deglobalization left the realm of the unimaginable. The following crisis, that of the coronavirus in 2020, discredited deindustrialization, the globalization of production, and the disengagement of the state, which were already losing legitimacy.

Crises occurred in the sphere of finance, but their source was in the productive sphere and they had repercussions on the real material, physical economy. Each time, in order to avoid a cascade of bankruptcies and the implosion of the system, state authorities intervened to organize the rescue of financial institutions by urgently creating money to advance in order to relieve balance sheets. The reaction was always the same: attempts to put out the fire by throwing cash at it. In the United States and elsewhere, "printing money" was in full swing, and that inflated the money supply. In what looked like doping, central banks injected liquidity by the billions, innovating by buying up debt ("monetization") and lowering interest rates to the floor to facilitate credit (read: indebtedness). Bank notes fell from the sky ("helicopter money") to directly provide means of payment without relying on banks, and Modern Monetary Theory justified the practice. Thrown in this way, money became "easy," while the economy was on monetary life support.

However, these new resources were not in demand in the depressed economy or were not reaching that economy; hence the strange phenomenon of negative rates. The new money remained in the financial sphere, driving up stock prices, accentuating the financialization of the economy, and paving the way for the next episode of turmoil. As for the money issued following the bursting of the subprime bubble, it translated into loans to states whose budgets had been affected by the crisis and who had to, among other things, intervene financially to save their financial institutions. The upshot was widespread over-indebtedness and near-bankruptcies, such as that of Greece which threatened the euro zone with implosion.

Ironically, the state, denigrated as obsolete by globalist thinking, was called upon to forestall disaster. During crises, the taxpayer was the last resort and public credit rescued private credit. Financial institutions offloaded their bad debts ("non-performing loans") by exchanging them for new money issued by central banks. Private debts were transformed into public debt, while the money supply rose sharply. The budget deficit of states and their debt increased. The severity of the 2008 crisis and the extent of government action revealed in broad daylight, the indispensable role of the state and its spectacular "comeback" after two decades of exaltation of market supremacy and promotion of an economy free from state interventionism. Ideology notwithstanding, it was a reminder of the fundamental, albeit veiled, fact that the economy is always framed, underpinned, and guaranteed by political power.

In addition to financialization on the national level, there was also financialization on the international scale, i.e., the extension of the geographical area in which capital operated. As an example of globalization, masses of volatile liquidity moved to be loaned on a short-term basis ("hot money") to financial institutions or states. The influx of considerable sums into the economy appreciated the national currency to levels that would soon be unsustainable. Devaluation or the anticipation of a depreciation caused foreign capital to flee the country—often taking refuge in the dollar, which appreciated—sending local currencies tumbling, widening the balance-of-payments deficit, and leaving banks, businesses, and national economies in disarray.

With no more than a few electronic transactions, national economies and those of comparable neighbors ("contagion") could be reduced to paralysis, leading to serial devaluations. This type of storm occurred in Mexico in 1994, the first occurrence of crises in globalized financial markets and the consequences of "sovereign risk," in Southeast Asia in 1997, in Russia and Brazil in 1998. Argentina fell victim to the backlash between 1998 and 2002.

The origins of large-scale movements of capital and the massification of the financial sphere dated back to the dissolution of the Bretton Woods system. The end of the fixed relationship with gold, floating exchange rates, and devaluation of the dollar definitively opened the floodgates to the trends which brought down the system of stable parities. Floating currencies fueled speculation on currency markets. In the United States, free rein was given to account imbalances—budgetary, commercial, and payments—which were now easier to cover by simply issuing dollars.

In Western countries, the lifting of exchange controls, the liberalization of financial markets through deregulation, and the decompartmentalization of financial institutions from 1979 onwards intensified global capital flows. From $339 billion in 1971-1975, they quintupled to $1,895 billion in 1981-1985, tripled to $5,541 billion in 1991-1995, then tripled again to $16,503 billion in 1995-2000. From around 6 percent of world GDP in 1980, the stock of FDI stood at around 22 percent in 2002.

Operations on financial markets ceased to be the counterpart of exchanges of goods and services and no longer had a function in the productive economy. Evolving in an autonomous circuit alongside the real economy, capital grew on its own. The volume of international capital movements far exceeded that of goods, which had been in the limelight during the decades of postwar growth. As for the rate of growth of capital, it was faster than that of international trade, itself higher than that of the world GDP.

In the early 1980s, annualized daily transactions on the New York foreign exchange market were equivalent to ten times the annual value of United States imports and exports, and twice the US GDP. During this decade, the Eurodollar market—in which financial institutions lent to each other—stood at $75,000 billion per year, or twenty-five times the value of world trade. In 1989, the sum of daily transactions in the world's foreign exchange markets represented almost forty times the daily value of world trade in goods and services. On the eve of the 2008 crisis, the multiple was fifty.

If one of the characteristics of the post-Bretton Woods period was the considerable increase in dollars in circulation, another was the greater presence of European and Japanese investors, particularly in the FDI category that was once a virtual United States monopoly. European and Japanese "multinationals," soon to be joined by South Koreans, carved out market shares. Three-quarters to four-fifths of FDI was still concentrated in the countries of the North. Until the 1970s, the United States was by far the largest exporter of capital. Devaluations of the dollar in 1971 and 1973 made assets in the United States less expensive for foreign buyers. A reversal of the trend set in: FDI flows towards the United States exceeded traditional flows towards Europe, as reflected in the stock table. The United States was now a net importer of FDI and its net international position in terms of cumulative investments moved into the negative zone.

During the 1970s, Western Europe overtook the United States as the world's leading source of FDI flows, then as the leading holder of

FDI stock
billions of $

	From the United States	To the United States
1950	11.8	3.4
1960	31.9	6.9
1970	75.5	13.3
1980	215.5	65.5
1986	259.9	209.3
1988	327.0	329.0

FDI stocks, even though the US still had more than any other single country and was home to the majority of the world's multinational firms. From three-quarters during the 1960s, its share fell to 41 percent in 1978, 24 percent in 1990, less than 20 percent in 1994, before rising again to 22 percent in 2002. In terms of the total stock of assets held by non-residents in the world (shares, bonds, loans, and cash), the American share decreased from one-half in 1960 to one-fifth in 1990.

Stock investment flows
Annual averages in billions of $

	1975-1979	1980-1984	1985-1989
Total incoming amount (14 industrial countries)	**3.6**	**10.8**	**23.1**
United States	1.5	3.4	8.6
Japan	0.6	3.5	(- 9.1)
9 major European countries	1.5	2.0	18.8
Total outgoing amount (14 industrial countries)	**1.2**	**8.7**	**36.6**
United States	0.2	1.7	4.1
Japan	0.1	0.2	9.2
9 major European countries	0.8	5.9	19.9

Bond investment flows
Annual averages in billions of $

	1975-1979	1980-1984	1985-1989
Total incoming amount (14 industrial countries)	**8.8**	**17.1**	**102.4**
United States	0.6	4.1	30.3
Japan	2.3	4.2	37.2
9 major European countries	3.9	5.9	29.3
Total outgoing amount (14 industrial countries)	**16.7**	**40.1**	**147.3**
United States	5.6	4.0	5.3
Japan	2.5	13.7	80.8
9 major European countries	8.6	21.7	59.6

Not only did the United States return to its nineteenth-century status as a net importer of capital, but it also settled into the position of the world's largest debtor, barely fifteen years after having been the leading creditor for more than half a century. It was also the main recipient of foreign capital. In 1984, the United States' net international balance (assets minus liabilities) became negative; by 2004, it represented 22 percent of GDP.

i. At the rentier stage

In 1971, the United States offensive that put an end to the Bretton Woods system had a commercial component (devaluation and protectionism) and a financial component (removal of all obstacles to the issuance of dollars). The trade aspect was abandoned because the decline in productivity and profitability of United States industry made it uncompetitive, regardless of the relief provided. Industry was sacrificed for the benefit of services and the transformation into the tertiary economy. All policy focused on the monetary and financial issues, namely the manipulation of the dollar and the expansion of the money supply through the exercise of seigniorage power to appropriate value from abroad. A major strategic and historical shift was confirmed. Less perceptible at first glance, it only became noticeable in the medium term. The face of the United States economy was changing fundamentally; its center of gravity shifted from production to the tertiary sector and finance.

Against all expectation or logic, the United States benefited from negative aggregates that for other countries would be debilitating handicaps. It was as if hegemony provided immunity from economic rules and constraints that were fully applicable to others. A major new development was that their deficits had become a bottomless pit destined to deepen immeasurably in the twenty-first century. In 2020, the deficit for goods was $922 billion, for goods and services $677 billion. At the same time, capital was being drained away by the swelling public debt, due in particular to enormous military spending, representing two-fifths of that of all the countries in the world. The federal government's debt tripled between 1980 and 1988. At 40 percent of GDP in 1985, the United States public debt stood at 64 percent in 2008 and reached 135 percent in 2020. As for private debt, it was of an equivalent amount.

Japan's trade surpluses were invested massively in United States Treasury bills and bonds. A new type of circuit was established and would be repeated with China two decades later: the negative trade balance of the United States was offset by the investment of the exporting countries' surpluses with their American client. What the United States lost in terms of production, it more than recovered in financial terms. Undermined in 1971, their supremacy was reaffirmed thanks to an unusual situation; the still exceptional status of the dollar which made it possible to draw resources from the rest of the world to the United States, allowing it to finance itself cheaply from the trade surpluses accumulated by foreign countries.

The privilege considered exorbitant during the 1960s, despite the formal link to gold, was even more so after the end of the Bretton Woods system because the disconnection from gold led to a dollar standard. The dollar remained the billing and settlement currency for half of international trade, even when the United States was not a party to the transactions, and even though it represented only 10 percent of world trade and 15 percent of world GDP. Today, the following are denominated in dollars: 40 percent of international payments via the banking clearing system SWIFT (Society for Worldwide Interbank Financial Telecommunications); 44 percent of foreign exchange transactions; two-thirds of issues on the bond market; three-fifths of international loans; three-fifths of the world's foreign exchange reserves. The dollar is far ahead of the euro, yen, pound sterling, and renminbi.

The result is that, thanks to the reach of the dollar, the United States retains the function of tutelary power despite the dissolution of the Bretton Woods regime. Industrial domination was succeeded by financial domination. Dollarization and the prevalence of the dollar made the currency the main instrument of United States globalist imperialism, the one through which blockades are imposed on targeted countries by the threat of "sanctions" against those who have relations with them.

From $3.37 billion in 1972, the US trade deficit soared from year to year, reaching $678.74 billion in 2020. Since this "overdraft" is structural, due to low productivity and lack of competitiveness, the United States is living beyond its means, with a daily need of $1.9 billion in new money from abroad. In the short term, indebtedness offsets stagnating or even falling real wages, while inequalities deepen, unemployment increases, and job insecurity becomes widespread. The fact remains that the United States consumes more than it produces, which should trigger speculative attacks on the dollar and its depreciation.

However, unusually, its value is strengthened and the power to import increased by more capital inflows. An intercontinental loop was created. To ward off the risks of exchange rate crises, foreign countries, particularly those in the South, accumulated dollar reserves and bought Treasury bills. Currently, a third of China's foreign exchange reserves are made up of United States government debt instruments. While putting these economies under the threat of a depreciation or devaluation of the dollar (or an imposed revaluation of their currency), the phenomenon maintains liquidity flows towards the United States. China (like Japan before it) thus sustains its exports and, by supporting its client's economy, protects its investments in the United States. The latter is in the historically unique position of overconsuming to facilitate the sale of what is produced elsewhere and of receiving foreign financial means to pursue this consumption, in other words, of enjoying a rent.

An original international economy was established, involving a drain of resources from abroad and external financing of balance of trade and payments deficits. The United States attracts global surpluses to its shores. Cheap external supplies seem inexhaustible, despite the unbalanced accounts. The demand for dollars and Treasury bills means the possibility to borrow at low rates in one's own currency. The United States is the only country that can run chronic payments deficits without having to raise interest rates, increase taxes or divest assets. The privilege arises from the replacement of gold by the dollar at the end of the Bretton Woods system.

The dizzying sums at stake for the public debt are beyond comprehension: (in billions of current \$) 398 in 1971, 1,000 in 1981, 4,000 in 1992, 10,000 in 2008, 20,000 in 2016, 28,600 in 2021, 34,630 in 2024 (GDP = 22,000, total world debt denominated in dollars = 100,000). There is a legislative debt ceiling, but the United States Congress has raised, revised or suspended it over seventy-eight times since 1960. The latest occurrence of this ritual was in June 2023. To this must be added the private debt of individuals, households, and companies of an equivalent amount.

The tree planted in 1971 after Bretton Woods bore fruit. With zero possibility of restitution and given that non-payment or repudiation would be a suicidal act of bringing down the columns of the temple of the world economy, indebtedness is structural, the overhang is long-term, and the debt de facto perpetual. All that remains is devaluation through inflation and/or depreciation of the dollar, i.e., a consequence of "quantitative easing," the current version of "money printing." In fact, contrary to all rationality, the maintenance of the construction or house of cards depends on faith in its sustainability and the obligation to guarantee it. All stakeholders are in a state of flight-forward or headlong rush. They have no interest in withdrawing, stopping financing, or requesting an audit which would force a declaration of bankruptcy and trigger a chain collapse. New lenders pay to remunerate old ones, in a large-scale reproduction of a Ponzi pyramid.

In this case, it is the American debtor who holds his creditors at his mercy and imposes his wishes on them. To question his credit or put the bankrupt into liquidation would amount to the bankruptcy of his lenders. A withdrawal of Chinese funds, a weapon of mass destruction and last resort, would lead to the free fall of the United States and world economies. A danger of a different kind would be a significant rise in the key interest rate, which was almost zero in 2020-2021. Countless debtors would owe billions they do not have, which would set off a crisis of the first order. The relatively limited rise in 2022-2023 sent shock waves through the system. Finally, the depreciation of the dollar could reduce the United States debt to the detriment of creditors.

Financial contribution from outside, that is the international side of the financialization of the economy, translates into the acquisition of goods and services, in other words value, without compensation. The country appropriates more value than it creates, a characteristic of imperialism. The United States is "exceptional," not least because it alone enjoys the privilege of having a structural deficit in its balance of accounts. It is the dowager of the late Bretton Woods system. As a cog in a new type of international rentier economy, it has a parasitic as well as an organic status. Like a queen bee in a hive, it has become fully rentier, divesting itself of productive sectors (deindustrialization) which are now more profitable elsewhere and importing more than ever what it consumes while being financed by its suppliers.

The corollary is the need for a coercive apparatus capable of securing that privilege, exercising coercion and repelling inevitable acts of insubordination or protest. Rentierism and military capabilities complement each other. Hence the colossal defense budgets which, at the same time, underpin the function of armed guarantor of a planetary imperialism coinciding with the world economy. The United States spends more than 40 percent of the world's military budgets on its armed forces, and as much as the ten other top spending countries combined. Nearly 800 military bases, spread across 130 countries, serve as launching pads of armed intervention, as needed. This does not prevent it from making its allies pay for its wars, such as the 1991 Gulf War financed by Japan and Saudi Arabia, or pressing them to pay more, as in the war in Ukraine.

j. Theorizing

The period ushered in by the crisis of the 1970s took theorizing about imperialism in new directions. A return to the sources of Marxism occurred, alongside the falling out of favor of the dependency school. It was criticized for having neglected dialectics, the dynamics of capital, and social classes, and given preference to a unilinear approach and formalist concepts inspired by functionalism and structuralism.

Modes of production and relations of production now took precedence over market exchanges between the center and the periphery; the sphere of production over the sphere of circulation; the appropriation of surplus value over the levy of economic surplus; the theory of value over unequal exchange. Asymmetrical relations with the metropolises could not mechanically determine the internal structures of dominated countries.

It is known that Marx did not do an in-depth study on the impact of the penetration of Western capitalism on precapitalist societies. His articles on colonialism gave an account of the destructuring of societies—that of India in particular—subjected to it and expressed his confidence that the colonial power carried out simultaneously, and independently of its will, a dual mission: dismantling the old society and laying down the indispensable conditions for its regeneration. He assumed that in the future the candidates for progress would follow the same path as those who preceded them. The most developed industrial country would show them the image of their future.

History did not follow this straight line; development proved to be a more bumpy, tortuous, and slow process than Marx believed. Be that as it may, the fact remains that the few opinions he expressed on the subject ran counter to the fundamental propositions of the dependency school. According to him, in the long term and despite the violence, or even in opposition to the intentions of the colonizers, the link with foreign capitalism would seem to entail renewal and progress, rather than stagnation and underdevelopment.

That was all it took for Bill Warren to latch on to Marx's writings in order to fire a violent salvo against the "dependentists." In *Imperialism: Pioneer of Capitalism* (1980), a book whose title gave away the thesis, he excoriated those who, in his opinion, had distorted Marx's ideas by refusing to recognize imperialism as the agent of the diffusion of capitalism. According to the author, Lenin had initiated this turn, followed by the Comintern, notably during its congress in 1928. For Warren, imperialism was a vehicle whose historical mission was to disseminate capitalism, as it was known in capitalist economies.

Calling underdevelopment a fiction, and dependency theory a nationalist mythology, Warren argued that imperialism bore no responsibility for the state of the Third World. He accumulated figures, tables and illustrations tending to show that industrialization had indeed taken place, that GNP per capita increased, and that living standards improved because, thanks to imperialism, capitalism had spread and taken root. Dependency theory was stood on its head.

This was no banal apology; imperialism had rarely been entitled to such a dithyrambic anthem. Reference to Marx was no more than rhetorical because the author joined the ranks of neoclassical economics. The theory of modernization refuted by the dependency school resurfaced as a lesson in Marxism. An essential corrective, Warren's work was flawed less by its polemical excesses—that was fair game—than by the crudeness of an out-of-context empiricism that equated accounting data with social transformations. Regarding the NICs, its main error consisted in attributing to foreign capital a development due primarily to local action, with which foreign capital was merely associated. In fact, FDI jumped on the bandwagon in East Asia, as it did in Western Europe during the postwar growth years.

Long before Warren's attack, Marxists were distancing themselves from dependency theory and some had criticized it. Leaving it aside, others, prompted by the extension of capitalism on a world scale, sought to explain the phenomenon by adapting Marxist concepts to new realities. Interpretations forked off: on the one hand, the modes of production; on the other, the internationalization of capital. Although enlightening on a theoretical level, they remained abstract because they were not based on concrete analyses.

In *Colonialisme, néocolonialisme et transition au capitalisme* (1971), Pierre-Philippe Rey proposed a model in which capitalism developed in the Third World through the articulation—a notion borrowed from Louis Althusser—of capitalist and precapitalist modes of production. The first drew labor and raw materials from the second. Precapitalist structures did not give way without resistance, but the growing needs of the metropolis, which had become imperialist, led it to favor the domination of the capitalist mode of production. The retreat of the precapitalist mode of production happened in stages: it was first reinforced, then destabilized, and finally eliminated. Third World countries were characterized by an unfinished transition to capitalism, not by underdevelopment.

However, an article by Hamza Alavi in *The Socialist Register* (1975) rejected the idea of two antagonistic modes of production within the same social formation. In peripheral capitalism, the interests of the metropolitan bourgeoisie, the national bourgeoisie, the feudalists, and the rural bourgeoisie coincided within a specific framework, the colonial mode of production. The absence of precise operating mechanisms did not facilitate the use of this concept, even if it gave rise to debates among Indian economists. In any case, the modes-of-production approach focused on internal conditions and put international factors in the background. It did, however, open the way to an analysis of the structuring of global capitalism that took into account both the countries where it was dominant and those where it was not.

The concept of internationalization of capital arose in opposition to current analyses of multinational firms. The proliferation of these companies following the Second World War was striking in its apparent novelty: direct investments, calls on local savings, relocation of production, internationalization of the production cycle, internalization of markets within the firm; so many elements that were difficult to integrate into previous approaches to international investment or capital export. All currents of thought, from empiricism to neoclassicism, strove to explain and take into consideration this unprecedented form of concentration of capital, centralization of management, and international division of labor.

Dissatisfied with the superficial nature of the demonstrations, Christian Palloix—in, among other publications, *L'internationalisation du capital: éléments critiques* (1975)—attempted to raise the debate to a more abstract level. The shift from appearances to deeper realities implied abandoning the perspective of the firm in favor of that of the sector or branch, then of capital itself. Microeconomics had to give way to the analysis of global processes; the study of the properties of capital had to replace that of the concrete or institutional forms that it can take. If capitalism became a global system, it was because of the intrinsic tendency of capital to valorize itself and pursue its accumulation. Multinational firms were only the latest agent of a dynamic operating outside them and partaking in the nature of capital.

Palloix conceptualized the internationalization of capital as a triple process corresponding to three circuits or cycles. Commodity capital, money capital, and productive capital extended successively on the world scene. The stage of the internationalization of productive capital marked the establishment of the capitalist mode of production on a global scale and the transition from the international economy to the world economy. The transition to the international was the inexorable expansion of capital in its social and geographical dimensions. Driven by competition, it spread wherever it could be profitably employed. This valorization internationalized because the law of value had an international content, and capital was subject to it.

For Palloix, the constraint of valorization and accumulation weighed on capital since its beginnings, and imperialism was inherent to the capitalist mode of production. Imperialism and international mode of accumulation were synonymous. Capitalism was evolutionary and passed through stages, each corresponding to a mode of generation and absorption of surplus, and the content of imperialism could not be considered as given and immutable. Capitalism was imperialist whatever its stage of development, even if the mechanisms varied according to the stages. The nature of imperialism lay in the external negation of the contradictions of the capitalist mode of production. As for international accumulation, it provided a way to overcome the constraints engendered by national accumulation.

Based on a solid grasp of the content of Marx's *Capital*, Palloix's finely crafted work brought Marxist analysis back to its primary building block, namely capital. *The Internationalization of Capital: Imperialism and Capitalist Development* (1987) by Berch Berberoglu followed in its wake. This trend, however, left a number of questions unanswered. Was there a difference between imperialism (a system) and the internationalization of capital (an intrinsic property of capital), especially since both involved the diffusion of the capitalist mode of production worldwide? If imperialism and capitalism were synonymous, there would be one concept too many. A theory that equated imperialism and the global economy would be of dubious utility.

Furthermore, was it possible to state unequivocally that the internationalization of capital led to the spatial extension of capital as a social relation? Did societies receiving foreign capital thereby become capitalist? This was plausible but there were so many obstacles, slowdowns, detours, even setbacks, along the way. Deviations and discontinuities were precisely the problem. The accomplishment or non-fulfillment of an ambiguous, complex, and conflicting process called for explanation. Palloix's theory did not sufficiently distance itself from a linear conception in which the globalization of the economy proceeded from a natural enlargement of the space of capital, without political intervention.

As it stood, the notion of internationalization of capital led to granting metropolitan capital the exclusive role in the transformation of the world. The movement was unilateral and unidirectional: the export of capital spread the capitalist mode of production, sparked industrialization, and created the proletariat. As in dependency theory, the initiating, promoting, and acting factor was external. The receiving society remained strictly passive, except that, for some observers, it was underdeveloped, for others, developed. The theory of the internationalization of capital could authorize the conclusion that development required the penetration of foreign capital. Theorists of modernization would find vindication here, were it not for the confidence of the proponents of the internationalization of capital that the spread of capitalism brought socialist revolution closer.

Marxist conceptions conflicted with liberal perspectives but were nonetheless plural. Where the latter detected no connection with capitalism and offered a multitude of interpretations, the former agreed that a relationship existed but there was no consensus about its nature. Capitalism was a multifaceted entity: an ideal construct, capable of being translated into concepts whose interaction allowed the creation of coherent models, it was also a concrete historical process, with a disorderly, tumultuous deployment not devoid of surprises. Its basic mechanisms did not automatically and at all times conform to the characteristics set by the theory.

No doubt they did so in the medium and long term. But history also knows the short term, that of actions and decisions taken in the light of clashes between opposing interests who have little regard for the formal arrangement of capitalism's models. Hence the difficulty Marxists have in directly linking the system's workings—which, all things considered, are within grasp—and its external manifestations in the real world. The challenge is theirs only since liberals do not see the economy as the substratum of society and underconsumptionists emphasize a specific malformation to which they subordinate everything else.

What mechanisms of capitalism produce pressures for territorial expansion? What are the consequences for the societies that engage in this outward spillover and for those on the receiving end? These are the fundamental questions posed by the Marxist tradition with regard to imperialism. The ambition is limitless because it requires the study of all levels of social reality, from both a diachronic and synchronic perspective. It should come as no surprise that the notable, and sometimes decisive, contributions that Marxism inspired have not exhausted the initial program.

Thinking on imperialism since the 1970s was marked by two main features: the influence of historical, material and ideological circumstances; and the confidentiality of reflection on imperialism compared to the "classical," most fertile period, at the beginning of the twentieth century or even the 1960s. International economic and political developments provided the impetus for theorizing, directed the gaze, and colored interpretations. What was produced corresponded to the state of the world and changed according to ongoing transformations. At the same time, the decline of left-wing currents and parties stripped this thinking of its main audience, so much so that it was relegated to the margins. The subject became a field of work for specialists rather than the content of a public debate that could lead to political action.

The responses to the crisis of the 1970s reordered capitalism at the cost of two far-reaching mutations. First, globalization moved an industry that had become unprofitable across borders. Unable to gainfully continue its operations on its home turf, economic activity migrated to more favorable climes. Second, tertiarization and financialization changed the face of the economy that had stayed put, and replaced vanishing production with services and an overblown financial function. Overhauling Western societies, these transformations shook the foundations that had been in place since the beginning of industrialization.

With analytical instruments ill-suited or lacking, thinking on imperialism was on hold for a while. On everyone's lips for decades—even for those who denied its existence —the term "imperialism" fell into disuse, evacuated by the intense globalist campaign. As early as 1983, in the afterword to *The Geometry of Imperialism*, the Marxist-leaning Giovanni Arrighi renounced the theory of imperialism and confined himself to the struggles for world hegemony. In 1990, the title of an article asked what had become of imperialism. In 1993, the *Radical History Review* (New York) organized a forum on the theme "Imperialism: A Useful Category of Historical Analysis?"

In addition to the post-1973 situation, there was the influence of dominant or mainstream thinking. Globalization, the neoliberal offensive, the dismantling of the USSR, the uniqueness of United States predominance, and the impression of a definitive victory for capitalism, viewed as definitive ("the end of history"), set the scene. Glorification of the market, economicism, disappearance of politics and states, end of nations, unification of the world, supranationality, and cosmopolitanism were all in vogue. The pressure exerted by the relentless promotion of liberal globalist ideology in the late twentieth century eventually infiltrated thinking about imperialism.

It was two authors from the left who gave this ideology, and the discourse associated with it, their most accomplished expression. Globalism was here at its peak, taken to its extreme limits. In *Empire* (2000), Michael Hardt and Antonio Negri argued that there was no longer any imperialism. A thing of the past, it had been replaced by the Empire, a global, transnational, deterritorialized, disembodied, and omnipresent entity. Based on nation-states, imperialism had given way to stateless, borderless Empire. Dematerialized and formless, it was everywhere and nowhere. There was no longer hierarchy in a universe synonymous with the global market, now leveled, homogenized, and networked, no more North or South, no more center or periphery. This development reflected the transition to the post-industrial economy and the intangible society of knowledge and information.

Futuristic, *Empire* was above all an idyllic, apologetic vision of neoliberal globalization. It did not describe the world of the present but the one that globalization was supposed to engender in the future. Imbued with postmodernism, it erased landmarks, rendering reality nebulous, ethereal, and elusive. All the clichés were repeated without embarrassment and the book was celebrated in the major United States media. Initially taken aback by such aplomb, critics were quick to reject what looked like a construction taking liberties with reality (for example, Atilio Boron, *Empire & impérialisme*, 2003). The fact remained that triumphant neoliberalism, which set the tone at the turn of the century, gave rise to the idea that capitalism no longer needed imperialism and states, and made it the issue occupying minds in intellectual circles interested in imperialism.

It was above all the evolution of the international situation and warmongering by the United States which were responsible for contradicting the assertions of Hardt and Negri by bringing back "classical" imperialism, moreover in its militarized form. The dismantling of the USSR, unipolarity, and a sense of impunity unleashed hegemonic impulses. Free rein was given to destabilization and military action to impose United States will on recalcitrant states. Uninhibited, neoconservatives and neoliberals came together to promote armed interventionism, some by praising expansionism outright, others by claiming to spread "Western values."

The return of the state and geopolitics—which, in fact, had never disappeared—brought them to the forefront at the beginning of the century. Inspired by globalism, the impression that domination henceforth would be purely economic, with no role for state action, left its mark but did not withstand the brutal manifestation of political and military factors. If the NATO war against Serbia (1999) did not provoke in-depth reflection, the global offensive launched by the United States government in the wake of the September 11, 2001, attacks proved that the state, politics, and war had not faded away.

It was preceded by the unreserved praise of imperialism on the part of "organic" intellectuals for whom it was a source of progress on all fronts, and regretted by the people who had lived under it. Likened to the Roman Empire, the British Empire was praised and the United States called upon to formally don the mantle of successor to bring order to a world where there were too many "failed" states incapable of self-government. Presented as self-evident, a "right to protect" was invoked, even if it barely concealed its affiliation with traditional imperialist interventionism, also cloaked in altruistic garb. Leaders who dared to oppose the imperial will were demonized, treated as criminals to be punished by armed interventionists setting themselves up as vigilantes, and dragged before special courts to make an example of them and assimilate aggression to the application of law.

Lodged within decision-making centers, the neoconservative current advocated a genuine, unbridled imperialism, highlighting military force and the willingness to use it in the service of an undisguised quest for power. The invasion and occupation of Iraq in 2003 was modeled on the age-old policy of the colonial empires of the past, an illustration of the fact that modern neocolonial imperialism can relapse to bygone colonial methods of military conquest, occupation and direct rule, if conditions allow. With this aggressive resurgence of the most classical forms of the state and Realpolitik, a yawning gap appeared between reality and musings about a postnational or postmodern world.

The first decade of the twenty-first century saw a succession of reminders of imperialism (a "new imperialism"), the economic interests that sustain it and the centrality of the role of the state. There were contributions from James Petras and Henry Veltmeyer (*Globalism Unmasked: Imperialism in the Twenty-First Century*, 2001; *Empire with Imperialism*, 2005; *Imperialism and Capitalism in the Twenty-First Century: A System in Crisis*, 2013) which focused less on the theory of imperialism than on the empirical exposition of its misdeeds and the structuring of the social classes on which it depended. Claude Serfati (*Impérialisme et militarisme: actualité du XXIe siècle*, 2006) underlined the key role played by the military function and the arms industry. In the same vein, John Rees (*Imperialism and Resistance*, 2006) provided an overview of certain major themes. With capitalism becoming universal, Ellen Meiksins Wood (*Empire of Capital*, 2003) and David Harvey (*The New Imperialism*, 2003, 2005) examined the relationship between two distinct but intersecting levels: on the one hand, the global dynamics of markets and economic control, and, on the other, the territorial logic of states and political control. Alex Callinicos (*Imperialism and Global Political Economy*, 2009) held that there was indeed a dialectical relation between the economy and the expansion of the state without it being a separation, because it was the same dynamic of the accumulation of capital.

This dichotomy may also have seemed forced insofar as the two levels interpenetrated and each integrated the needs of the other. Still, it continued to raise questions, even giving rise to one-sided, sometimes reductionist interpretations. Thus William I. Robinson ("Beyond the Theory of Imperialism: Global Capitalism and the Transnational State," 2007) believed national capitalism and states to be dead, the world now being that of multinational corporations without nationality and a transnationalized capital in the hands of a new transnational capitalist class. That would be going beyond the entente between national capitalists envisaged by Kautsky. Capitalism would need neither the state nor imperialism.

However, Leo Panitch and Sam Gindin (*The Making of Global Capitalism*, 2013) produced a political study which placed the state at the heart of the analysis and insisted on the primacy of the United States, the only imperial state and the one enjoying complete autonomy. It acted more as the guarantor of global capitalism than of its own interests. Incorporating the rest of the world through globalization, the informal US empire transcended geopolitical rivalries and interimperialist conflicts. For Claudio Katz (*Sous l'empire du capital: L'impérialisme aujourd'hui*, 2011, 2017), the end of these conflicts and the changes in capitalism justified the abandonment of the classical interpretations of the Marxists of the beginning of the twentieth century, without however taking away the relevance of the notion of imperialism.

The perspective changed with John Smith (*Imperialism in the Twenty-First Century*, 2016) and Zak Cope (*Divided World Divided Class: Global Political Economy and the Stratification of Labour Under Capitalism*, 2015; *The Wealth of (Some) Nations: Imperialism and the Mechanics of Value Transfer*, 2019). Like the "dependentists" before them, the two authors found imperialism in center-periphery relations, the difference being that the Third World was now in the era of industrialization and the "colonial pact" belonged to a distant past. The object of study was delocalized production in the South. "Super-exploitation" of poorly paid labor and net transfer of resources towards the North were the substance of imperialism. As for the highlighting of financialization, it owed a lot to François Chesnais (*La mondialisation du capital*, 1997), Michael Hudson (*Super Imperialism: The Origins and Fundamentals of U.S. World Dominance,* 1972, 2003) and Costas Lapavitsas (*Financialization in Crisis*, ed., 2012).

Retrospect and perspective

Subsequent to the Second World War, imperialism underwent the most significant transformation in its history since the mercantilist era. It ceased to be synonymous with the quest for colonies. The possession of colonial empires had been the hallmark of mercantilist and neomercantilist imperialism from the end of the fifteenth century to the mid-twentieth century. Even in the liberal and free trade era of the nineteenth century, during which empires were supposed to have lost favor from the point of view of economic and political doctrine, acquired colonies were retained. After 1945, it was no longer possible to keep populations under formal tutelage against their will.

The beginnings of dissociation between imperialism and colonial empires could be perceived as early as the nineteenth century within a framework which remained that of neomercantilist colonial imperialism. At first, the free-trade imperialism that emerged with industrialization aimed to sell goods on all markets, since those of the colonies were no longer sufficient to absorb increased production. It was always imperialist because the "opening" of new markets was a process of coercion and often violence, especially towards the countries of the South. Then, at the end of the nineteenth century, the export of capital became more important than that of goods.

Capital ignored borders and was more attracted to politically sovereign countries than to colonies held by the country of origin of exported capital. Nevertheless, empires were not dissolved. During the neomercantilist era, which extended from the 1870s to 1945, the traditional template of colonial imperialism coexisted and intertwined with the seeds of new practices of domination through capital. Marked by decolonization, the period after 1945 saw the separation of colonial imperialism—direct control now becoming impracticable—from the imperialism of indirect control, notably by capital.

On another major level, postcolonial imperialism was distinguished by the fact that it applied to both developed and less developed countries. Colonial imperialism was specific to overseas possessions in situations of compulsory economic complementarity. It did not concern countries with a level of development similar to that of the colonizer. Postcolonial imperialism applied as much to former colonies as to former metropolises. All were subject to informal control policies that could be as effective as the formal methods of the past.

Finally, postcolonial imperialism contrasted with its predecessor on a third level. Until the twentieth century, imperialism was embodied in territorially delimited colonial possessions, in full continuity with the imperial models of the past to which mercantilism and neomercantilism brought doctrinal consecration. Empires existed side by side and shared the surface of the earth according to the balance of power.

However, the new imperialism without colonies knew no borders; it was planetary. Capitalism, production, and markets were globalized. Imperial methods and practices adapted to this. Domination was no longer exercised through primacy over a space reserved and off-limits to others. It involved projection onto the entire world and the integration, willing or unwilling, of old and new rivals into a system of hierarchical control governed by the hegemonic power. Globalization did not render imperialism obsolete; it updated it. In globalized capitalism, the object was to reach a higher rank in the hierarchy ("value chain") or to reconfigure globalization, which is where China is heading. The framework was not, however, immutable and the repercussions of globalization gave rise to tensions which led to renegotiation and redistribution. It remains to be seen to what extent globalization would withstand a severe crisis.

WHERE ARE WE NOW?

This journey into the past and the present establishes the definition of imperialism as *a system of international economic transfers by extra-economic means*. It stems from unequal development and inequality in power relations. Domination and coercion are intrinsic to it. It is underpinned and guaranteed by the state and its military means. The modalities of transfers vary according to social structures (modes of production) and the identity of the actors who generate the imperialist phenomenon. Imperialism can be colonial or non-colonial, regional or global, primary or sophisticated, precapitalist or capitalist, with several metropolises or with a single one, multi-center or single-center with subordinate annexes.

To the extent that there is a system of taking possession of resources (land, raw materials, manufactured goods, capital, labor generated by a workforce) maintained through the co-optation of local ruling strata, pressure, threats or violence, there is imperialism. The upshot is a generic description consistent with the uniqueness of the phenomenon, but also applicable differently depending on the periods and contexts, from the past to the present. The obstacle of piecemeal definitions, limited to particular contexts, valid in some cases but not in others, is overcome.

The historical approach has the merit of anchoring analysis in reality at all times. It is a reminder that imperialism is less an idea than a concrete process. It allows observation diachronically and raises awareness of both the continuities and the changes that defined its course through time and space. It is based on the fact that, however worthwhile they may be as a stimulus to thought, existing theories on imperialism come up against situations that escape them or that they cannot fully explain. Hence the decision to resort to history to review the tangible manifestations of imperialism, a necessary journey in order to formulate generalizations rooted in space and time.

At the base, there is the favorable balance of power from which advantage is taken for economic ends. Expressed crudely and without circumlocution, imperialism is like racketeering and high-level extortion. Imperialists are the great powers of their time, the ones that are the most developed and have the means of coercion to enforce an order of which they are the first beneficiaries, without necessarily being the only ones. Availing themselves of the power differential, they use it to extract advantages that would not be easily accessible to them by licit channels.

Asymmetry allows increased exploitation compared to what is possible domestically. Power is converted into economic gains. At the heart of imperialism lies the capacity to coerce by force, ultimately of a military nature. However, although essential, it is not sufficient. Force must be based on economic, political, social, and technical structures which make the great powers of the moment more active and efficient entities than the others. It must also leave part of the gains to the local elites who administer the regions of the imperial domain.

Imperialism has a history that shapes it. It is marked by stages, themselves determined by the succession of economic, political, and social structures which generate imperialism. From its original version, akin to buccaneering and plundering, to organized forms of undisguised extraction, to the camouflaged and continuous pumping of distant wealth, imperialism emanates from the economic systems and states which give it its specific form.

Precapitalist and premodern imperialism is the most elementary version, catering to dominant castes and social strata, normally landed, in search of tribute and slave labor. With the gradual advent of capitalism, modern imperialism crystallizes in forms depending on the configuration of the capitalism in question. Under the commercial capitalism of the sixteenth to eighteenth centuries, it is strictly colonial and embodied in colonies acquired by force, most often by war, with the whole system justified by mercantilist doctrine. Western Europe, especially the Atlantic seaboard, is the first to achieve capitalism. A gap widens between it and the rest of the world. The effect is long-lasting. It enjoys for a long time a power surplus that it fully uses to subjugate and exploit less developed regions of the world. This is the *sine qua non* condition of imperialism.

Industrial capitalism goes through two phases. In the first, at the beginning of the nineteenth century, it is liberal, based on free enterprise and less inclined towards colonial expansion. It proclaims itself to be "anti-imperialist," without however stopping acquisitions of colonies or letting go of the colonies bequeathed to it by mercantilist imperialism born of commercial capitalism. It adds to its panoply informal free-trade imperialism, through which economic control and drainage are achieved by indirect means and without formal political tutelage.

In the second phase, which begins towards the end of the nineteenth century, the concentration of firms gives rise to oligopolies indifferent or hostile to freedom of enterprise and more favorable to organized markets and protectionism. In addition to trade, which had been the substance of international economic relations until then, there is the mounting importance of the export of capital, an activity destined to undergo unlimited expansion. The colonial policy inherited from commercial capitalism is intensified, colonial possessions are enlarged, the world is carved up and divided between some ten powers. As the interests of each can only be served at the expense of others, frictions fanning belligerence multiply, leading to two world wars.

The transparency and readability of imperialism fade in today's world. An object for ostentation and celebration in the ancient behavior of states, it is less visible since the end of the Second World War. Marked by the primacy of the United States, which by default became the premier imperial center, by the control now extended to developed countries after having been extended only to less developed countries, and by decolonization, the postwar period is one of expectation, of wait-and-see, imposed by the need to rally useful support in the context of competition with the USSR. This period draws to its end with the economic crisis of the 1970s. A final period opens; postcolonial, postindustrial, and financial, it is the current era. What emerges is a reorganization of Western economies under the aegis of neoliberalism and including deindustrialization, relocation, financialization, and the promotion of globalization through multinational firms and the mobility of capital.

The territorial base of imperialism broadens; the scale and depth are greater. As the colonial empires that existed from the sixteenth to the twentieth centuries were unable to resist decolonization, they are replaced by a global model, intended to integrate the world economy under the aegis of the United States. The extraction channel, formerly commercial, then industrial, is now financial and monetary. Exploitation of the status of the dollar allows it to be issued without restriction and without it representing real economic activity, while the United States money market acts as a suction pump of money capital from outside.

The United States has piled up an astronomical debt that cannot be repaid and possesses free means of payment to import goods and services. United States capitalism has now achieved rentier status, a fate similar to that of its British and Dutch predecessors. After a commercial and productive era, settling into the role of beneficiary of a financial advantage appears to be a historical constant.

Is imperialism a necessity or a choice? This was a burning question since Lenin confronted Kautsky and has remained divisive ever since. For the first, imperialism is a policy for which others could be substituted. For the second, it is an unavoidable development in capitalism because it is the last stage of its evolution. What does the study of the past tell us? On the one hand, oligopolies and the export of capital do not mechanically mean the existence of imperialism. The Scandinavian countries, Switzerland or Luxembourg have not taken the imperialist route, even if they and their companies are part and parcel of foreign imperialisms better equipped than they are. As states, they lack the dimension of great powers seeking hegemony and economically exploiting their political advantages.

Contrariwise, history does not reveal cases of great powers able to take advantage of their situation to gain economic advantage who have abstained from doing so. Imperialism is the path to relatively quick and easy enrichment for countries that have the appropriate means of coercion. There is no historical period in which it was not taken. Near or distant targets are not difficult to reach. For a power that loses its imperialist ramifications, another replaces it at short notice. This means that if imperialism is not necessary according to an inexorable logic, the permanence of imperialism is empirically verified.

The history of imperialism does not belong to the past alone; it persists in the present. Currently, the scale of imperialism is globalized. The juxtaposition of territorially circumscribed empires, which was the

WHERE ARE WE NOW? • 339

configuration of previous centuries, is no more. The United States, the greatest power, strives to rule the world within the framework of a universal imperialism encompassing all economies, also known as neoliberal globalization. The aim is to integrate them, not to equalize conditions, which would cancel out the advantages gained from unequal development. The structure is hegemonic and hierarchical: the United States directing center and regional extensions (Europe, Japan) are tertiarized and financialized economies; the rest of the world hosts the production base (here processing industries, there raw materials). In this orchestra, there is a conductor and musicians occupying their places.

The bonus for the dominant power is the possibility of enjoying a situational rent, in this case that of the dollar, to take in more wealth from the rest of the world than it provides and to live beyond its means. Thus positioned, it is at the top of the food chain. Hegemony also confers the privilege of exceptionalism, to which are attached the de facto suspension of law, the ability to lay down rules and apply one's jurisprudence to others, and impunity through non-membership in international jurisdictions.

Setting up the system is painful. Liberalism has to be imposed, notably by the International Monetary Fund, the World Bank, and the World Trade Organization. National economies are dismantled and chopped to pieces for sale or closure of production units. Societies are disjointed. Some states are domesticated and provincialized, their sovereignty flouted, while others implode.

The implementation of the new order is contentious and contested. The main obstacle lies in countries that do not bend or only partially bend to hierarchical globalization. These countries are reluctant to relinquish their economic powers and/or to abandon their sovereignty and independence. They are duly subjected to coercion: demonization ("Axis of evil"), embargoes ("sanctions"), destabilization, attempts to change their regimes, wars (by proxy or direct), invasions. They have to be brought down in order to widen the field of action of globalized imperialism. Failing that, they have to be rendered dysfunctional by the collapse of their states, the disarticulation of their societies, and the disintegration of their nations into premodern entities—confessional, ethnic, tribal. Hence the serial wars in various forms.

The United States has been in a state of permanent war since 1945, in its quest to globalize its sphere of influence. From 1945 to 1979, it waged wars more to avoid losing countries, which would become independent or join the opposing bloc, than to expand its own. The dismantling of the USSR was the signal to go on the offensive.

The war against Iraq of 1990-1991, ostensibly over the occupation of Kuwait, was in reality an opportunity to showcase to the world the consequences that would befall anyone who dared to cross the United States. Featuring a display of ultramodern weaponry previously reserved for use against the USSR, an electronic show, a big-time video game, the conflict was waged with complete impunity against a weaker adversary. The formation of a coalition of countries anxious to be associated with the hegemon, the instrumentalization of the United Nations and a media frenzy with a single message gave the impression of a crusade led by the forces of good ("the international community") against the forces of evil ("the dictator"). Virtue combined with omnipotence. This war is the founding act of the new unipolar world order and a textbook for the conduct of post-Cold War conflicts.

The dismantling of Yugoslavia and the war against Serbia in 1999 are in the same vein. The attacks of September 11, 2001, triggered an unlimited and endless war which, under the guise of fighting terrorism, targeted the Muslim and Arab world. The invasions-occupations of Afghanistan (2001) and Iraq (2003) were to be followed by those of Iran and Syria. Despite the extremely favorable balance of power, they turned into quagmires. The surprise was nasty. Disarmed populations found ways to make the stabilization of occupations impossible. The loss of soldiers in the occupying army terminated the doctrine of zero American deaths, developed as a counter to the "Vietnam syndrome," and turned public opinion against these foreign adventures.

The United States had to review its military plans. Preparations to wage two conventional wars at the same time became unrealistic and were thus abandoned. On the contrary, it was realized that the regular forces, despite their offensive means, are incapable of controlling conquered populations and territories. Waged without them, future wars will be of a hybrid nature, indirect and by proxy. If Libya was destroyed, Syria resisted until 2024, and Yemen took the offensive against Saudi Arabia. This meant that the military lever, the ultimate guarantor of imperialism, was worn down. Ineffective and in every respect counterproductive, conventional war was replaced by shadow warfare, waged by special forces and local auxiliaries. The intent was not so much to invade and occupy target countries—unattainable objectives—than to destabilize, dismantle or create chaos.

To this end, economic warfare takes over. In the past, economic aid was used to win over recalcitrant countries and to sway the undecided. It gave way to economic coercion, as globalization exposed countries to the risk of having their dependence on the outside turned against them. Taking advantage of its economic omnipresence and especially that of the dollar, the United States seeks to subdue its enemies by cracking down on those who maintain economic relations with them. In 2017, the *Countering America's Adversaries through Sanctions Act* (CAATSA) put extra-economic instruments at the center of United States foreign policy. Identical to blockades, "sanctions" differ only in name, since "blockade" is equivalent to an act of war. Despite the difficulties they cause, the desired political effect on Russia, Iran, North Korea or Venezuela has not been achieved.

While the failure of the offensive strategy of the 1990s to 2000s undermined the United States position, the economic crisis of 2008 removed its ideological justification and revealed the flaws of neoliberal globalization. Finally, on the international scene, while the United States was bogged down in peripheral wars against weak countries, two large states, Russia and China, made known their refusal to accept the role of subordinates and cogs of the neoliberal globalization. Russia got back on its feet; China got stronger. Both asserted their interests, their independence, and their sovereignty, positions that are antithetical to Americentric globalization.

Both also challenge unipolarity. Their Eurasian project would shift the world's center of gravity eastward, rebalance the global economy, and put an end to five centuries of predominance of the Atlantic zone. From being expansionist, United States policy is now that of a dominant power struggling to prevent defections and cow its rivals. From colonial-type wars of the 1990s-2000s, almost all of which were lost in the end despite overwhelming military superiority, the United States is bringing classic wars between great powers back to the forefront. Its attention is now focused on confronting China and Russia, to the point where the conflicts of the past twenty years seem to be on the way out. The exception, and it is momentous, is the century-old conflict in Palestine which came back to center stage on October 7, 2023, with worldwide repercussions. It is worth recalling the beginning of the twentieth century when the gaze of European powers shifted from colonial expeditions to clashes between them.

The analogy between the post-1945 and post-1990 periods is also striking. In the aftermath of World War II, the United States was well placed to exercise global hegemony and benefit from globalized imperialism. The presence of the USSR and, later, the People's Republic of China, put this prospect beyond reach. The United States confronted both. After the dismantling of the USSR, globalized imperialism became possible again. The *National Security Strategy for the New Century* (December 1998) proclaimed that the goal of the United States is to lead the world and that it would not tolerate challenges from any country or group of countries. NATO, UN, and other international institutions were enlisted.

But the "window of opportunity" closed a quarter of a century later when military failures multiplied in quasi-colonial wars, the economic crisis of 2008 delegitimized the type of economy embodied by the United States, and Russia and China resisted. The three antagonists are the same but the reasons for the confrontation have changed. Once a systems struggle between capitalism and socialism, the conflict now unfolds within capitalism and concerns the organization of the world and the respective places of the great powers within it. It reflects the exacerbation of the dichotomy between unipolarity and multipolarity, unicentrism and polycentrism, unilateralism and multilateralism. It calls into question the solidity of the international alignment established after the end of the Cold War under the aegis of the United States.

The foundations of the struggle are new. The East-West conflict was a competition between two industrial-productivist systems, each displaying its achievements and offering the world its prescriptions for economic development and the rise of living standards. It is not emphasized enough that both ran out of steam at the same time in the 1960s and 1970s, although it turned out that the Soviet system was the harder hit. The current American-Chinese conflict is not about bringing to heel a recalcitrant, formerly perceived as a harmless satellite, but a possible rival with the potential to supplant the hegemon. The economic struggle pits the American financial-rentier system against the Chinese industrial-productivist system. Both are globalist because the economy is on a global scale and territorially delimited neomercantilist empires are a thing of the past. In a nutshell, the conflict is between rentierism and productivism. Will the outcome ensure the continuation of the first or its replacement by the second? Will globalization remain neoliberal or will it be reconfigured? Will the directing center of globalization remain in the United States or will it devolve on China? Will there be a hegemonic succession? Questions that remain unanswered at present.

Pushing back and reducing rivals and rebels to bring them into line or, failing that, to destroy them, is the axis of the policy of the United States, implemented as much as possible by the mobilization of its allies and associates. As the hegemonic power and main beneficiary of the status quo, it understands that the changes underway, in particular the shift of the pivot of the world economy from the West to Asia, from the Atlantic to Eurasia, undermine its preponderance. If it is unable to subjugate or co-opt them, how can it halt the advance of fast-growing economies?

United States international policy is to thwart this unfavorable development through actions likely to put rival and rebellious countries on the defensive by exploiting internal fault lines or international disputes, without excluding pressure and military operations. Wars of destabilization and destructuring, through direct intervention or by proxy, must be understood from this perspective. They consist either of expanding the American sphere or of preventing withdrawals to the benefit of divergent constructions. It is about the defense of the established order through an offensive strategy. Hence the paradox— but it is only apparent—of a dominant power, normally conservative, disrupting the international status quo because its trajectory does not suit it.

A case in point is the United States policy aimed at separating Europe and Russia. Economically complementary, they were moving closer together out of mutual interest and could ultimately form with China the Eurasian bloc so feared by the United States. Geopolitical levers are used to upset the unfavorable course of economic development. This is the logic behind the conflict in Ukraine. The integration of Ukraine into the American system since the 2014 regime change in Kiev threatened Russia on its southern flank and tightened its encirclement by way of NATO expansion. Russia finally reacted in 2021-2022, allowing the United States to achieve the severance of economic relations between Europe and Russia, the recovery of its control of Europe, and the possibility of damaging Russia by embroiling it in a war waged by Ukrainian intermediaries.

On the horizon for over a decade, the showdown between the great powers is underway. It comes out of the realm of the unthinkable and looks set to continue after the proxy conflict in Ukraine. On the Asian front, preparations against China are proceeding in broad daylight. The stakes are enormous, nothing less than the extension or the demise of postcolonial imperialism with a universal vocation and of the unipolar order. In Ukraine, the conflict is not without paradoxical developments. Not only were the "sanctions" blunted but they have also instated the de-dollarization that some were already calling for. It is now shown that the dollar is not indispensable. While the Russian economy has been expelled from Americentric globalization, the fact that it held its own and is doing well proves that it is possible to function outside the dollar framework. Globalization is being sapped precisely by those who are its prime movers and beneficiaries. A turn is being taken in the direction of deglobalization. The far-reaching American-Russian conflict in Ukraine is determining the future of imperialism and world geopolitics.

The dollar remains a nerve center. On its primacy and the ability to issue it at will rests American economic privilege. For all practical purposes, a unilateral abandonment of the dollar by one or more countries would be tantamount to a *casus belli* for the United States, so dependent is its hegemony and the pumping of wealth from the outside world on the extraordinary status of its currency. Among the causes of NATO's intervention in Libya in 2011 was this country's desire to replace the dollar with the gold dinar and propose it as the currency of the African continent.

Beyond the international clashes and what would emerge from them is the question of leaving or not leaving the present globalized capitalist-imperialist order. The working class/industrial proletariat has been concentrated in Europe since the nineteenth century. Its demands bore fruit many times but did not bring down capitalism; it reinvented itself and survived, without putting an end to the reproduction of the imbalances and disorders that characterize it. The very specific Soviet experience lasted three-quarters of a century, longer than its precursor the Commune, but it did not succeed in perpetuating itself. The life of regimes inspired by the Soviet model has not been any longer. Major historical changes occur at particular junctures, when the necessary conditions are in place. Once a favorable situation has passed, there is a waiting period before others materialize.

It so happened that the communist parties which came to power did so in countries where the primary task was not the establishment of socialism, but first and foremost the recovery of failing national capitalisms (in the West) or the creation of socioeconomic preconditions that should have been the work of capitalism (in Russia, Eastern Europe, and the countries of the South). The socialist goal was subordinated to the unavoidable task of overcoming historical backwardness, eliminating underdevelopment, and struggling for development. Paradoxically, and without this being their ultimate objective, the socialist regimes in Russia, Eastern Europe, and the South laid the material foundations for the capitalism that would grow after their overthrow at the end of the twentieth century. The detour via socialism and its voluntarist action will have facilitated the advent of capitalism in places where it had not progressed *motu proprio*.

Today the ranks of the Western working class are thinned out by deindustrialization and tertiarization. It is everywhere on the defensive, and union organizations are weakened. The majority of the world's workers are employed in factories in the South and are rarely unionized. Is the Western cycle of working-class history dating back to the industrial revolution definitively closed? Is a new one beginning in the non-Western world? Will it follow the same path: awareness, unionization, political organization? What programs and alliances will emerge within the South and, beyond it, with compatible forces in the North? What will be their stance on imperialism? These questions, and many others, can only be answered in the future because the historical era of neoliberal capitalism and contemporary imperialism continues to unfold.

Historical perspective can shed light on the alternation between phases of globalization and deglobalization in the evolution of imperialism. Great Britain acted as the linchpin of globalization in the era of free trade imperialism as long as it was uncontested at the summit of the world economy and, at the same time, its main beneficiary. It made free trade virtually an ideology, even a cult, to be urged on others or forced on them at gunpoint. But hegemony is never eternal, and as soon as Germany and the United States caught up with it at the end of the nineteenth century and became serious competitors capable of taking markets away from British manufacturers, free trade suddenly appeared less appealing. Speaking for British industry, Joseph Chamberlain launched a campaign to restrict it by throwing up tariffs to hinder foreign competition. A blow would be dealt to the globalization that Britain had so ardently espoused. This was outright heresy in the sanctuary of free trade. It failed at the beginning of the twentieth century because Britain could not let go of its far-flung interests in the world. The breakdown of globalization did occur with the First World War and in the 1930s in the midst of an acute economic depression. Was it the demise of globalization? Only temporarily. In many respects, the Depression and the Second World war turned out to be cathartic experiences marked by pain and bloodshed but setting the stage for a new postwar phase of globalization.

Fast forward to the closing years of the twentieth century and the beginning of the twenty-first with the United States underpinning globalization and profiting greatly from it. Again, a near-ideology morphed into a quasi-religious creed persistently pressed on the world by all means, fair and foul. United States-centered globalization was touted as the ultimate panacea for humanity with no alternative even imaginable. Yet, the course of history again upset facile assertions. Parts of the rest of the world managed to develop despite American-conducted globalization and gradually came to look beyond the role assigned to them of cogs in the wheel of the United States. Large countries emerged as independent economic powers, China foremost among them. United States primacy, an unquestioned dogma, was unexpectedly on the way to being a thing of the past. Also unanticipated was the refusal of large segments of the American public to accept the relocation abroad of the country's industries and the jobs they provided. Globalization lost what luster it may have had. "Populist" political forces set about reversing it, including in the United States. As with free-trade Britain a century earlier, the apostle of globalization turned to protectionism and set in motion a process of deglobalization. Policies are touted as deriving from timeless truths when they favor their advocates, and are discarded when they cease to do so.

The Trump phenomenon is the upshot of the recognition that globalization does not guarantee the longevity of United States planetary imperialism. It pursues the same objectives as the global-izers did, namely American hegemony, but by a different path, one replacing "progressive" demagoguery, subversion, manipulation and multilateralist rhetoric by bellicose nationalism, bullying, bluster, and undisguised extortion. Distortions, disinformation and "narrative" control through heavy and continuous propaganda diligently echoed 24/7 by the mainstream media are vital components common to both. Trump's intention is to skew the rules and make friend and foe alike pay more for the restoration of the unravelling position of the United States. Like Britain a century earlier, the United States is less and less economically competitive. It is losing its capacity to bend others to its will or to enlist them in its network. It is flailing in all directions against changing reality.

Globalizers had sought to make up for deficiencies by harming others and spreading chaos wherever they could in the hope that, ultimately, the United States would remain the only one standing. With Trump, the United States is going a step further in the belief that the only possible path to remaining preponderant is to revise the economic system it previously championed. It is switching to protectionism, using tariffs to increase government revenues and hoping that the raising of the price of imports and, consequently, the lowering of real wages would draw into the United States productive capacities that had migrated in the past half century. Profitability will be the criterion for companies and investors. But a crucial issue not addressed is how goods produced could be purchased by consumers with diminished real incomes and a declining standard of living.

If Trump's project is carried through, globalization will be slowed down and may grind to a halt. Economic collapse and out and out shooting wars to impose hegemony should not be ruled out. Barring those eventualities, deglobalization would represent a phase that will not be permanent. The scale of production, the size of markets, the universal source of inputs of today's economy point to globalization of some sort, as the outcome of the reordering of the world econ-omy. Hierarchical, single-center globalization is not the only form. The United States model is discredited and has fewer and fewer supporters beyond Western ruling circles who have mortgaged their countries, embraced the function of vassals and staked their future on it. Horizontal, polycentric forms of globalization are conceivable and could eventually come into being. But a precondition will be the neutralization and elimination of imperialism, even of capitalism itself.

10 June 2025

SELECT BIBLIOGRAPHY ON IMPERIALISM

A bibliography on imperialism would fill several volumes. The selection below is indicative. It includes titles of books relevant to the themes developed in this book.

ADDO, Herb. *Imperialism: The Permanent State of Capitalism*. Tokyo: United Nations University, 1986.

AMIN, Samir. *Accumulation on a World Scale: A Critique of the Theory of Underdevelopment*. New York: Monthly Review Press, 1974 [1970].

Ibid. Imperialism and Unequal Development, New York: Monthly Review Press, 1977 [1976].

ARON, Raymond. *Peace and War: A Theory of International Relations*. Garden City: Doubleday, 1966 [1962].

ARRIGHI, Giovanni. *The Geometry of Imperialism: The Limits of Hobson's Paradigm*. Translated from Italian by Patrick Camiller. London: NLB, 1978.

BARAN, Paul A. and Paul M. Sweezy, *Monopoly Capital*. New York: Monthly Review Press, 1966.

BARONE, Charles A. *Marxist Thought on Imperialism: Survey and critique*. Armonk, New York: M. E. Sharpe, 1985.

BERBEROGLU, Berch. *The Internationalization of Capital: Imperialism and Capitalist Development on a World Scale*. New York: Praeger, 1987.

BLEANEY, Michael. *Underconsumption Theories: A History and Critical Analysis*. New York: International Publishers, 1976.

BORON, Atilio A. *Empire & impérialisme: Une lecture critique de Michael Hardt et Antonio Negri*. Paris: L'Harmattan, 2003.

BUKHARIN, Nikolai. *L'économie mondiale et l'impérialisme: Esquisse économique*. Paris: Anthropos, 1969 (1918, written in 1915]

BREWER, Anthony. *Marxist Theories of Imperialism*. London: Routledge & Kegan Paul, 1980.

BROWN, Michael Barratt. *The Economics of Imperialism*. Harmondsworth: Penguin, 1974.

BUHLER, Pierre. *La puissance au XXIe siècle*. Paris: CNRS Éditions, 2011.

CAIN, Peter. *Hobson and Imperialism: Radicalism, New Liberalism and Finance, 1887-1938*. Oxford: Oxford University Press, 2002.

CAIN, P. J. and A. G. Hopkins. *British Imperialism, 1688-2000*. Harlow: Longman, 2002 [1993].

CALLINICOS, Alex. *Imperialism and Global Political Economy*. Cambridge: Polity, 2009.

CHESNAIS, François. *La mondialisation du capital*. Paris: Syros, 1997.

CHILCOTE, Ronald H. (ed.). *The Political Economy of Imperialism: Critical Appraisals*. Lanham: Rowman & Littlefield, 2000.

COPE, Zak. *The Wealth of (Some) Nations: Imperialism and the Mechanics of Value Transfer*. London: Pluto Press, 2019.

DOCKÈS, Pierre. *L'internationale du capital*. Paris: Presses universitaires de France, 1975.

DOYLE, Michael W. *Empires*. Ithaca and London: Cornell University Press, 1986.

EMMANUEL, Arghiri. *L'échange inégal: Essai sur les antagonismes dans les rapports internationaux*. Paris: Maspéro, 1978.

ETEMAD, Bouda. *De l'utilité des empires: Colonisation et prospérité de l'Europe*. Paris, Armand Colin, 2005.

Ibid. La possession du monde: Poids et mesures de la colonisation. Brussels: Complexe, 2000.

ETHERINGTON, Norman. *Theories of Imperialism: War, Conquest and Capital*. London: Croom Helm. 1984.

FRANK, André Gunder. *Capitalism and Underdevelopment in Latin America*. New York: Monthly Review Press, 1969.

HARDT, Michael and Antonio Negri. *Empire*. Cambridge, Mass.: Harvard University Press, 2000.

HARVEY, David. *The New Imperialism*. Oxford: Oxford University Press, 2005 [2003].

HILFERDING, Rudolf. *Finance Capital: A Study of the Latest Phase of Capitalist Development*. Tom Bottomore, ed. London: Routledge & Kegan Paul, 1981 [1910].

HOBSON, J. A. *Imperialism: A Study*. London: Allen & Unwin, 1938 [1902].

HODGART, Alan. *The Economics of Imperialism*. London: Edward Arnold, 1977.

HUDSON, Michael. *Super Imperialism: The Origins and Fundamentals of US World Dominance*. London: Pluto 2003 [1972].

JALÉE, Pierre. *L'impérialisme en 1970*. Paris: Maspéro, 1970.

KATZ, Claudio. *Sous l'empire du capital: L'impérialisme aujourd'hui*. Translated from Castilian (Argentina) by Lucile Daumas. Unspecified: M Éditeur, 2011.

KAUTSKY, Karl, "Ultra-imperialism," *New Left Review*, 59, January-February 1970, p. 41-46.

KENNEDY, Paul. *The Rise and Fall of the Great Powers*. New York: Random House, 1987.

KEYNES, John Maynard. *The General Theory of Employment, Interest and Money*. New York: Harcourt, Brace, and company, 1936.

KIERNAN, V. G. *Marxism and Imperialism*. London: Edward Arnold, 1974.

KOEBNER, Richard and Helmut Dan Schmidt. *Imperialism: The Story and Significance of a Political Word, 1840-1960,* Cambridge: Cambridge University Press, 2010.

LANDES, David S. *The Wealth and Poverty of Nations: Why Some Are so Rich and Some so Poor.* New York: W. W. Norton, 1998.

LAPAVITSAS, Costas (ed.). *Financialization in Crisis*. Leiden: Brill, 2012.

LATOUCHE, Serge. *Critique de l'impérialisme*. Paris: Anthropos, 1979.

LAURENS, Henry. *L'empire et ses ennemis: La question impériale dans l'histoire*. Paris: Seuil, 2009.

LENIN, *Imperialism, the Highest Stage of Capitalism: A Popular Outline* (1916). Many editions. *Selected Works*. Volume 1, Moscow: Progress Publishers, 1963, p. 667-766. Written in 1916.

LUXEMBURG, Rosa. *The Accumulation of Capital*. Translated from German by Agnes Schwarzschild. London: Routledge & Kegan Paul, 1951 [1913].

MAGDOFF, Harry. *Imperialism without Colonies*. New York: Monthly Review Press, 1969.

Ibid., The Age of Imperialism and the Economics of U. S. Foreign Policy. New York: Monthly Review Press, 2003.

MALTHUS, Thomas Robert. *Principles of Political Economy*. London: W. Pickering, 1836 [1821].

MARSEILLE, Jacques. *Empire et capitalisme français: Histoire d'un divorce*. Paris: Albin Michel, 1984.

MARX, Karl and F. Engels. *Textes sur le colonialisme*. Moscow: Éditions du progrès, 1977.

MILL, John Stuart. *Principles of Political Economy*. Toronto and London: University of Toronto Press and Routledge & Kegan Paul, 1965 [1848].

MOMMSEN, Wolfgang J. *Theories of Imperialism*. New York: Random House, 1980.

MÜNKLER, Herfried. *Empires*. Translated from German by Patrick Camiller. Cambridge: Polity, 2007 [2005].

NOONAN, Murray. *Marxist Theories of Imperialism: A History*. London: I. B. Tauris, 2017.

OWEN, Roger and Bob Sutcliffe (eds.). *Studies in the Theory of Imperialism*. London: Longman, 1972.

PALLOIX, Christian. *L'économie mondiale capitaliste et les firmes multinationales*. Paris: Maspéro, 1975.

Ibid. L'internationalisation du capital: Éléments critiques. Paris: Maspéro, 1975.

PANITCH, Leo Panitch and Sam Gindin. *The Making of Global Capitalism: The Political Economy of American Empire.* New York: Verso, 2013.

PARSONS, Timothy H. *The Rule of Empires.* Oxford: Oxford University Press, 2010.

PETRAS, James and Henry Veltmeyer. *Empire with Imperialism: The Globalizing Dynamics of Neo-Liberal Capitalism.* Black Point and London: Fernwood and Zed, 2005.

Ibid. Globalism Unmasked: Imperialism in the 21ˢᵗ Century, Black Point and London: Fernwood and Zed, 2001.

Ibid. Imperialism and Capitalism in the Twenty-First Century: A system in crisis. Farnham: Ashgate, 2013.

POLYCHRONIOU, Chronis. *Marxist Perspectives on Imperialism: A Theoretical Analysis.* New York: Praeger, 1991.

POMERANZ, Kenneth. *The Great Divergence: China, Europe, and the Making of the Modern World Economy.* Princeton: Princeton University Press, 2000.

Radical History Review, 57, fall 1993. Special issue on imperialism.

REES, John. *Imperialism and Resistance.* London and New York: Routledge, 2006.

REY, Pierre-Philippe. *Colonialisme, néocolonialisme et transition au capitalisme.* Paris: Maspéro, 1971.

RICARDO, David. *On the Principles of Political Economy and Taxation.* Kitchener: Batoche Books, 2001 [1817].

SAY, Jean-Baptiste. *Traité d'économie politique.* Paris: Deterville, 1819 [1803].

SCHUMPETER, Joseph. *Imperialism and Social Classes.* New York: Augustus M. Kelley, 1951 [1919].

SERFATI, Claude. *Impérialisme et militarisme: Actualité du 21ᵉ siècle.* Lausanne: Éditions Page deux, 2004.

SISMONDI, J. C. L. Simonde de. *Nouveaux principes d'économie politique.* Paris: Calmann-Lévy, 1971 [1819].

SMITH, Adam. *An Inquiry into the Nature and Causes of the Wealth of Nations.* Oxford: Oxford University Press, 1976 [1776].

SMITH, John. *Imperialism in the Twenty-First Century,* New York: Monthly Review Press, 2016.

SZENTES, Tamas. *Theories of World Capitalist Economy.* Budapest: Academy Kiado, 1985.

SZYMANSKI, Albert. *The Logic of Imperialism.* New York: Praeger, 1981.

VALIER, Jacques. *Sur l'impérialisme.* Paris: Maspéro, 1975.

WARREN, Bill. *Imperialism: Pioneer of Capitalism.* London: NLB, 1980.

WOOD, Ellen Meiksins. *Empire of Capital.* London: Verso, 2003.

INDEX

ALSO FROM BARAKA BOOKS

SYRIA: ANATOMY OF REGIME CHANGE
Jeremy Kuzmarov and Dan Kovalik
(Foreword by Oliver Stone)

RAZING PALESTINE
PUNISHING SOLIDARITY AND DISSENT IN CANADA
An Anthology Edited by Leila Marshy

PATRIOTS, TRAITORS AND EMPIRES
THE STORY OF KOREA'S STRUGGLE FOR FREEDOM
Stephen Gowans

RWANDA AND THE NEW SCRAMBLE FOR AFRICA
FROM TRAGEDY TO USEFUL IMPERIAL FICTION
Robin Philpot

SLOUCHING TOWARDS SIRTE
NATO'S WAR ON LIBYA AND AFRICA
Maximilian C. Forte

A DISTINCT ALIEN RACE
THE UNTOLD STORY OF FRANCO-AMERICANS
David Vermette

MONTREAL, CITY OF SECRETS
CONFEDERATE OPERATIONS IN
MONTREAL DURING THE AMERICAN CIVIL WAR
Barry Sheehy

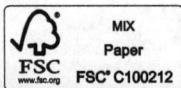

FSC
www.fsc.org

MIX
Paper
FSC® C100212

Printed by Imprimerie Gauvin
Gatineau, Québec